Oh My Goddess!

ああ女神さまっ Sympathy for the Devil

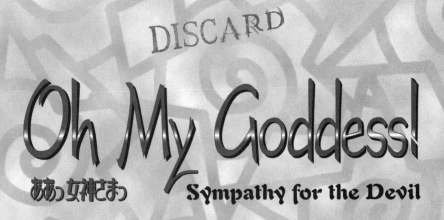

Oh My Goddess!

ああ女神さま **Sympathy for the Devil**

STORY AND ART BY

Kosuke Fujishima

TRANSLATION BY

Alan Gleason, Toren Smith, & Dana Lewis

LETTERING AND TOUCH-UP BY

L. Lois Buhalis, Tom Orzechowski, Susie Lee, & PC Orz

DARK HORSE COMICS®

OHM

PUBLISHER
Mike Richardson

SERIES EDITORS
Peet Janes, Greg Vest, & Dave Chipps

COLLECTION EDITOR
Suzanne Taylor

COLLECTION DESIGNERS
Julie Eggers Gassaway & Amy Arendts

English version produced by Studio Proteus for Dark Horse Comics, Inc.

OH MY GODDESS! Volume V: Sympathy for the Devil

This book collects *Oh My Goddess!* Part I issue six, Part II issues one and two, and Specials "Sympathy for the Devil," "Mystical Engine," and "Valentine Rhapsody."

Published by
Dark Horse Comics, Inc.
10956 SE Main Street
Milwaukie, OR 97222

First edition: May 1998
ISBN: 1-56971-329-4

5 7 9 10 8 6
Printed in Canada

The Scales of Love

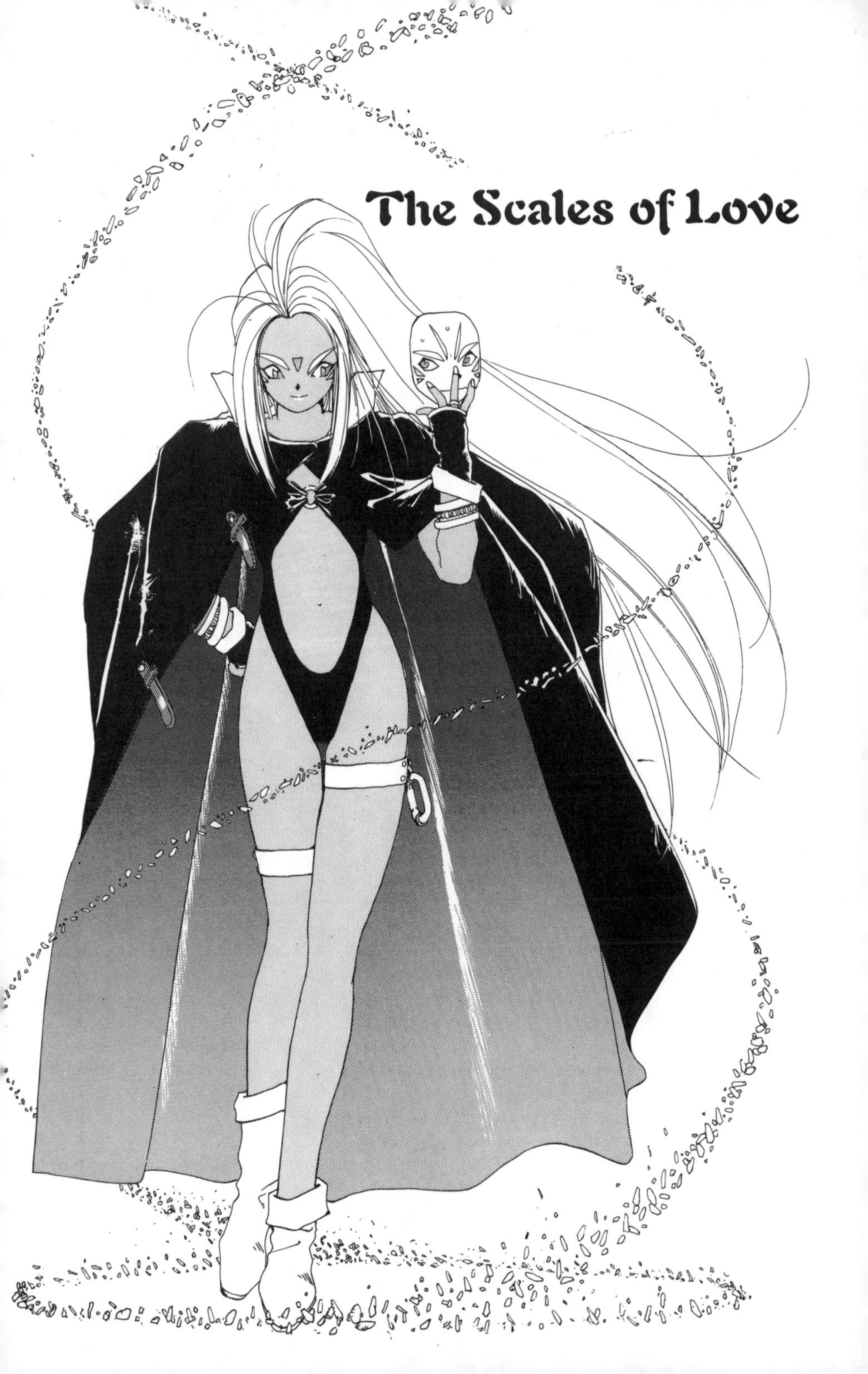

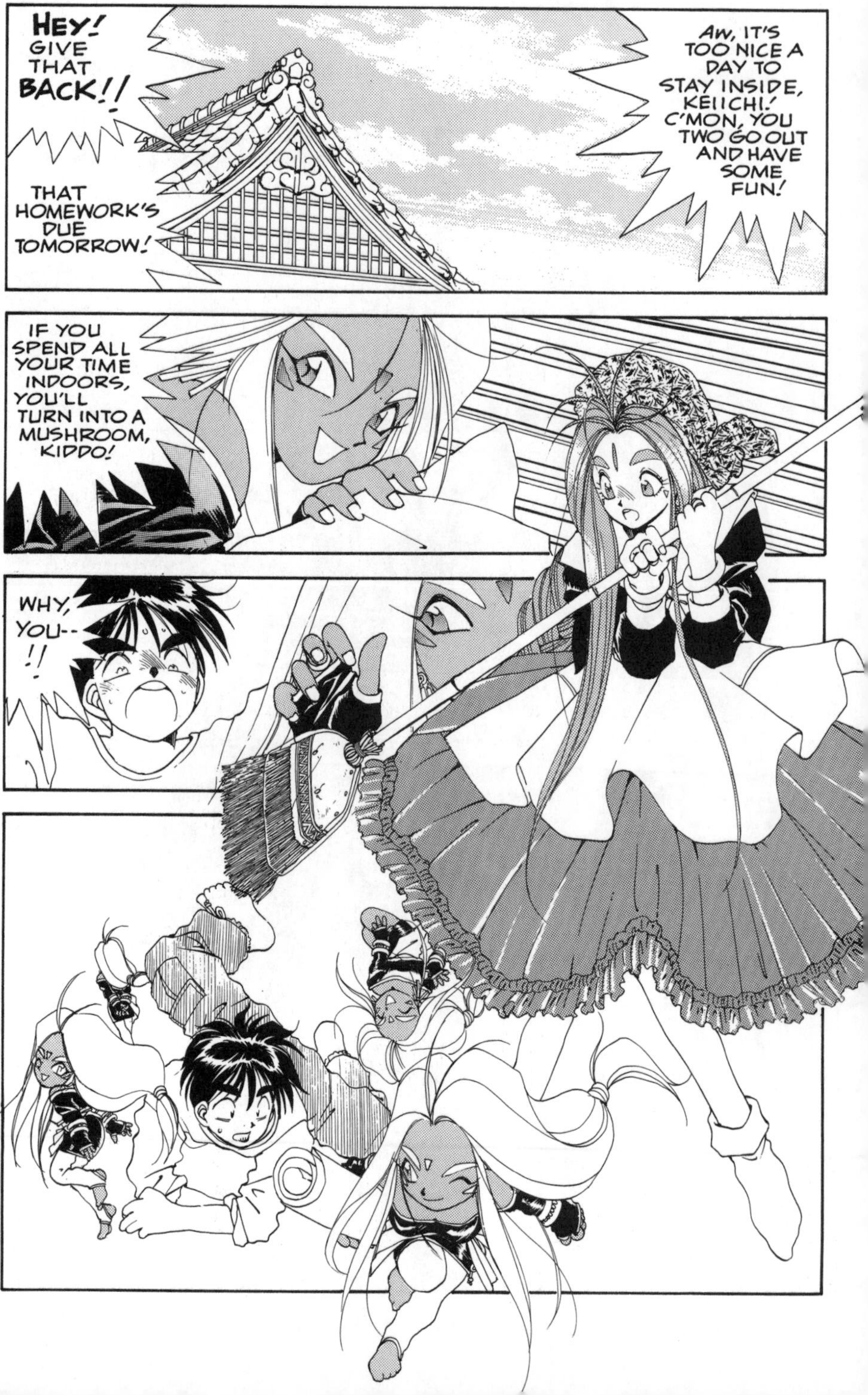
HEY! GIVE THAT BACK!!
THAT HOMEWORK'S DUE TOMORROW!
AW, IT'S TOO NICE A DAY TO STAY INSIDE, KEIICHI! C'MON, YOU TWO GO OUT AND HAVE SOME FUN!
IF YOU SPEND ALL YOUR TIME INDOORS, YOU'LL TURN INTO A MUSHROOM, KIDDO!
WHY, YOU-- !!

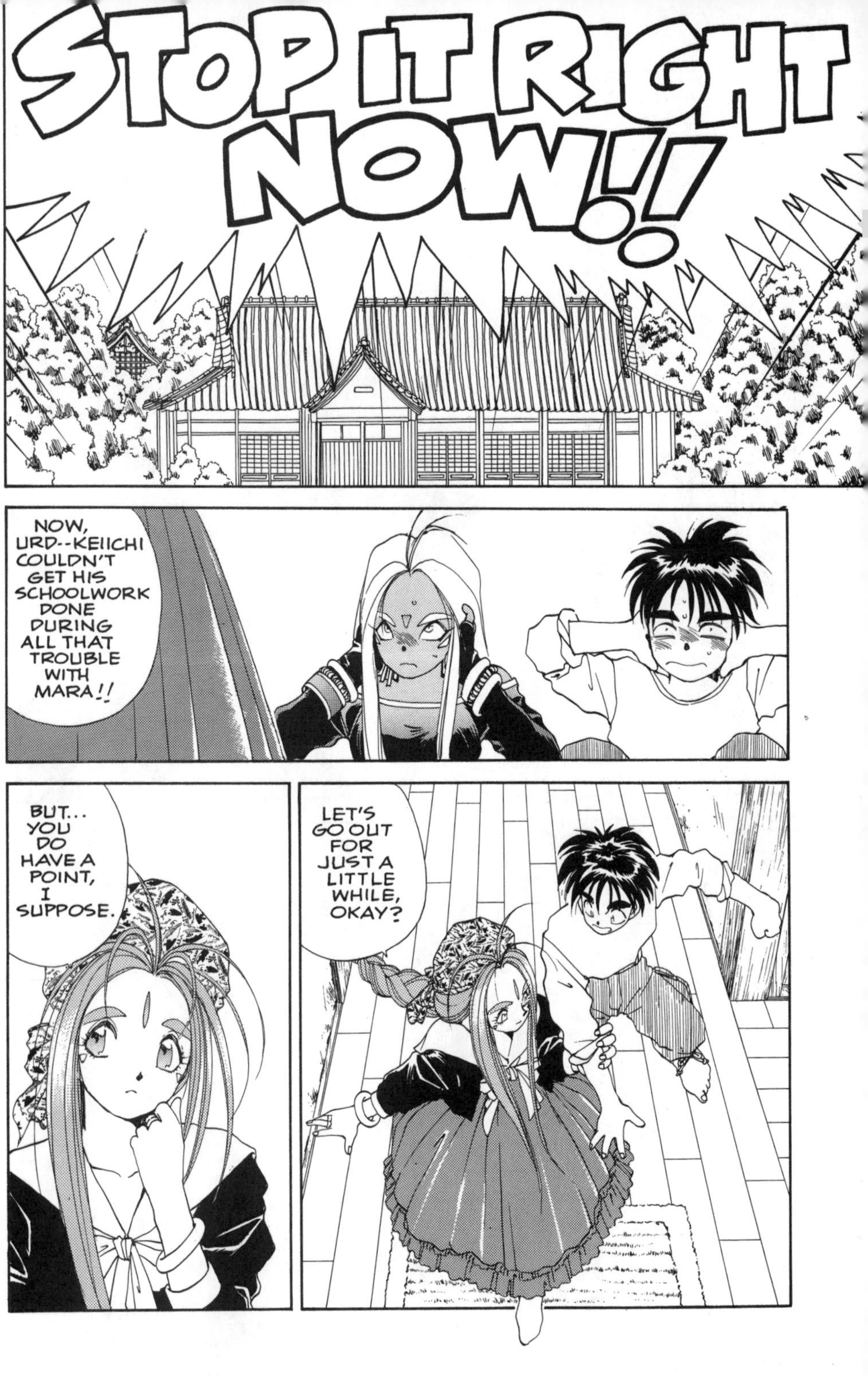
STOP IT RIGHT NOW!!
NOW, URD--KEIICHI COULDN'T GET HIS SCHOOLWORK DONE DURING ALL THAT TROUBLE WITH MARA!!
BUT... YOU DO HAVE A POINT, I SUPPOSE.
LET'S GO OUT FOR JUST A LITTLE WHILE, OKAY?

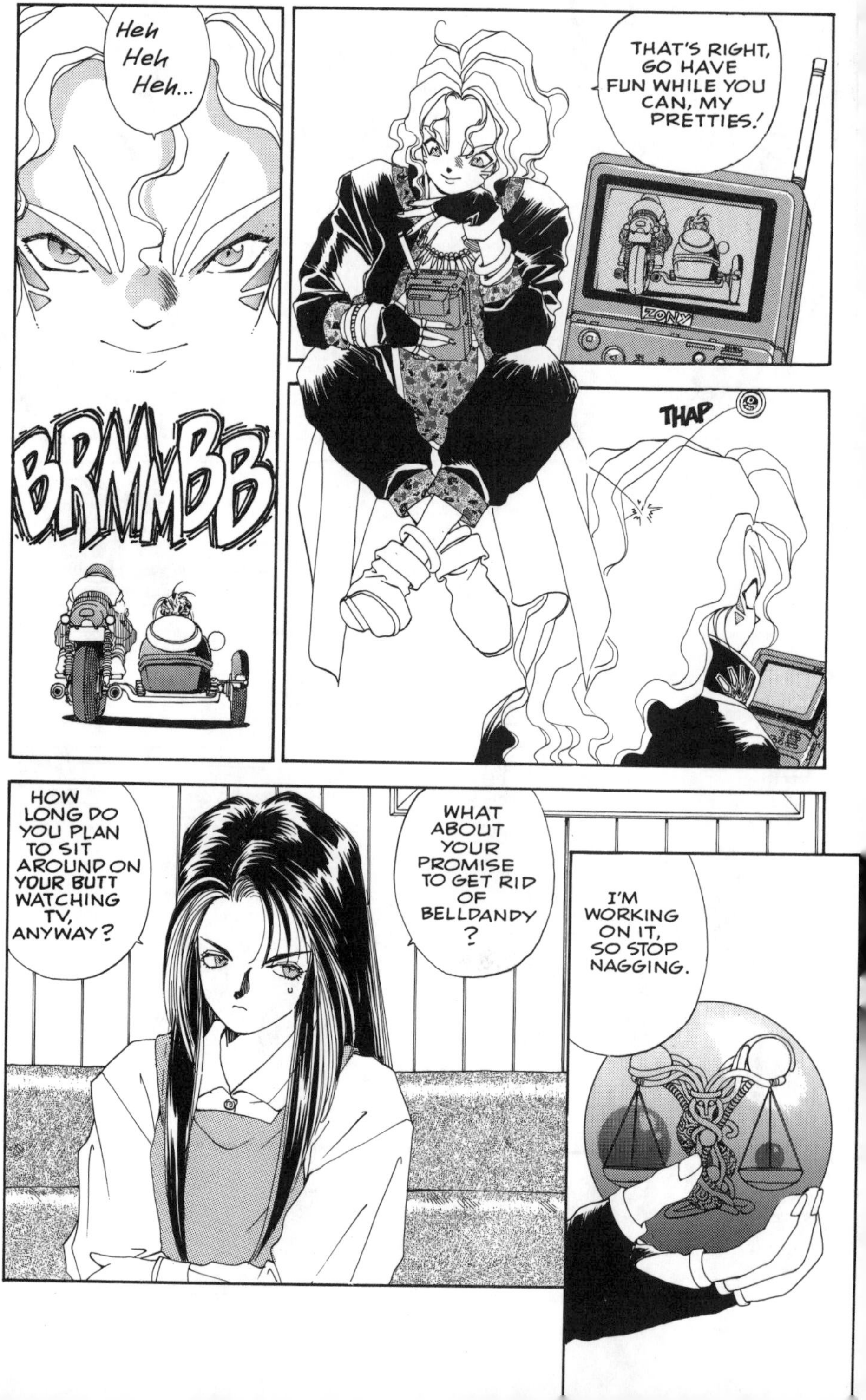
Heh Heh Heh...
BRMMBB
THAT'S RIGHT, GO HAVE FUN WHILE YOU CAN, MY PRETTIES!
ZONY
THAP
HOW LONG DO YOU PLAN TO SIT AROUND ON YOUR BUTT WATCHING TV, ANYWAY?
WHAT ABOUT YOUR PROMISE TO GET RID OF BELLDANDY?
I'M WORKING ON IT, SO STOP NAGGING.

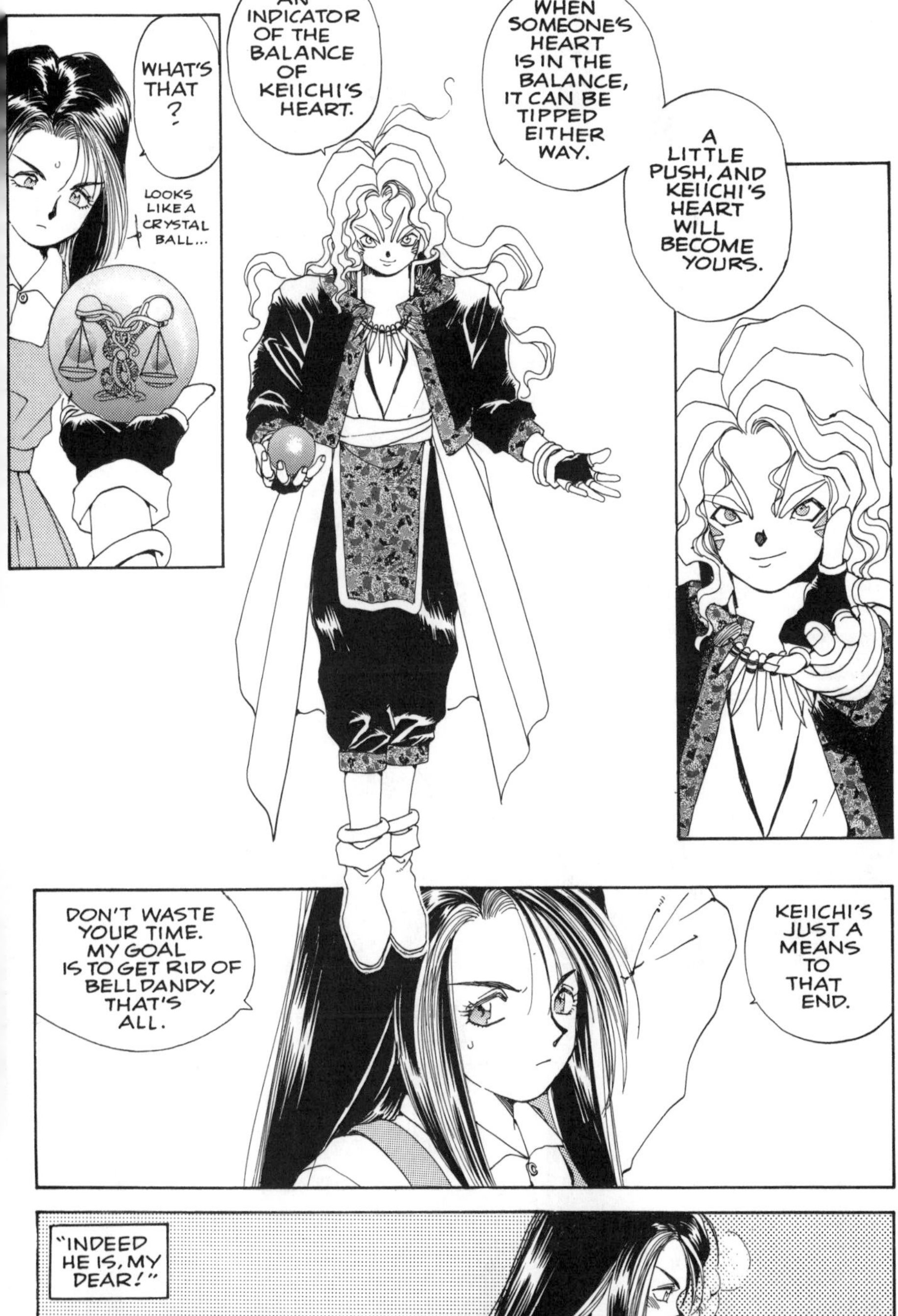
WHAT'S THAT ?
LOOKS LIKE A CRYSTAL BALL...
AN INDICATOR OF THE BALANCE OF KEIICHI'S HEART.
WHEN SOMEONE'S HEART IS IN THE BALANCE, IT CAN BE TIPPED EITHER WAY.
A LITTLE PUSH, AND KEIICHI'S HEART WILL BECOME YOURS.
DON'T WASTE YOUR TIME. MY GOAL IS TO GET RID OF BELLDANDY, THAT'S ALL.
KEIICHI'S JUST A MEANS TO THAT END.
"INDEED HE IS, MY DEAR!"

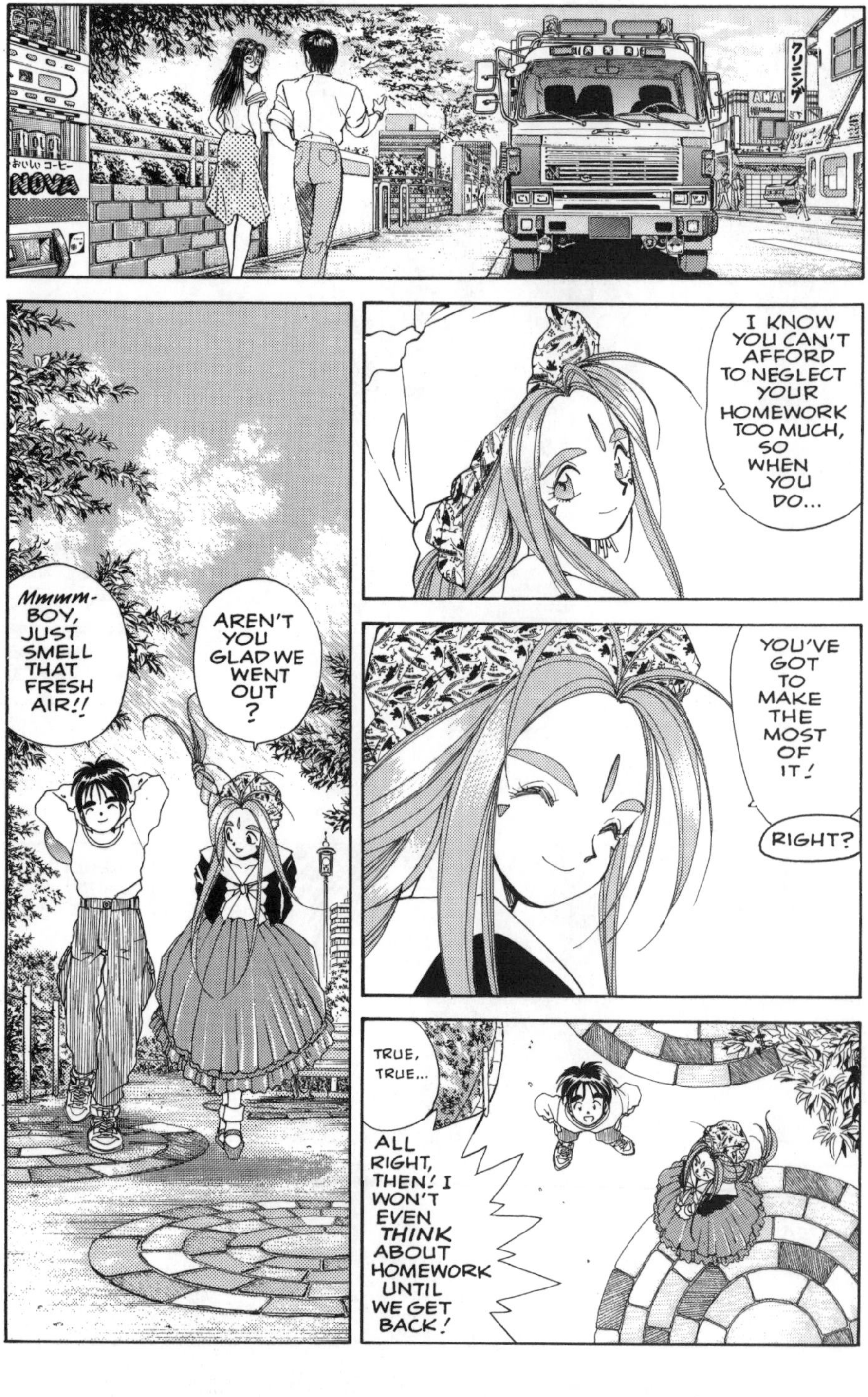
おいしい コーヒー
NOVA
クリーニング
Mmmm-BOY, JUST SMELL THAT FRESH AIR!!
AREN'T YOU GLAD WE WENT OUT?
I KNOW YOU CAN'T AFFORD TO NEGLECT YOUR HOMEWORK TOO MUCH, SO WHEN YOU DO...
YOU'VE GOT TO MAKE THE MOST OF IT!
RIGHT?
TRUE, TRUE...
ALL RIGHT, THEN! I WON'T EVEN THINK ABOUT HOMEWORK UNTIL WE GET BACK!

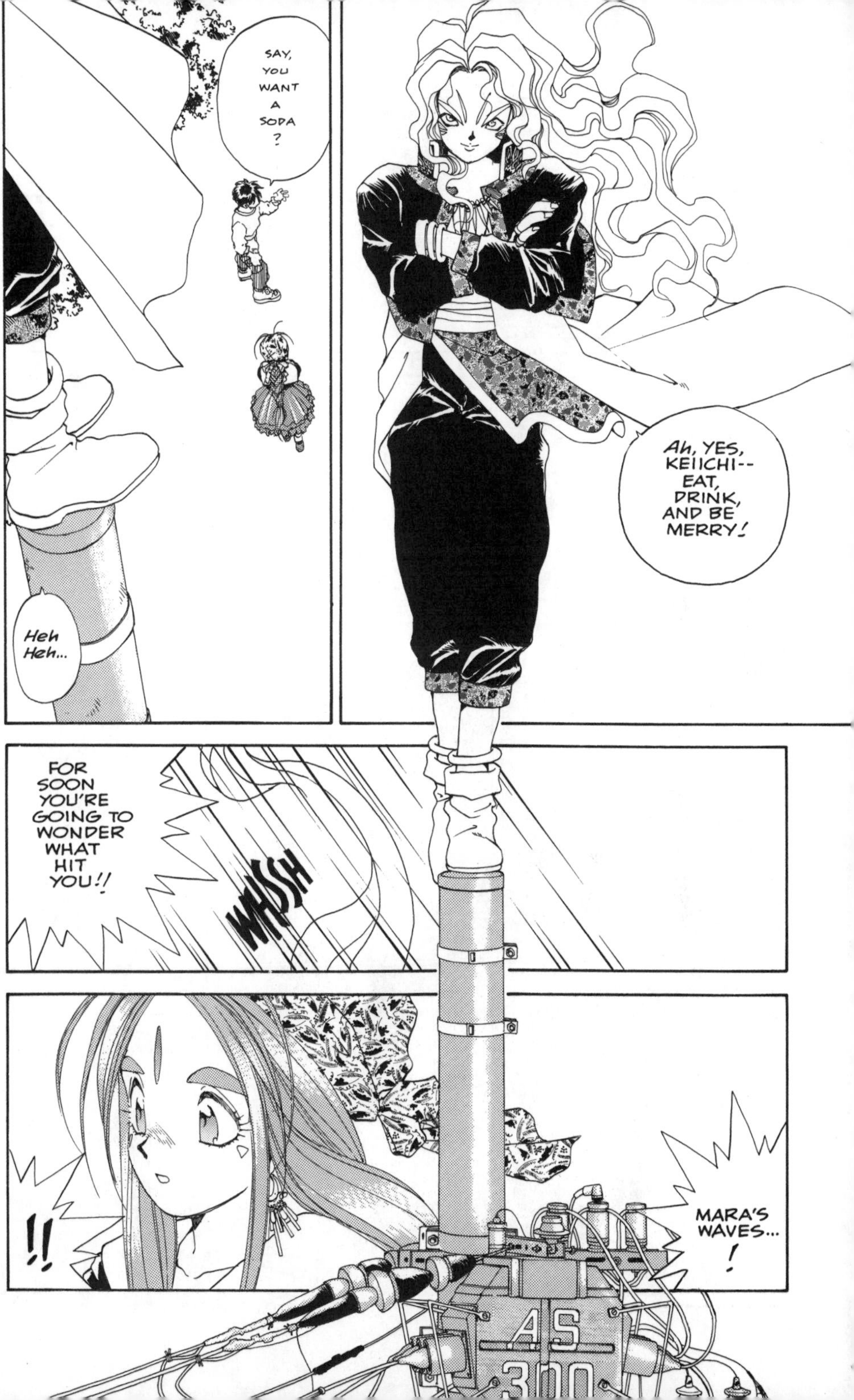
SAY, YOU WANT A SODA?
Heh Heh...
Ah, YES, KEIICHI--EAT, DRINK, AND BE MERRY!
FOR SOON YOU'RE GOING TO WONDER WHAT HIT YOU!!
WHOSH
!!
MARA'S WAVES...!
AS
300

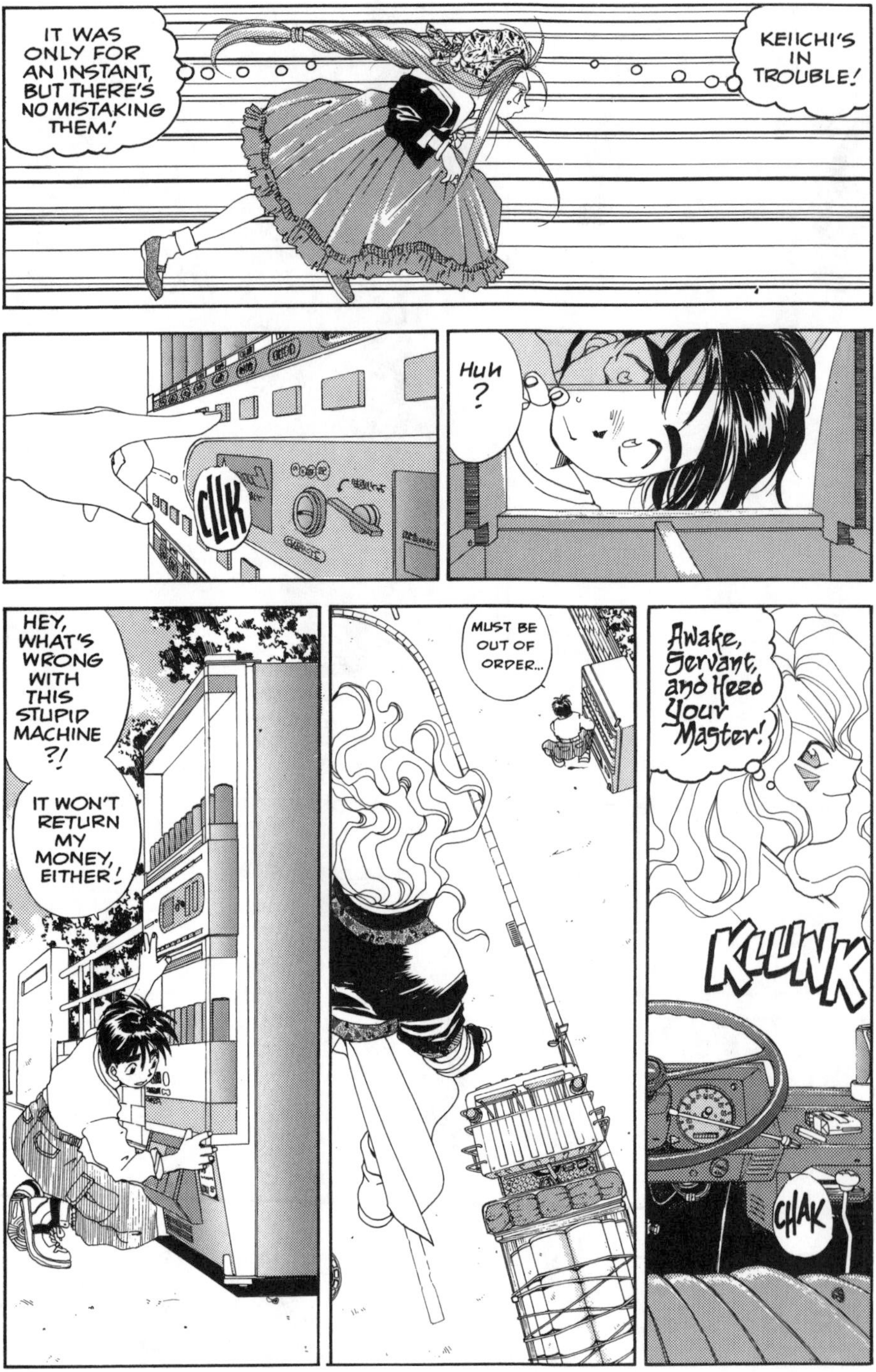
IT WAS ONLY FOR AN INSTANT, BUT THERE'S NO MISTAKING THEM!
KEIICHI'S IN TROUBLE!
CLIK
Huh ?
HEY, WHAT'S WRONG WITH THIS STUPID MACHINE ?!
IT WON'T RETURN MY MONEY, EITHER!
MUST BE OUT OF ORDER...
Awake, Servant, and Heed Your Master!
KLUNK
CHAK

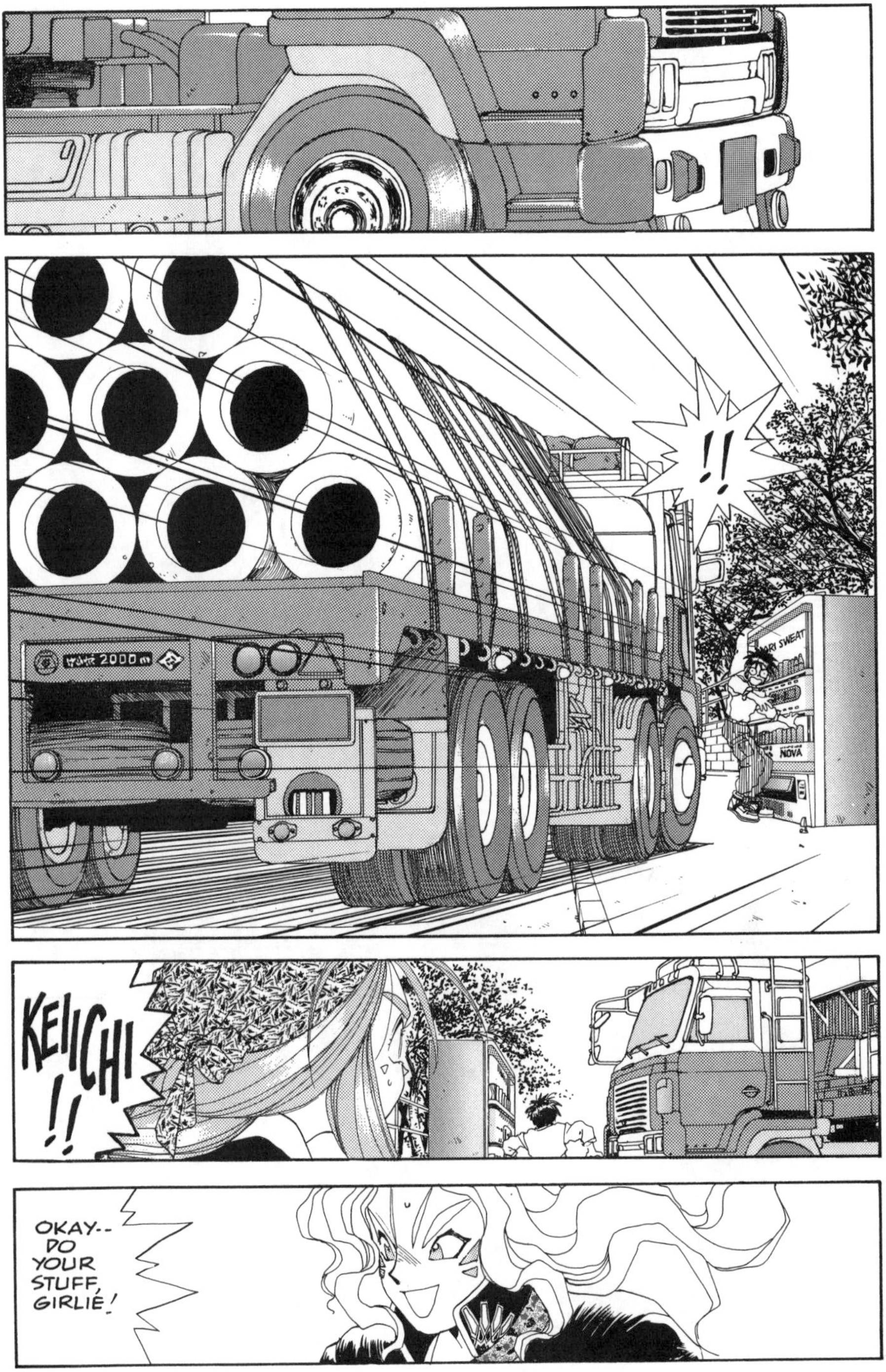
!!
NOVA
KEIICHI !!
OKAY-- DO YOUR STUFF, GIRLIE!

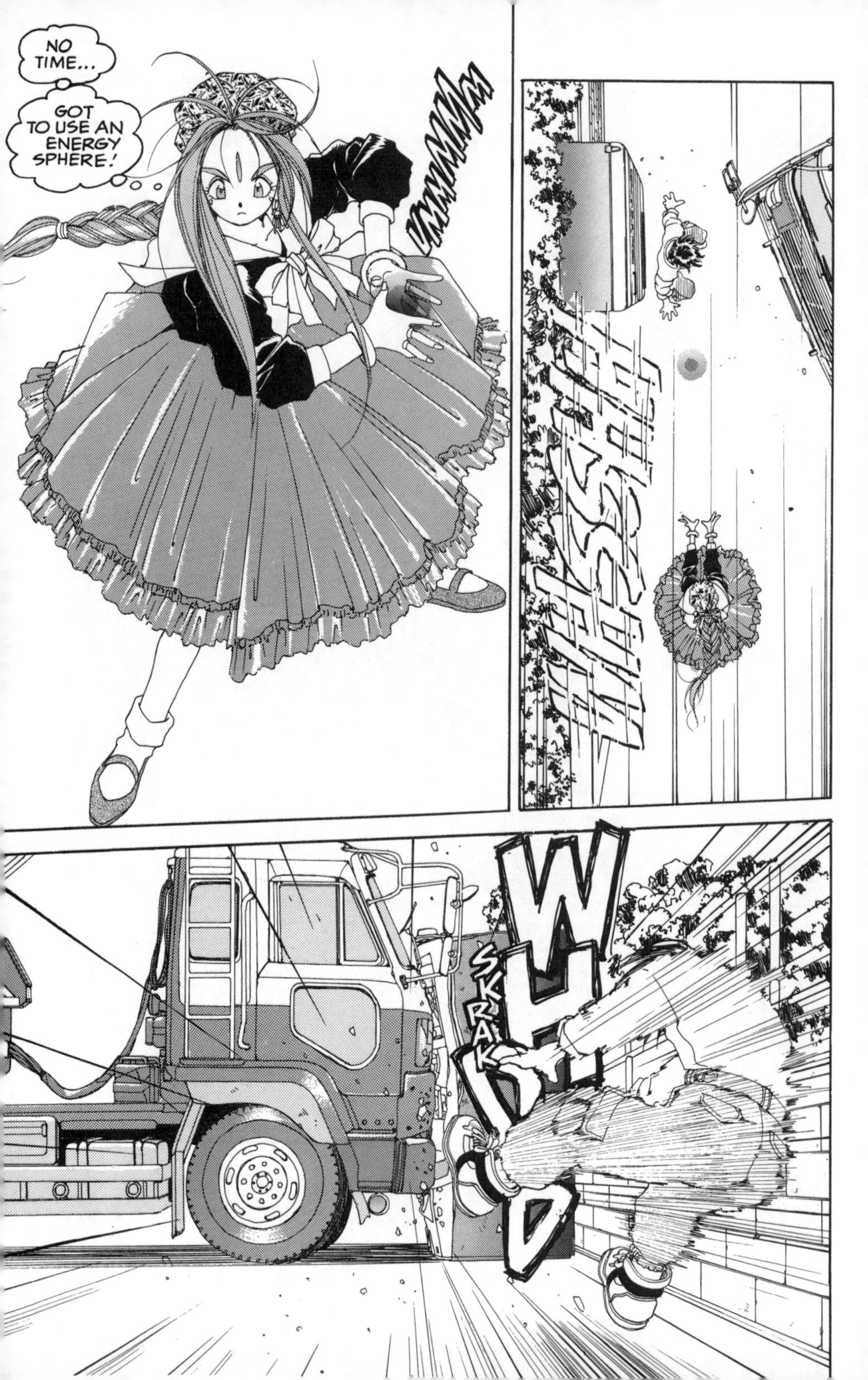
NO TIME...
GOT TO USE AN ENERGY SPHERE!
SKRAK

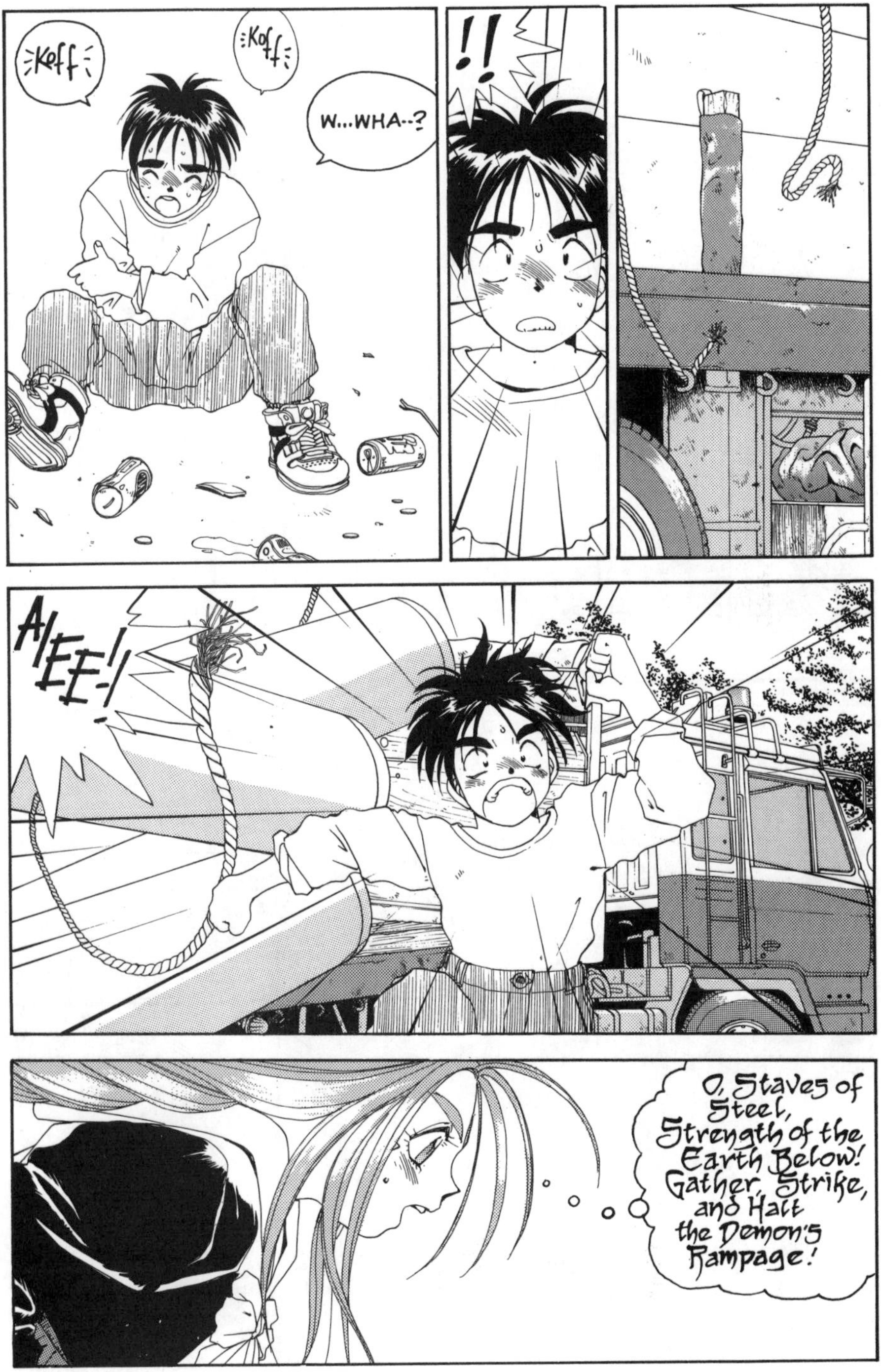
Koff
Koff
W...WHA--?
!!
AIEE-!!
O, Staves of Steel, Strength of the Earth Below! Gather, Strike, and Halt the Demon's Rampage!

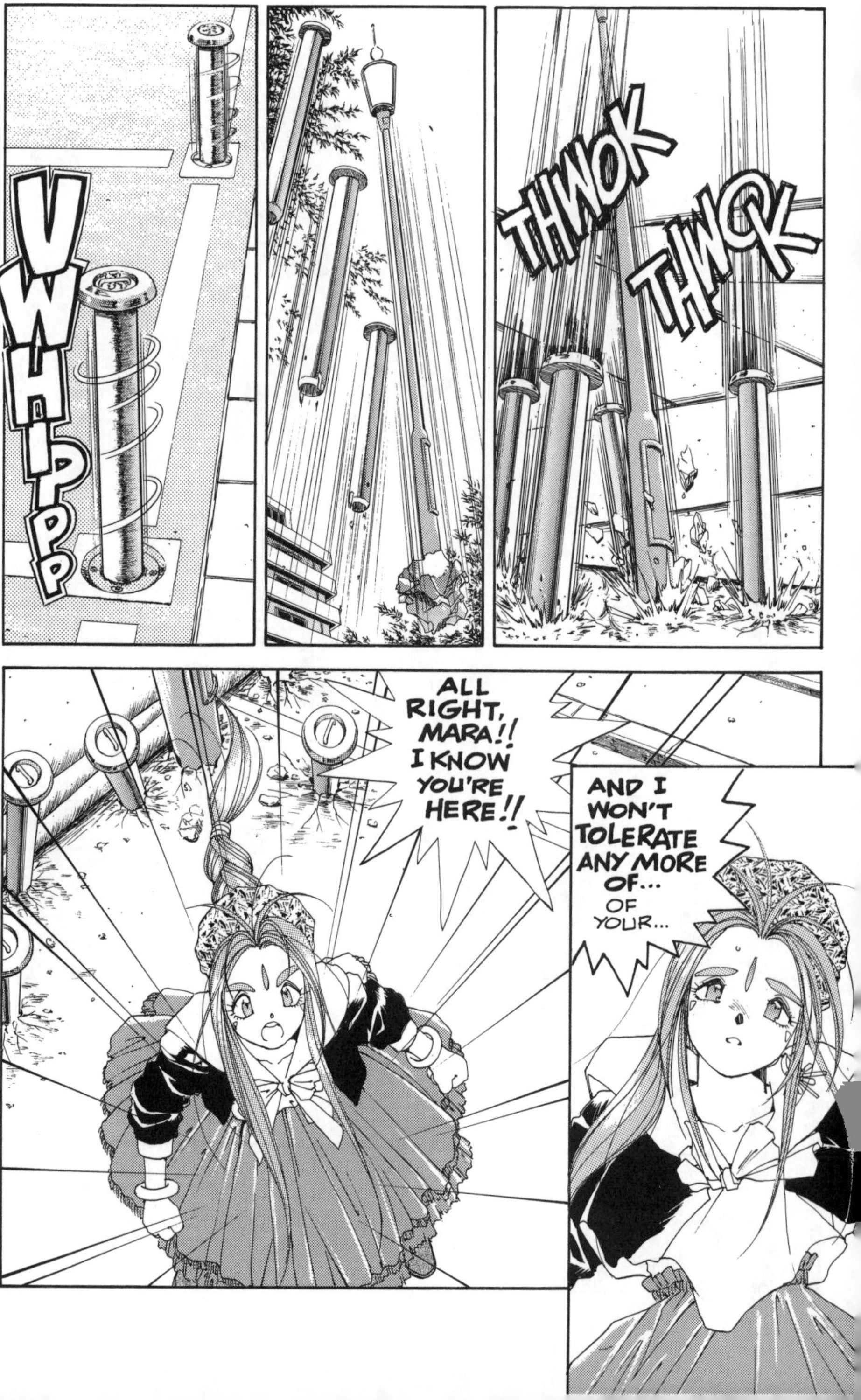
VWHIPPP
THWOK
THWOK
ALL RIGHT, MARA!! I KNOW YOU'RE HERE!!
AND I WON'T TOLERATE ANY MORE OF... OF YOUR...

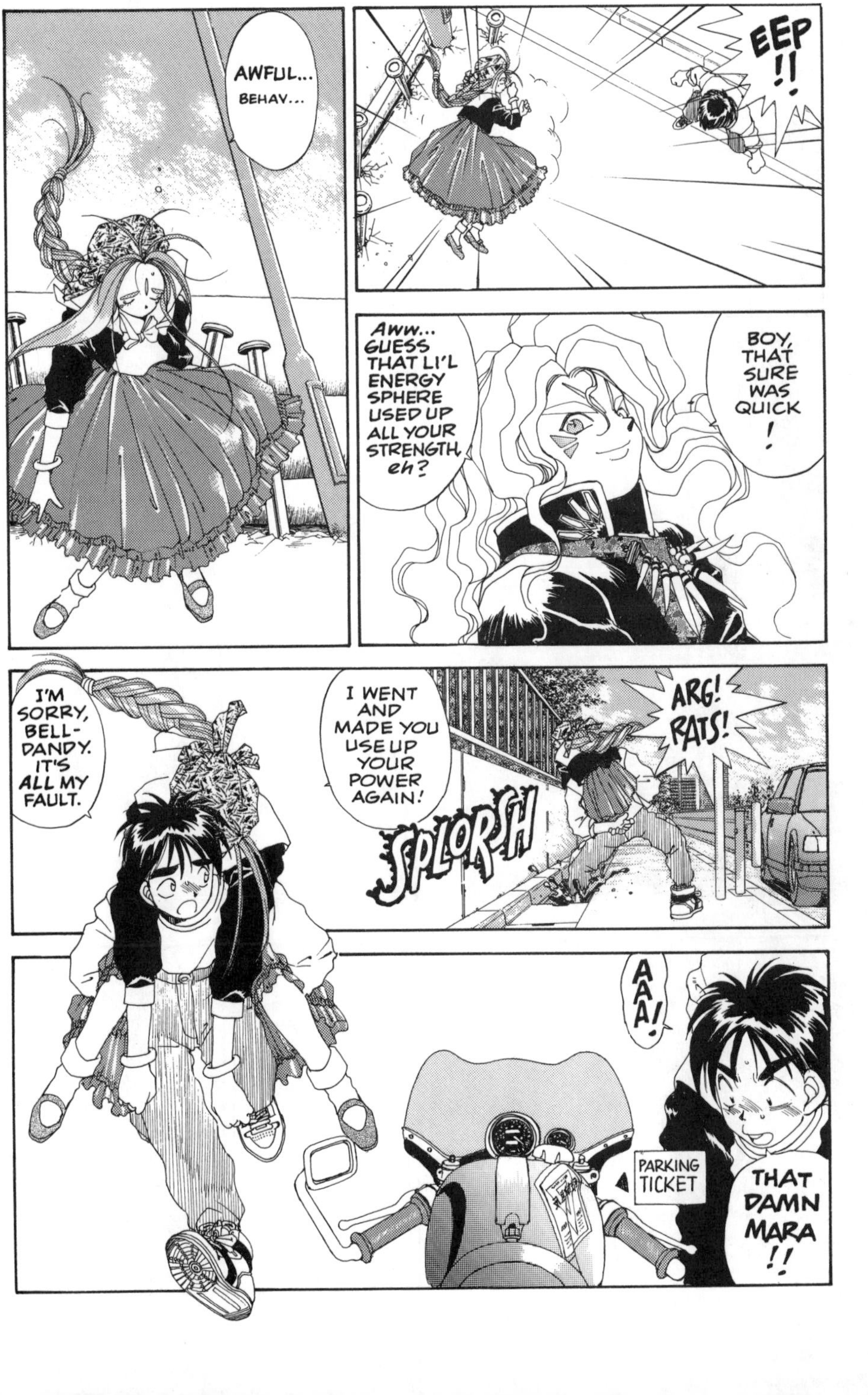
AWFUL... BEHAV...
EEP!!
Aww... GUESS THAT LI'L ENERGY SPHERE USED UP ALL YOUR STRENGTH, eh?
BOY, THAT SURE WAS QUICK!
I'M SORRY, BELL-DANDY. IT'S ALL MY FAULT.
I WENT AND MADE YOU USE UP YOUR POWER AGAIN!
SPLORSH
ARG! RATS!
AAA!
PARKING TICKET
THAT DAMN MARA!!

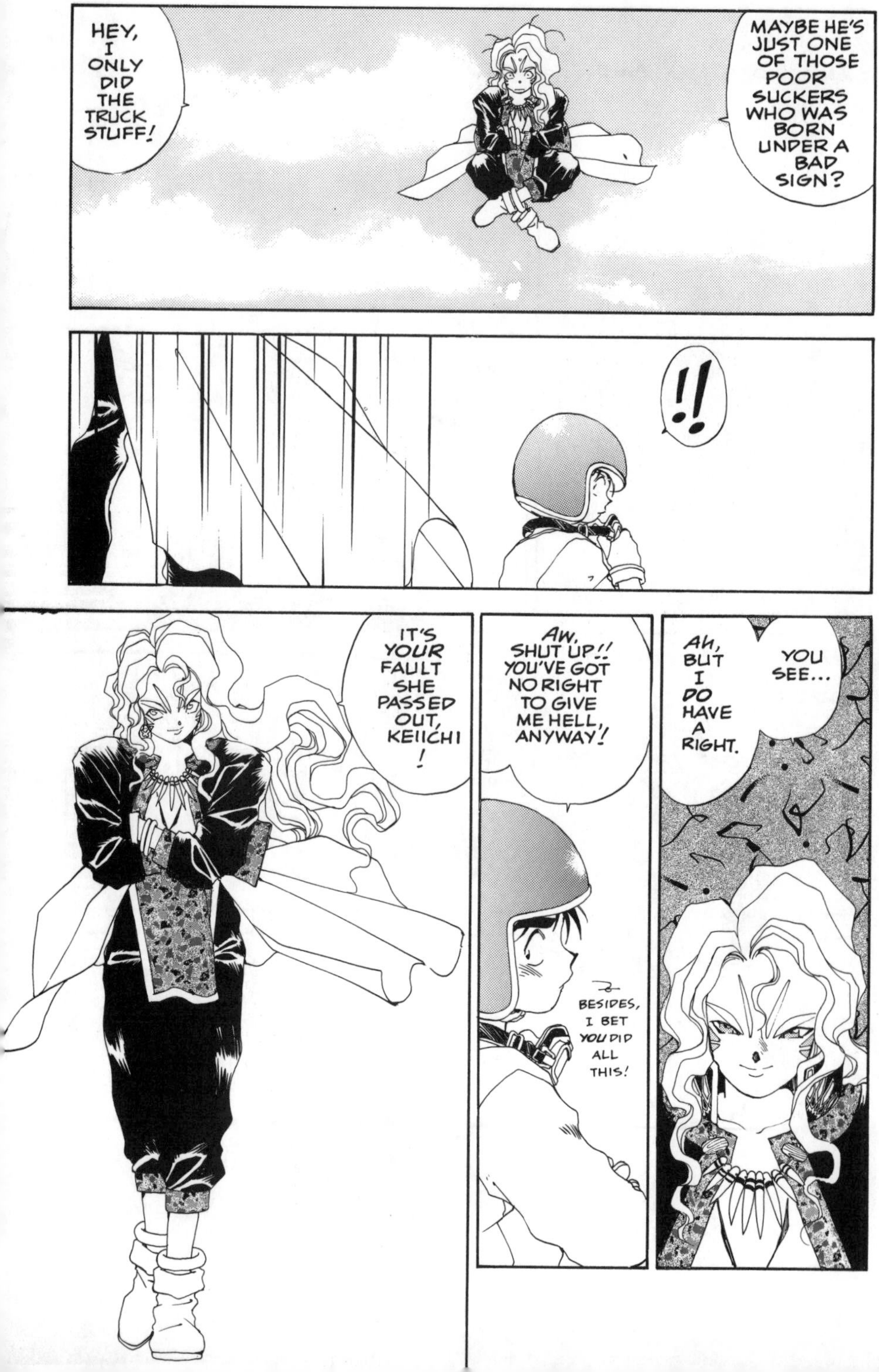

HEY, I ONLY DID THE TRUCK STUFF!
MAYBE HE'S JUST ONE OF THOSE POOR SUCKERS WHO WAS BORN UNDER A BAD SIGN?
!!
IT'S YOUR FAULT SHE PASSED OUT, KEIICHI!
AW, SHUT UP!! YOU'VE GOT NO RIGHT TO GIVE ME HELL, ANYWAY!
BESIDES, I BET YOU DID ALL THIS!
AH, BUT I DO HAVE A RIGHT.
YOU SEE...

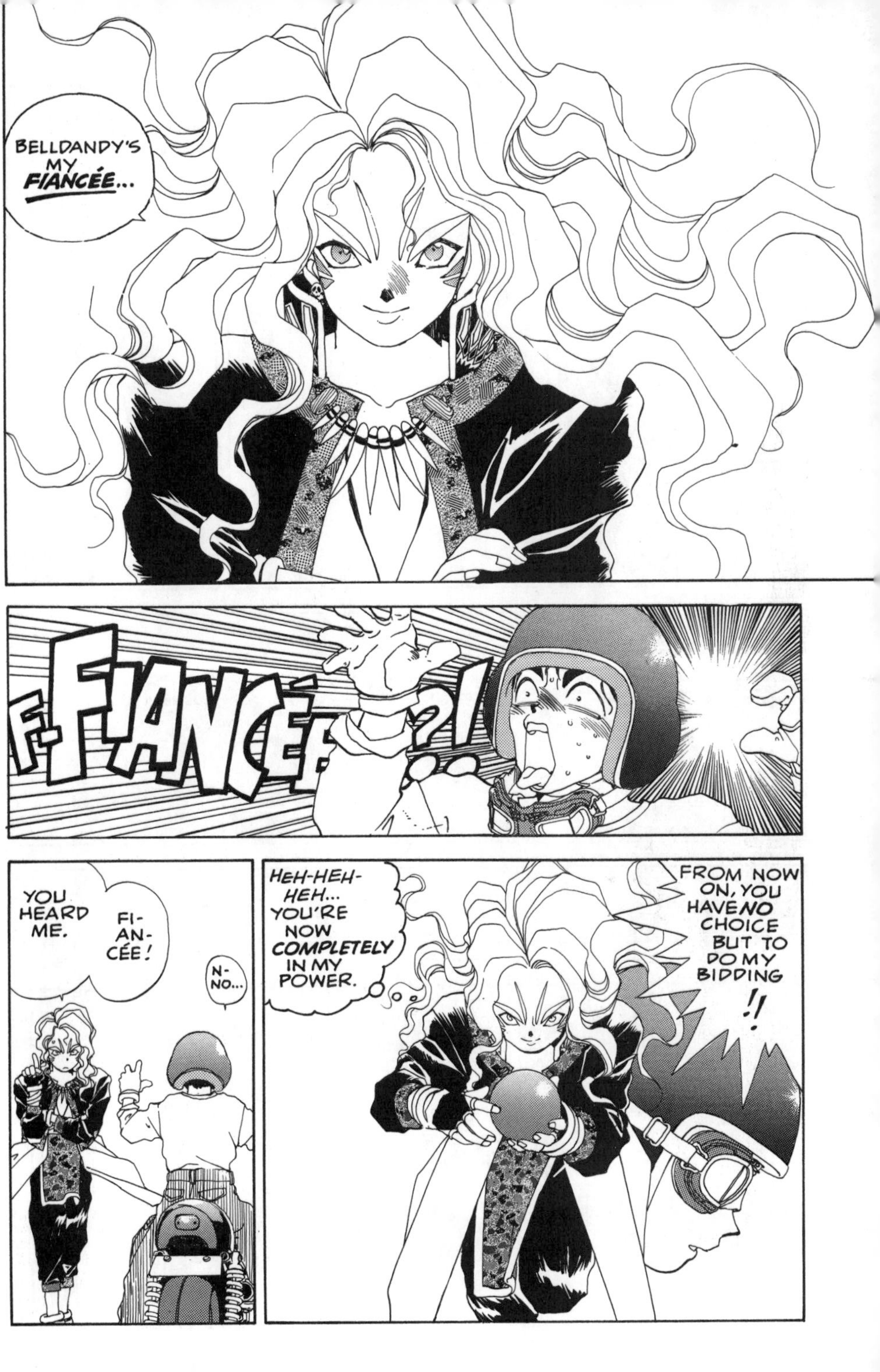
BELLDANDY'S MY FIANCÉE...
F-FIANCÉE?!
YOU HEARD ME.
FI-AN-CÉE!
N-NO...
HEH-HEH-HEH... YOU'RE NOW COMPLETELY IN MY POWER.
FROM NOW ON, YOU HAVE NO CHOICE BUT TO DO MY BIDDING
!!

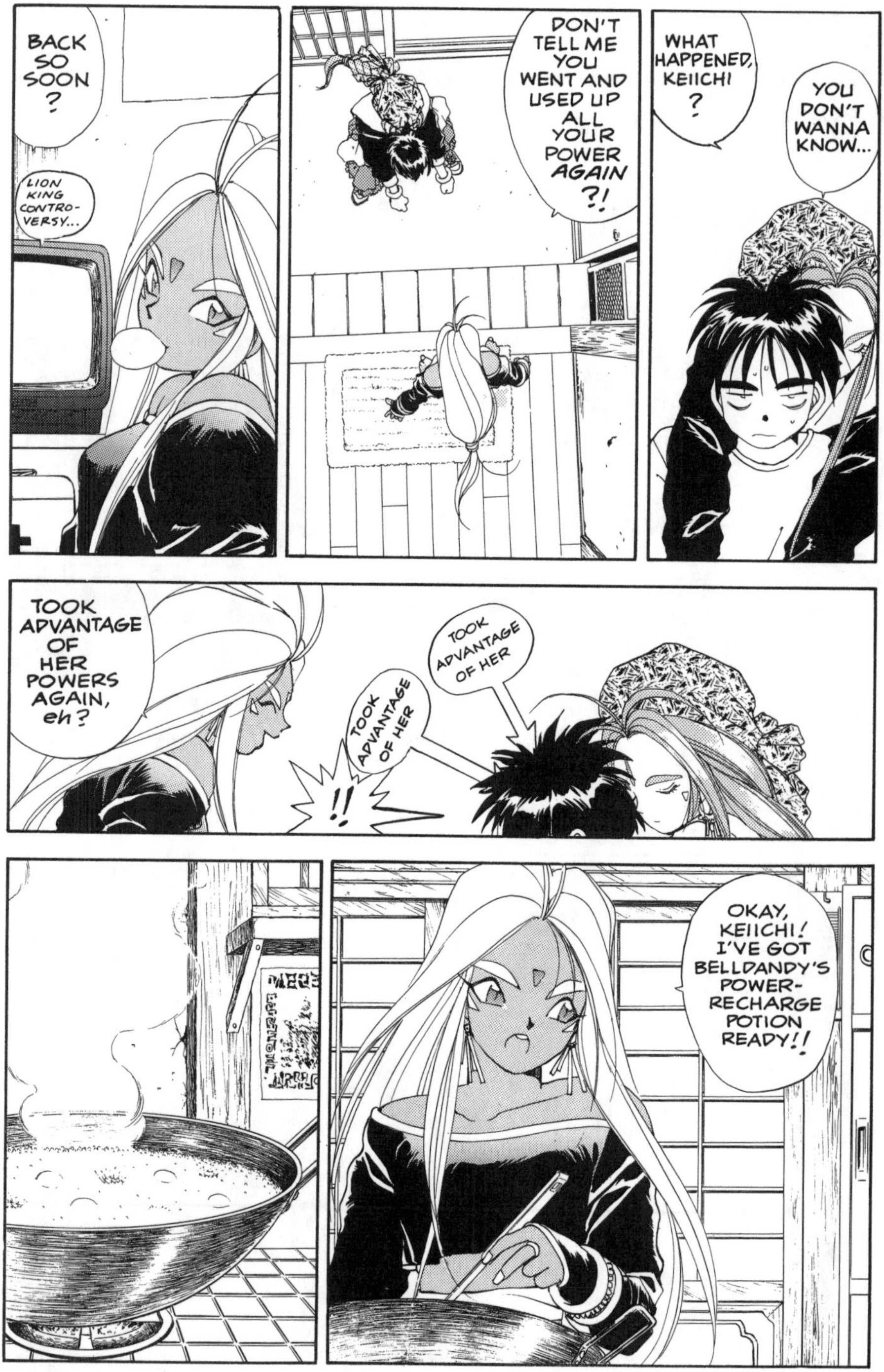
BACK SO SOON?
LION KING CONTRO-VERSY...
DON'T TELL ME YOU WENT AND USED UP ALL YOUR POWER AGAIN?!
WHAT HAPPENED, KEIICHI?
YOU DON'T WANNA KNOW...
TOOK ADVANTAGE OF HER POWERS AGAIN, eh?
!!
TOOK ADVANTAGE OF HER
TOOK ADVANTAGE OF HER
OKAY, KEIICHI! I'VE GOT BELLDANDY'S POWER-RECHARGE POTION READY!!

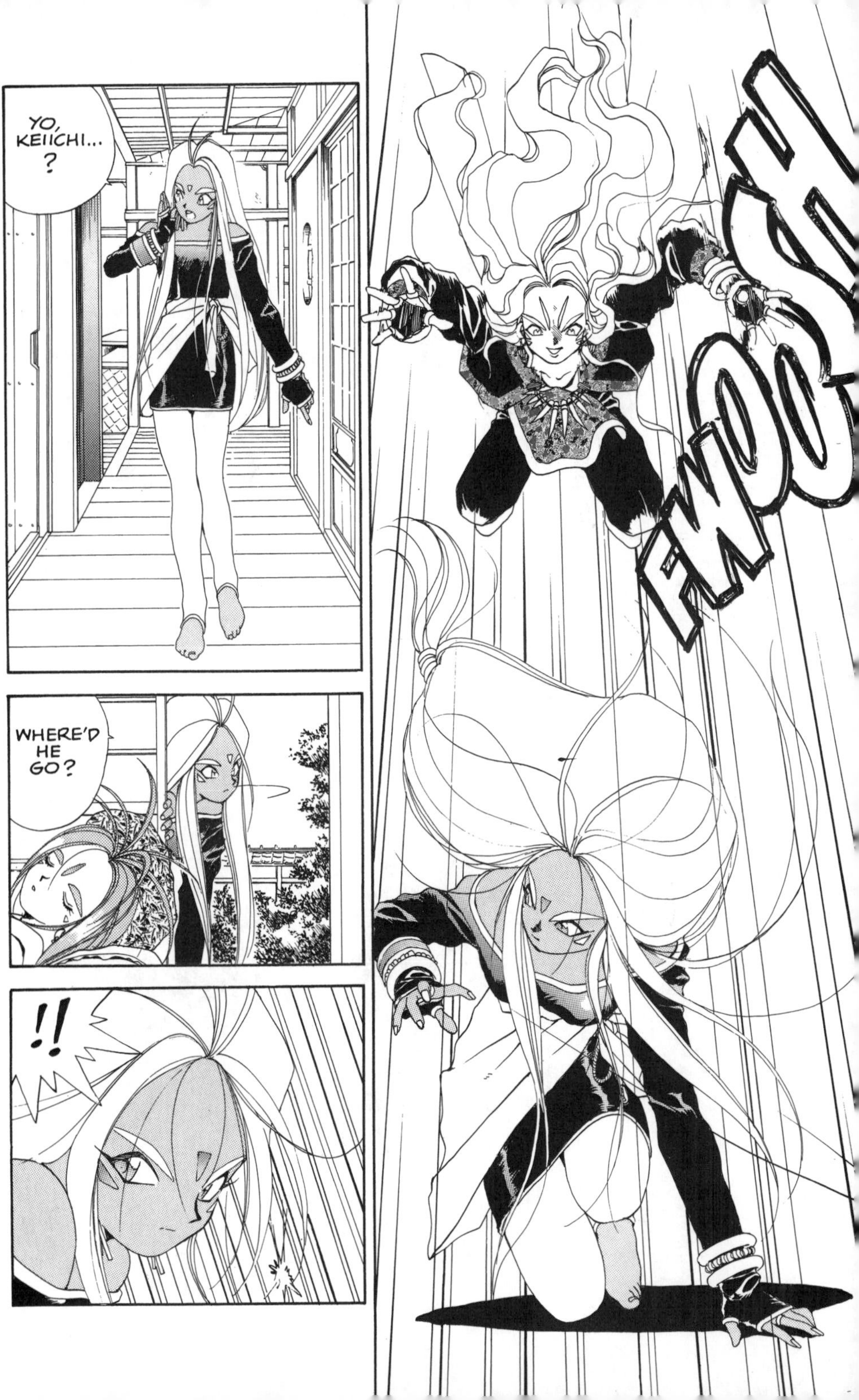

YO, KEIICHI... ?
WHERE'D HE GO?
!!
FWOOSH!

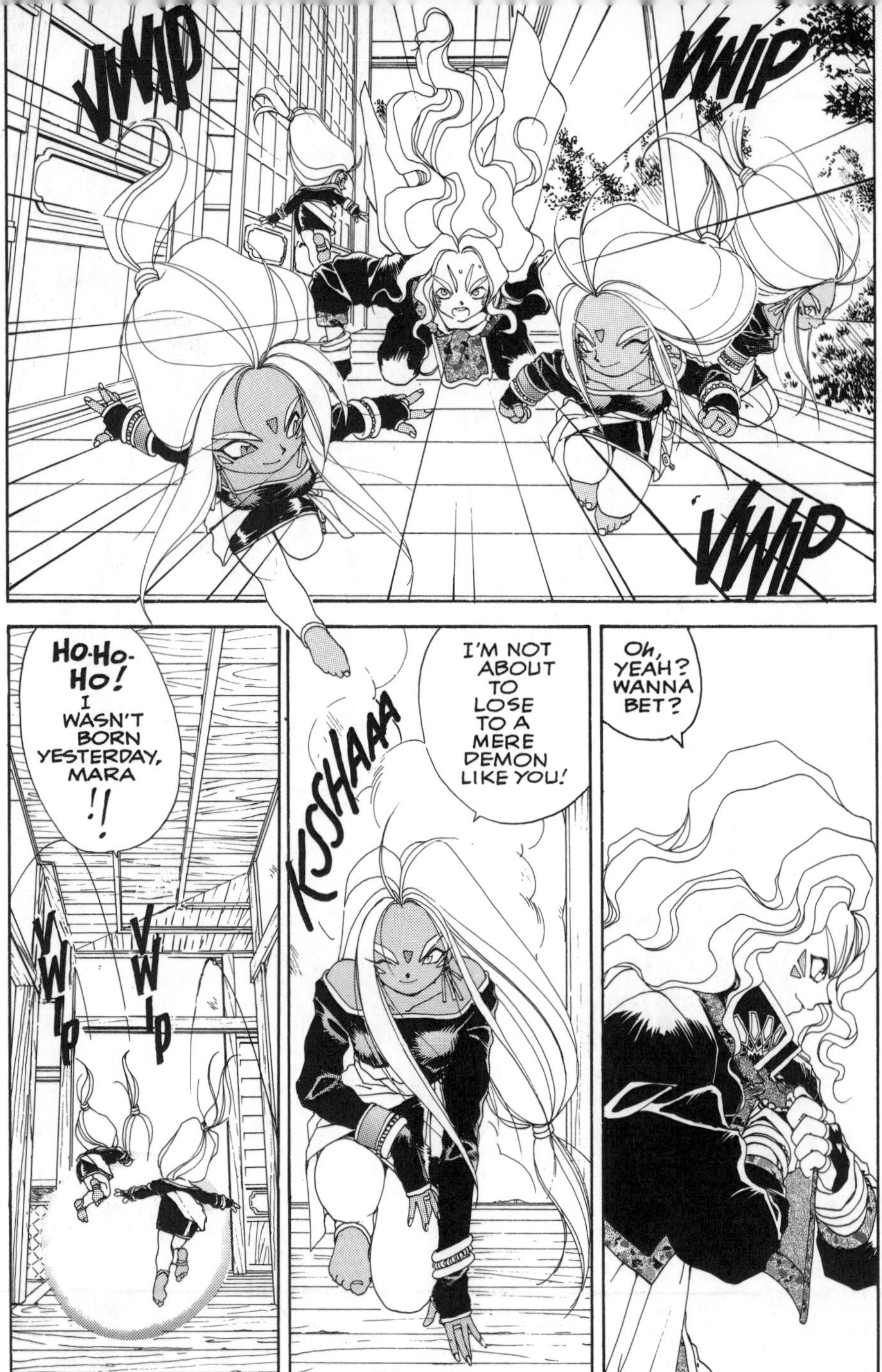
VWIP
VWIP
VWIP
HO-HO-HO! I WASN'T BORN YESTERDAY, MARA !!
VWIP
VWIP
KSSHAAA
I'M NOT ABOUT TO LOSE TO A MERE DEMON LIKE YOU!
Oh, YEAH? WANNA BET?

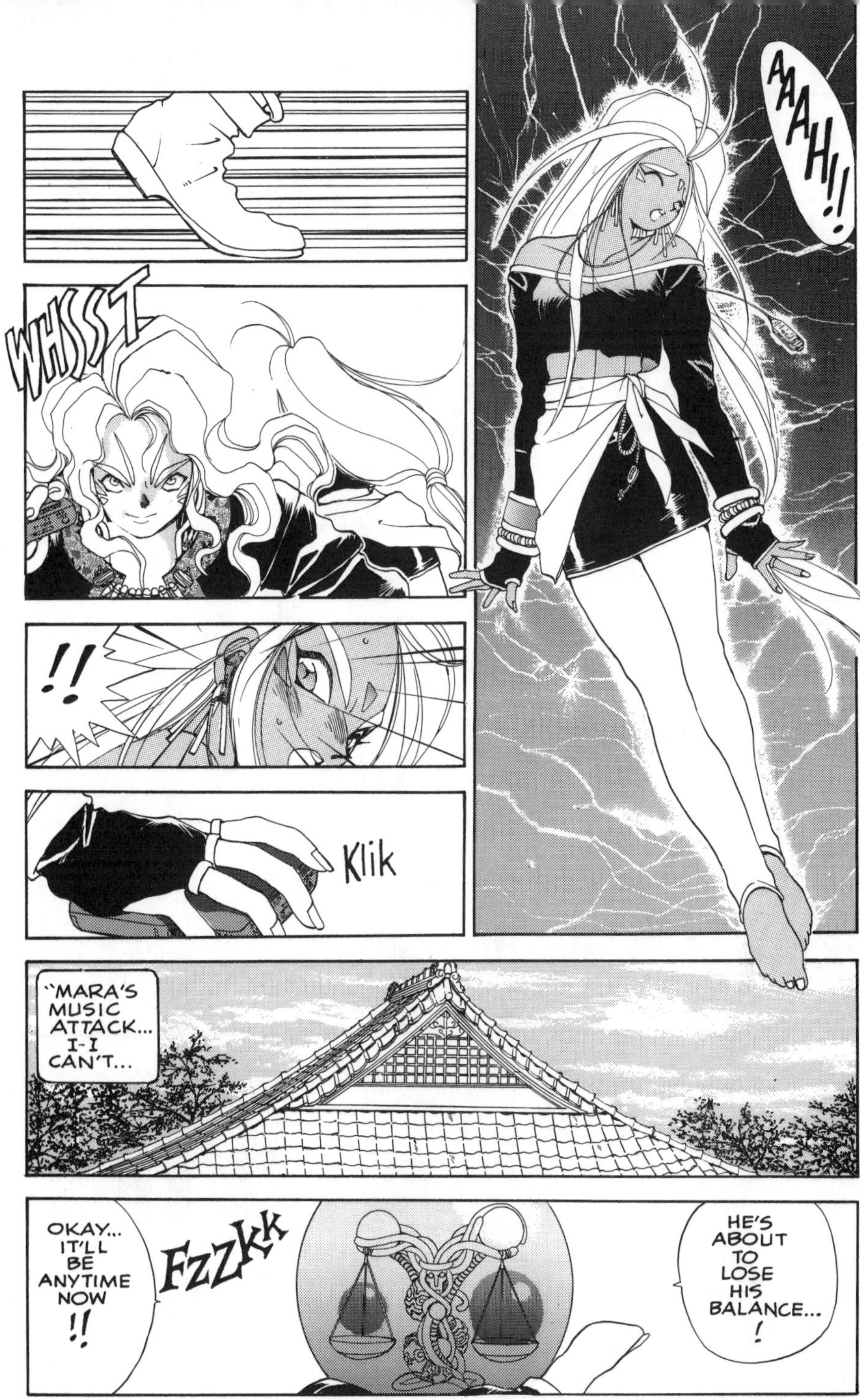
WHSST
!!
Klik
AAAAH!!
"MARA'S MUSIC ATTACK... I-I CAN'T...
OKAY... IT'LL BE ANYTIME NOW !!
FZZKK
HE'S ABOUT TO LOSE HIS BALANCE... !

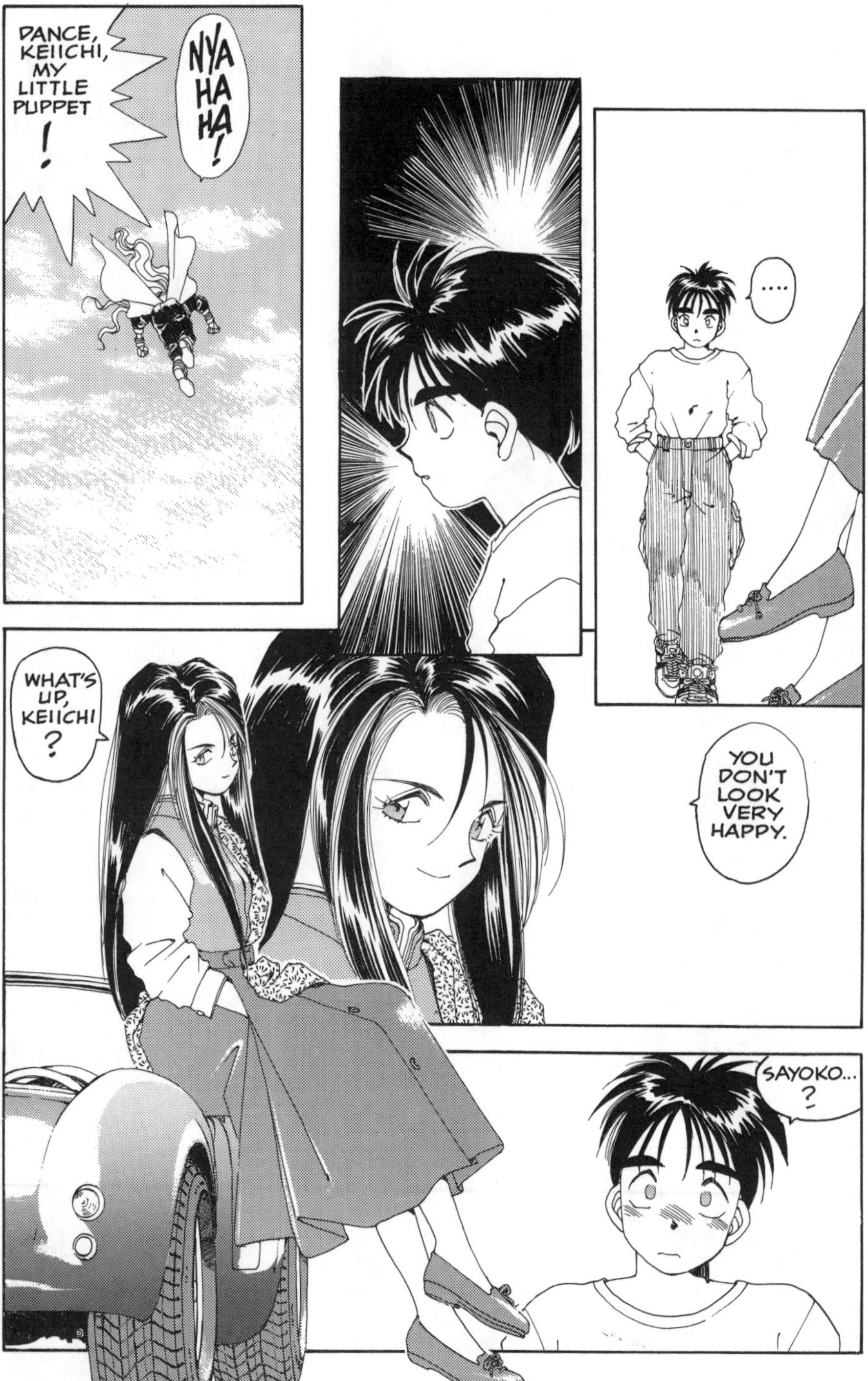
DANCE, KEIICHI, MY LITTLE PUPPET!
NYAHAHAHA!
....
WHAT'S UP, KEIICHI?
YOU DON'T LOOK VERY HAPPY.
SAYOKO...?

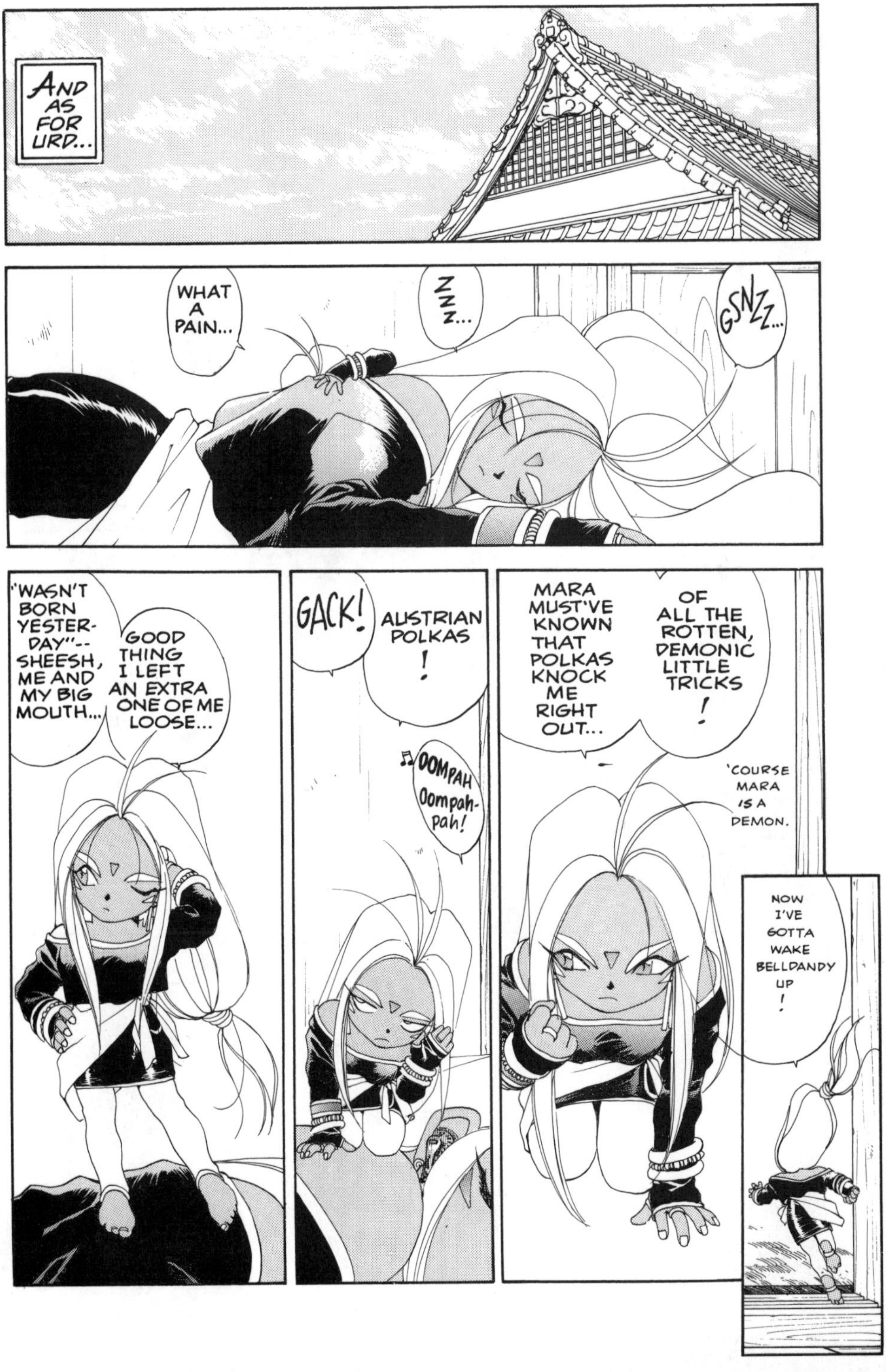
AND AS FOR URD...
WHAT A PAIN...
ZZZ...
GSNZZZ...
"WASN'T BORN YESTER-DAY"-- SHEESH, ME AND MY BIG MOUTH...
GOOD THING I LEFT AN EXTRA ONE OF ME LOOSE...
GACK!
AUSTRIAN POLKAS!
OOMPAH Oompahpah!
MARA MUST'VE KNOWN THAT POLKAS KNOCK ME RIGHT OUT...
OF ALL THE ROTTEN, DEMONIC LITTLE TRICKS!
'COURSE MARA IS A DEMON.
NOW I'VE GOTTA WAKE BELLDANDY UP!

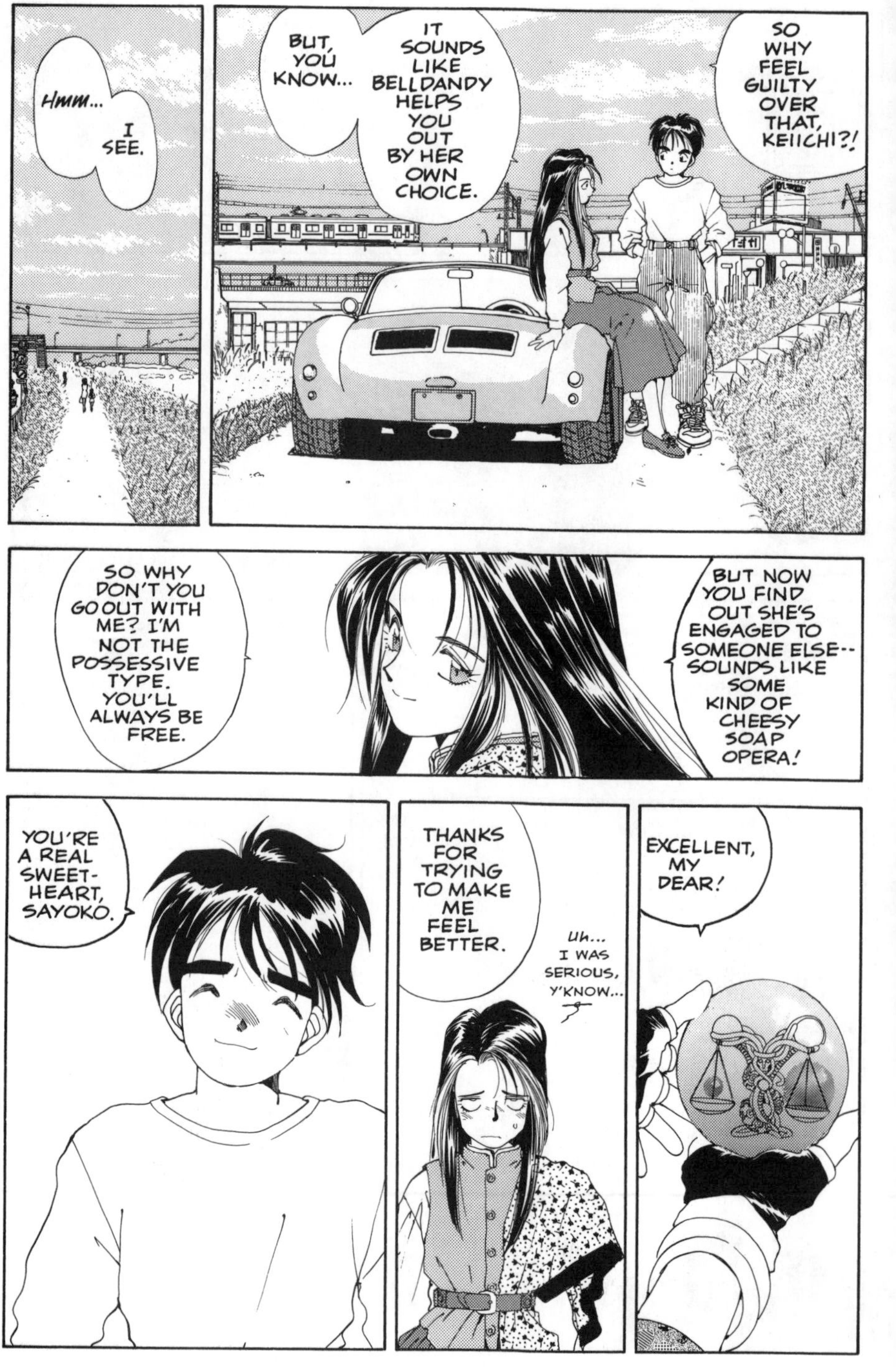
Hmm... I SEE.
BUT, YOU KNOW...
IT SOUNDS LIKE BELLDANDY HELPS YOU OUT BY HER OWN CHOICE.
SO WHY FEEL GUILTY OVER THAT, KEIICHI?!
SO WHY DON'T YOU GO OUT WITH ME? I'M NOT THE POSSESSIVE TYPE. YOU'LL ALWAYS BE FREE.
BUT NOW YOU FIND OUT SHE'S ENGAGED TO SOMEONE ELSE--SOUNDS LIKE SOME KIND OF CHEESY SOAP OPERA!
YOU'RE A REAL SWEET-HEART, SAYOKO.
THANKS FOR TRYING TO MAKE ME FEEL BETTER.
UH... I WAS SERIOUS, Y'KNOW...
EXCELLENT, MY DEAR!

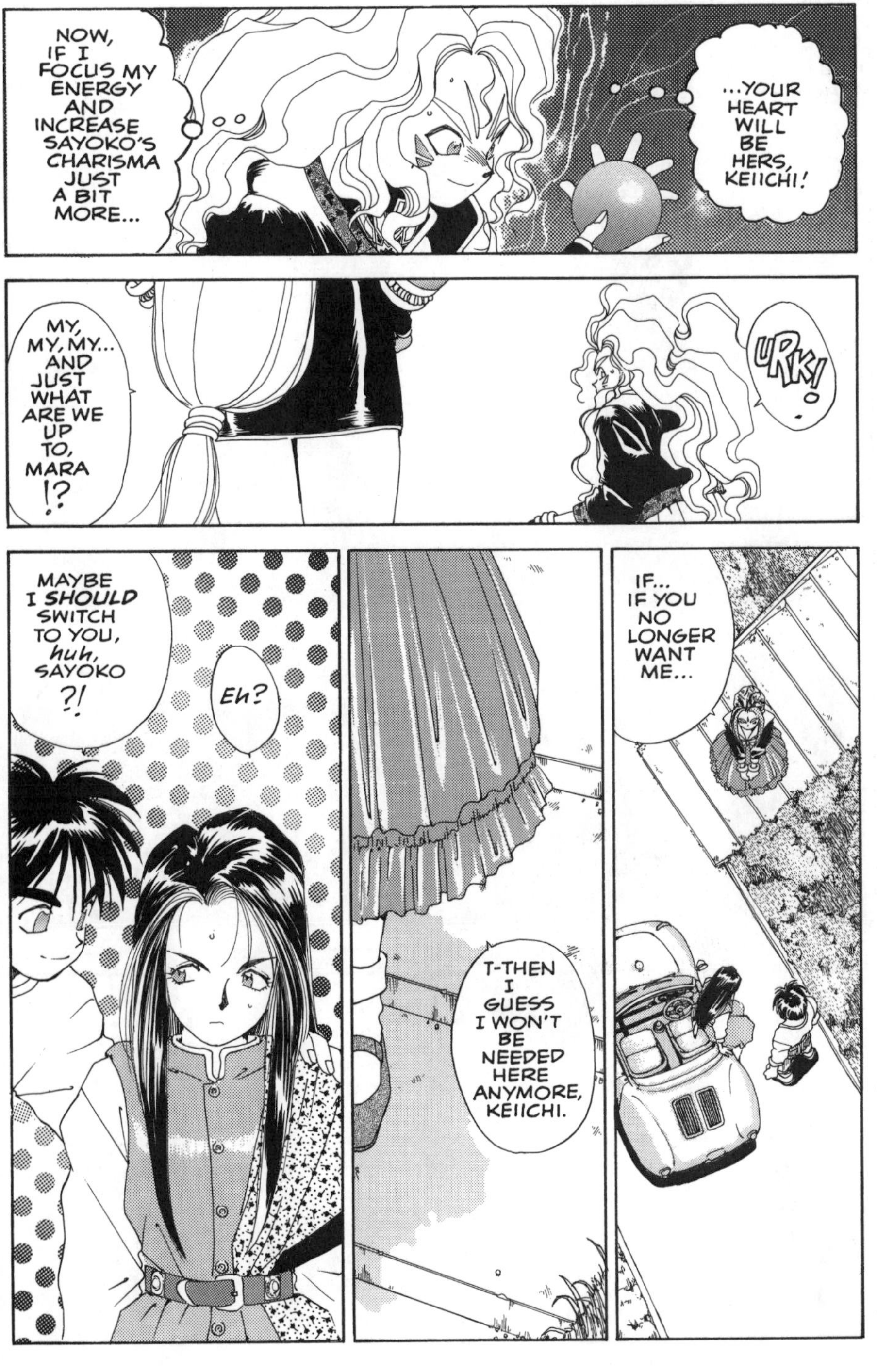
NOW, IF I FOCUS MY ENERGY AND INCREASE SAYOKO'S CHARISMA JUST A BIT MORE...
...YOUR HEART WILL BE HERS, KEIICHI!
MY, MY, MY... AND JUST WHAT ARE WE UP TO, MARA!?
URK!
MAYBE I SHOULD SWITCH TO YOU, huh, SAYOKO?!
Eh?
T-THEN I GUESS I WON'T BE NEEDED HERE ANYMORE, KEIICHI.
IF... IF YOU NO LONGER WANT ME...

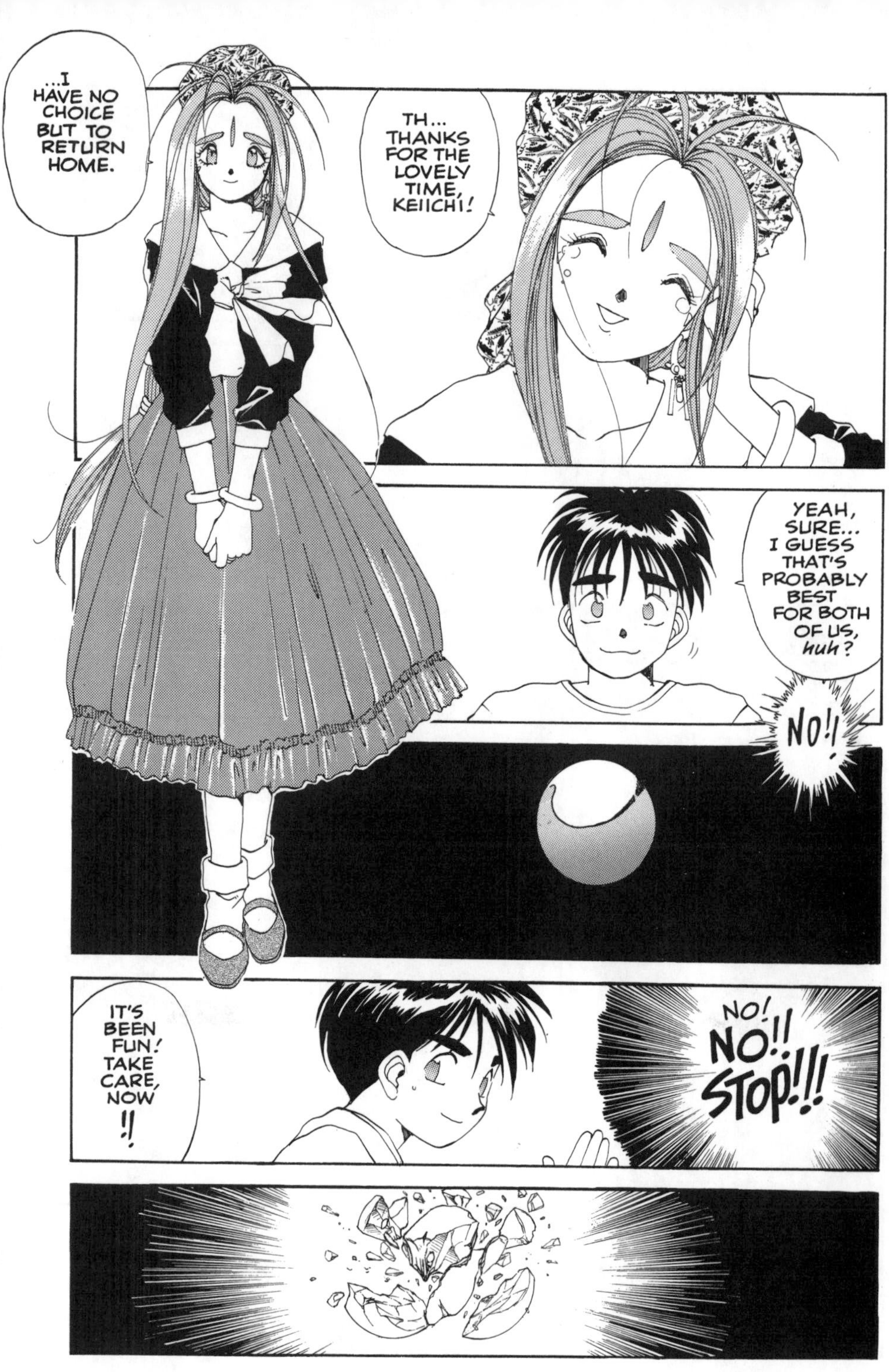

...I HAVE NO CHOICE BUT TO RETURN HOME.
TH... THANKS FOR THE LOVELY TIME, KEIICHI!
YEAH, SURE... I GUESS THAT'S PROBABLY BEST FOR BOTH OF US, huh?
NO!!
IT'S BEEN FUN! TAKE CARE, NOW!!
NO! NO!! STOP!!!

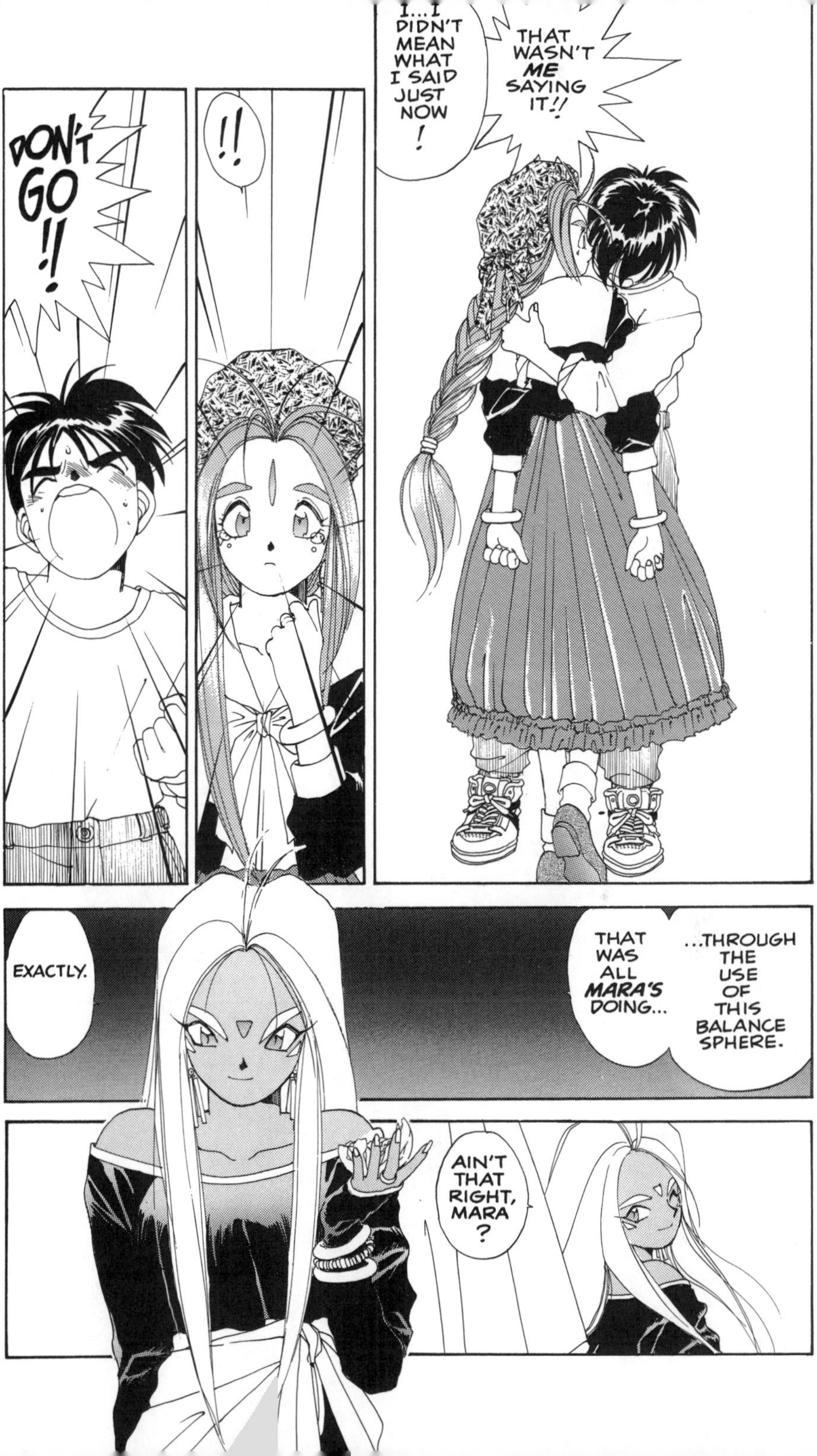
DON'T GO!!
!!
I...I DIDN'T MEAN WHAT I SAID JUST NOW!
THAT WASN'T ME SAYING IT!!
EXACTLY.
THAT WAS ALL MARA'S DOING...
...THROUGH THE USE OF THIS BALANCE SPHERE.
AIN'T THAT RIGHT, MARA?

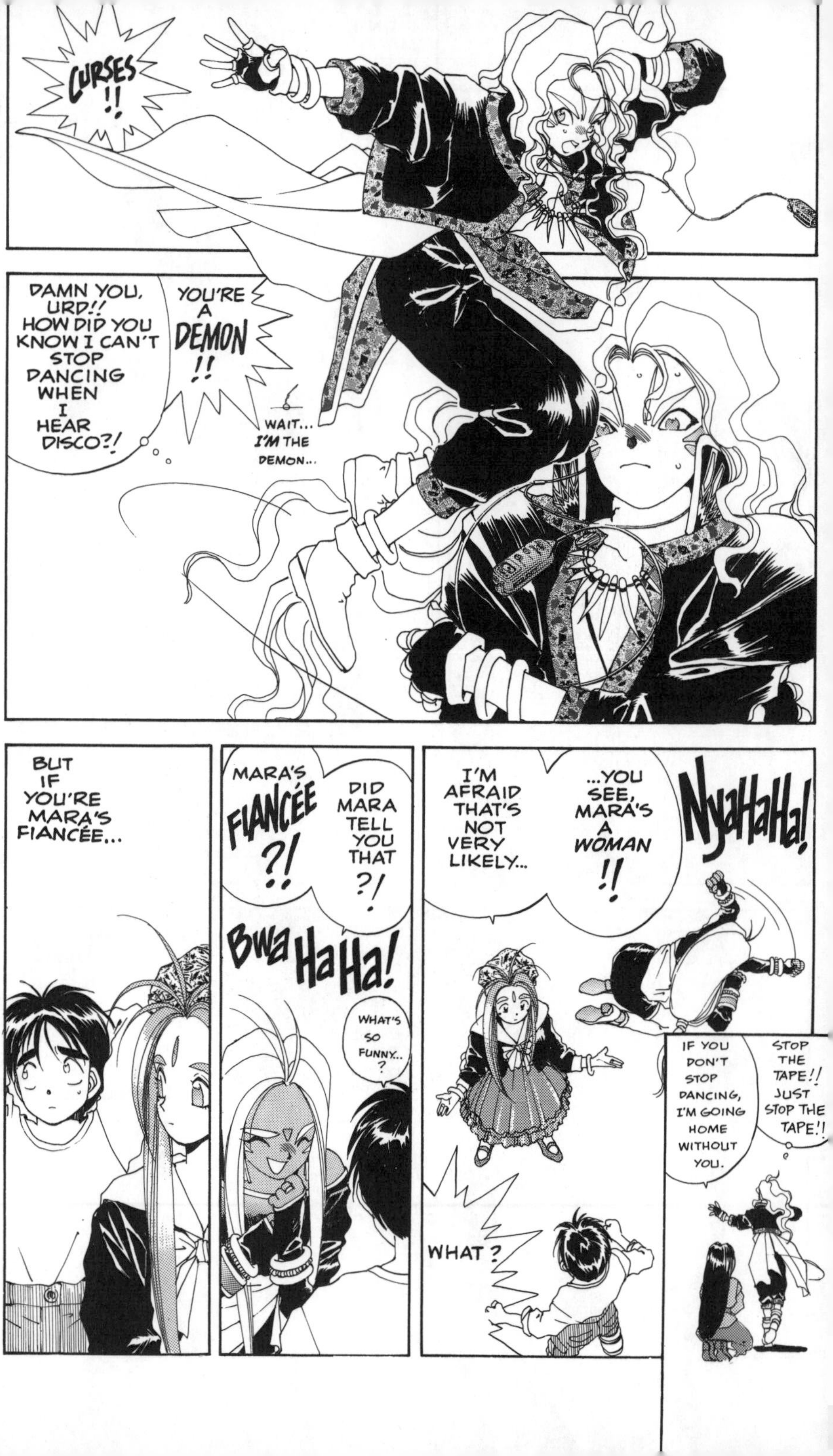
CURSES!!
DAMN YOU, URD!! HOW DID YOU KNOW I CAN'T STOP DANCING WHEN I HEAR DISCO?!
YOU'RE A DEMON!!
WAIT... I'M THE DEMON...
BUT IF YOU'RE MARA'S FIANCÉE...
MARA'S FIANCÉE?!
DID MARA TELL YOU THAT?!
BWAHAHA!
WHAT'S SO FUNNY...?
I'M AFRAID THAT'S NOT VERY LIKELY...
...YOU SEE, MARA'S A WOMAN!!
NYAHAHA!
WHAT?
IF YOU DON'T STOP DANCING, I'M GOING HOME WITHOUT YOU.
STOP THE TAPE!! JUST STOP THE TAPE!!

Sympathy for the Devil

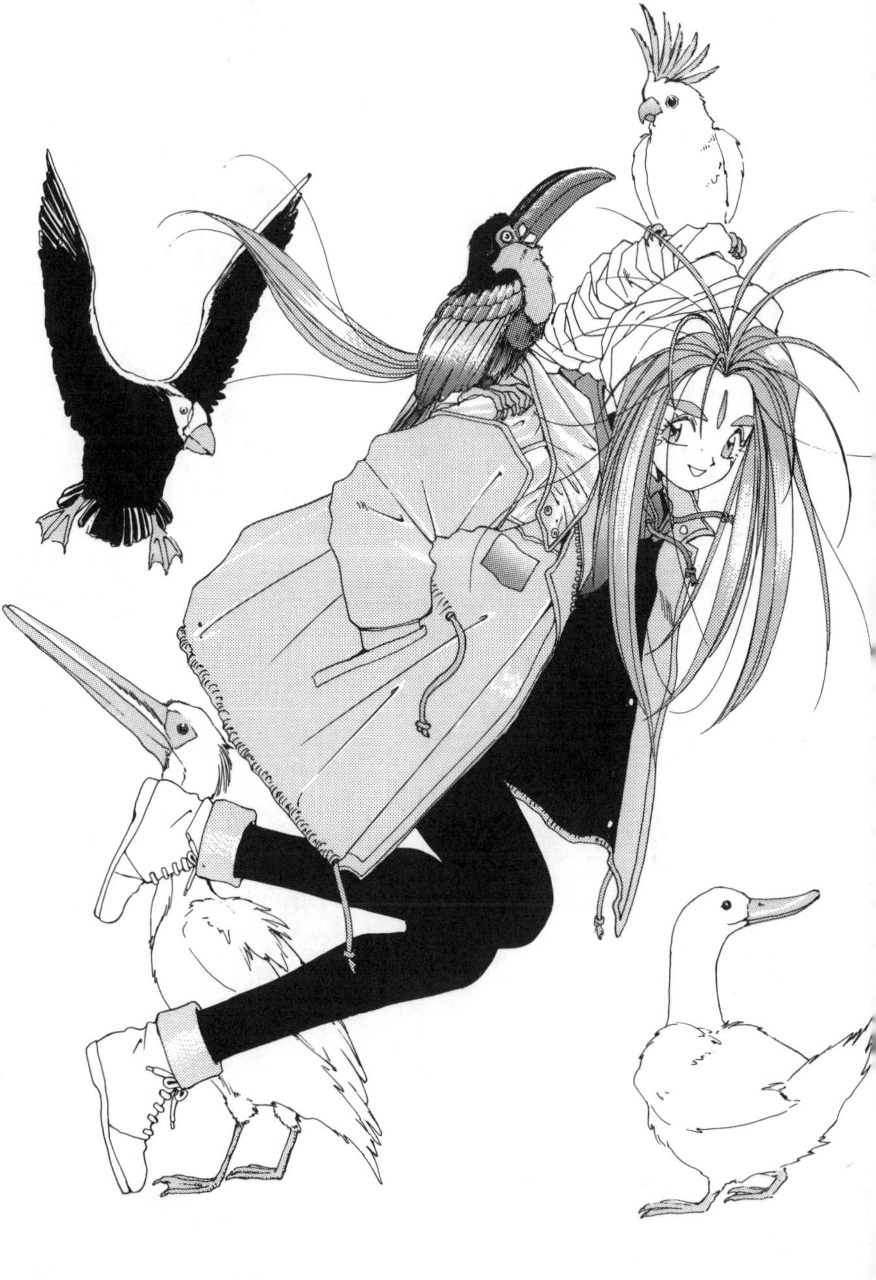

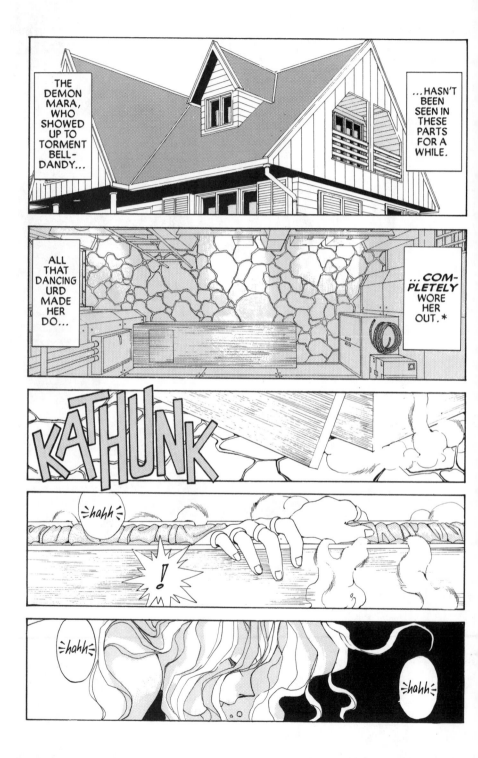

THE DEMON MARA, WHO SHOWED UP TO TORMENT BELL-DANDY...

...HASN'T BEEN SEEN IN THESE PARTS FOR A WHILE.

ALL THAT DANCING URD MADE HER DO...

...COM-PLETELY WORE HER OUT. *

KATHUNK

≒hahh≒

！

≒hahh≒

≒hahh≒

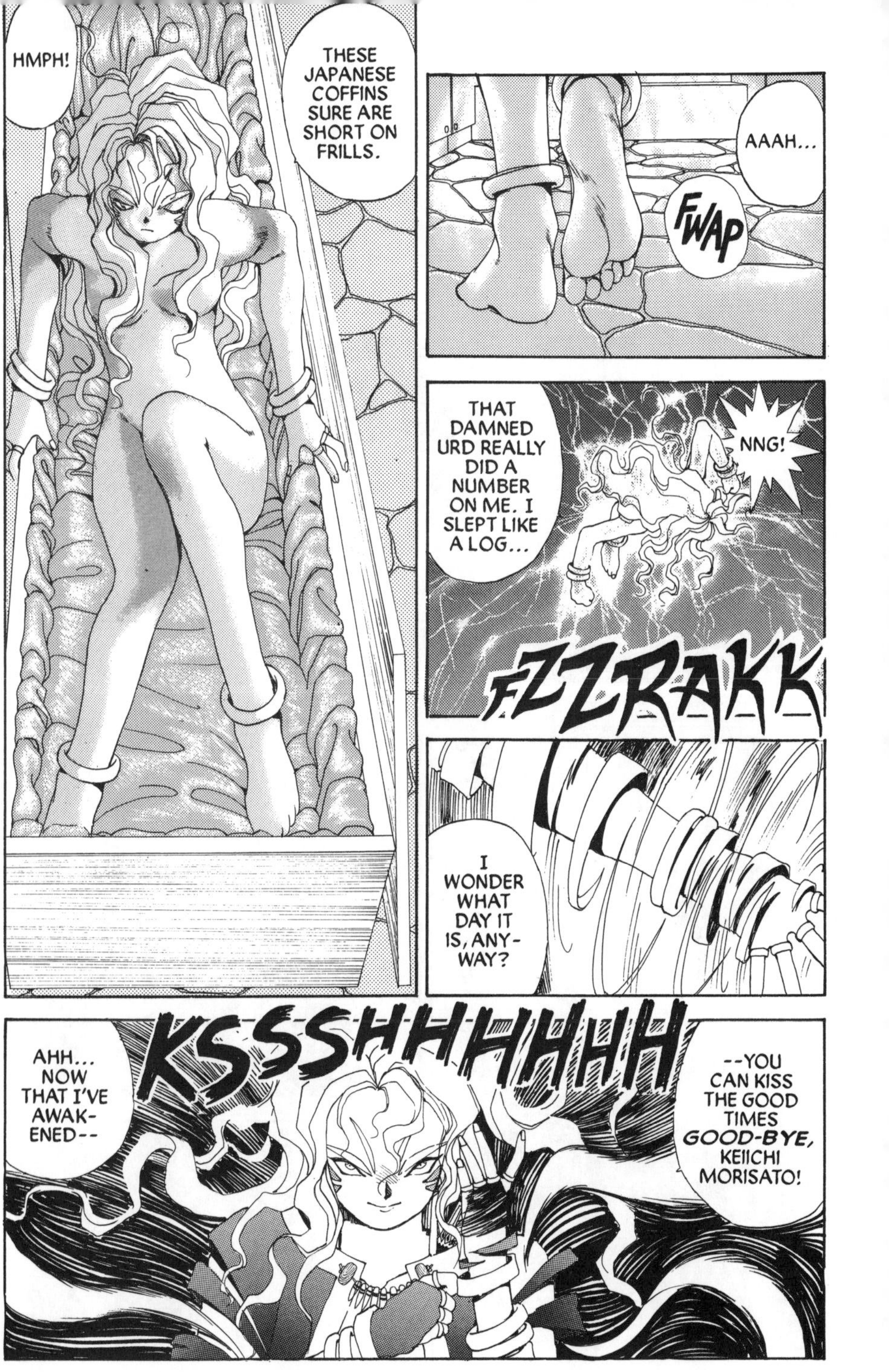
HMPH!
THESE JAPANESE COFFINS SURE ARE SHORT ON FRILLS.
AAAH...
FWAP
THAT DAMNED URD REALLY DID A NUMBER ON ME. I SLEPT LIKE A LOG...
NNG!
FZZRAKK
I WONDER WHAT DAY IT IS, ANY-WAY?
KSSSHHHHHH
AHH... NOW THAT I'VE AWAK-ENED--
--YOU CAN KISS THE GOOD TIMES *GOOD-BYE,* KEIICHI MORISATO!

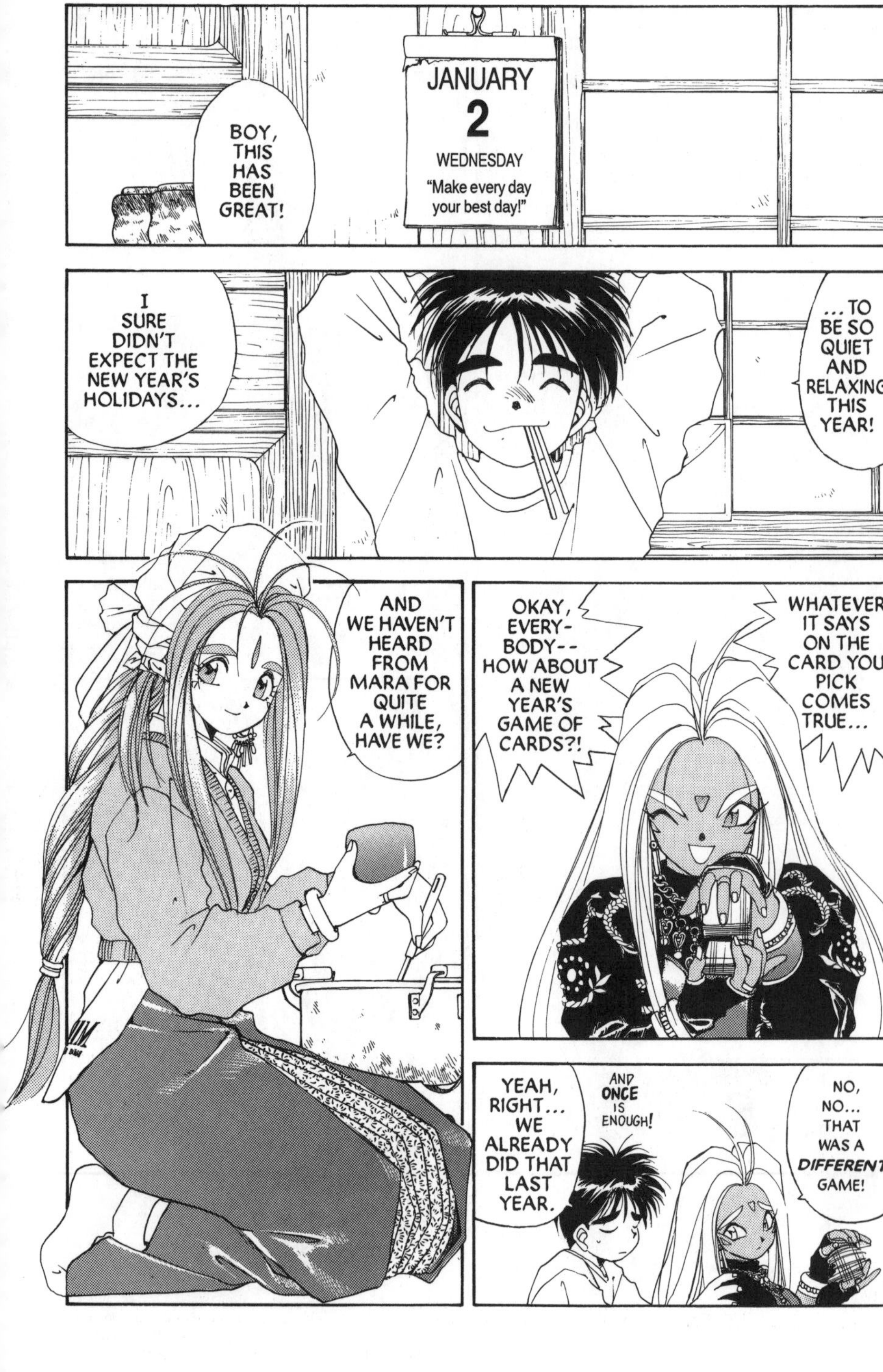
BOY, THIS HAS BEEN GREAT!
JANUARY
2
WEDNESDAY
"Make every day your best day!"
I SURE DIDN'T EXPECT THE NEW YEAR'S HOLIDAYS...
...TO BE SO QUIET AND RELAXING THIS YEAR!
AND WE HAVEN'T HEARD FROM MARA FOR QUITE A WHILE, HAVE WE?
OKAY, EVERY-BODY--HOW ABOUT A NEW YEAR'S GAME OF CARDS?!
WHATEVER IT SAYS ON THE CARD YOU PICK COMES TRUE...
YEAH, RIGHT... WE ALREADY DID THAT LAST YEAR.
AND ONCE IS ENOUGH!
NO, NO... THAT WAS A DIFFERENT GAME!

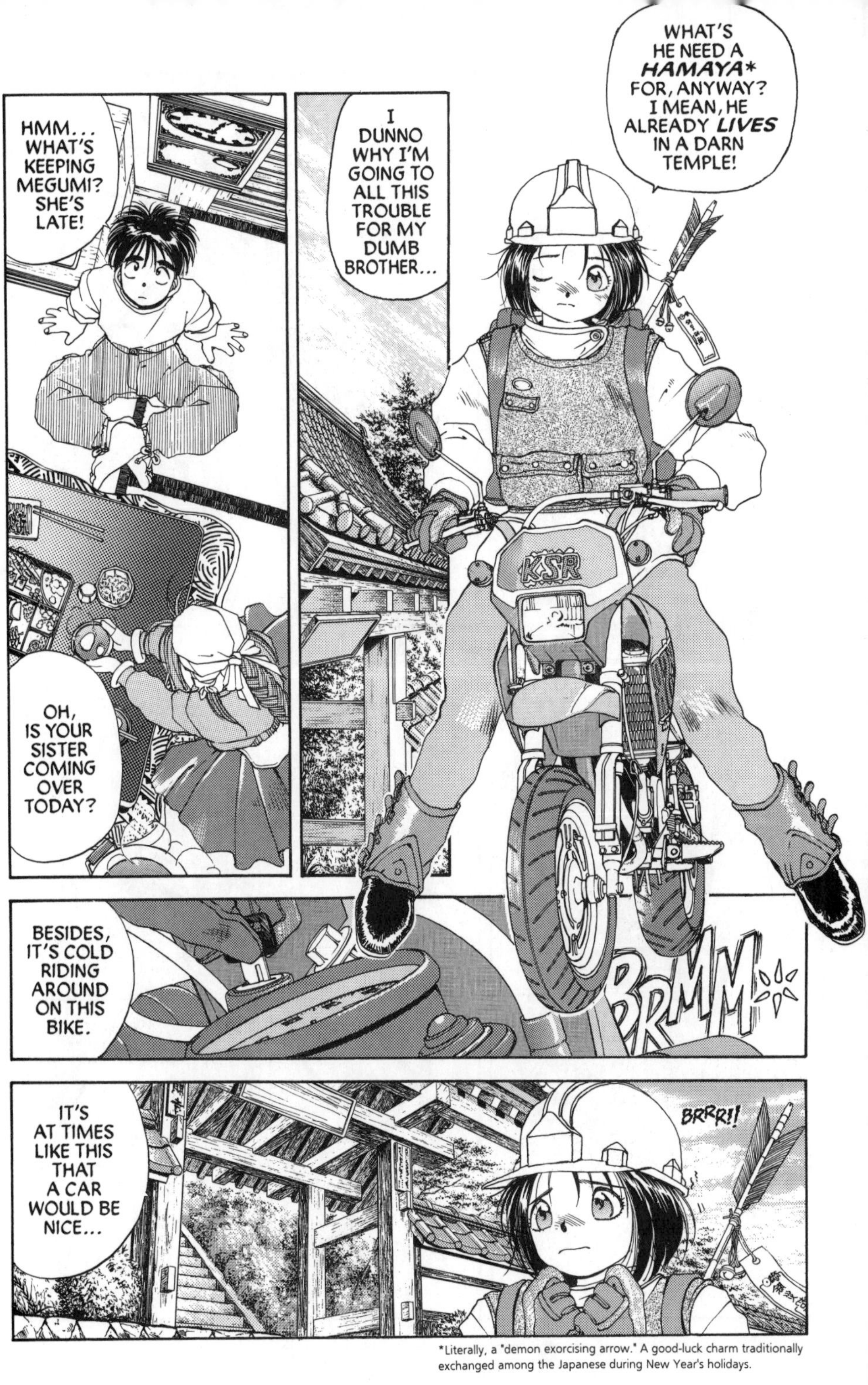
HMM... WHAT'S KEEPING MEGUMI? SHE'S LATE!
OH, IS YOUR SISTER COMING OVER TODAY?
I DUNNO WHY I'M GOING TO ALL THIS TROUBLE FOR MY DUMB BROTHER...
WHAT'S HE NEED A HAMAYA* FOR, ANYWAY? I MEAN, HE ALREADY LIVES IN A DARN TEMPLE!
BESIDES, IT'S COLD RIDING AROUND ON THIS BIKE.
BRMMM
IT'S AT TIMES LIKE THIS THAT A CAR WOULD BE NICE...
BRRR!!

*Literally, a "demon exorcising arrow." A good-luck charm traditionally exchanged among the Japanese during New Year's holidays.

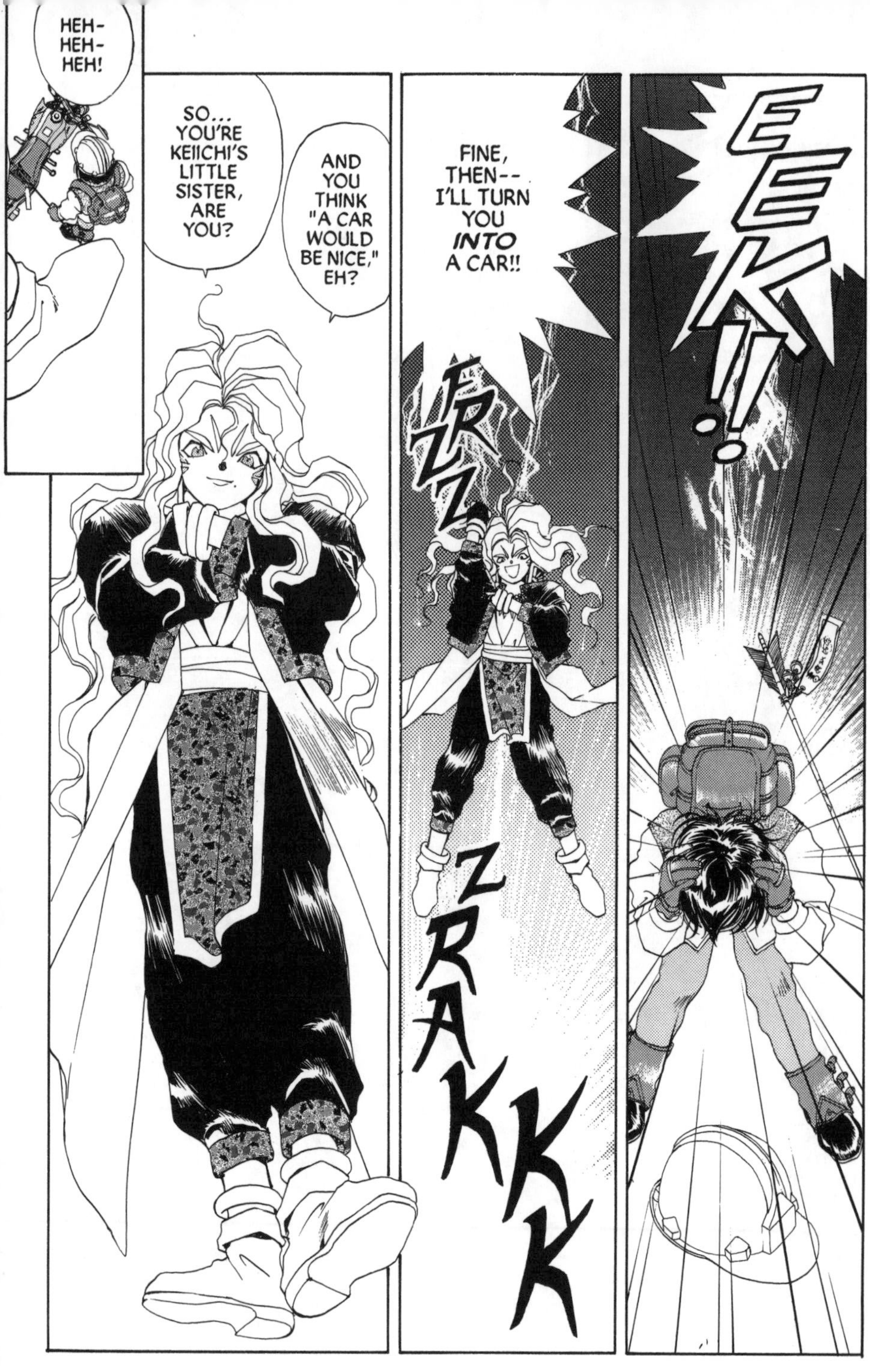
HEH-HEH-HEH!
SO... YOU'RE KEIICHI'S LITTLE SISTER, ARE YOU?
AND YOU THINK "A CAR WOULD BE NICE," EH?
FINE, THEN-- I'LL TURN YOU *INTO* A CAR!!
FRZZ
ZRAKKKK
EEEK!!!

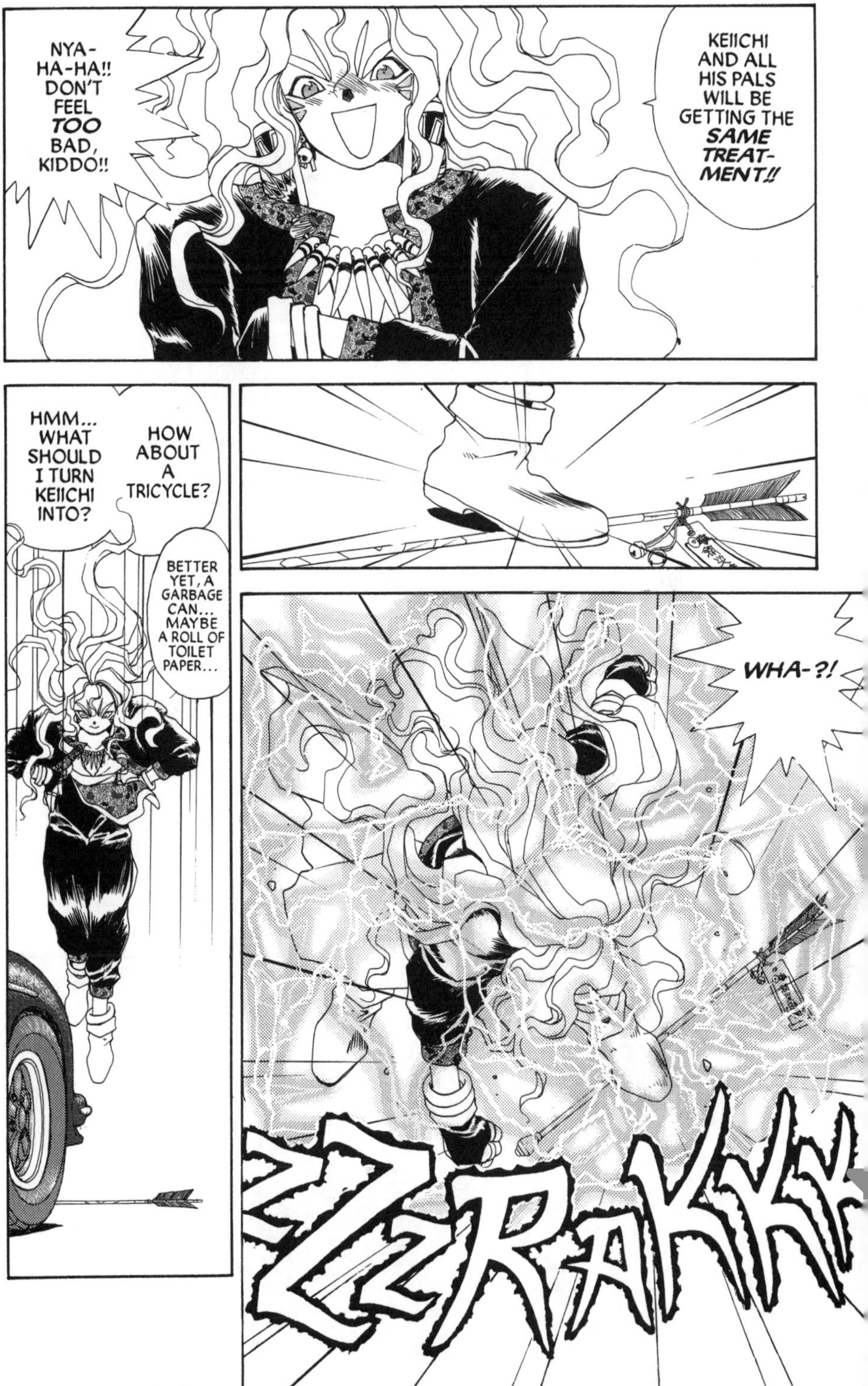
NYA-HA-HA!! DON'T FEEL *TOO* BAD, KIDDO!!
KEIICHI AND ALL HIS PALS WILL BE GETTING THE *SAME TREAT-MENT!!*
HMM... WHAT SHOULD I TURN KEIICHI INTO?
HOW ABOUT A TRICYCLE?
BETTER YET, A GARBAGE CAN... MAYBE A ROLL OF TOILET PAPER...
WHA-?!
ZZRAKK

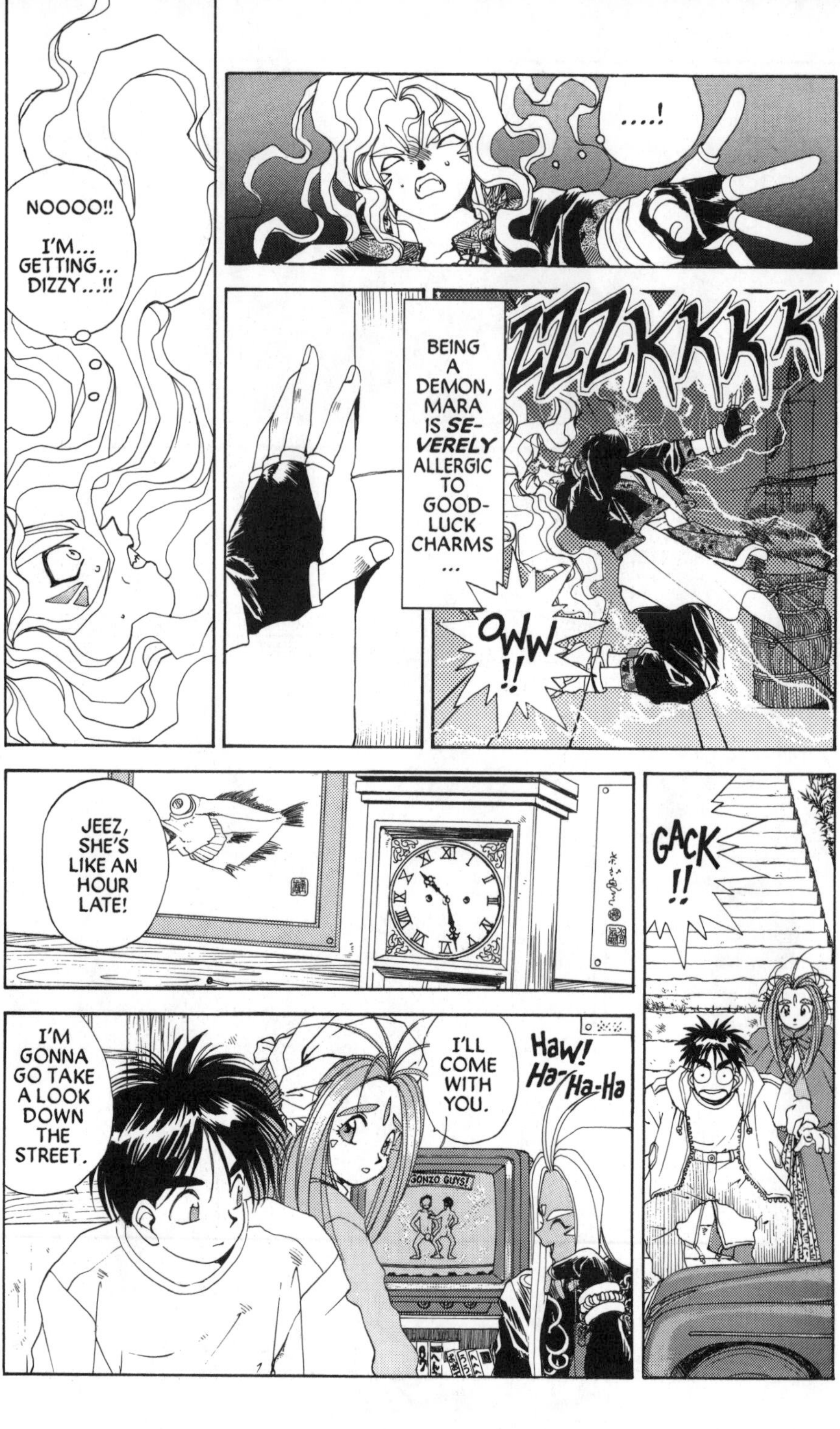
NOOOO!! I'M... GETTING... DIZZY...!!
....!
BEING A DEMON, MARA IS *SE-VERELY* ALLERGIC TO GOOD-LUCK CHARMS ...
ZZZKKKK
OWW !!
JEEZ, SHE'S LIKE AN HOUR LATE!
I'M GONNA GO TAKE A LOOK DOWN THE STREET.
I'LL COME WITH YOU.
GONZO GUYS!
HAW! HA-HA-HA
GACK !!

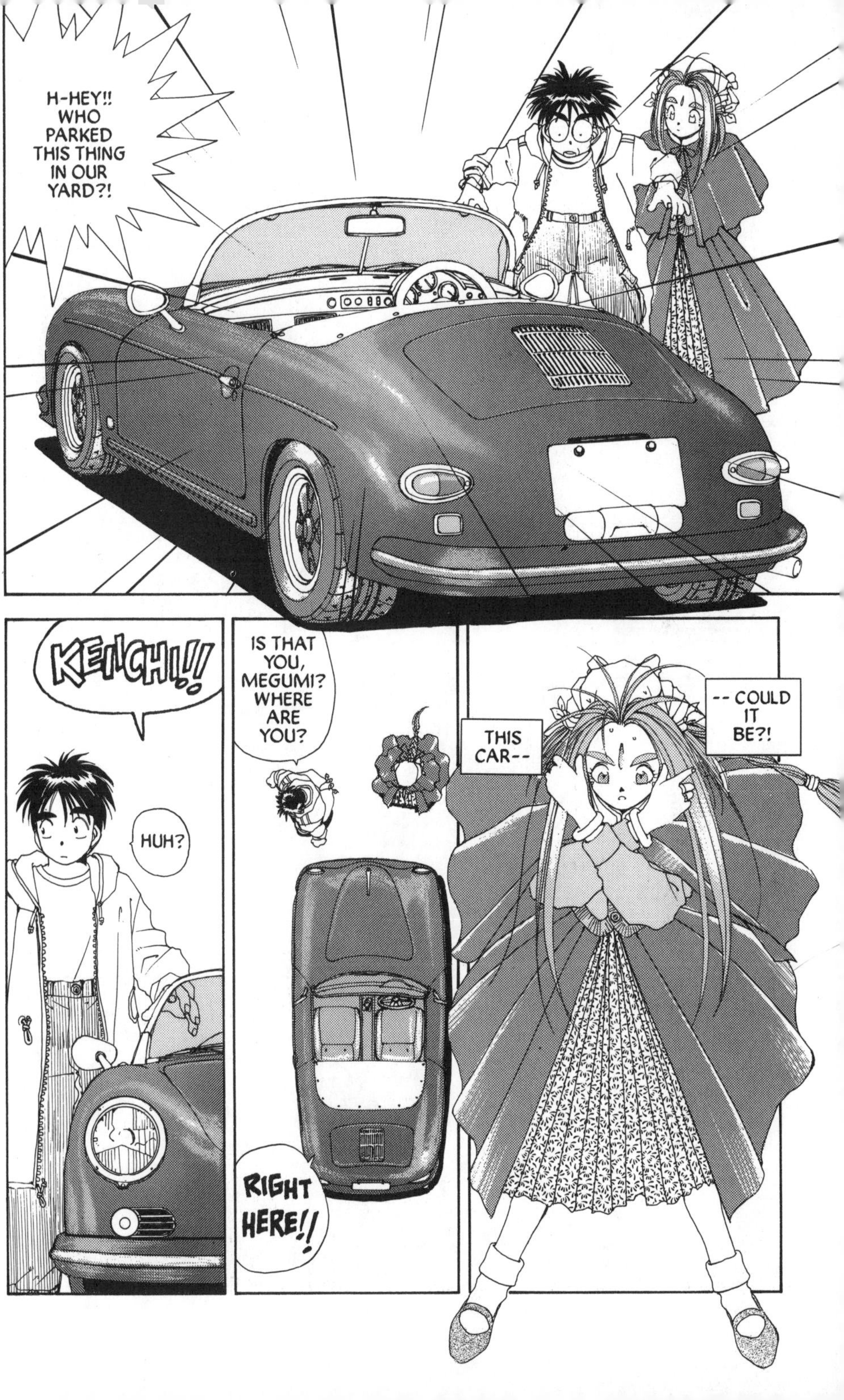
H-HEY!! WHO PARKED THIS THING IN OUR YARD?!
KEIICHI!!!
HUH?
IS THAT YOU, MEGUMI? WHERE ARE YOU?
RIGHT HERE!!
THIS CAR--
-- COULD IT BE?!

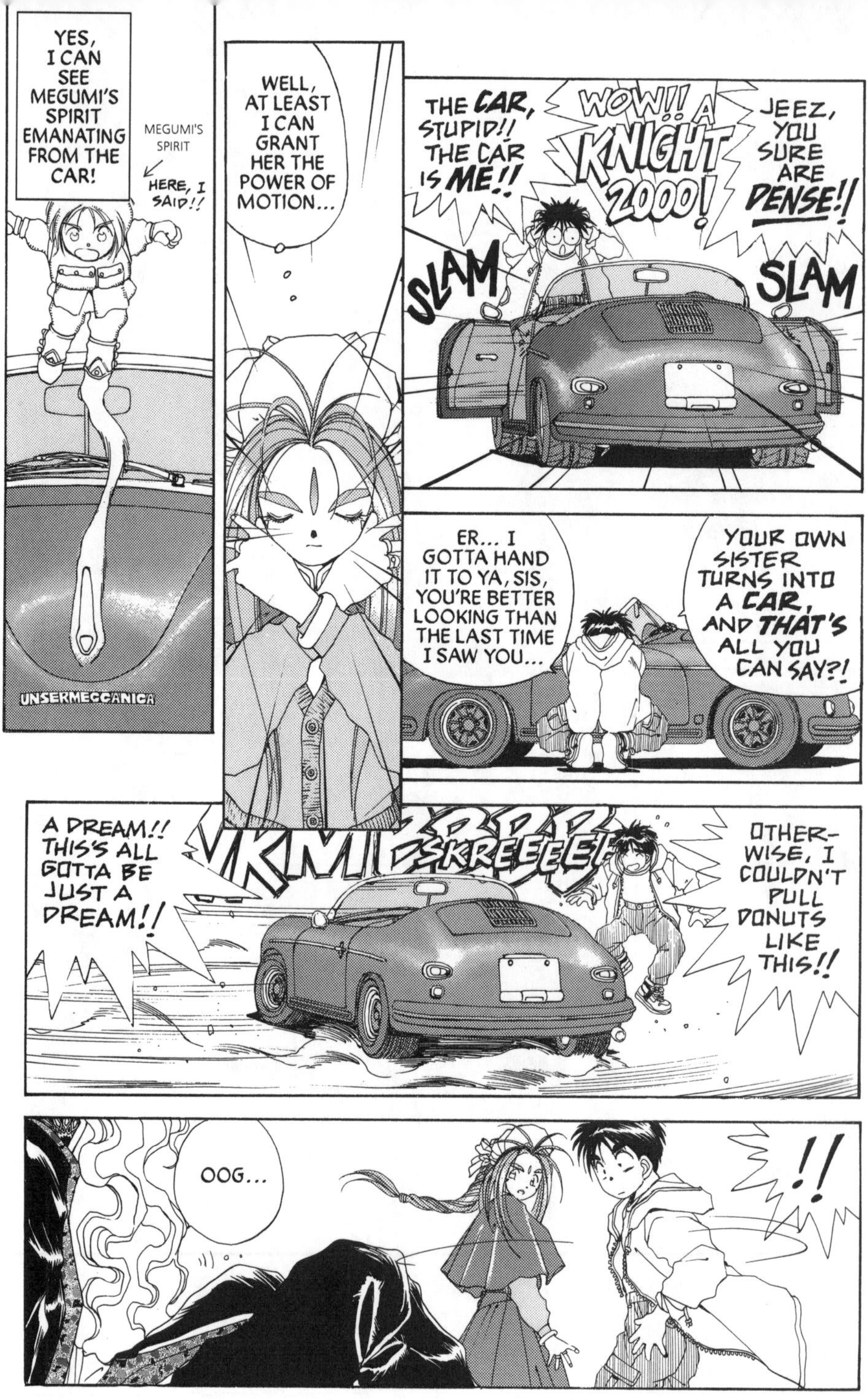
YES, I CAN SEE MEGUMI'S SPIRIT EMANATING FROM THE CAR!
MEGUMI'S SPIRIT
HERE, I SAID!!
UNSERMECCANICA
WELL, AT LEAST I CAN GRANT HER THE POWER OF MOTION...
THE CAR, STUPID!! THE CAR IS ME!!
WOW!! A KNIGHT 2000!
JEEZ, YOU SURE ARE DENSE!!
SLAM
SLAM
ER... I GOTTA HAND IT TO YA, SIS, YOU'RE BETTER LOOKING THAN THE LAST TIME I SAW YOU...
YOUR OWN SISTER TURNS INTO A CAR, AND THAT'S ALL YOU CAN SAY?!
A DREAM!! THIS'S ALL GOTTA BE JUST A DREAM!!
VKMM
BBBB
SKREEEEE
OTHER-WISE, I COULDN'T PULL DONUTS LIKE THIS!!
OOG...
!!

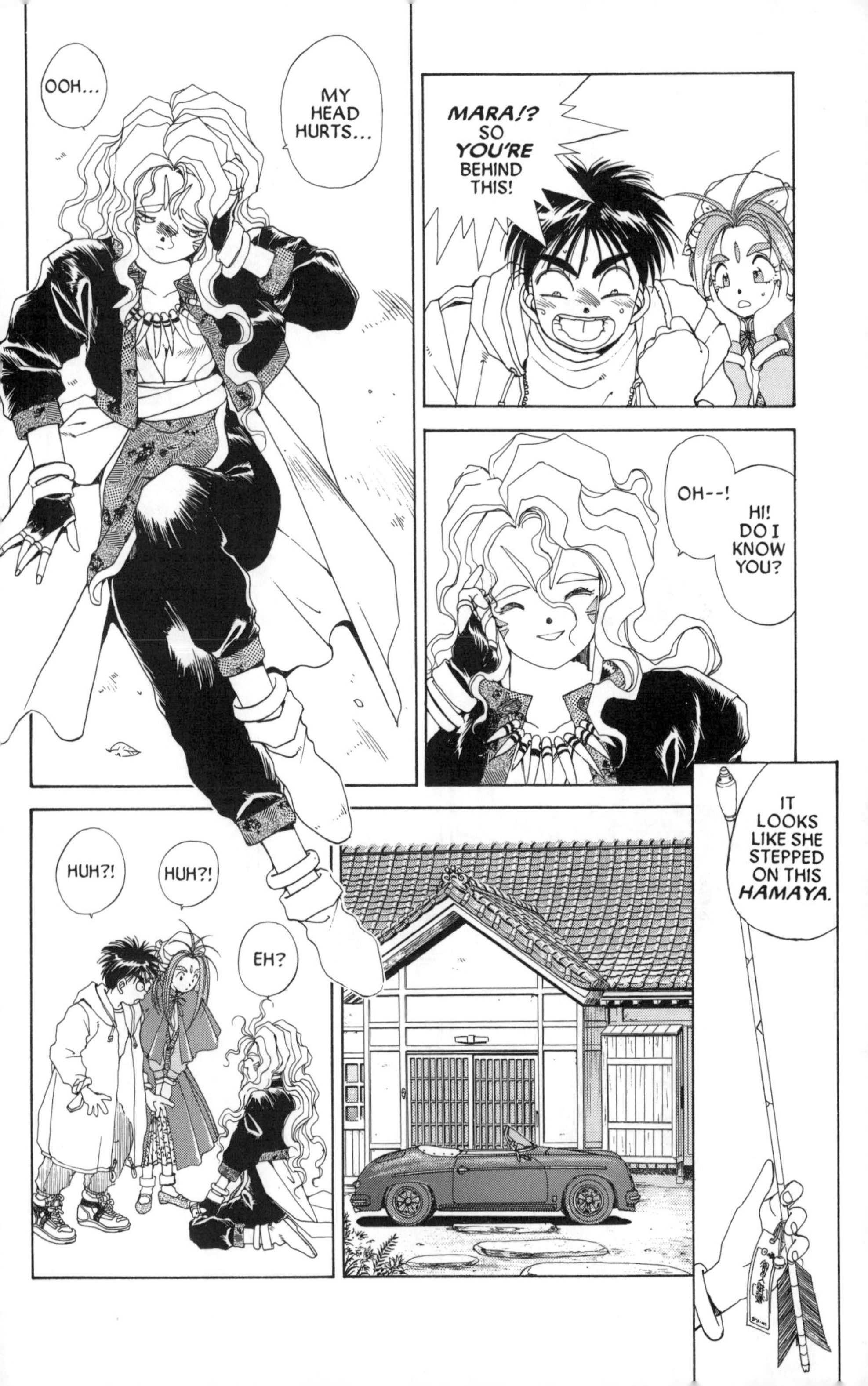
OOH...
MY HEAD HURTS...
MARA!? SO YOU'RE BEHIND THIS!
OH--!
HI! DO I KNOW YOU?
HUH?!
HUH?!
EH?
IT LOOKS LIKE SHE STEPPED ON THIS HAMAYA.

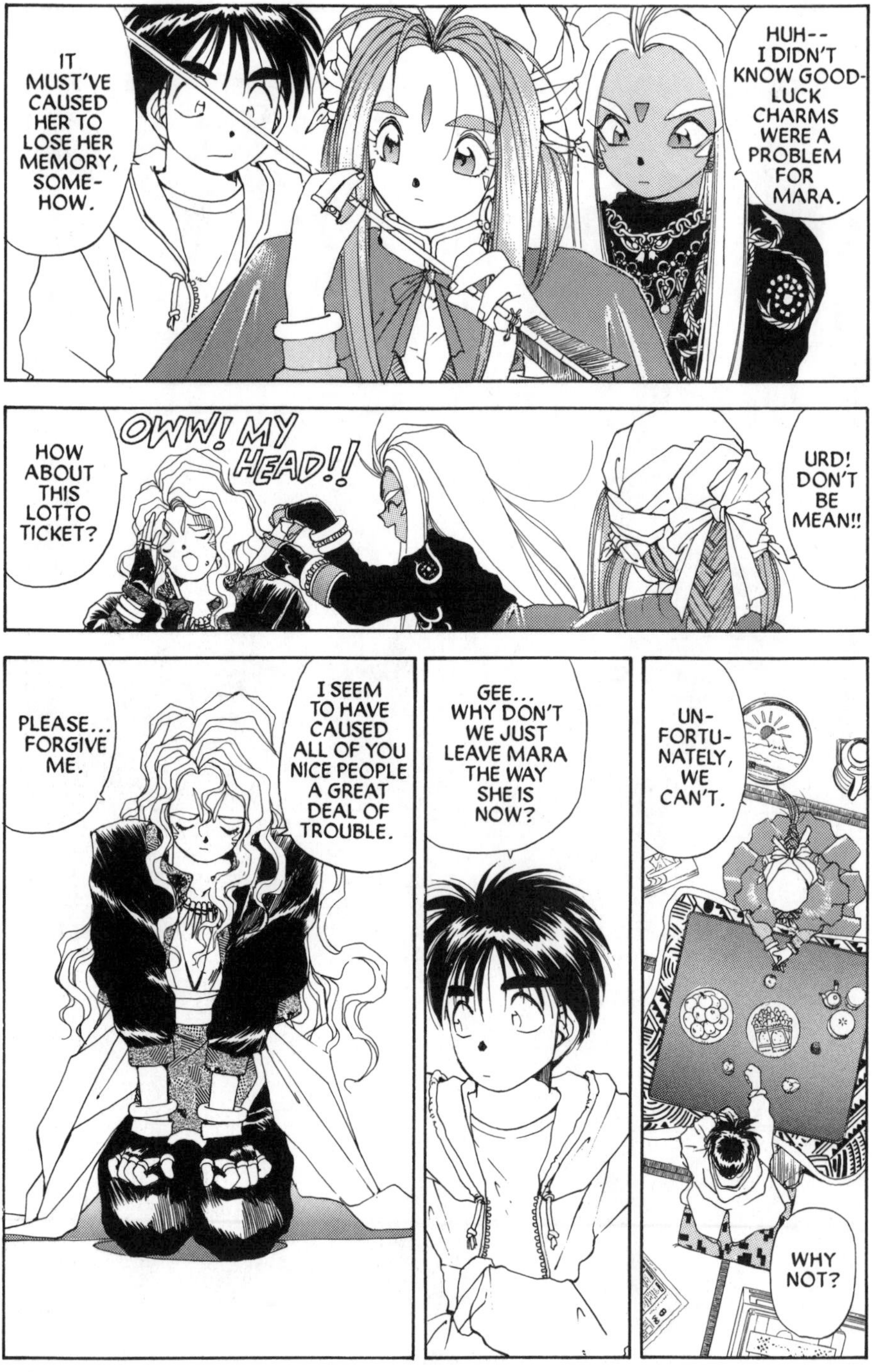
IT MUST'VE CAUSED HER TO LOSE HER MEMORY, SOME-HOW.
HUH-- I DIDN'T KNOW GOOD-LUCK CHARMS WERE A PROBLEM FOR MARA.
HOW ABOUT THIS LOTTO TICKET?
OWW! MY HEAD!!
URD! DON'T BE MEAN!!
PLEASE... FORGIVE ME.
I SEEM TO HAVE CAUSED ALL OF YOU NICE PEOPLE A GREAT DEAL OF TROUBLE.
GEE... WHY DON'T WE JUST LEAVE MARA THE WAY SHE IS NOW?
UN-FORTU-NATELY, WE CAN'T.
WHY NOT?

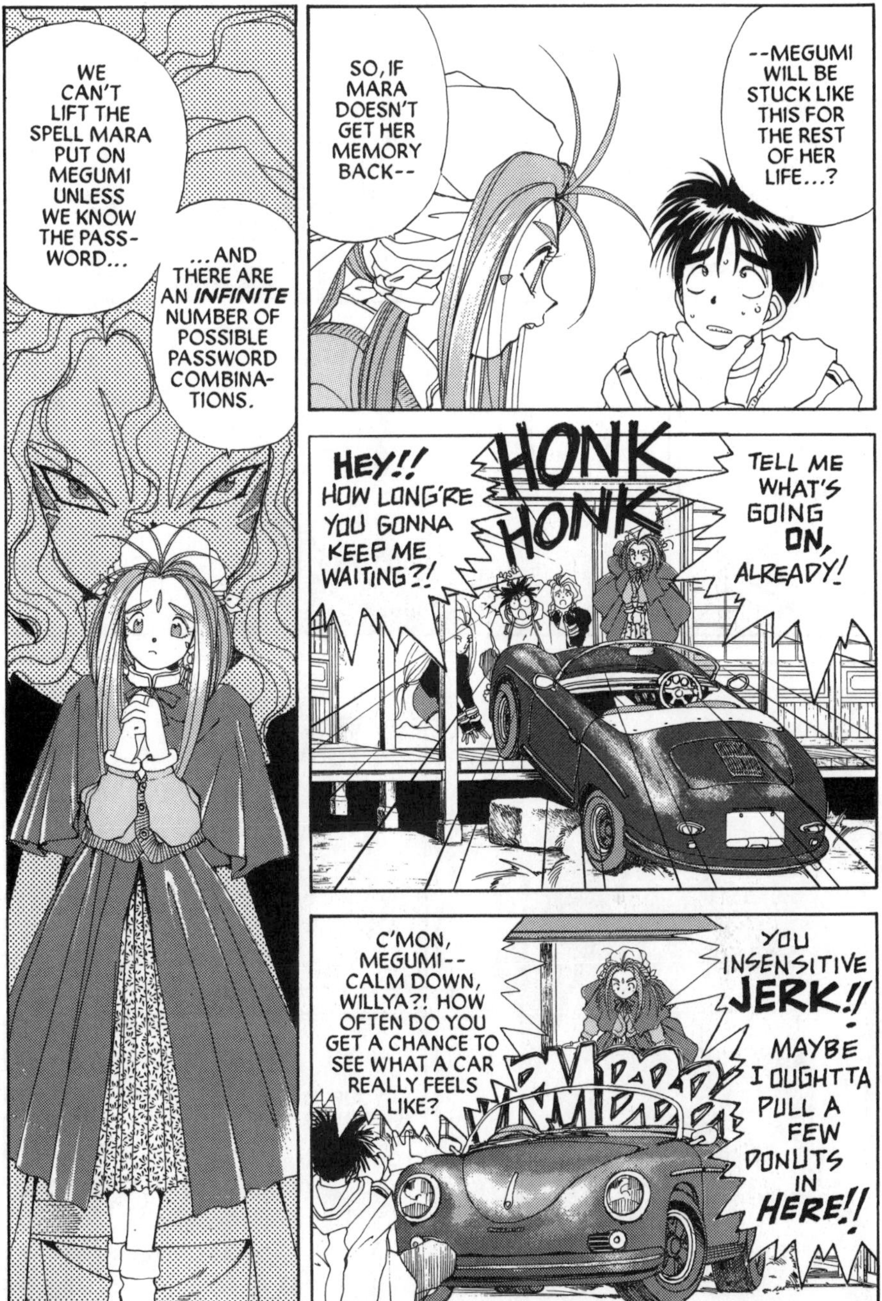
WE CAN'T LIFT THE SPELL MARA PUT ON MEGUMI UNLESS WE KNOW THE PASS-WORD...
...AND THERE ARE AN *INFINITE* NUMBER OF POSSIBLE PASSWORD COMBINA-TIONS.
SO, IF MARA DOESN'T GET HER MEMORY BACK--
--MEGUMI WILL BE STUCK LIKE THIS FOR THE REST OF HER LIFE...?
HEY!! HOW LONG'RE YOU GONNA KEEP ME WAITING?!
HONK HONK
TELL ME WHAT'S GOING ON, ALREADY!
C'MON, MEGUMI-- CALM DOWN, WILLYA?! HOW OFTEN DO YOU GET A CHANCE TO SEE WHAT A CAR REALLY FEELS LIKE?
YOU INSENSITIVE JERK!!
MAYBE I OUGHTTA PULL A FEW DONUTS IN HERE!!

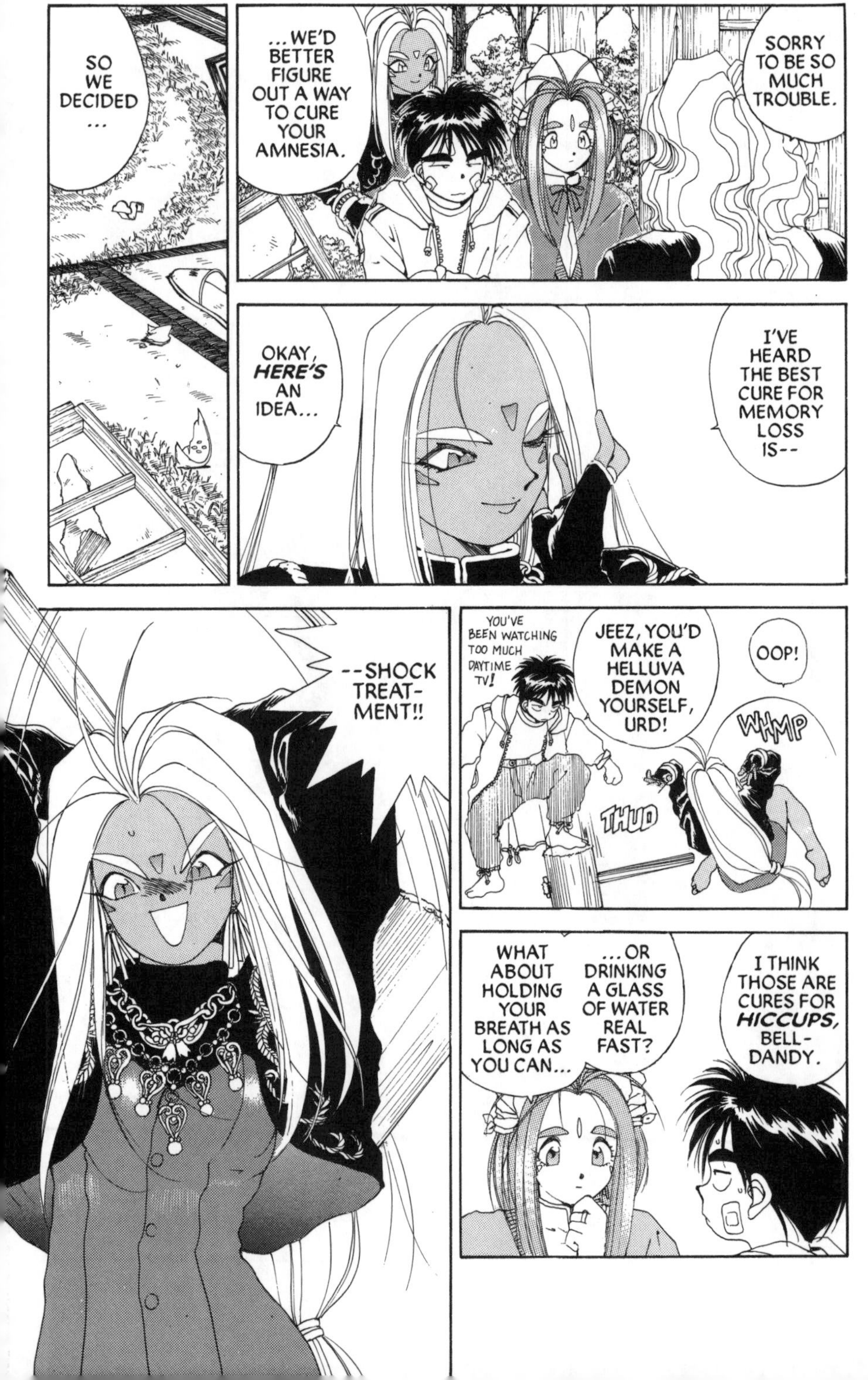
SO WE DECIDED ...
...WE'D BETTER FIGURE OUT A WAY TO CURE YOUR AMNESIA.
SORRY TO BE SO MUCH TROUBLE.
OKAY, *HERE'S* AN IDEA...
I'VE HEARD THE BEST CURE FOR MEMORY LOSS IS--
--SHOCK TREAT-MENT!!
YOU'VE BEEN WATCHING TOO MUCH DAYTIME TV!
JEEZ, YOU'D MAKE A HELLUVA DEMON YOURSELF, URD!
OOP!
WHMP
THUD
WHAT ABOUT HOLDING YOUR BREATH AS LONG AS YOU CAN...
...OR DRINKING A GLASS OF WATER REAL FAST?
I THINK THOSE ARE CURES FOR *HICCUPS,* BELL-DANDY.

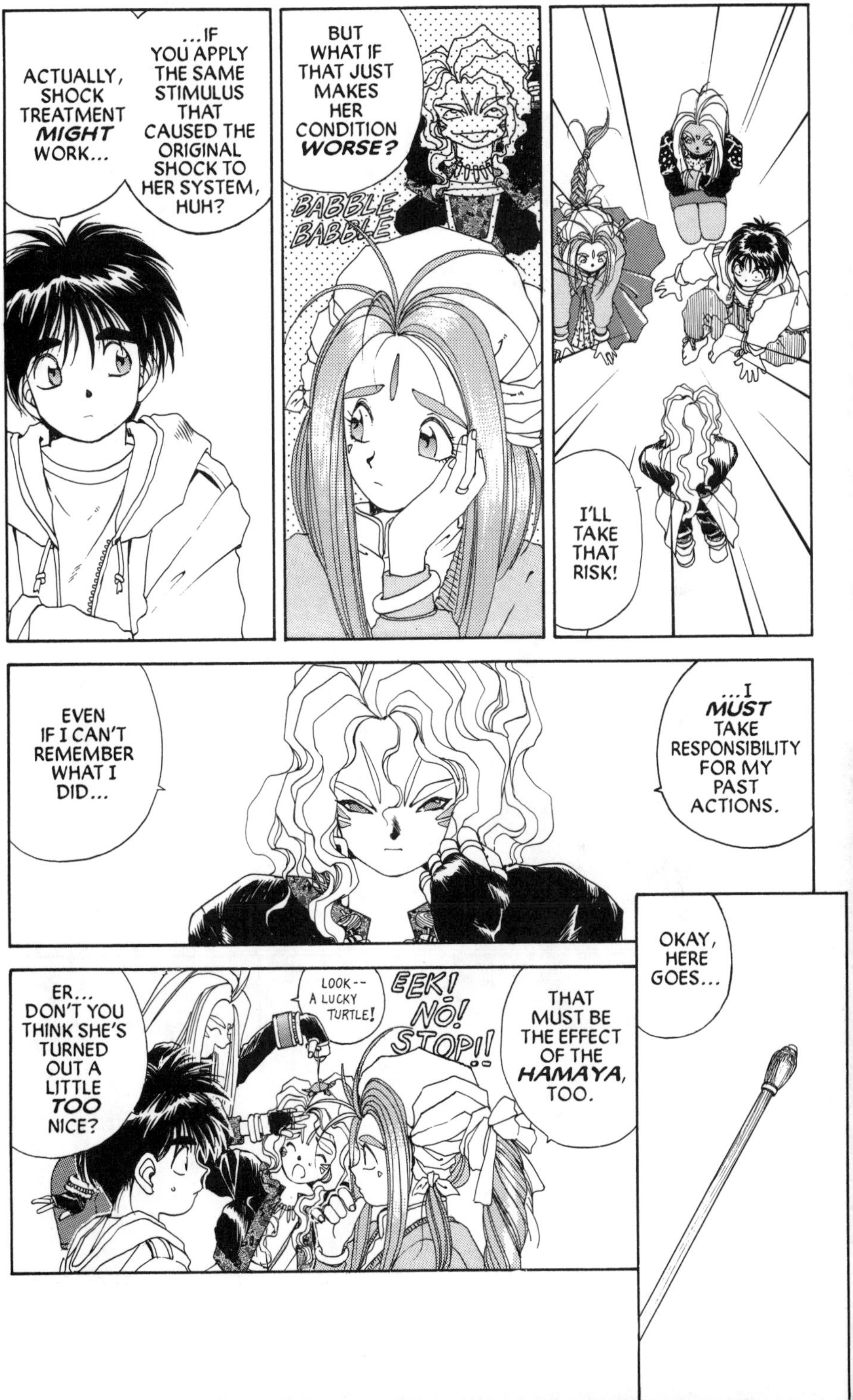
ACTUALLY, SHOCK TREATMENT MIGHT WORK...
...IF YOU APPLY THE SAME STIMULUS THAT CAUSED THE ORIGINAL SHOCK TO HER SYSTEM, HUH?
BUT WHAT IF THAT JUST MAKES HER CONDITION WORSE?
BABBLE BABBLE
I'LL TAKE THAT RISK!
EVEN IF I CAN'T REMEMBER WHAT I DID...
...I MUST TAKE RESPONSIBILITY FOR MY PAST ACTIONS.
ER... DON'T YOU THINK SHE'S TURNED OUT A LITTLE TOO NICE?
LOOK-- A LUCKY TURTLE!
EEK! NO! STOP!!
THAT MUST BE THE EFFECT OF THE HAMAYA, TOO.
OKAY, HERE GOES...

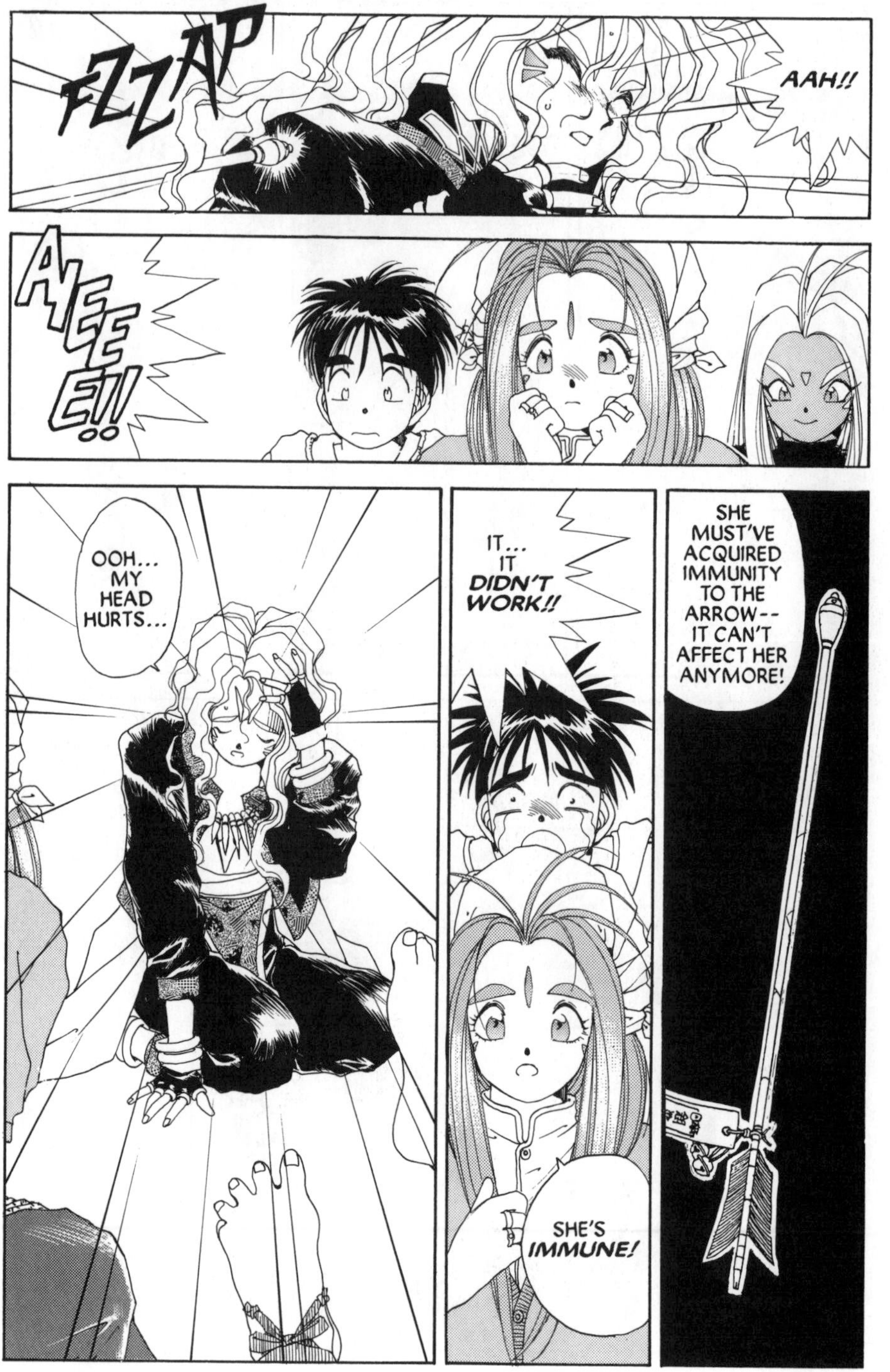
FZZAP
AAH!!
AIEEEE!!
OOH... MY HEAD HURTS...
IT... IT DIDN'T WORK!!
SHE'S IMMUNE!
SHE MUST'VE ACQUIRED IMMUNITY TO THE ARROW-- IT CAN'T AFFECT HER ANYMORE!

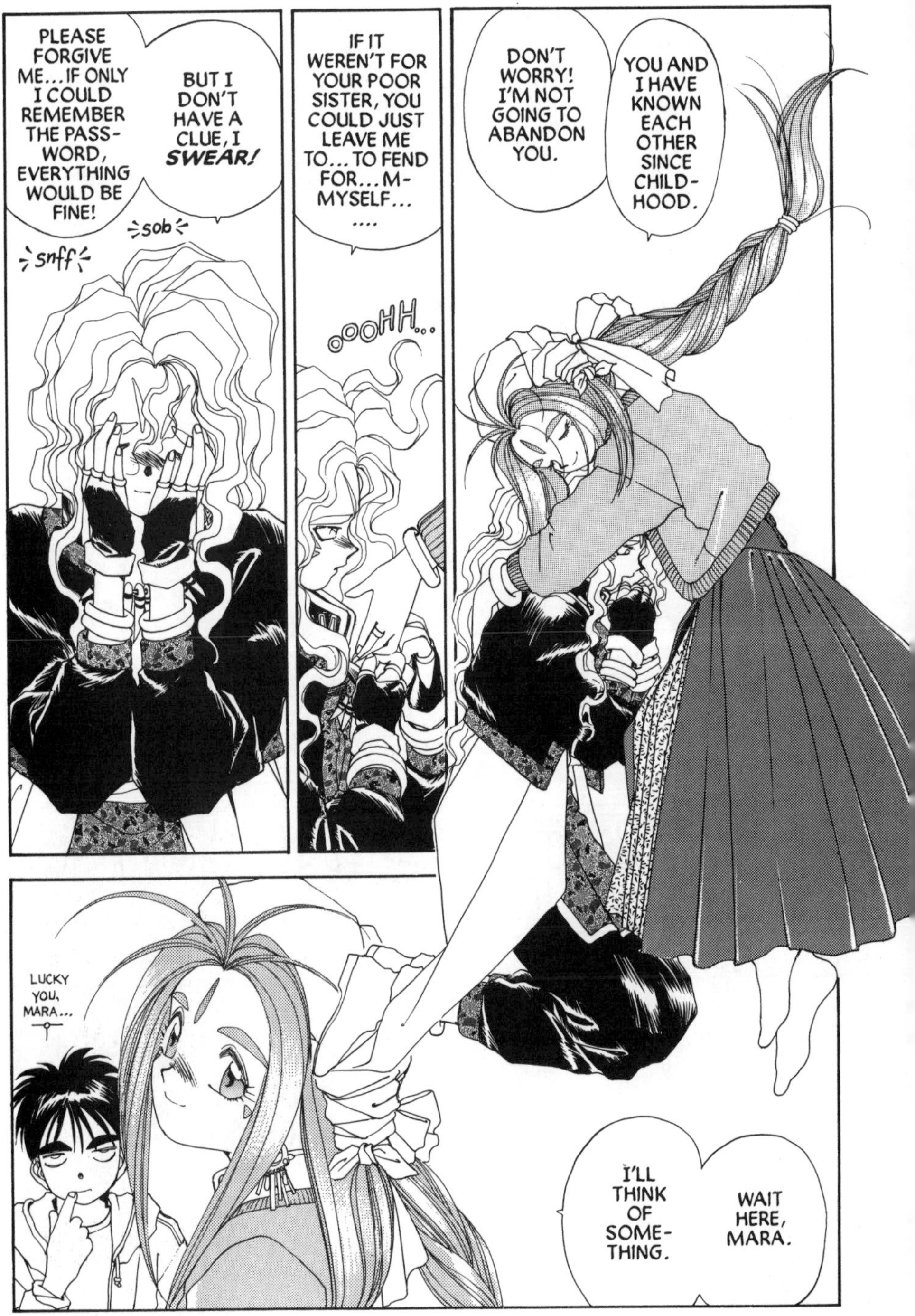
PLEASE FORGIVE ME... IF ONLY I COULD REMEMBER THE PASS-WORD, EVERYTHING WOULD BE FINE!
BUT I DON'T HAVE A CLUE, I SWEAR!
sob
snff
IF IT WEREN'T FOR YOUR POOR SISTER, YOU COULD JUST LEAVE ME TO... TO FEND FOR... M-MYSELF... ....
oooHH...
DON'T WORRY! I'M NOT GOING TO ABANDON YOU.
YOU AND I HAVE KNOWN EACH OTHER SINCE CHILD-HOOD.
LUCKY YOU, MARA...
I'LL THINK OF SOME-THING.
WAIT HERE, MARA.

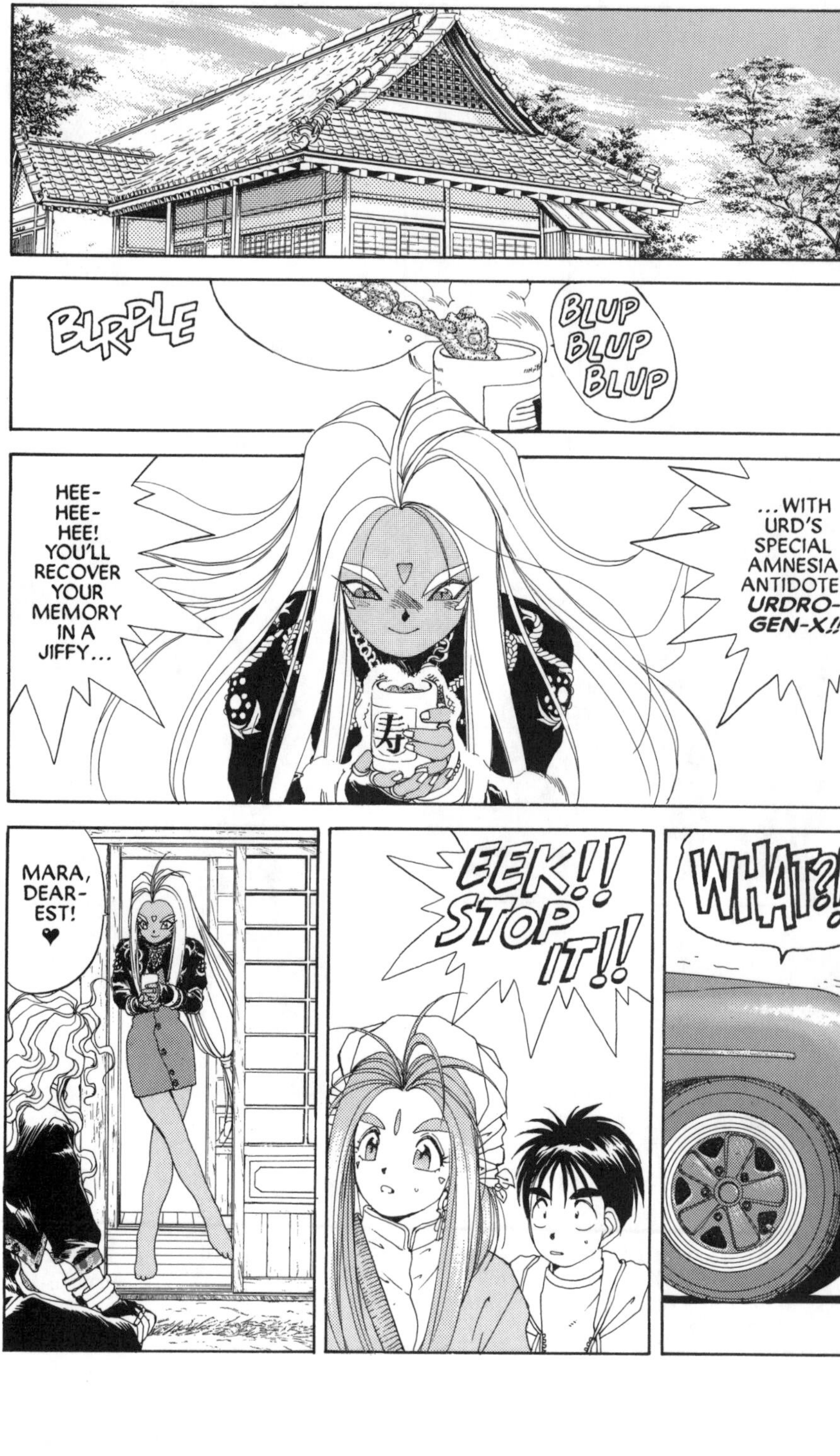
BLRPLE
BLUP BLUP BLUP
HEE-HEE-HEE! YOU'LL RECOVER YOUR MEMORY IN A JIFFY...
...WITH URD'S SPECIAL AMNESIA ANTIDOTE, URDRO-GEN-X!!
MARA, DEAR-EST! ♥
EEK!! STOP IT!!
WHAT?!

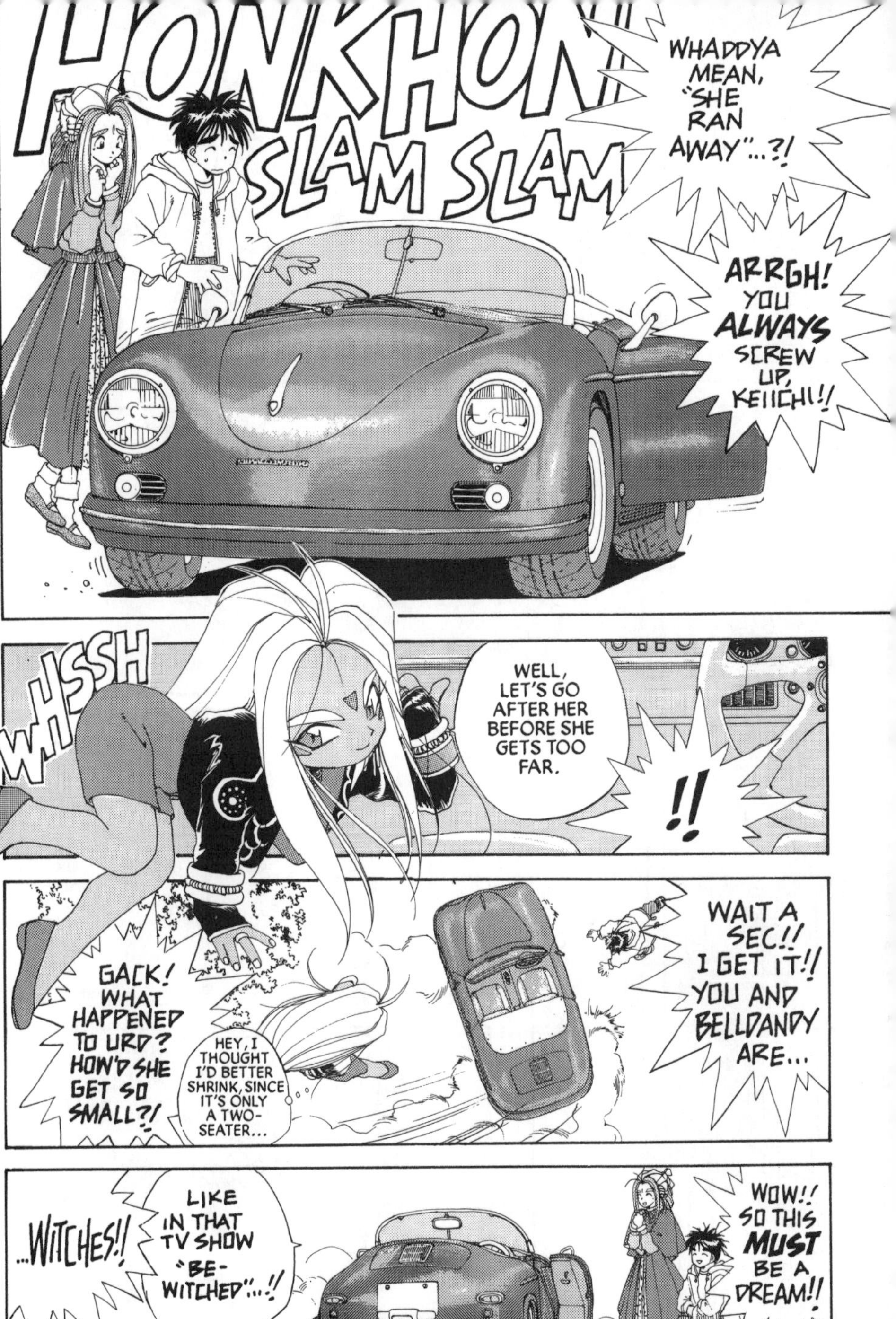
HONK HONK
SLAM SLAM
WHADDYA MEAN, "SHE RAN AWAY"...?!
ARRGH! YOU ALWAYS SCREW UP, KEIICHI!!
WHSSH
WELL, LET'S GO AFTER HER BEFORE SHE GETS TOO FAR.
!!
WAIT A SEC!! I GET IT!! YOU AND BELLDANDY ARE...
GACK! WHAT HAPPENED TO URD? HOW'D SHE GET SO SMALL?!
HEY, I THOUGHT I'D BETTER SHRINK, SINCE IT'S ONLY A TWO-SEATER...
WOW!! SO THIS MUST BE A DREAM!!
LIKE IN THAT TV SHOW "BE-WITCHED"...!!
...WITCHES!!

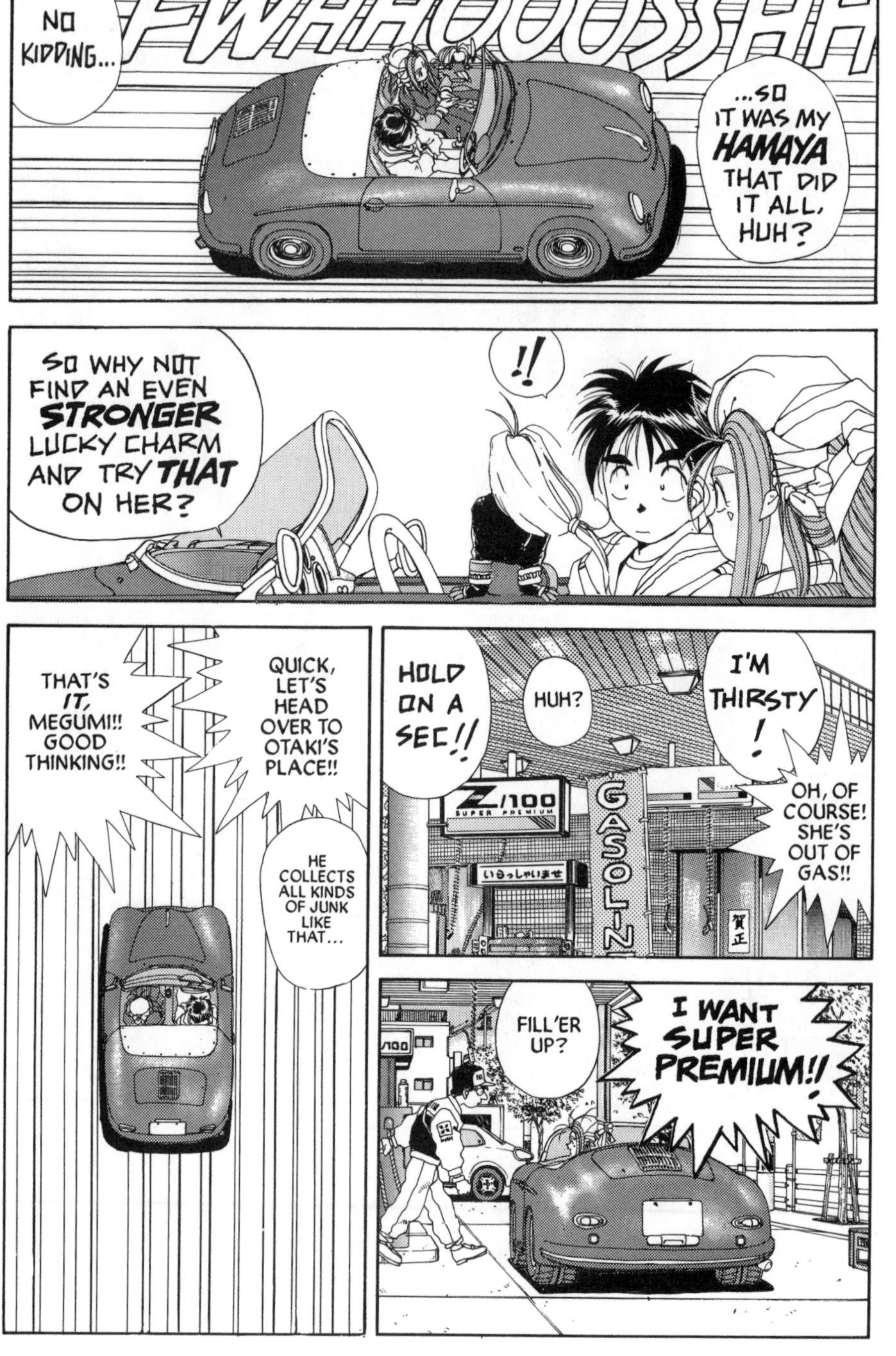
NO KIDDING...
FWHHOOOSSHH
...SO IT WAS MY HAMAYA THAT DID IT ALL, HUH?
SO WHY NOT FIND AN EVEN STRONGER LUCKY CHARM AND TRY THAT ON HER?
!!
THAT'S IT, MEGUMI!! GOOD THINKING!!
QUICK, LET'S HEAD OVER TO OTAKI'S PLACE!!
HE COLLECTS ALL KINDS OF JUNK LIKE THAT...
HOLD ON A SEC!!
HUH?
I'M THIRSTY!
Z/100 SUPER PREMIUM
GASOLIN
いらっしゃいませ
賀正
OH, OF COURSE! SHE'S OUT OF GAS!!
FILL'ER UP?
I WANT SUPER PREMIUM!!

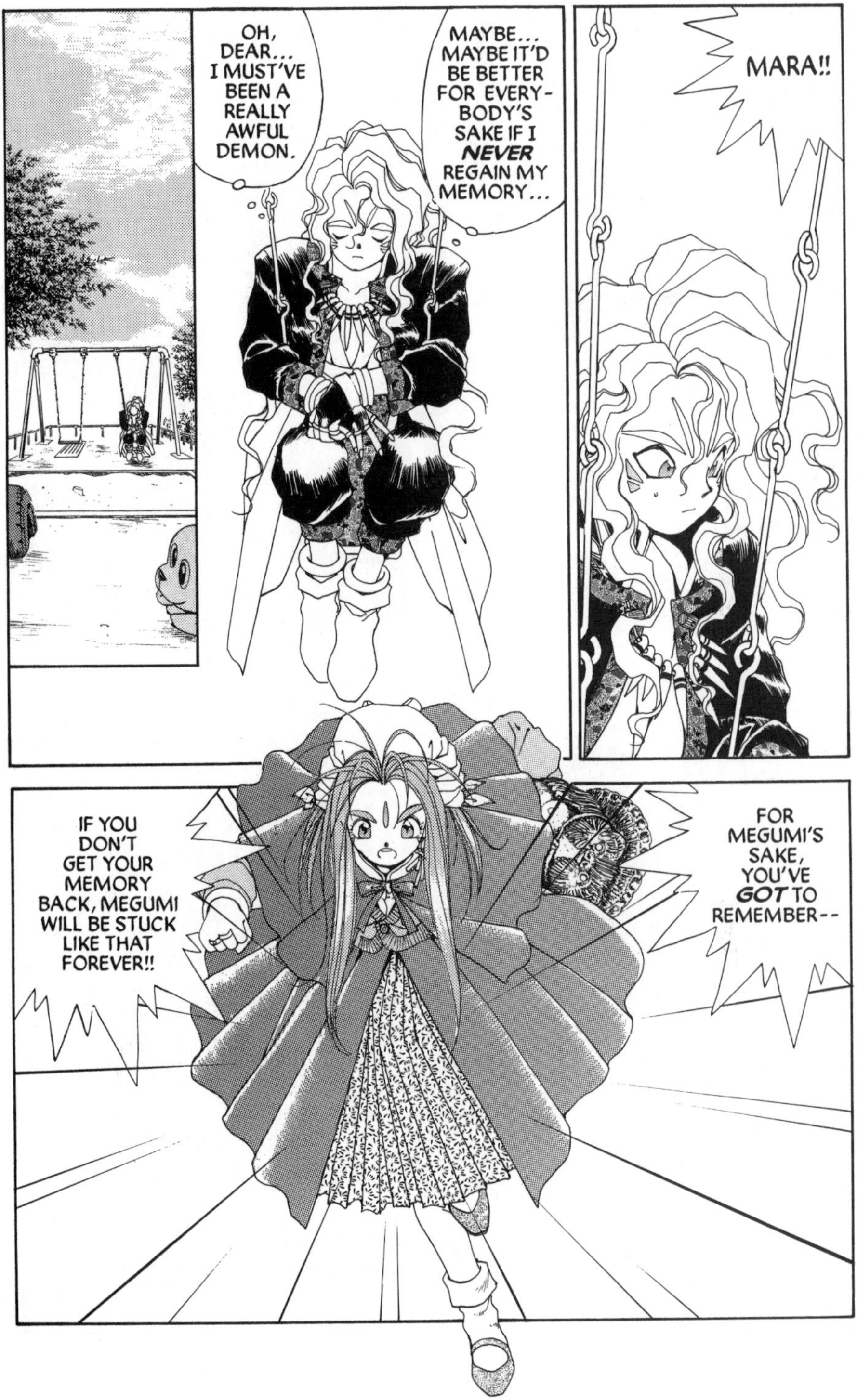
OH, DEAR... I MUST'VE BEEN A REALLY AWFUL DEMON.
MAYBE... MAYBE IT'D BE BETTER FOR EVERY-BODY'S SAKE IF I NEVER REGAIN MY MEMORY...
MARA!!
IF YOU DON'T GET YOUR MEMORY BACK, MEGUMI WILL BE STUCK LIKE THAT FOREVER!!
FOR MEGUMI'S SAKE, YOU'VE GOT TO REMEMBER--

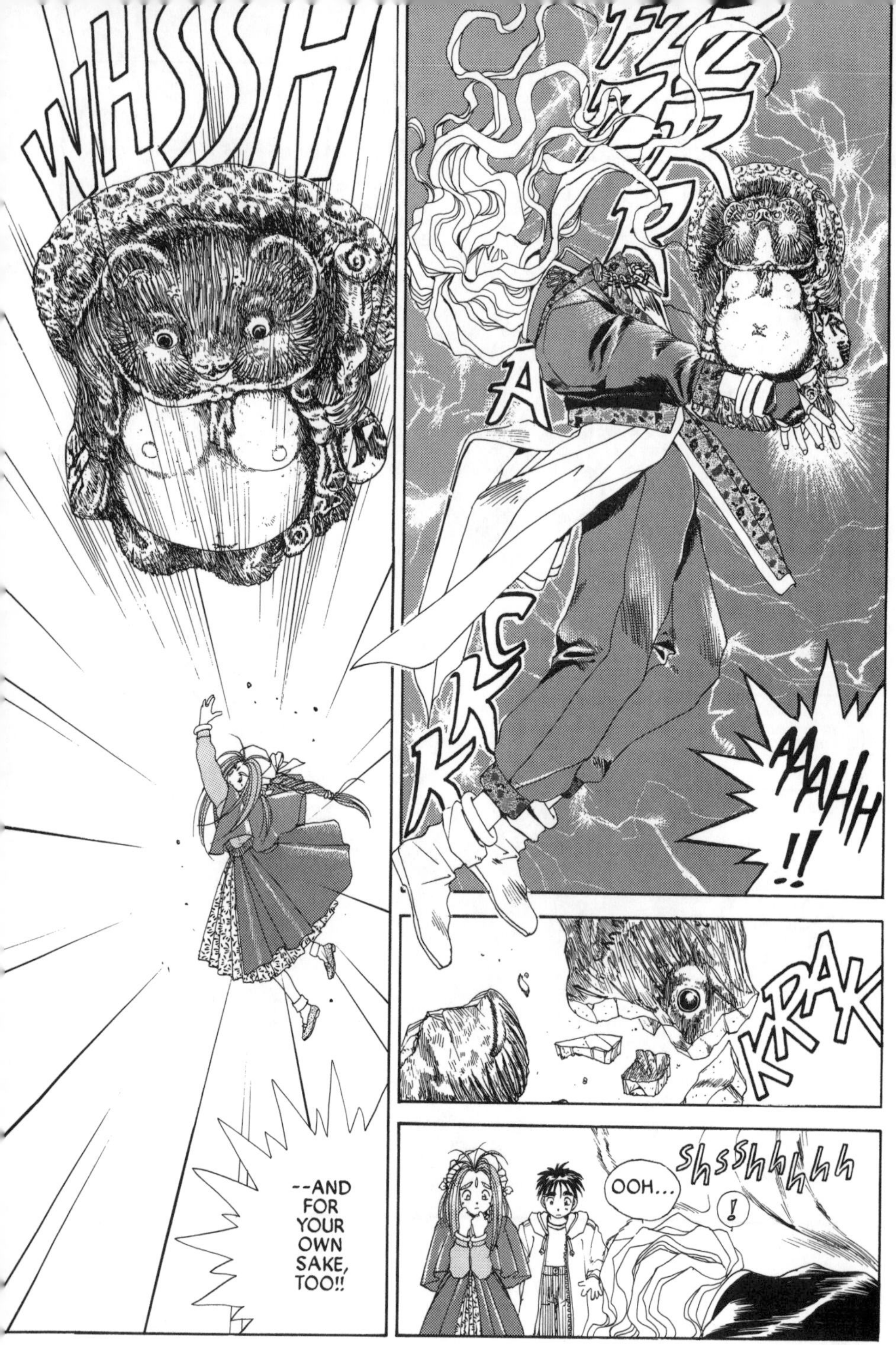
WHSSH
--AND FOR YOUR OWN SAKE, TOO!!
KKC
AAAAHH!!
KRAK
OOH...
shsShhhhhh
!

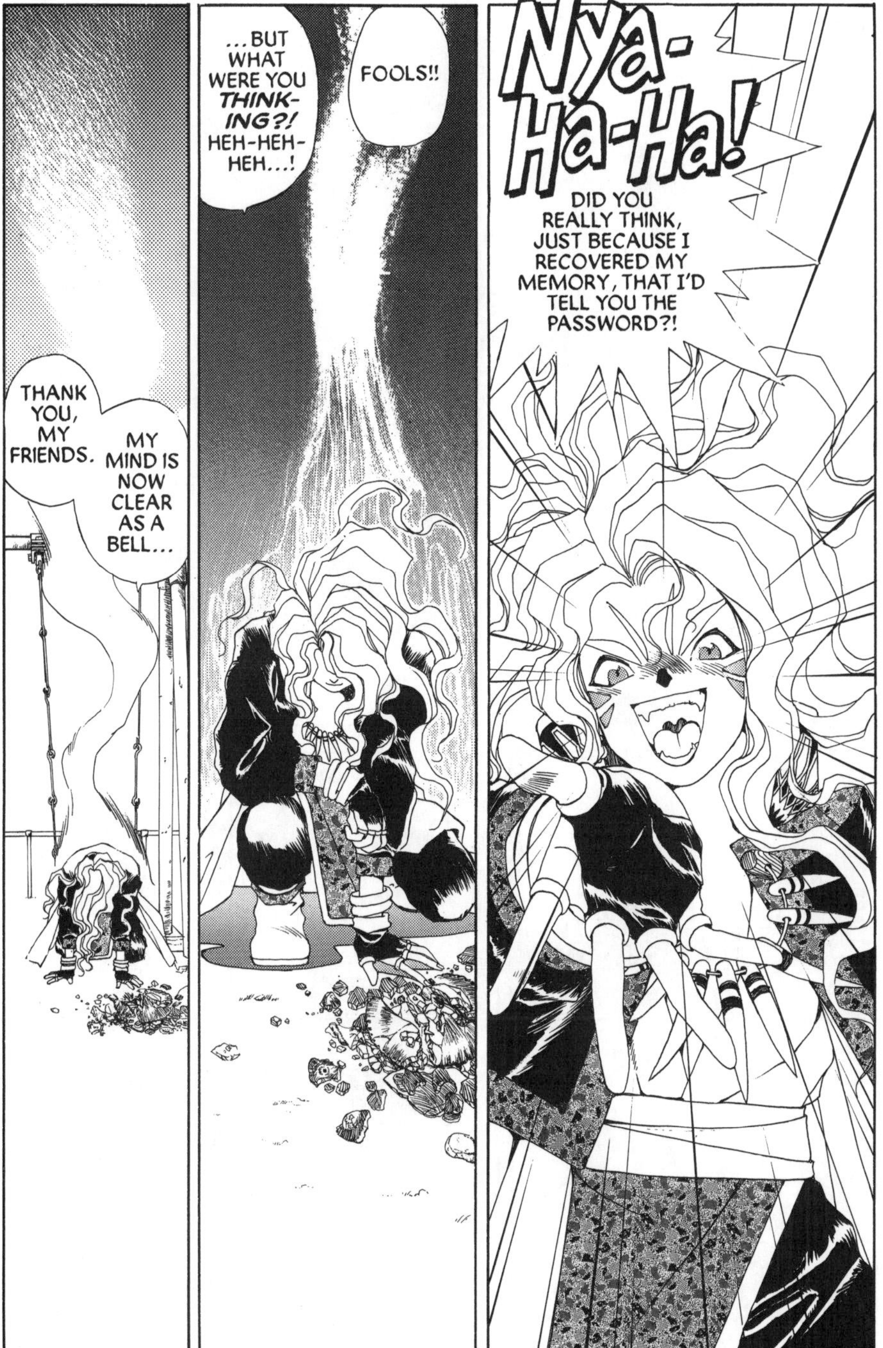
THANK YOU, MY FRIENDS.
MY MIND IS NOW CLEAR AS A BELL...
...BUT WHAT WERE YOU *THINKING?!* HEH-HEH-HEH...!
FOOLS!!
Nya-Ha-Ha!
DID YOU REALLY THINK, JUST BECAUSE I RECOVERED MY MEMORY, THAT I'D TELL YOU THE PASSWORD?!

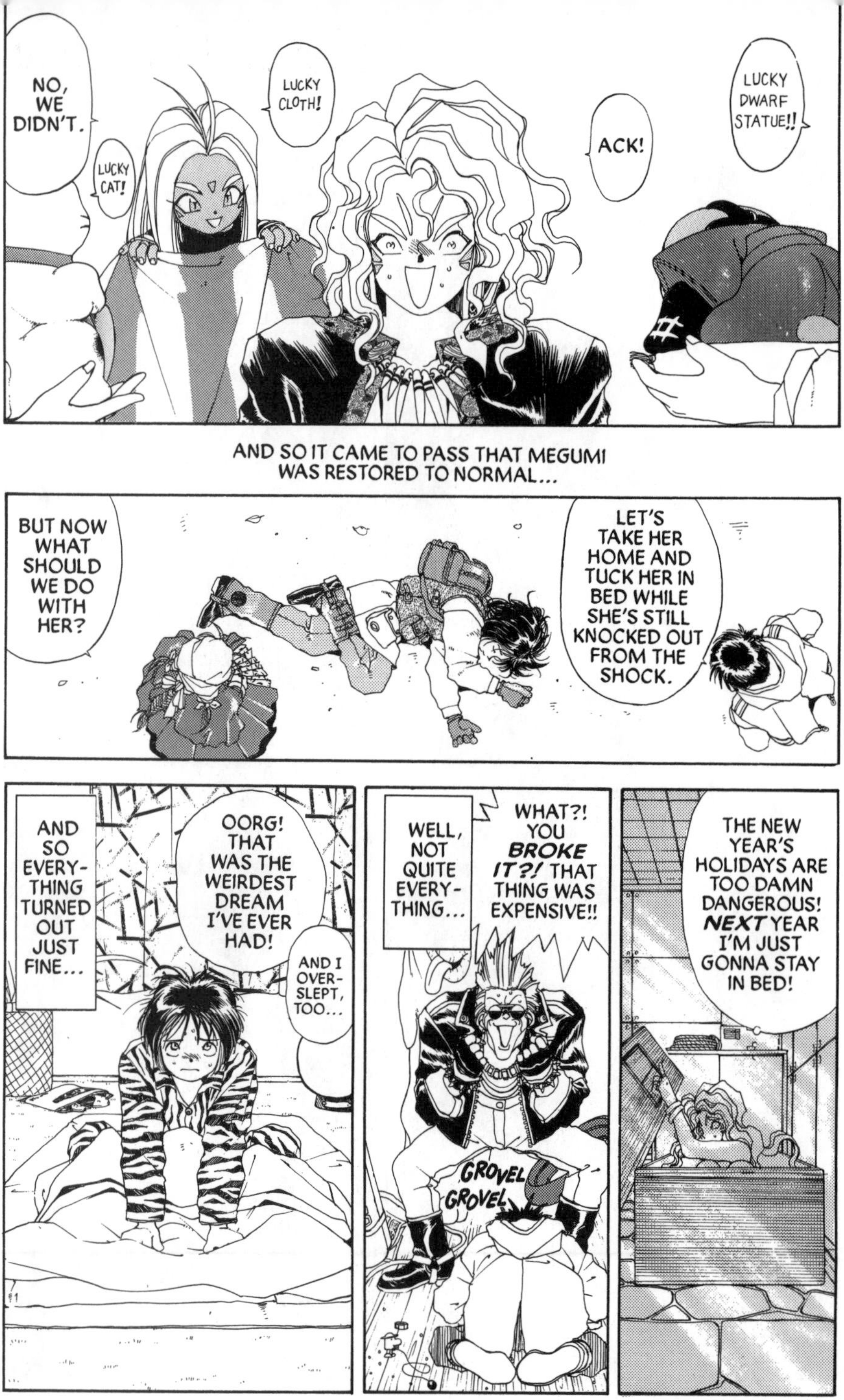
NO, WE DIDN'T.
LUCKY CAT!
LUCKY CLOTH!
ACK!
LUCKY DWARF STATUE!!
AND SO IT CAME TO PASS THAT MEGUMI WAS RESTORED TO NORMAL...
BUT NOW WHAT SHOULD WE DO WITH HER?
LET'S TAKE HER HOME AND TUCK HER IN BED WHILE SHE'S STILL KNOCKED OUT FROM THE SHOCK.
AND SO EVERY-THING TURNED OUT JUST FINE...
OORG! THAT WAS THE WEIRDEST DREAM I'VE EVER HAD!
AND I OVER-SLEPT, TOO...
WELL, NOT QUITE EVERY-THING...
WHAT?! YOU *BROKE IT?!* THAT THING WAS EXPENSIVE!!
GROVEL
GROVEL
THE NEW YEAR'S HOLIDAYS ARE TOO DAMN DANGEROUS! *NEXT* YEAR I'M JUST GONNA STAY IN BED!

Mystical Engine

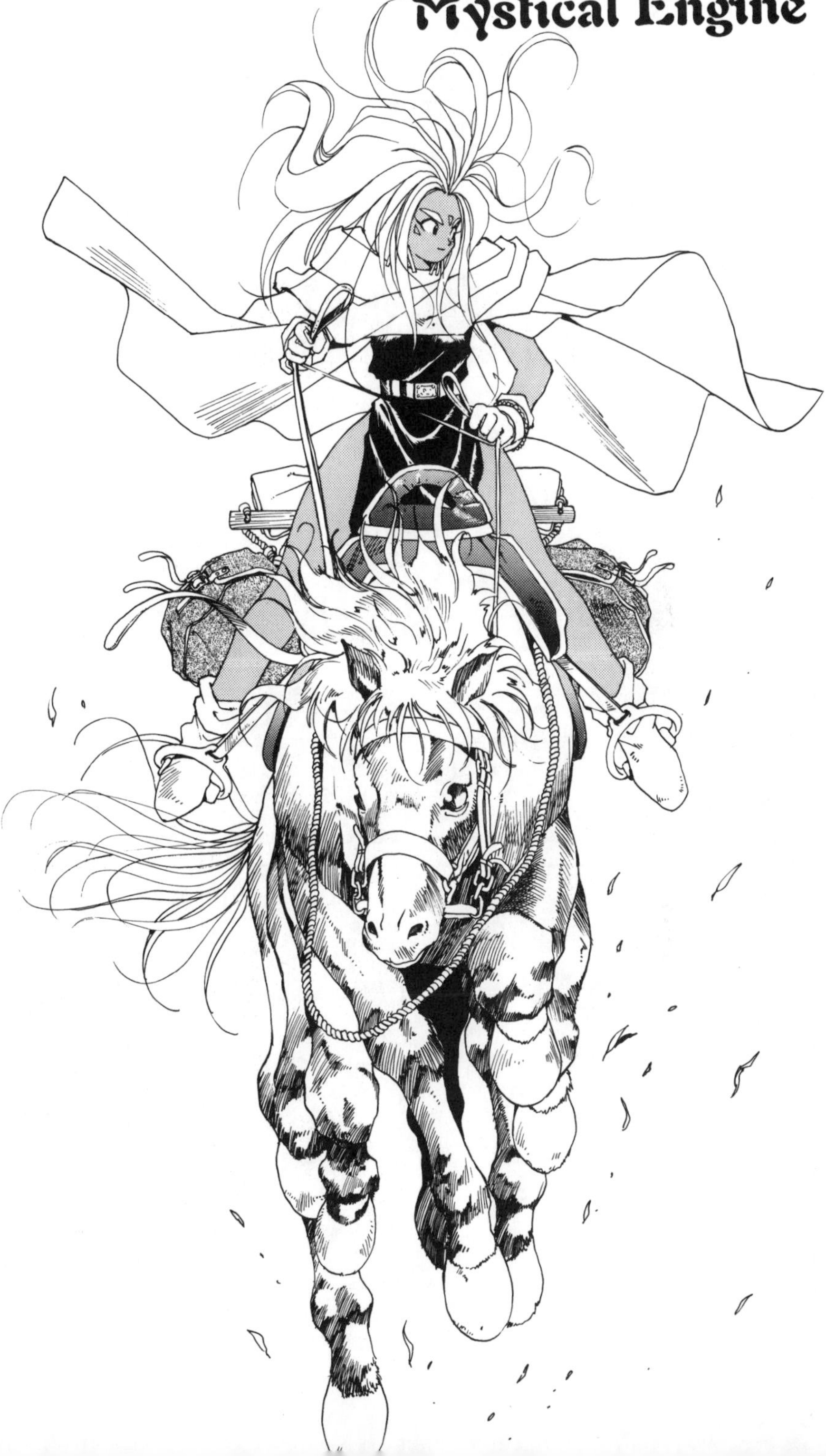

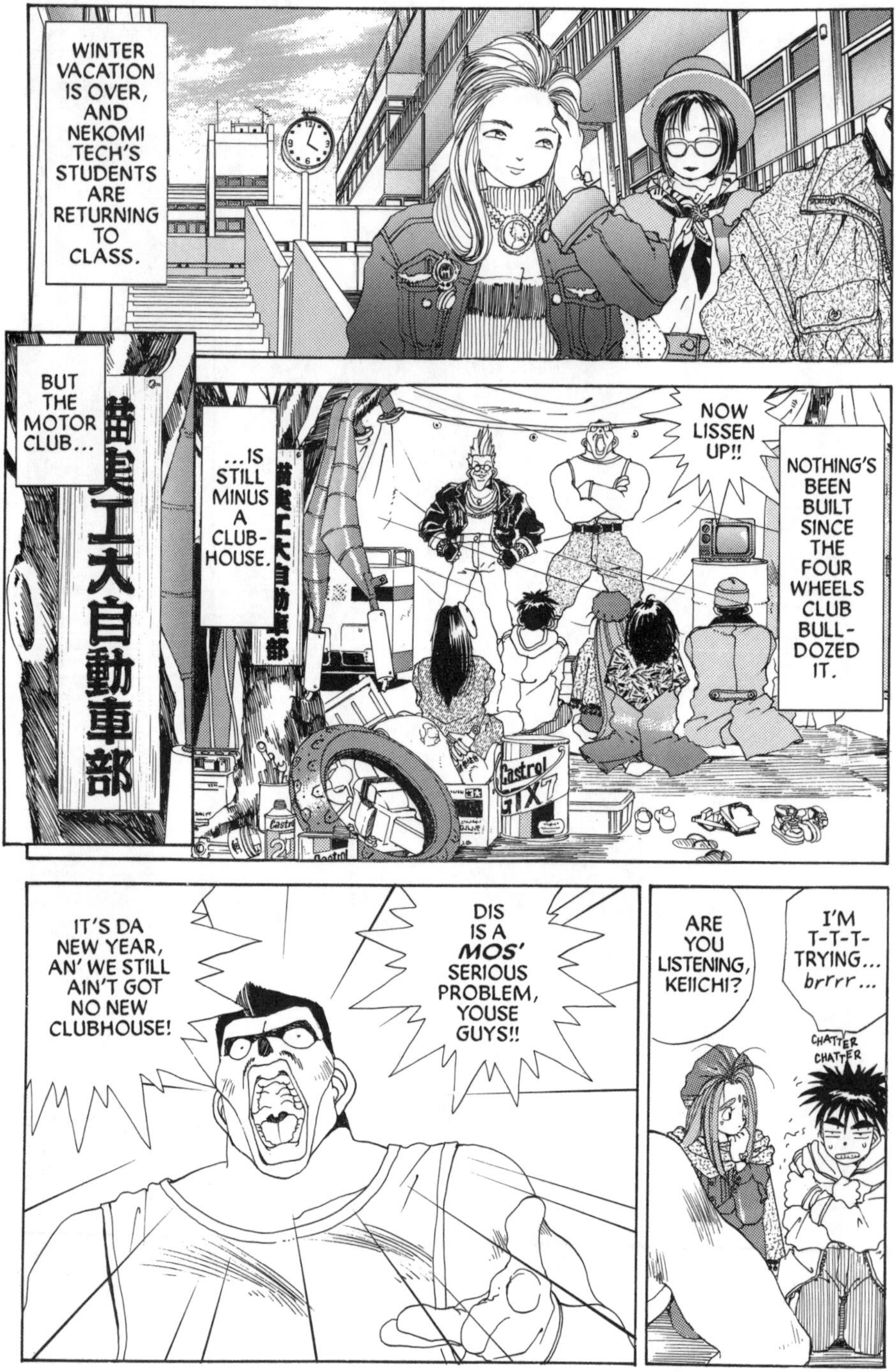
WINTER VACATION IS OVER, AND NEKOMI TECH'S STUDENTS ARE RETURNING TO CLASS.
BUT THE MOTOR CLUB...
猫実工大自動車部
...IS STILL MINUS A CLUB-HOUSE.
NOW LISSEN UP!!
NOTHING'S BEEN BUILT SINCE THE FOUR WHEELS CLUB BULL-DOZED IT.
Castrol GTX7
IT'S DA NEW YEAR, AN' WE STILL AIN'T GOT NO NEW CLUBHOUSE!
DIS IS A *MOS'* SERIOUS PROBLEM, YOUSE GUYS!!
ARE YOU LISTENING, KEIICHI?
I'M T-T-T-TRYING... *brrrr...*
CHATTER CHATTER

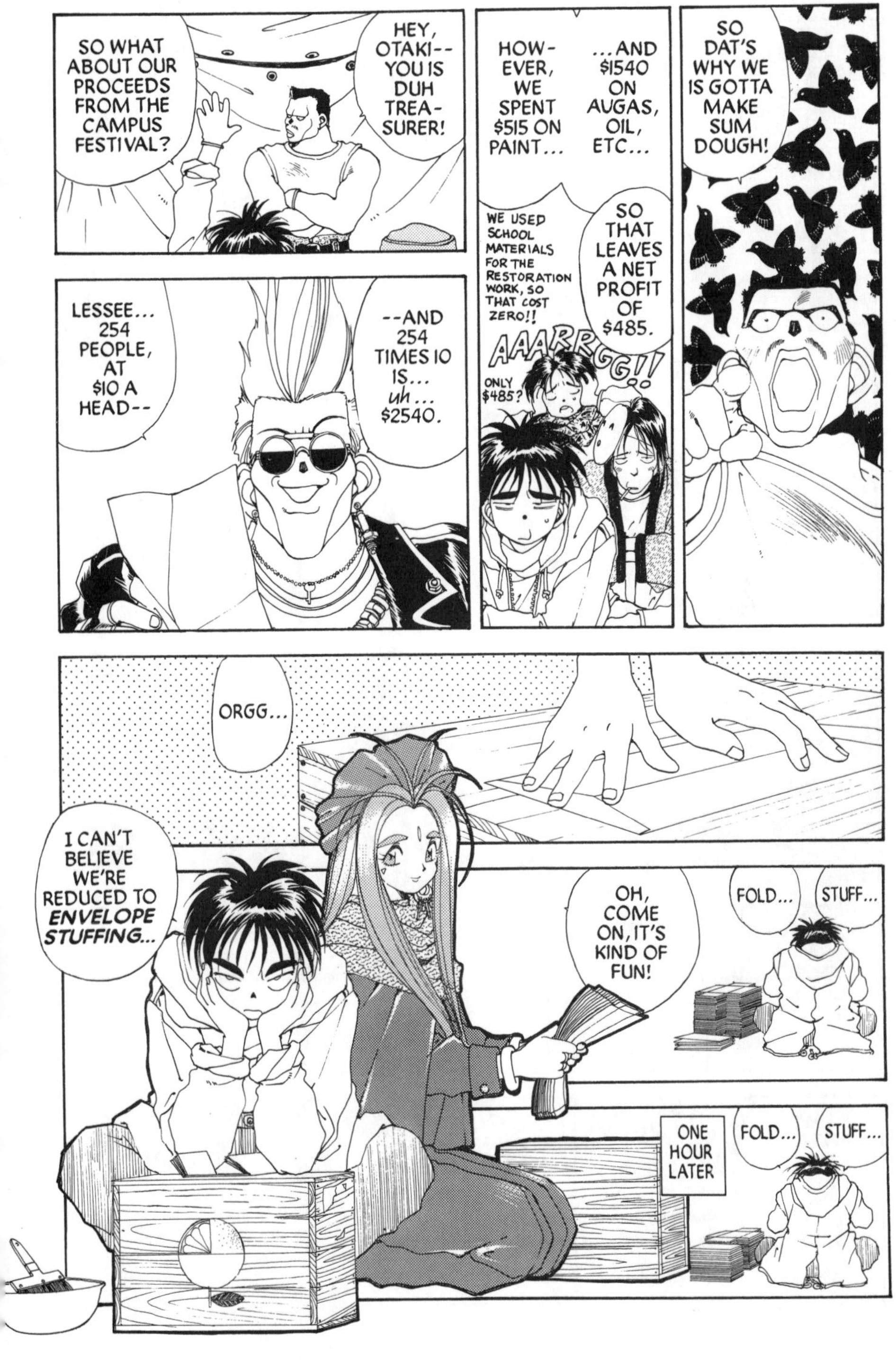
SO WHAT ABOUT OUR PROCEEDS FROM THE CAMPUS FESTIVAL?
HEY, OTAKI-- YOU IS DUH TREASURER!
HOW- EVER, WE SPENT $515 ON PAINT...
...AND $1540 ON AUGAS, OIL, ETC...
WE USED SCHOOL MATERIALS FOR THE RESTORATION WORK, SO THAT COST ZERO!!
SO THAT LEAVES A NET PROFIT OF $485.
SO DAT'S WHY WE IS GOTTA MAKE SUM DOUGH!
LESSEE... 254 PEOPLE, AT $10 A HEAD--
--AND 254 TIMES 10 IS... uh... $2540.
AAARRGG!!
ONLY $485?
ORGG...
I CAN'T BELIEVE WE'RE REDUCED TO ENVELOPE STUFFING...
OH, COME ON, IT'S KIND OF FUN!
FOLD...
STUFF...
ONE HOUR LATER
FOLD...
STUFF...

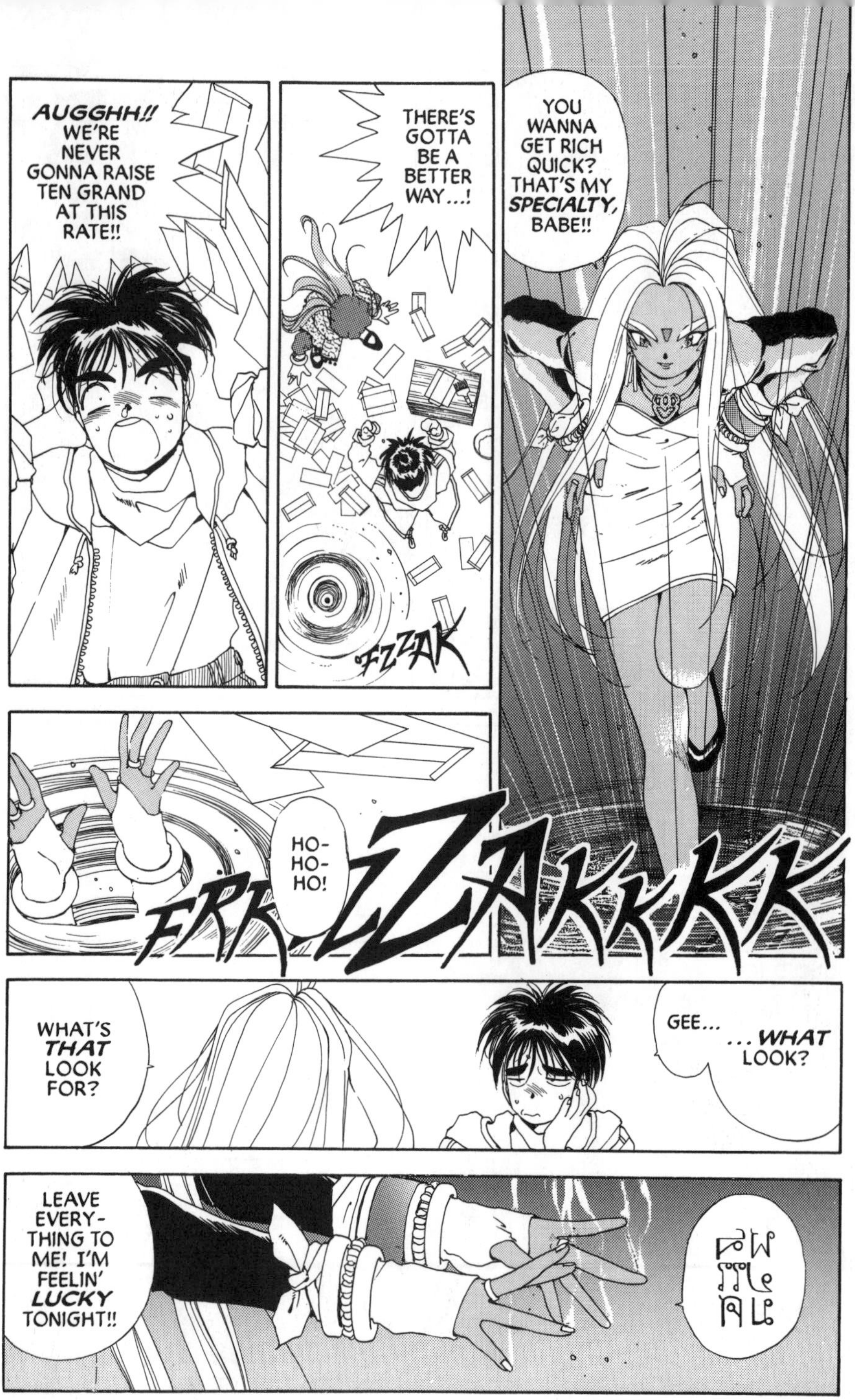
AUGGHH!! WE'RE NEVER GONNA RAISE TEN GRAND AT THIS RATE!!
THERE'S GOTTA BE A BETTER WAY...!
FZZAK
HO-HO-HO!
YOU WANNA GET RICH QUICK? THAT'S MY SPECIALTY, BABE!!
FRRZZAKKKK
WHAT'S THAT LOOK FOR?
GEE...
...WHAT LOOK?
LEAVE EVERYTHING TO ME! I'M FEELIN' LUCKY TONIGHT!!

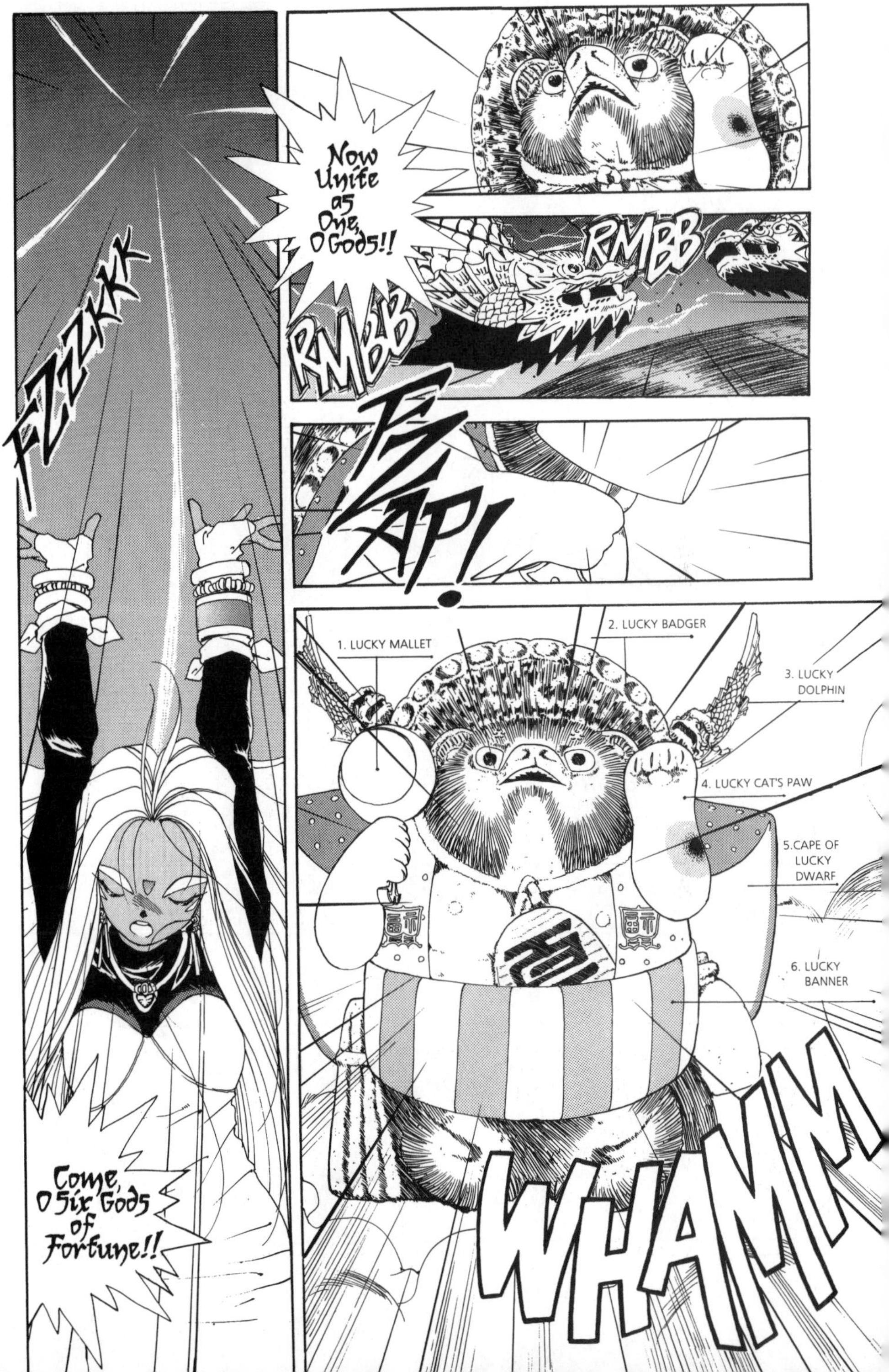
FZZZKKK
Come, O Six Gods of Fortune!!
Now Unite as One, O Gods!!
RMBB
RMBB
FSZAP!
1. LUCKY MALLET
2. LUCKY BADGER
3. LUCKY DOLPHIN
4. LUCKY CAT'S PAW
5.CAPE OF LUCKY DWARF
6. LUCKY BANNER
WHAMM

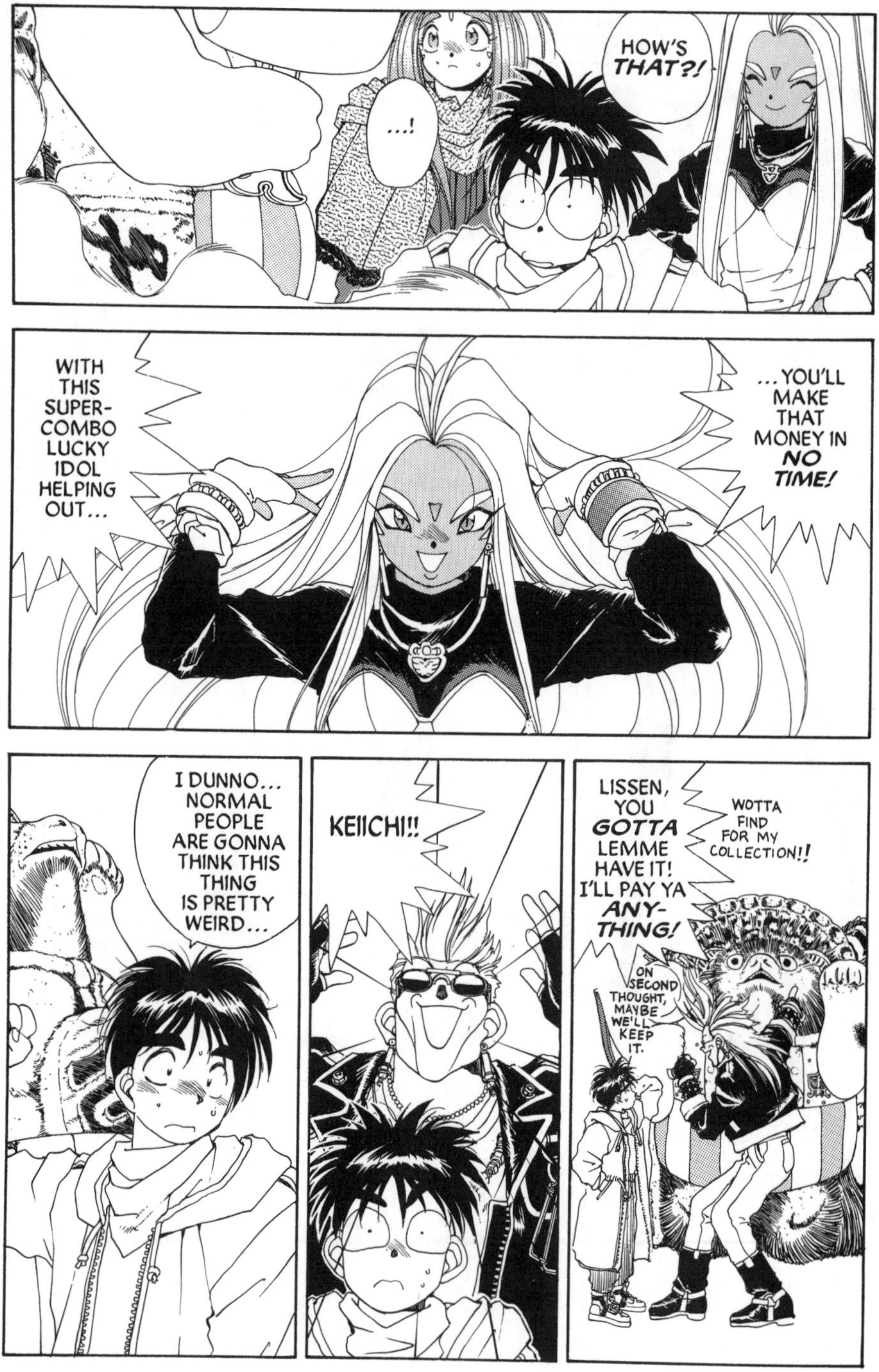
...!
HOW'S THAT?!
WITH THIS SUPER-COMBO LUCKY IDOL HELPING OUT...
...YOU'LL MAKE THAT MONEY IN NO TIME!
I DUNNO... NORMAL PEOPLE ARE GONNA THINK THIS THING IS PRETTY WEIRD...
KEIICHI!!
LISSEN, YOU GOTTA LEMME HAVE IT! I'LL PAY YA ANY-THING!
WOTTA FIND FOR MY COLLECTION!!
ON SECOND THOUGHT, MAYBE WE'LL KEEP IT.

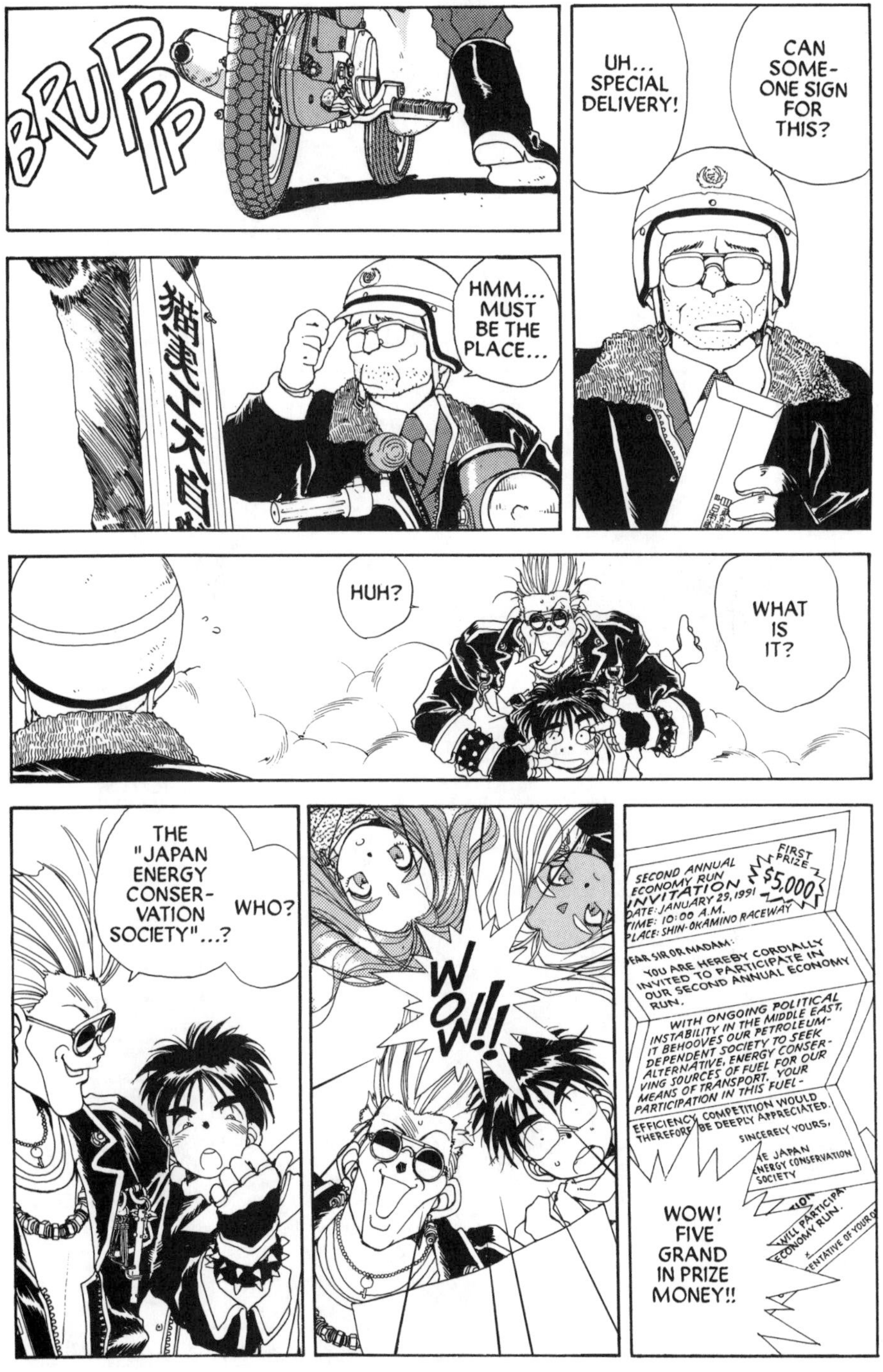
BRUPPP
HMM... MUST BE THE PLACE...
UH... SPECIAL DELIVERY!
CAN SOME-ONE SIGN FOR THIS?
HUH?
WHAT IS IT?
THE "JAPAN ENERGY CONSER-VATION SOCIETY"...?
WHO?
WOW!!
SECOND ANNUAL ECONOMY RUN INVITATION
FIRST PRIZE $5,000
DATE: JANUARY 29, 1991
TIME: 10:00 A.M.
PLACE: SHIN-OKAMINO RACEWAY
EAR SIR OR MADAM:
YOU ARE HEREBY CORDIALLY INVITED TO PARTICIPATE IN OUR SECOND ANNUAL ECONOMY RUN.
WITH ONGOING POLITICAL INSTABILITY IN THE MIDDLE EAST, IT BEHOOVES OUR PETROLEUM-DEPENDENT SOCIETY TO SEEK ALTERNATIVE, ENERGY CONSER-VING SOURCES OF FUEL FOR OUR MEANS OF TRANSPORT. YOUR PARTICIPATION IN THIS FUEL-EFFICIENCY COMPETITION WOULD THEREFORE BE DEEPLY APPRECIATED.
SINCERELY YOURS,
HE JAPAN ENERGY CONSERVATION SOCIETY
WOW! FIVE GRAND IN PRIZE MONEY!!

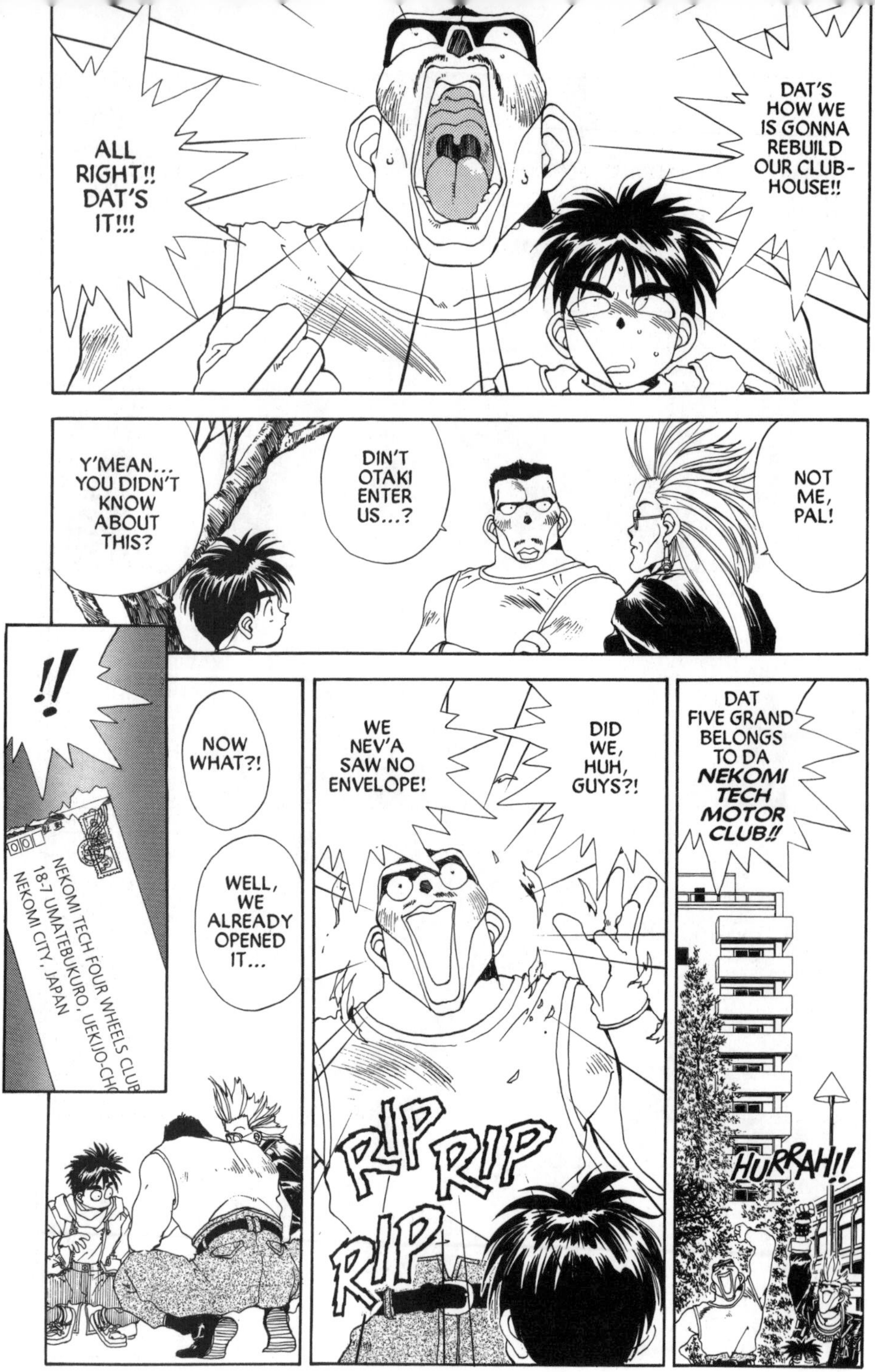
ALL RIGHT!! DAT'S IT!!!
DAT'S HOW WE IS GONNA REBUILD OUR CLUB-HOUSE!!
Y'MEAN... YOU DIDN'T KNOW ABOUT THIS?
DIN'T OTAKI ENTER US...?
NOT ME, PAL!
!!
NEKOMI TECH FOUR WHEELS CLUB
18-7 UMATEBUKURO, UEKIJO-CHO
NEKOMI CITY, JAPAN
NOW WHAT?!
WELL, WE ALREADY OPENED IT...
WE NEV'A SAW NO ENVELOPE!
DID WE, HUH, GUYS?!
RIP RIP RIP
DAT FIVE GRAND BELONGS TO DA *NEKOMI TECH MOTOR CLUB!!*
HURRAH!!

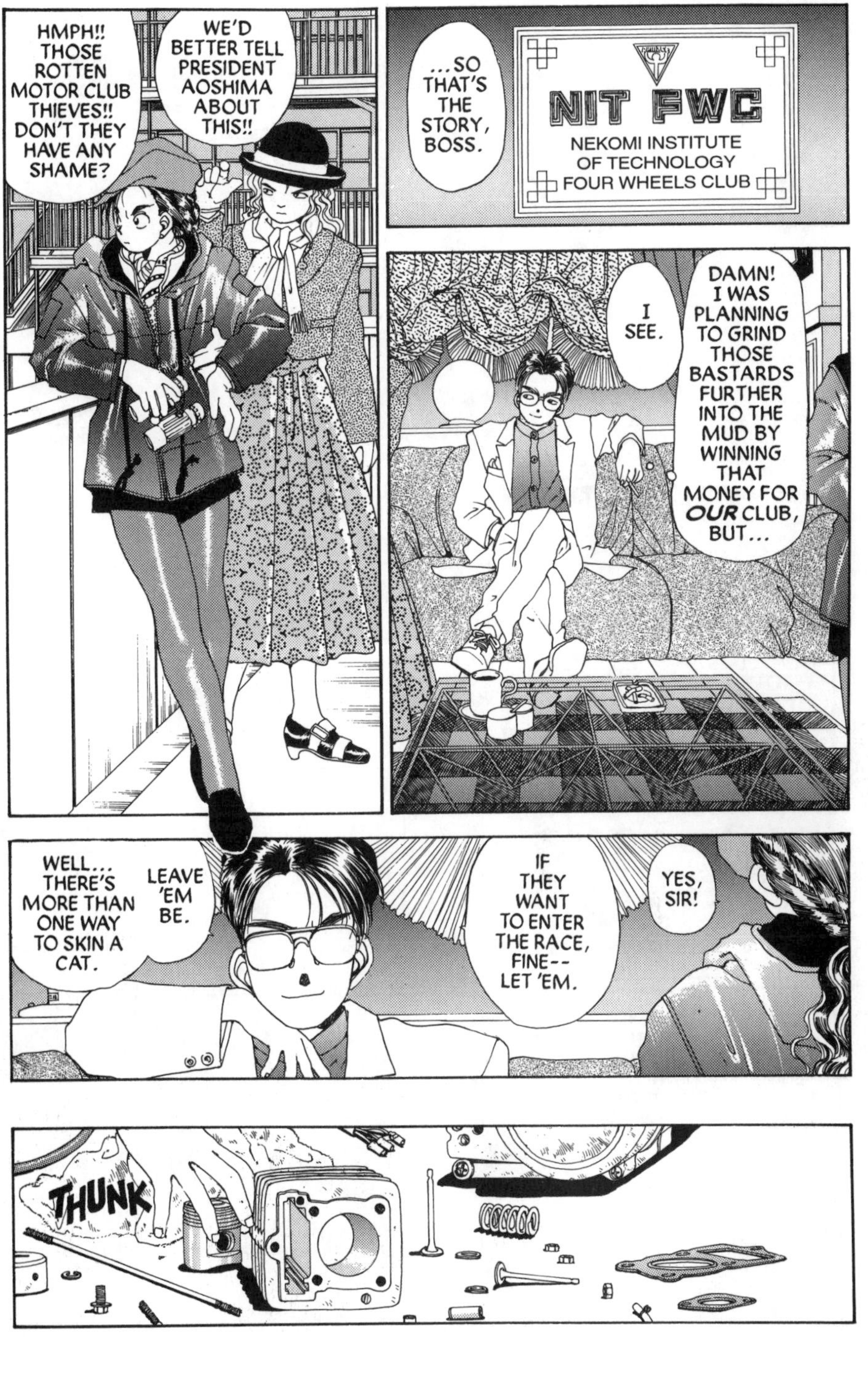
HMPH!! THOSE ROTTEN MOTOR CLUB THIEVES!! DON'T THEY HAVE ANY SHAME?
WE'D BETTER TELL PRESIDENT AOSHIMA ABOUT THIS!!
...SO THAT'S THE STORY, BOSS.
NIT FWC
NEKOMI INSTITUTE OF TECHNOLOGY FOUR WHEELS CLUB
I SEE.
DAMN! I WAS PLANNING TO GRIND THOSE BASTARDS FURTHER INTO THE MUD BY WINNING THAT MONEY FOR OUR CLUB, BUT...
WELL... THERE'S MORE THAN ONE WAY TO SKIN A CAT.
LEAVE 'EM BE.
IF THEY WANT TO ENTER THE RACE, FINE-- LET 'EM.
YES, SIR!
THUNK

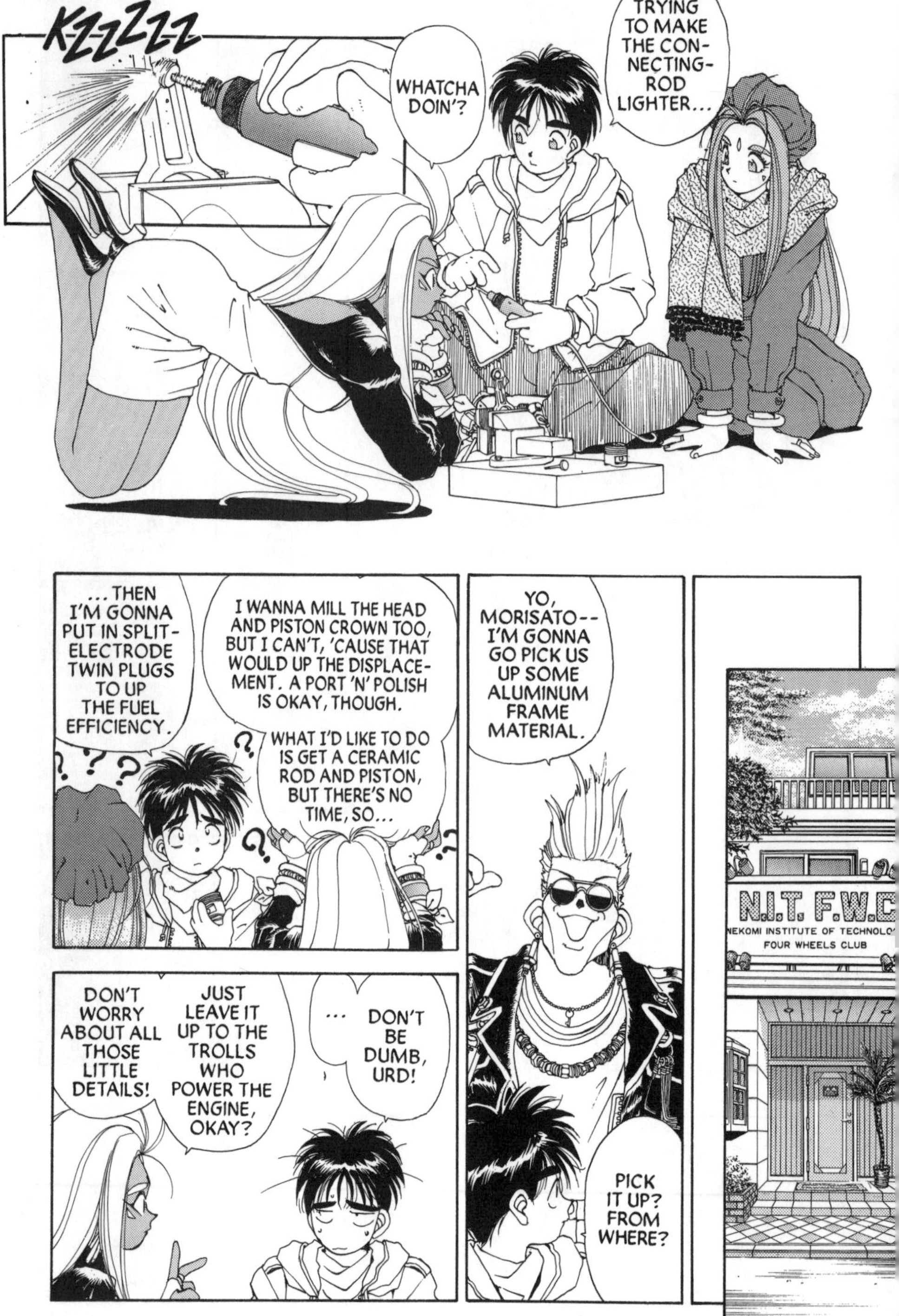
KZZZZZZ
WHATCHA DOIN'?
TRYING TO MAKE THE CON-NECTING-ROD LIGHTER...
...THEN I'M GONNA PUT IN SPLIT-ELECTRODE TWIN PLUGS TO UP THE FUEL EFFICIENCY.
I WANNA MILL THE HEAD AND PISTON CROWN TOO, BUT I CAN'T, 'CAUSE THAT WOULD UP THE DISPLACE-MENT. A PORT 'N' POLISH IS OKAY, THOUGH.
WHAT I'D LIKE TO DO IS GET A CERAMIC ROD AND PISTON, BUT THERE'S NO TIME, SO...
DON'T WORRY ABOUT ALL THOSE LITTLE DETAILS!
JUST LEAVE IT UP TO THE TROLLS WHO POWER THE ENGINE, OKAY?
... DON'T BE DUMB, URD!
YO, MORISATO-- I'M GONNA GO PICK US UP SOME ALUMINUM FRAME MATERIAL.
PICK IT UP? FROM WHERE?
N.I.T. F.W.C
NEKOMI INSTITUTE OF TECHNOLO
FOUR WHEELS CLUB

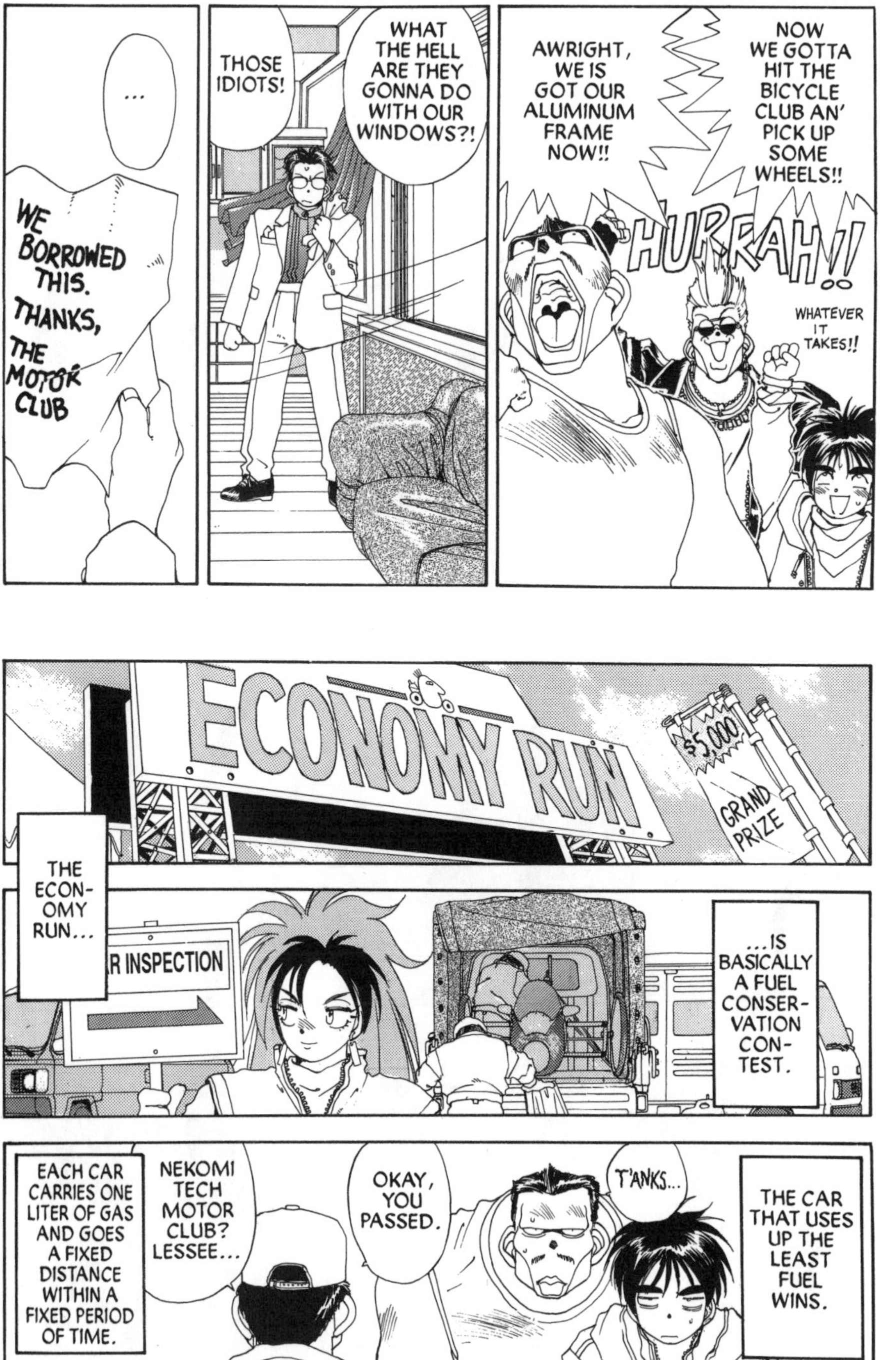

...
WE BORROWED THIS. THANKS, THE MOTOR CLUB
THOSE IDIOTS!
WHAT THE HELL ARE THEY GONNA DO WITH OUR WINDOWS?!
AWRIGHT, WE IS GOT OUR ALUMINUM FRAME NOW!!
NOW WE GOTTA HIT THE BICYCLE CLUB AN' PICK UP SOME WHEELS!!
HURRAH!!
WHATEVER IT TAKES!!
ECONOMY RUN
$5,000
GRAND PRIZE
THE ECONOMY RUN...
R INSPECTION
...IS BASICALLY A FUEL CONSERVATION CONTEST.
EACH CAR CARRIES ONE LITER OF GAS AND GOES A FIXED DISTANCE WITHIN A FIXED PERIOD OF TIME.
NEKOMI TECH MOTOR CLUB? LESSEE...
OKAY, YOU PASSED.
T'ANKS...
THE CAR THAT USES UP THE LEAST FUEL WINS.

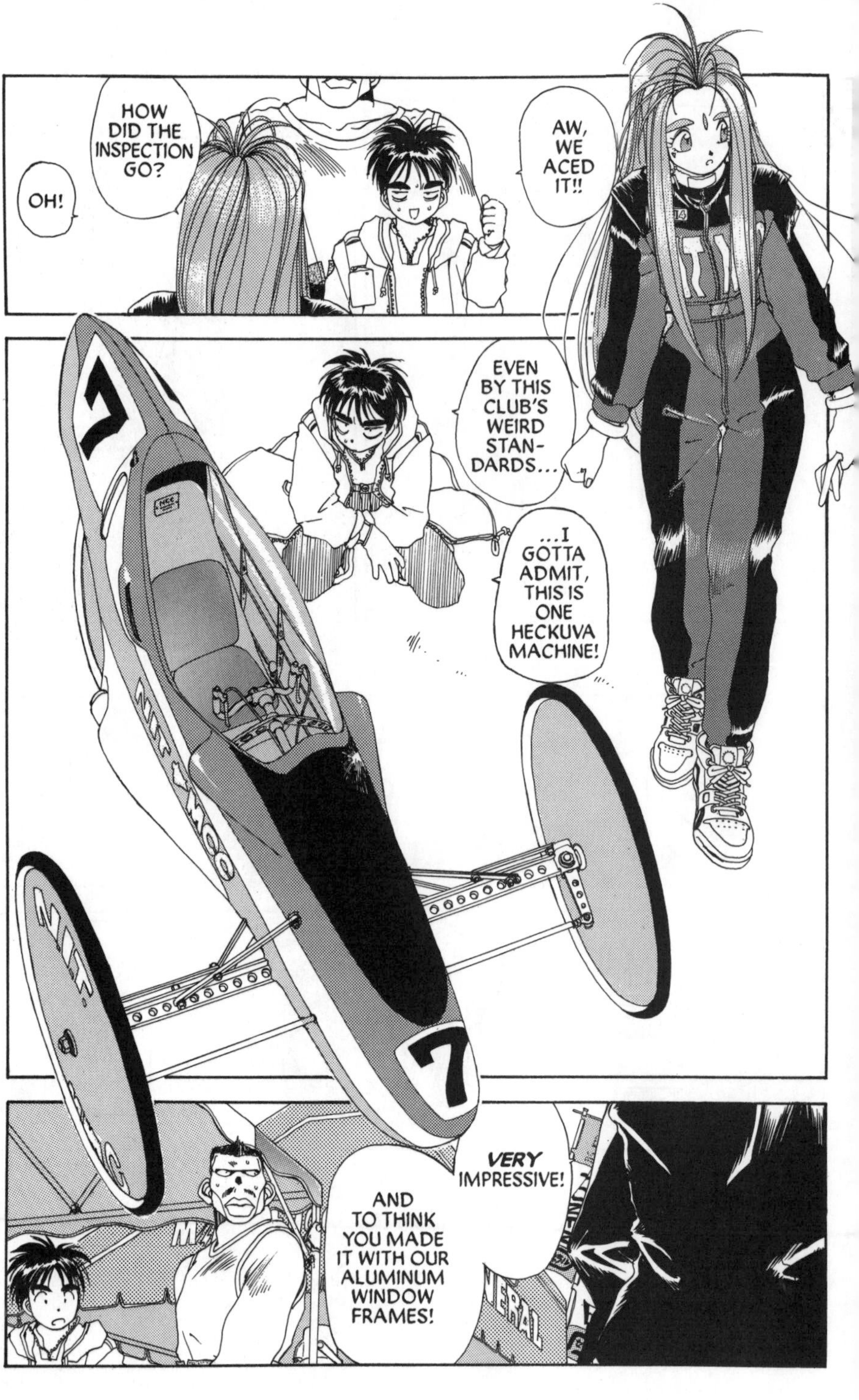
OH!
HOW DID THE INSPECTION GO?
AW, WE ACED IT!!
EVEN BY THIS CLUB'S WEIRD STAN-DARDS...
...I GOTTA ADMIT, THIS IS ONE HECKUVA MACHINE!
VERY IMPRESSIVE!
AND TO THINK YOU MADE IT WITH OUR ALUMINUM WINDOW FRAMES!

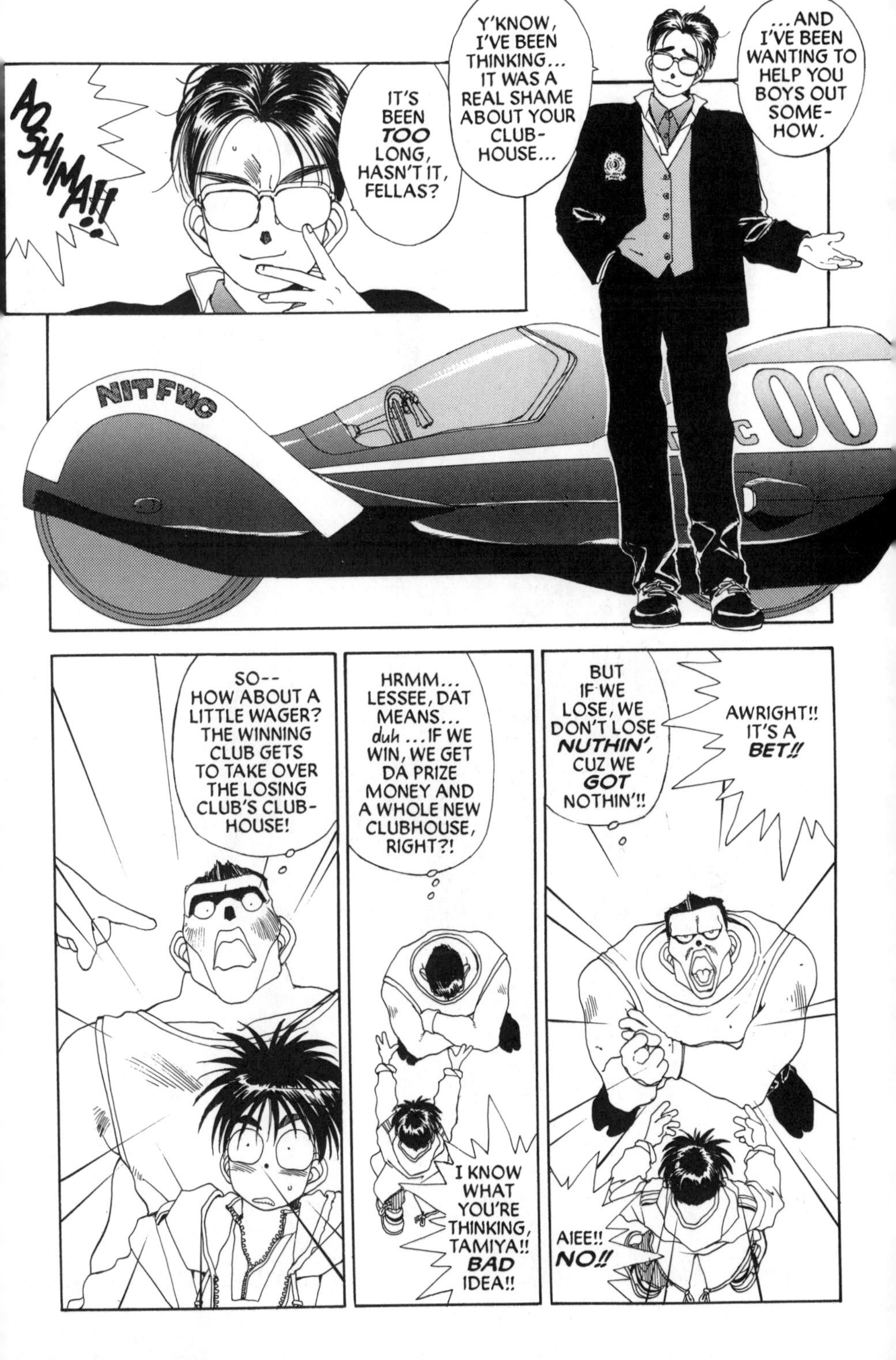
AOSHIMA!!
IT'S BEEN TOO LONG, HASN'T IT, FELLAS?
Y'KNOW, I'VE BEEN THINKING... IT WAS A REAL SHAME ABOUT YOUR CLUB-HOUSE...
...AND I'VE BEEN WANTING TO HELP YOU BOYS OUT SOME-HOW.
NIT FWC
00
SO-- HOW ABOUT A LITTLE WAGER? THE WINNING CLUB GETS TO TAKE OVER THE LOSING CLUB'S CLUB-HOUSE!
HRMM... LESSEE, DAT MEANS... duh ...IF WE WIN, WE GET DA PRIZE MONEY AND A WHOLE NEW CLUBHOUSE, RIGHT?!
I KNOW WHAT YOU'RE THINKING, TAMIYA!! BAD IDEA!!
BUT IF WE LOSE, WE DON'T LOSE NUTHIN', CUZ WE GOT NOTHIN'!!
AWRIGHT!! IT'S A BET!!
AIEE!! NO!!

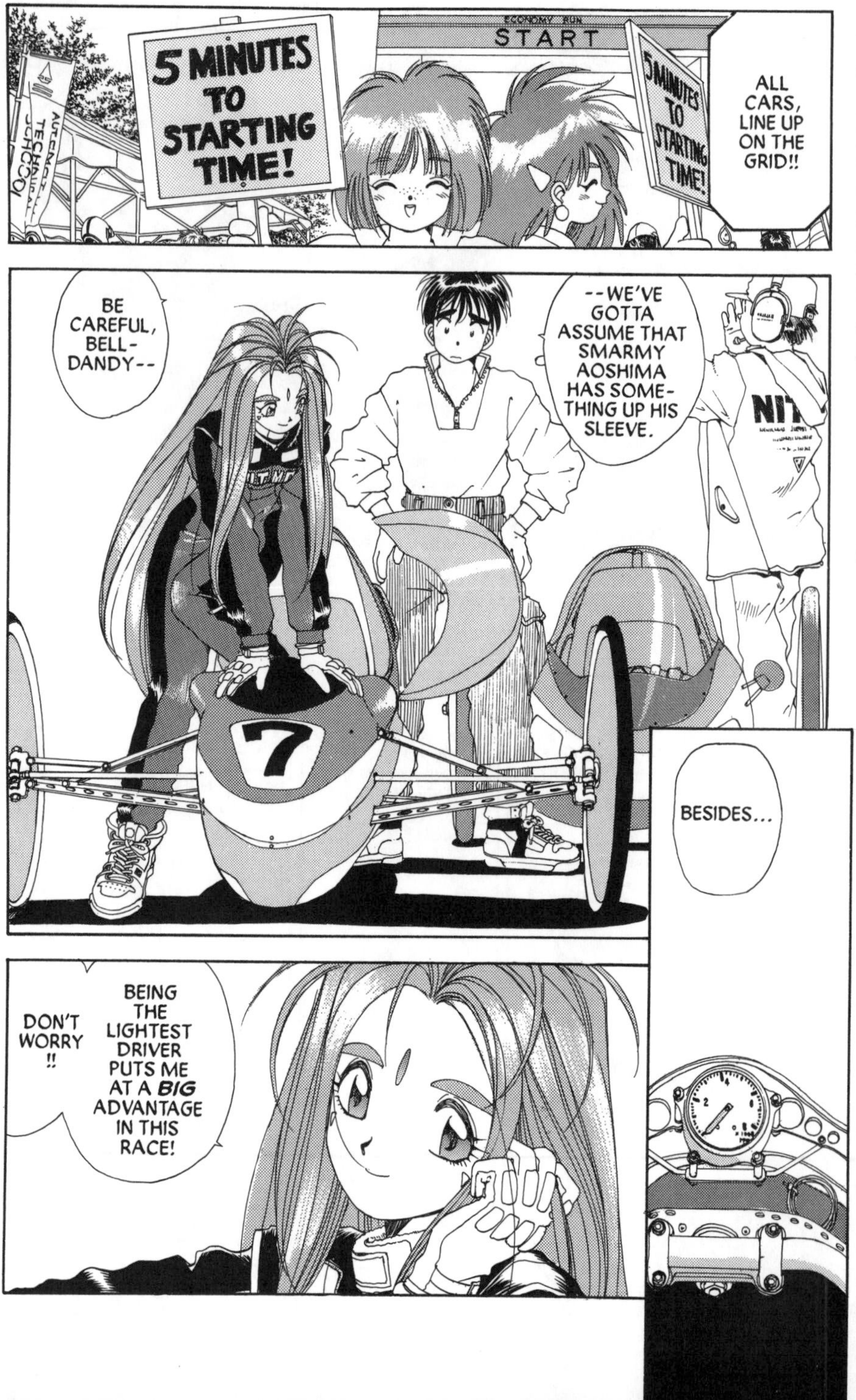
ALL CARS, LINE UP ON THE GRID!!
5 MINUTES TO STARTING TIME!
ECONOMY RUN
START
5 MINUTES TO STARTING TIME!
--WE'VE GOTTA ASSUME THAT SMARMY AOSHIMA HAS SOME-THING UP HIS SLEEVE.
BE CAREFUL, BELL-DANDY--
BESIDES...
BEING THE LIGHTEST DRIVER PUTS ME AT A *BIG* ADVANTAGE IN THIS RACE!
DON'T WORRY!!

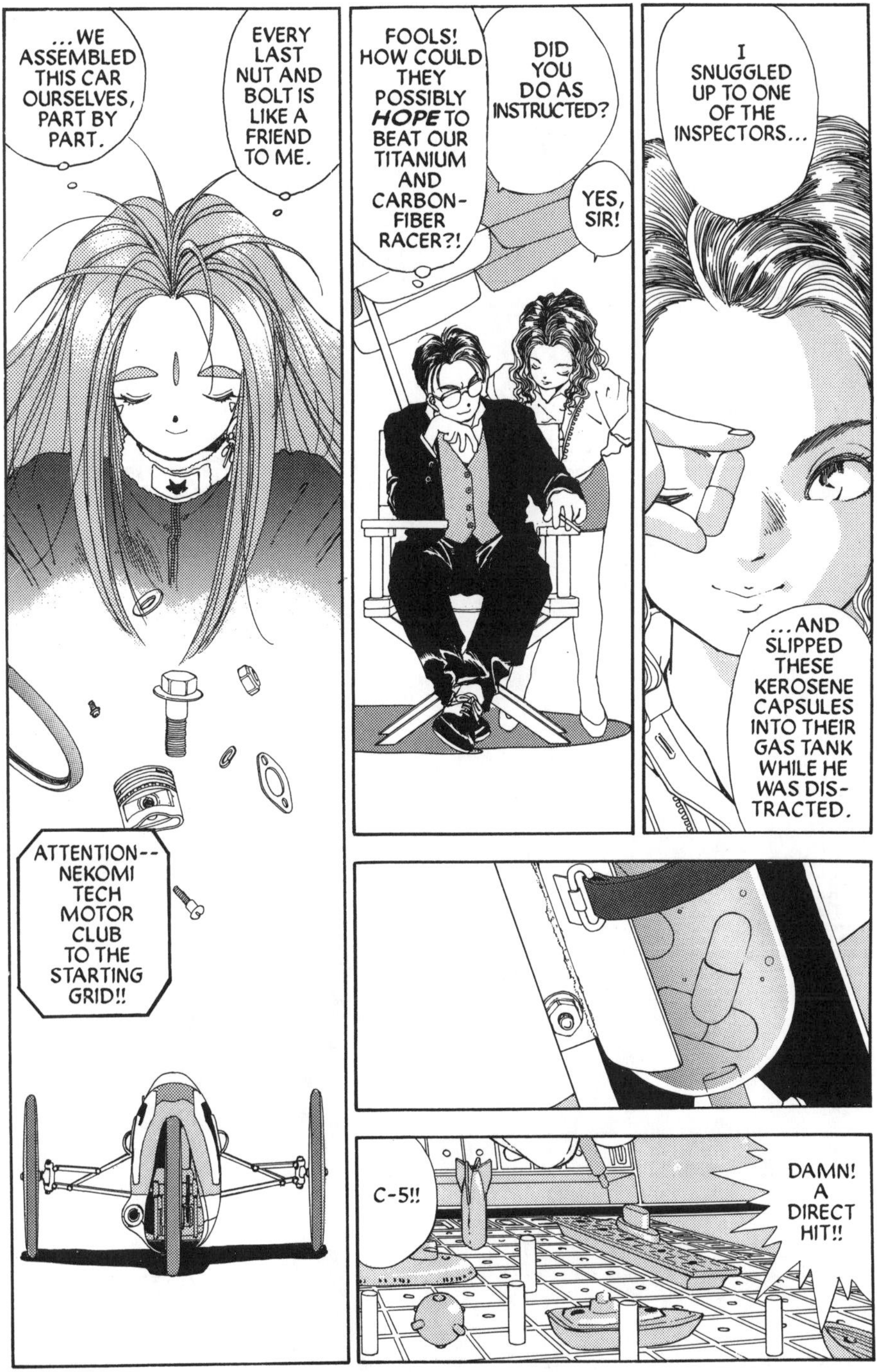
...WE ASSEMBLED THIS CAR OURSELVES, PART BY PART.
EVERY LAST NUT AND BOLT IS LIKE A FRIEND TO ME.
ATTENTION-- NEKOMI TECH MOTOR CLUB TO THE STARTING GRID!!
FOOLS! HOW COULD THEY POSSIBLY *HOPE* TO BEAT OUR TITANIUM AND CARBON-FIBER RACER?!
DID YOU DO AS INSTRUCTED?
YES, SIR!
I SNUGGLED UP TO ONE OF THE INSPECTORS...
...AND SLIPPED THESE KEROSENE CAPSULES INTO THEIR GAS TANK WHILE HE WAS DIS-TRACTED.
C-5!!
DAMN! A DIRECT HIT!!

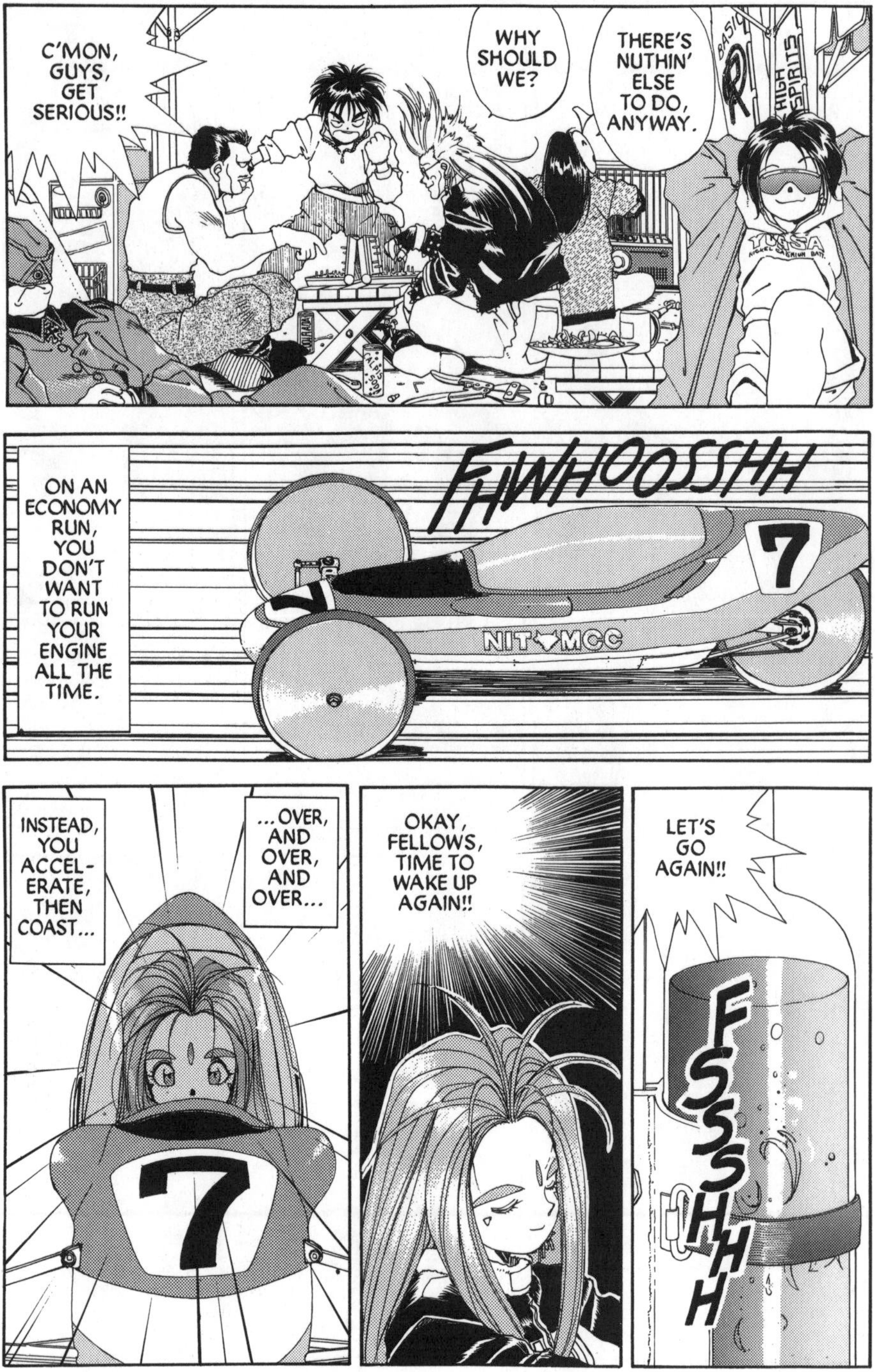
C'MON, GUYS, GET SERIOUS!!
WHY SHOULD WE?
THERE'S NUTHIN' ELSE TO DO, ANYWAY.
BASIC
HIGH SPIRITS
YUASA
ON AN ECONOMY RUN, YOU DON'T WANT TO RUN YOUR ENGINE ALL THE TIME.
FHWHOOSSHH
7
NIT MCC
INSTEAD, YOU ACCEL-ERATE, THEN COAST...
...OVER, AND OVER, AND OVER...
7
OKAY, FELLOWS, TIME TO WAKE UP AGAIN!!
LET'S GO AGAIN!!
FSSSHHHH

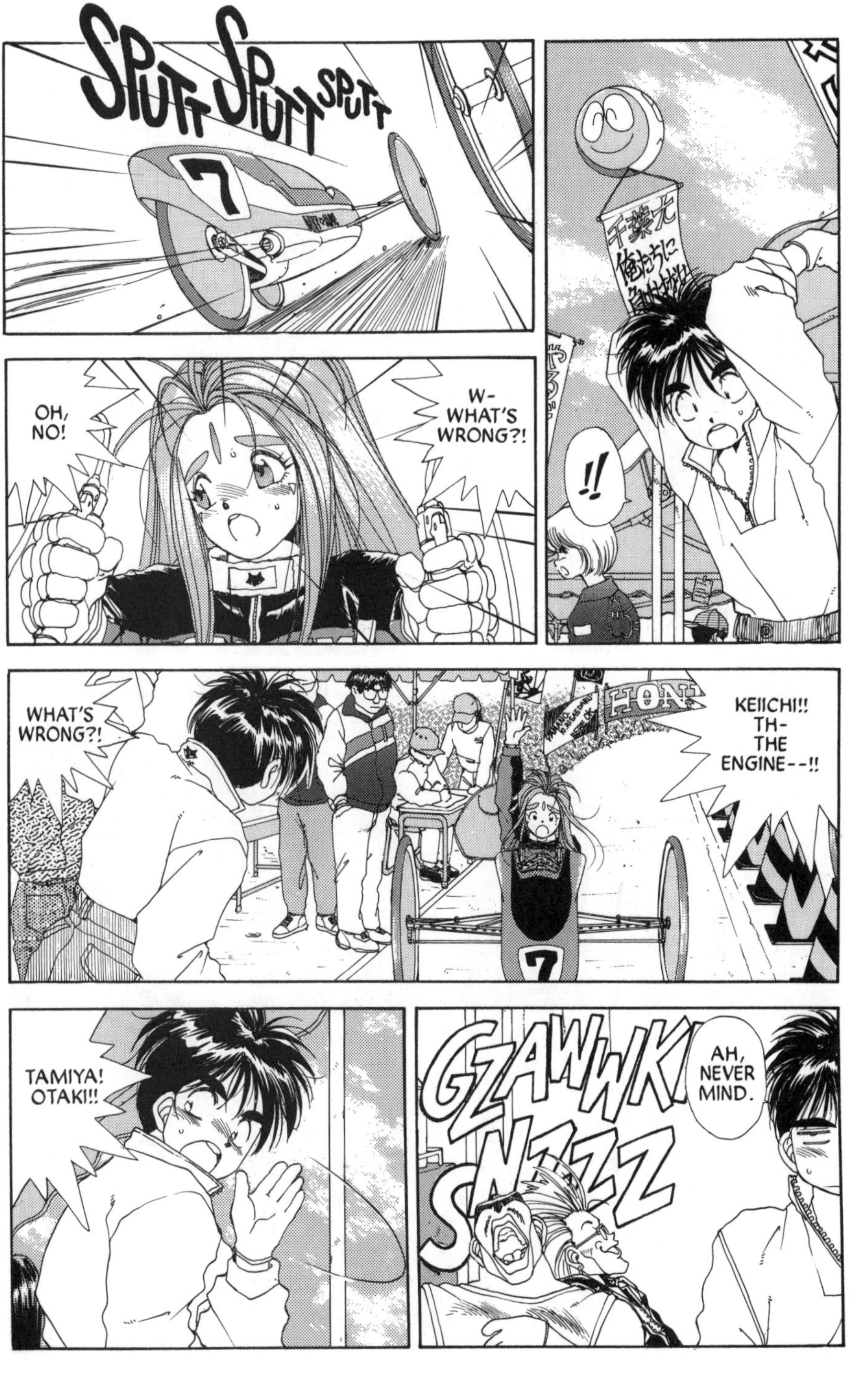
SPUTT SPUTT SPUTT
OH, NO!
W- WHAT'S WRONG?!
!!
WHAT'S WRONG?!
KEIICHI!! TH- THE ENGINE--!!
TAMIYA! OTAKI!!
GZAWWK!
SNZZZ
AH, NEVER MIND.

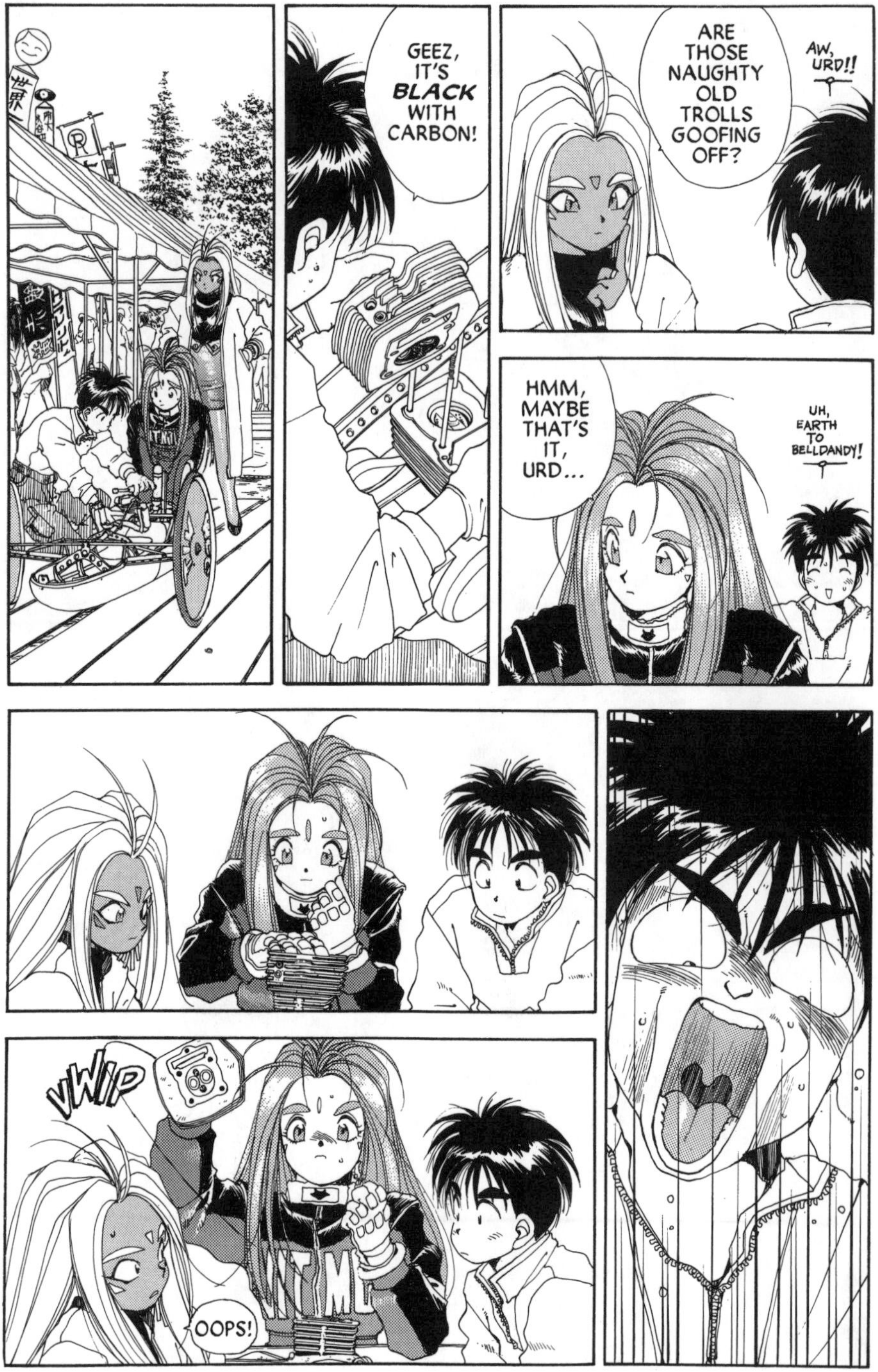
GEEZ, IT'S BLACK WITH CARBON!
ARE THOSE NAUGHTY OLD TROLLS GOOFING OFF?
AW, URD!!
HMM, MAYBE THAT'S IT, URD...
UH, EARTH TO BELLDANDY!
VWIP
OOPS!

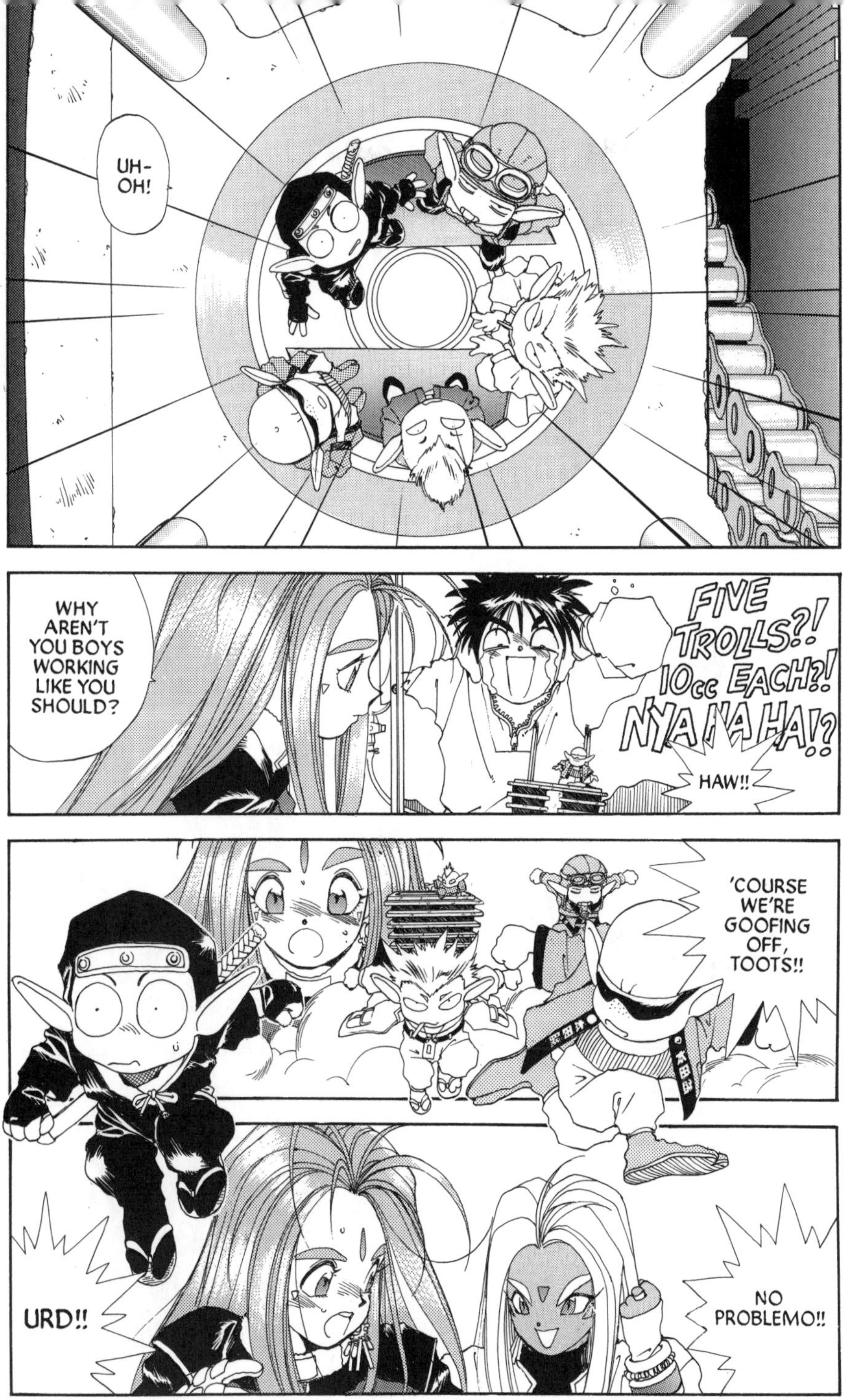
UH-OH!
WHY AREN'T YOU BOYS WORKING LIKE YOU SHOULD?
FIVE TROLLS?! 10cc EACH?! NYA HA HA!?
HAW!!
'COURSE WE'RE GOOFING OFF, TOOTS!!
URD!!
NO PROBLEMO!!

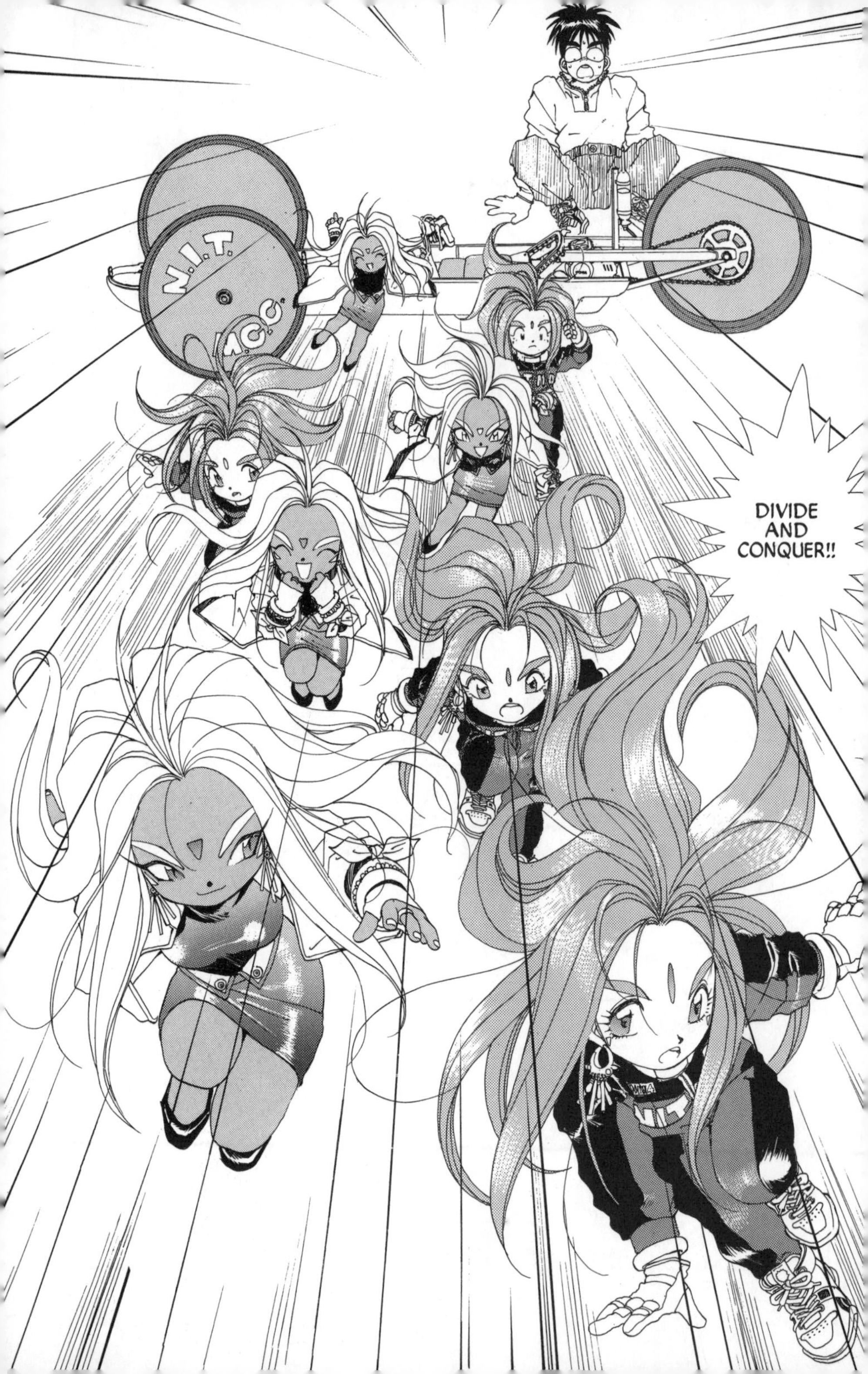
M.I.T.
M.C.C.
DIVIDE AND CONQUER!!

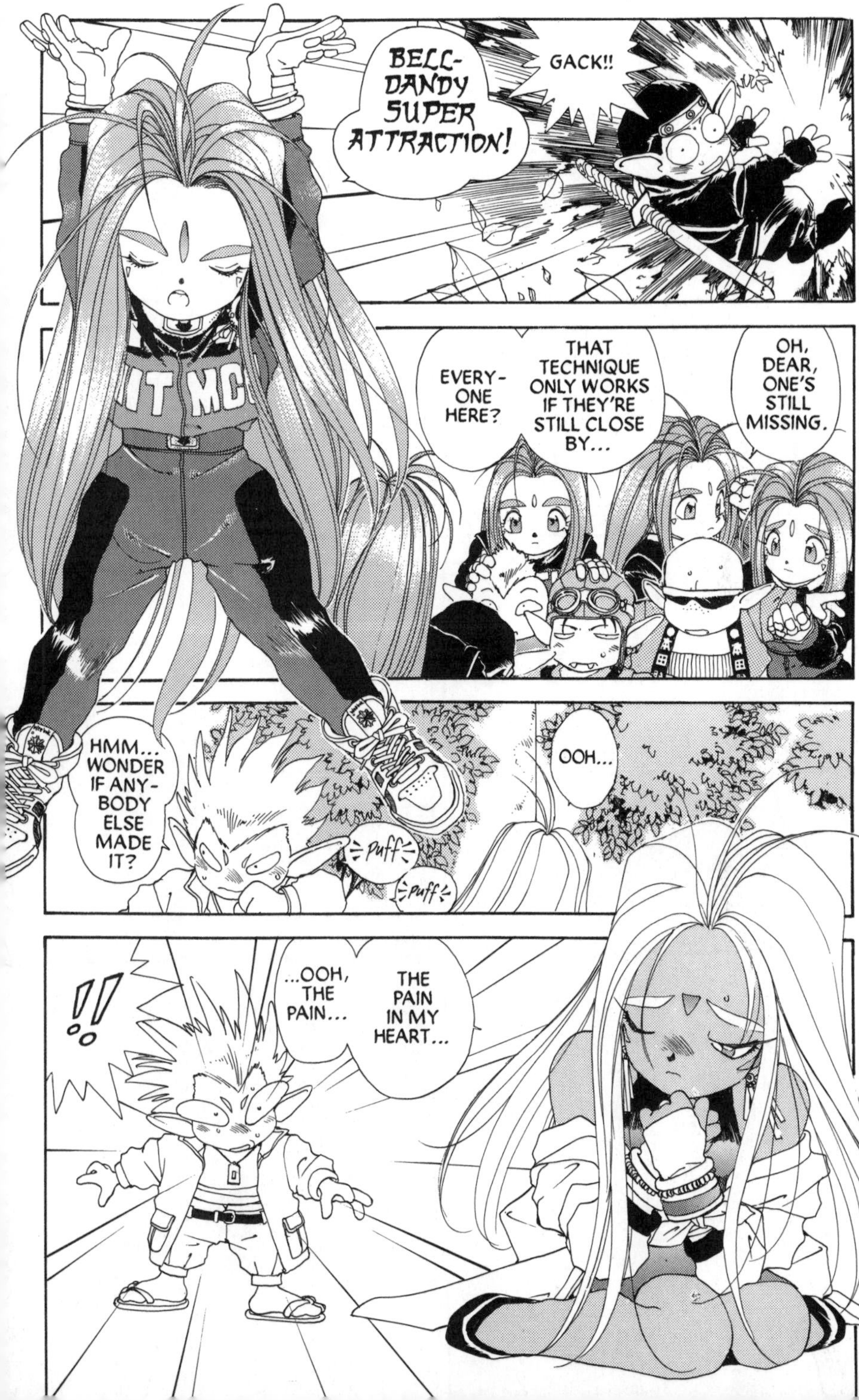
BELL-DANDY SUPER ATTRACTION!
GACK!!
EVERY-ONE HERE?
THAT TECHNIQUE ONLY WORKS IF THEY'RE STILL CLOSE BY...
OH, DEAR, ONE'S STILL MISSING.
HMM... WONDER IF ANYBODY ELSE MADE IT?
puff
puff
OOH...
!!
...OOH, THE PAIN...
THE PAIN IN MY HEART...

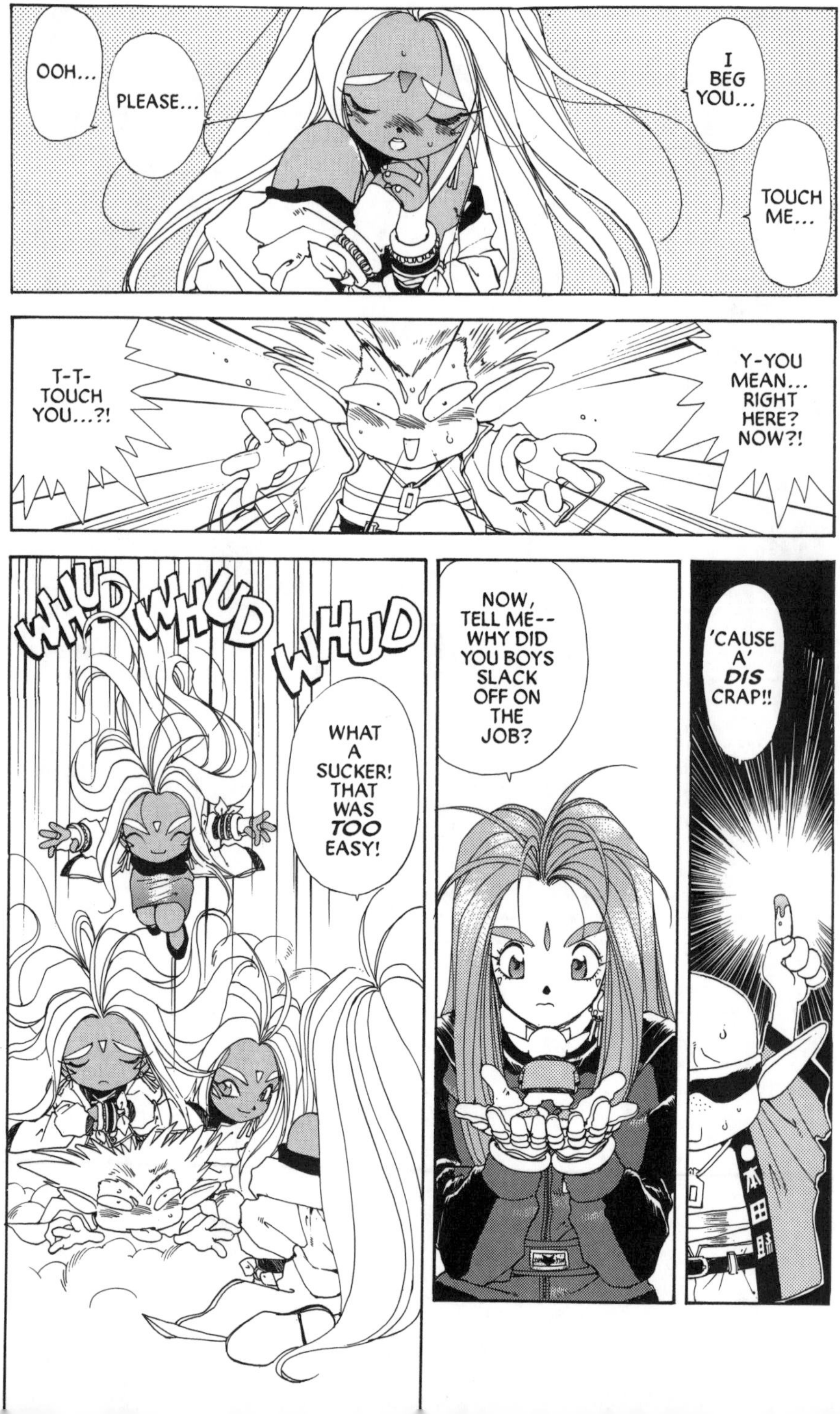

OOH...
PLEASE...
I BEG YOU...
TOUCH ME...
T-T-TOUCH YOU...?!
Y-YOU MEAN... RIGHT HERE? NOW?!
WHUD WHUD WHUD
WHAT A SUCKER! THAT WAS *TOO* EASY!
NOW, TELL ME-- WHY DID YOU BOYS SLACK OFF ON THE JOB?
'CAUSE A' ***DIS*** CRAP!!

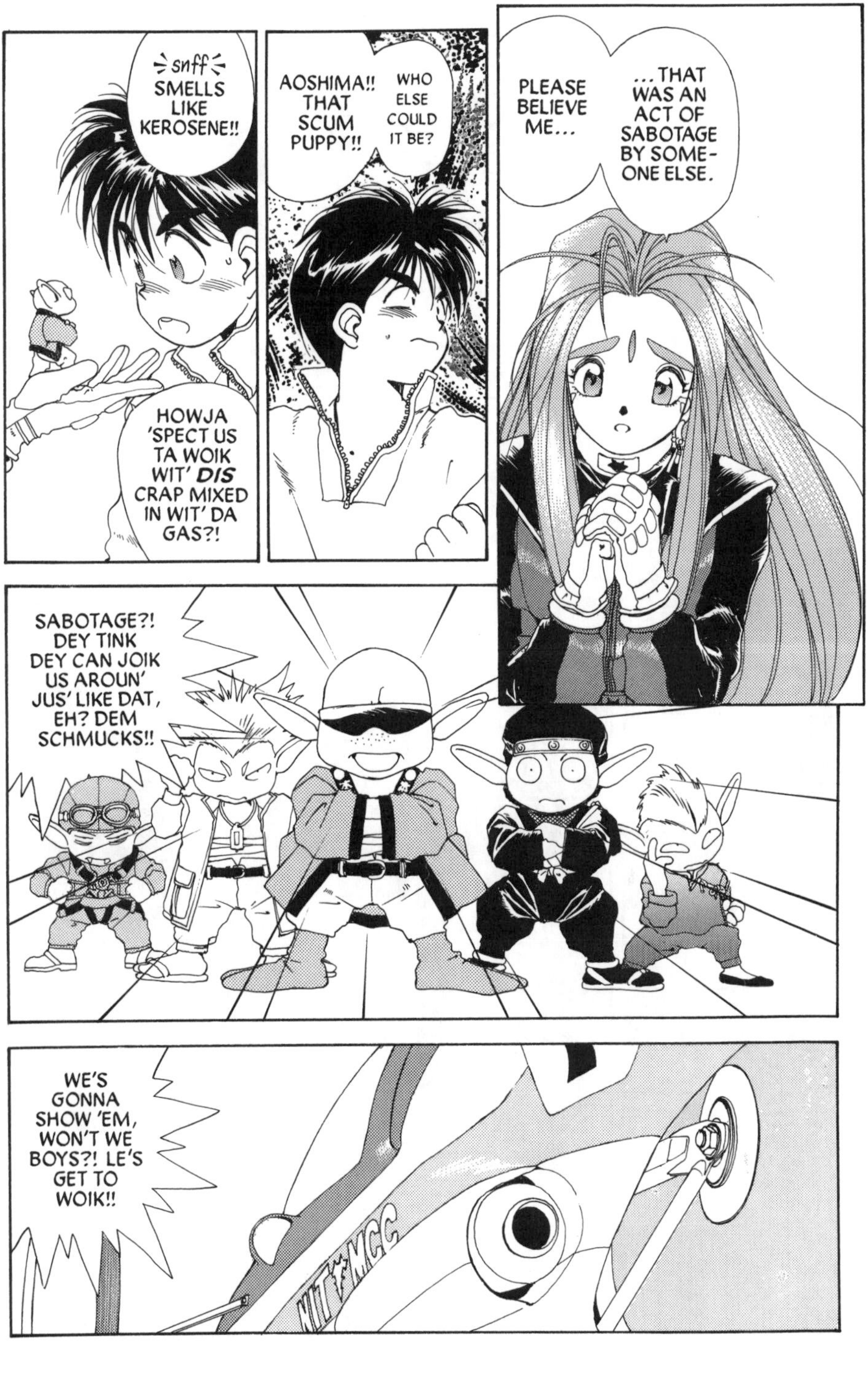
snff
SMELLS LIKE KEROSENE!!
HOWJA 'SPECT US TA WOIK WIT' *DIS* CRAP MIXED IN WIT' DA GAS?!
AOSHIMA!! THAT SCUM PUPPY!!
WHO ELSE COULD IT BE?
PLEASE BELIEVE ME...
...THAT WAS AN ACT OF SABOTAGE BY SOME-ONE ELSE.
SABOTAGE?! DEY TINK DEY CAN JOIK US AROUN' JUS' LIKE DAT, EH? DEM SCHMUCKS!!
WE'S GONNA SHOW 'EM, WON'T WE BOYS?! LE'S GET TO WOIK!!
MCC

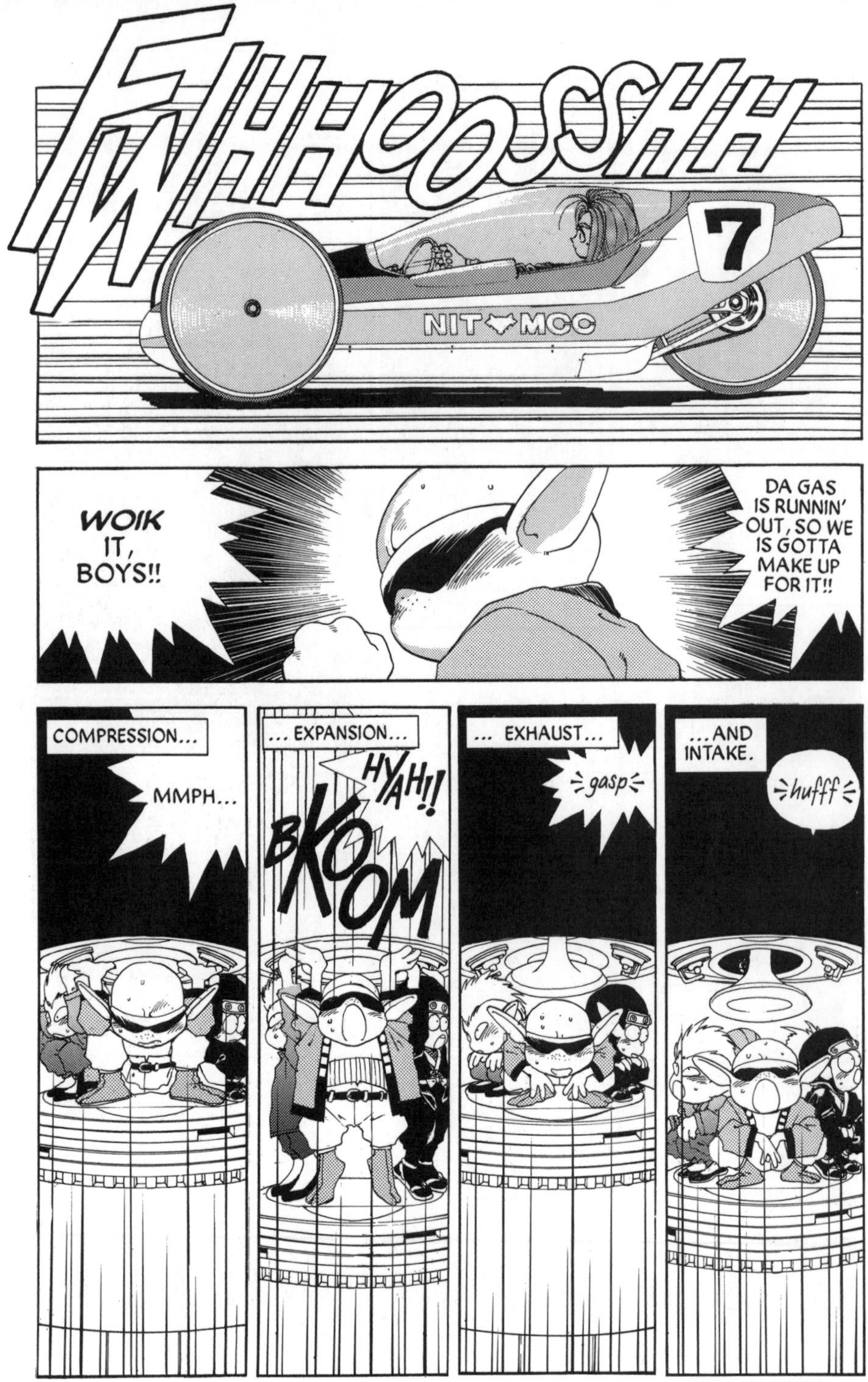
FWHHOOSSHH
7
NIT MCC
WOIK IT, BOYS!!
DA GAS IS RUNNIN' OUT, SO WE IS GOTTA MAKE UP FOR IT!!
COMPRESSION...
MMPH...
...EXPANSION...
HYAH!!
BKOOM
... EXHAUST...
gasp
...AND INTAKE.
hufff
(REPEAT 1500 TIMES PER MINUTE = 3000RPM)

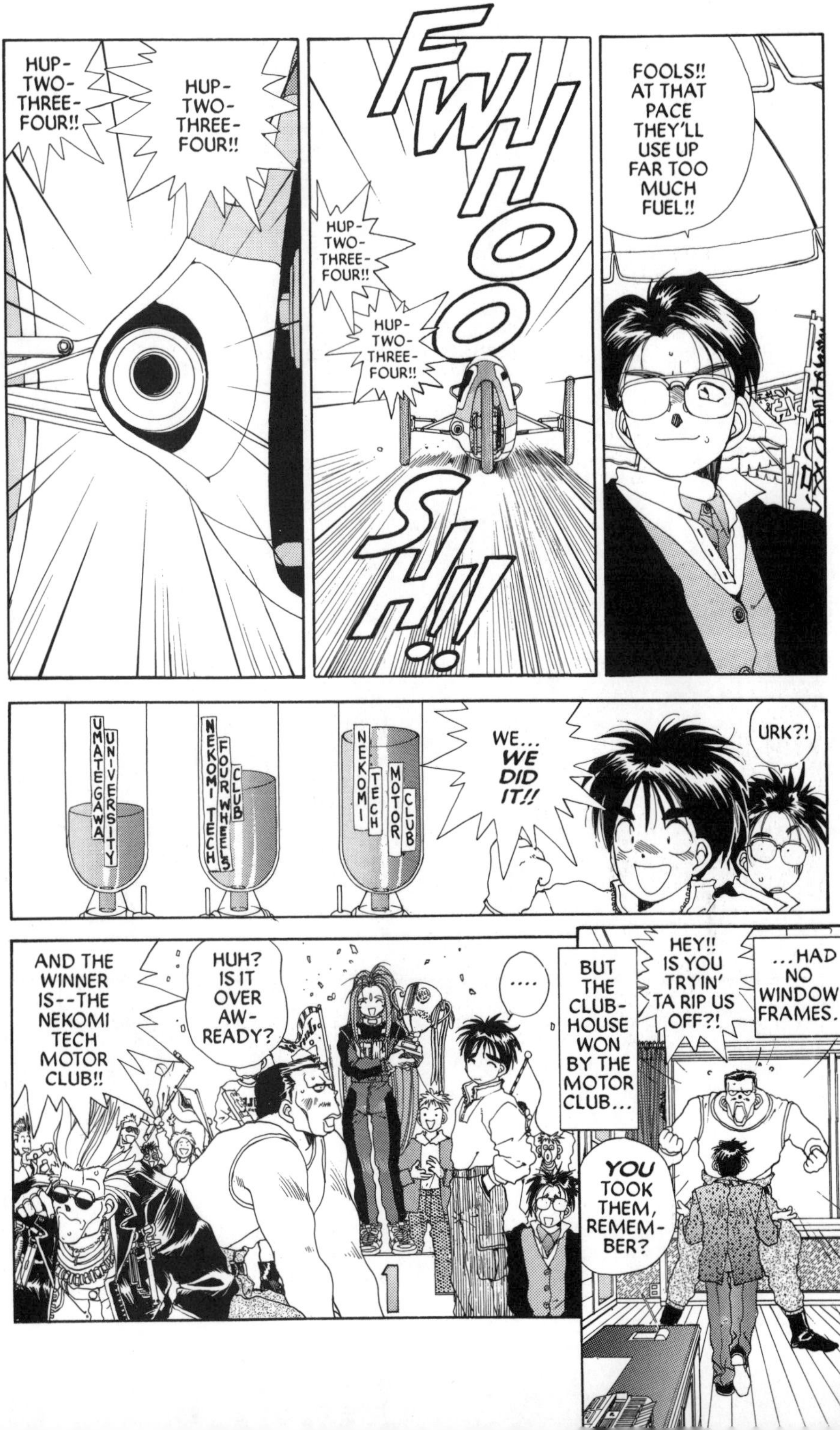
HUP-TWO-THREE-FOUR!!
HUP-TWO-THREE-FOUR!!
FWHOOOSH!!
HUP-TWO-THREE-FOUR!!
HUP-TWO-THREE-FOUR!!
FOOLS!! AT THAT PACE THEY'LL USE UP FAR TOO MUCH FUEL!!
UMATEGAWA UNIVERSITY
NEKOMI TECH FOUR WHEELS CLUB
NEKOMI TECH MOTOR CLUB
WE... WE DID IT!!
URK?!
AND THE WINNER IS--THE NEKOMI TECH MOTOR CLUB!!
HUH? IS IT OVER AW-READY?
....
BUT THE CLUB-HOUSE WON BY THE MOTOR CLUB...
HEY!! IS YOU TRYIN' TA RIP US OFF?!
...HAD NO WINDOW FRAMES.
YOU TOOK THEM, REMEMBER?
1

Valentine Rhapsody

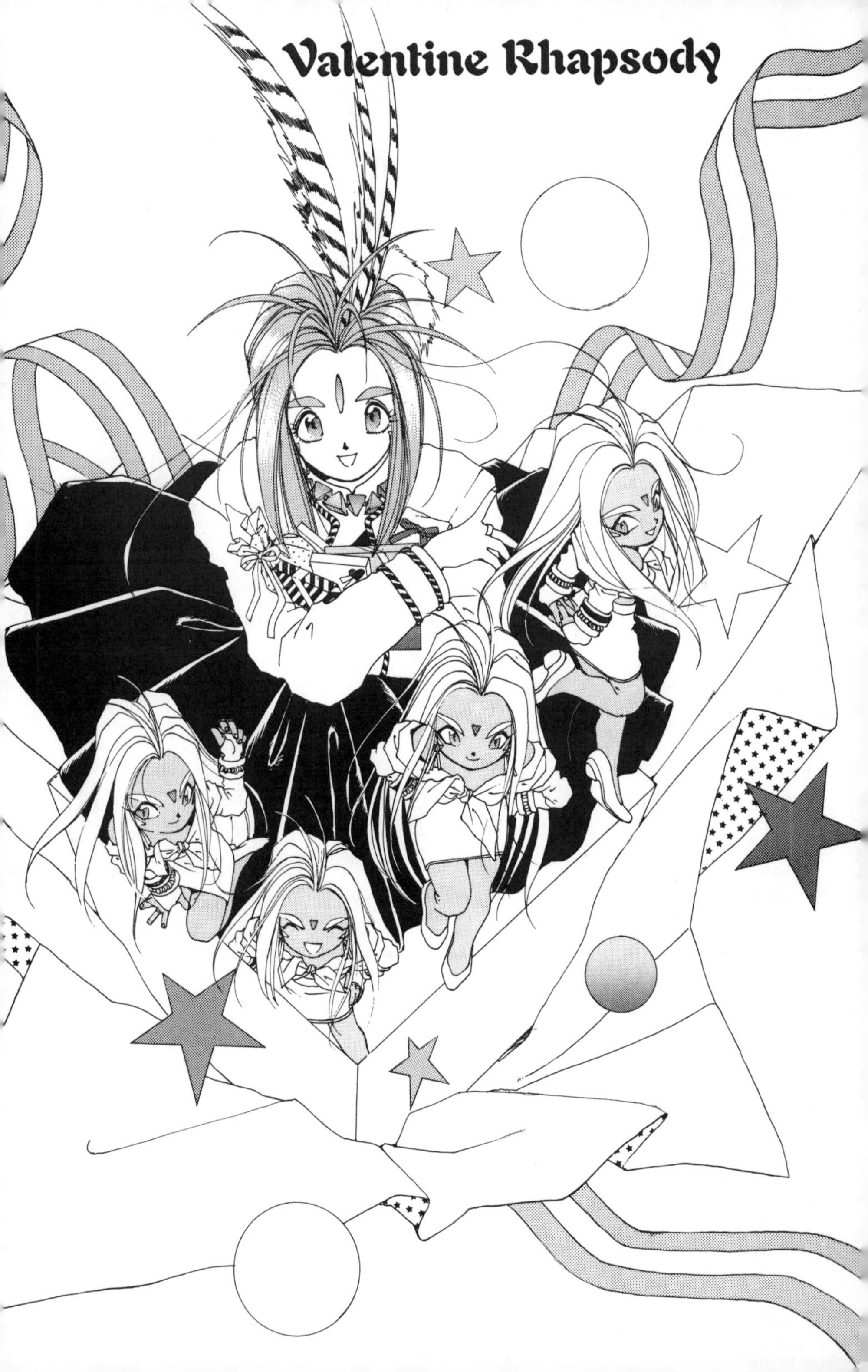

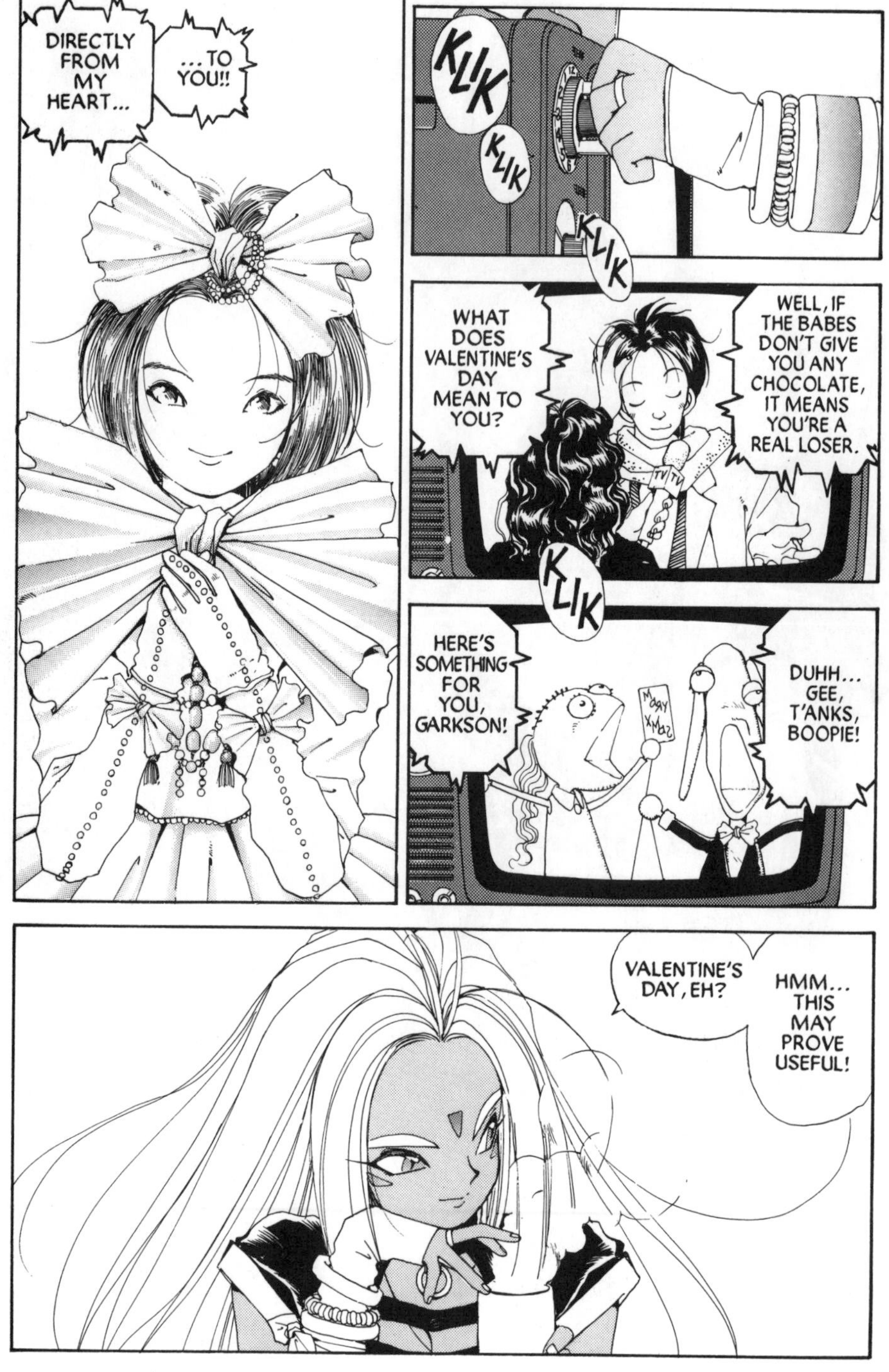
DIRECTLY FROM MY HEART...
...TO YOU!!
KLIK
KLIK
KLIK
WHAT DOES VALENTINE'S DAY MEAN TO YOU?
WELL, IF THE BABES DON'T GIVE YOU ANY CHOCOLATE, IT MEANS YOU'RE A REAL LOSER.
KLIK
HERE'S SOMETHING FOR YOU, GARKSON!
DUHH... GEE, T'ANKS, BOOPIE!
VALENTINE'S DAY, EH?
HMM... THIS MAY PROVE USEFUL!

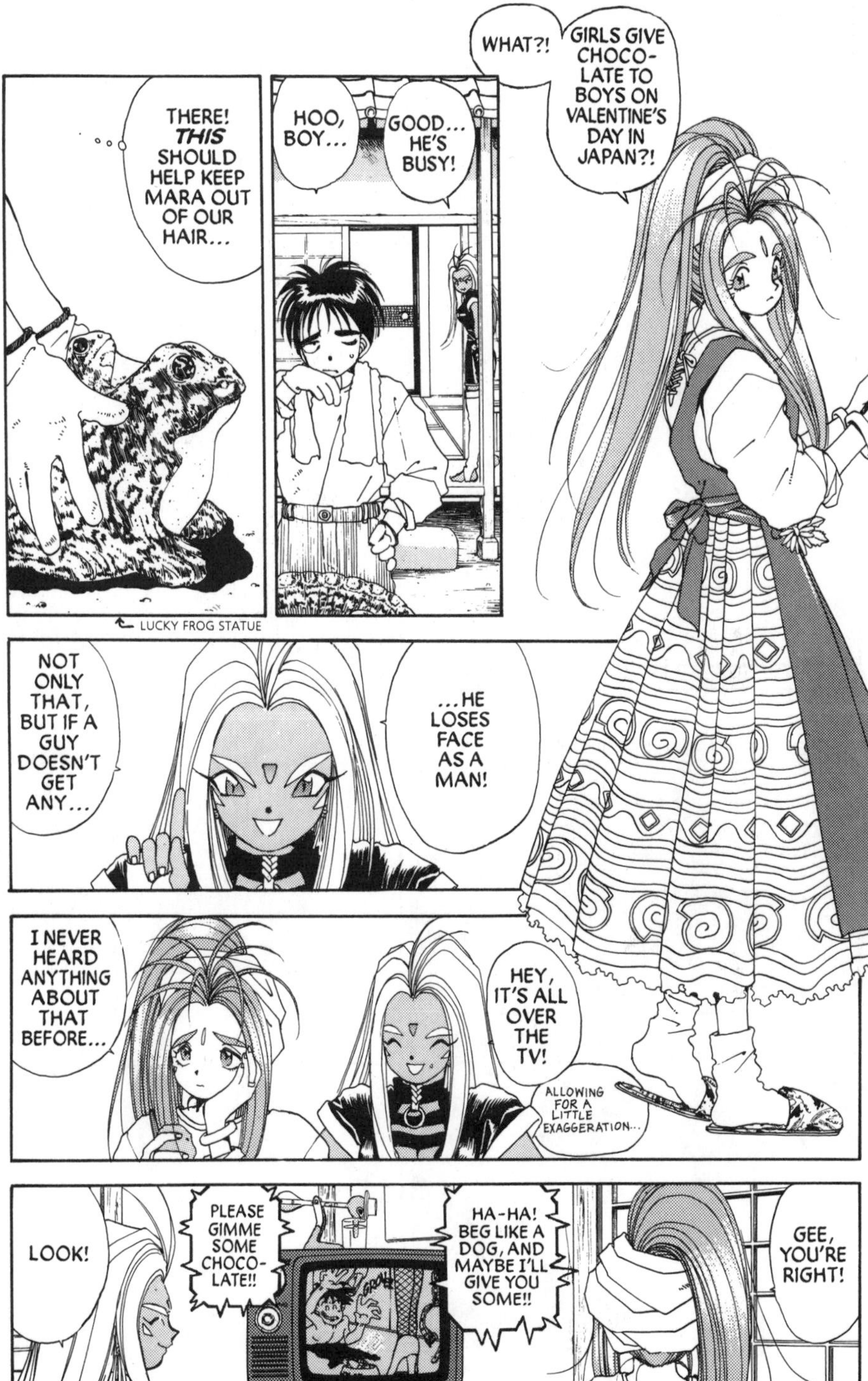
THERE! THIS SHOULD HELP KEEP MARA OUT OF OUR HAIR...
LUCKY FROG STATUE
HOO, BOY...
GOOD... HE'S BUSY!
WHAT?!
GIRLS GIVE CHOCOLATE TO BOYS ON VALENTINE'S DAY IN JAPAN?!
NOT ONLY THAT, BUT IF A GUY DOESN'T GET ANY...
...HE LOSES FACE AS A MAN!
I NEVER HEARD ANYTHING ABOUT THAT BEFORE...
HEY, IT'S ALL OVER THE TV!
ALLOWING FOR A LITTLE EXAGGERATION...
LOOK!
PLEASE GIMME SOME CHOCOLATE!!
HA-HA! BEG LIKE A DOG, AND MAYBE I'LL GIVE YOU SOME!!
GEE, YOU'RE RIGHT!

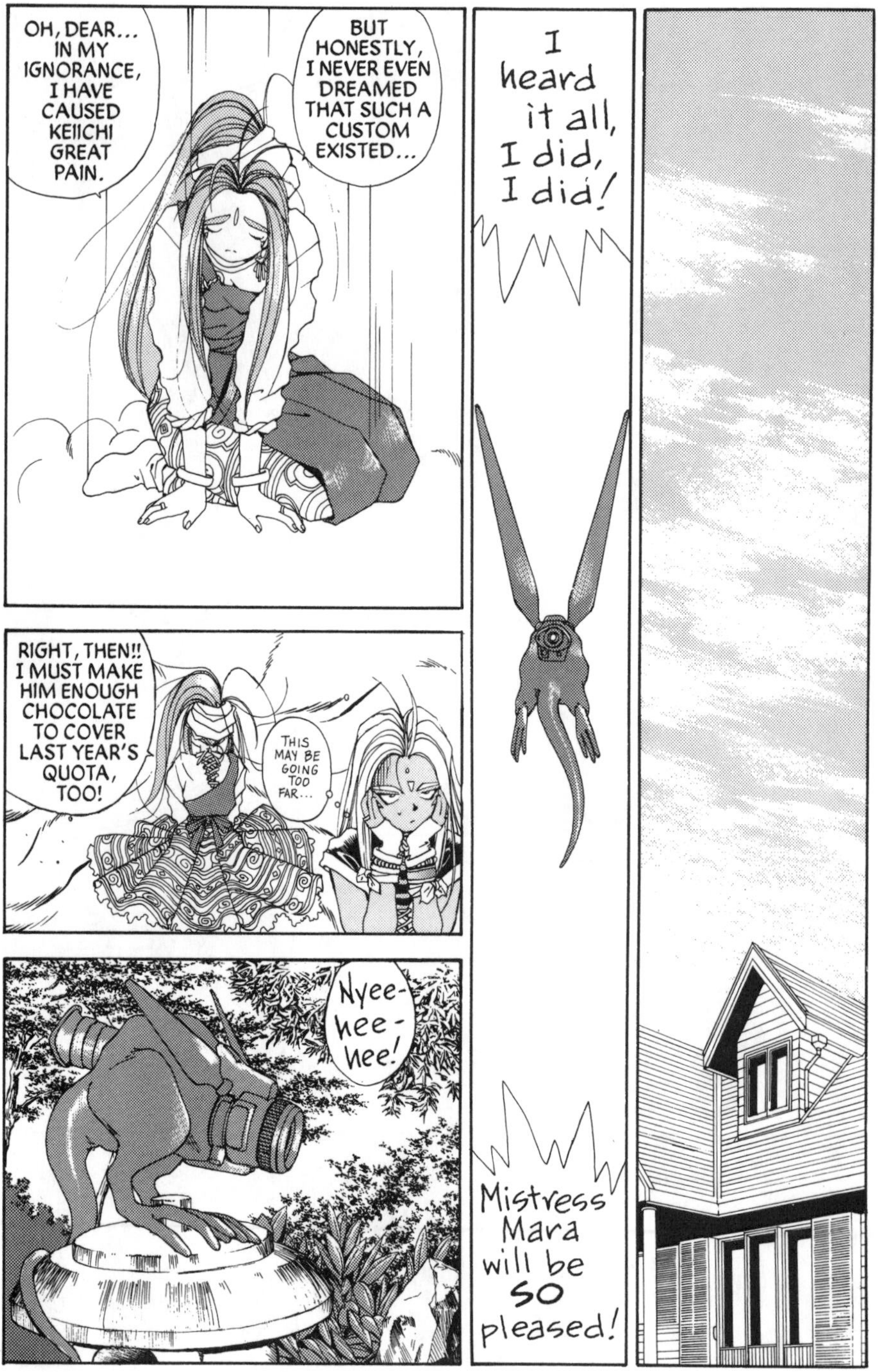
OH, DEAR... IN MY IGNORANCE, I HAVE CAUSED KEIICHI GREAT PAIN.
BUT HONESTLY, I NEVER EVEN DREAMED THAT SUCH A CUSTOM EXISTED...
RIGHT, THEN!! I MUST MAKE HIM ENOUGH CHOCOLATE TO COVER LAST YEAR'S QUOTA, TOO!
THIS MAY BE GOING TOO FAR...
Nyee-hee-hee!
I heard it all, I did, I did!
Mistress Mara will be SO pleased!

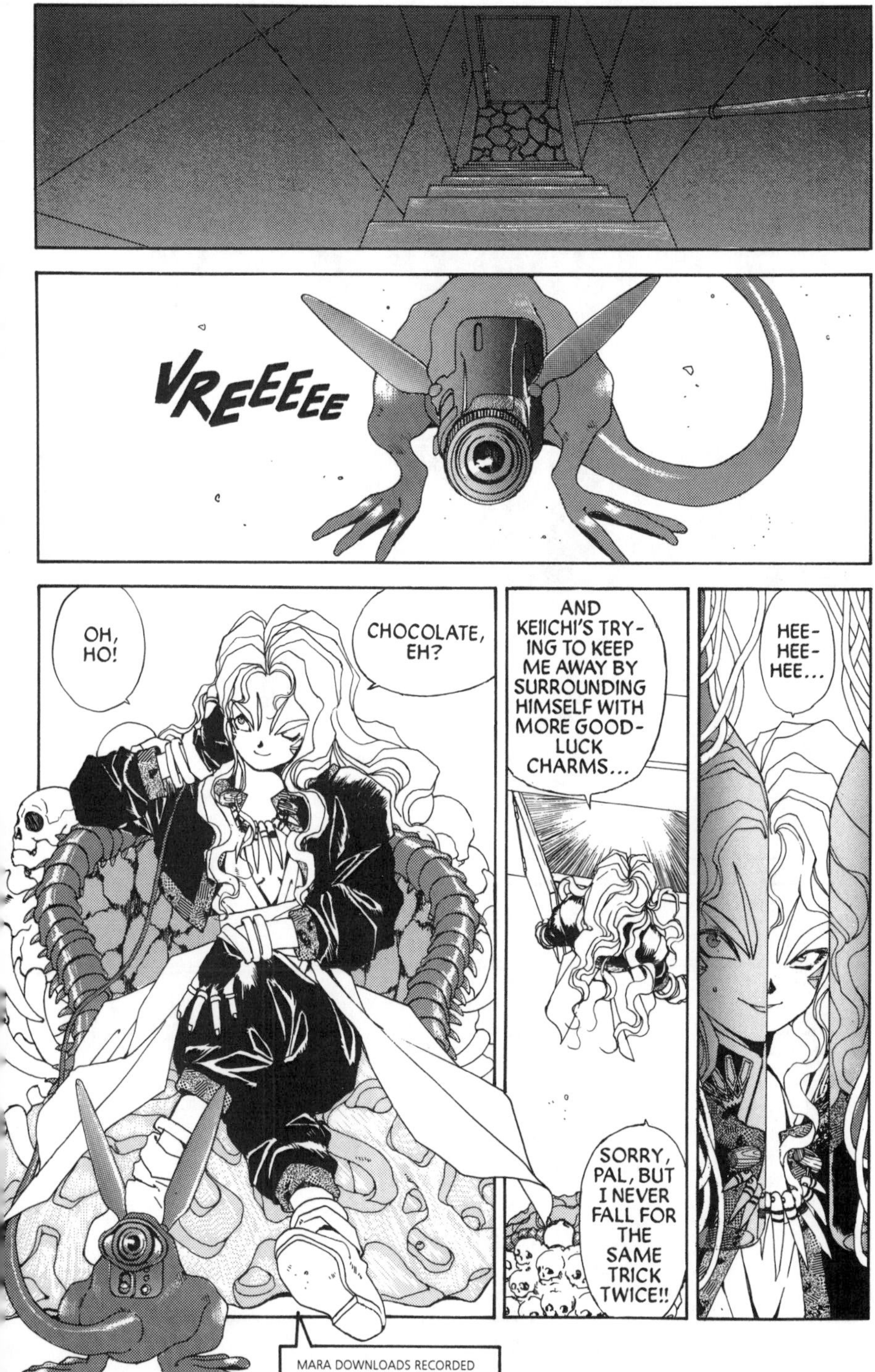
VREEEEEE
OH, HO!
CHOCOLATE, EH?
MARA DOWNLOADS RECORDED DATA VIA THE SPY'S TAIL.
AND KEIICHI'S TRYING TO KEEP ME AWAY BY SURROUNDING HIMSELF WITH MORE GOOD-LUCK CHARMS...
SORRY, PAL, BUT I NEVER FALL FOR THE SAME TRICK TWICE!!
HEE-HEE-HEE...

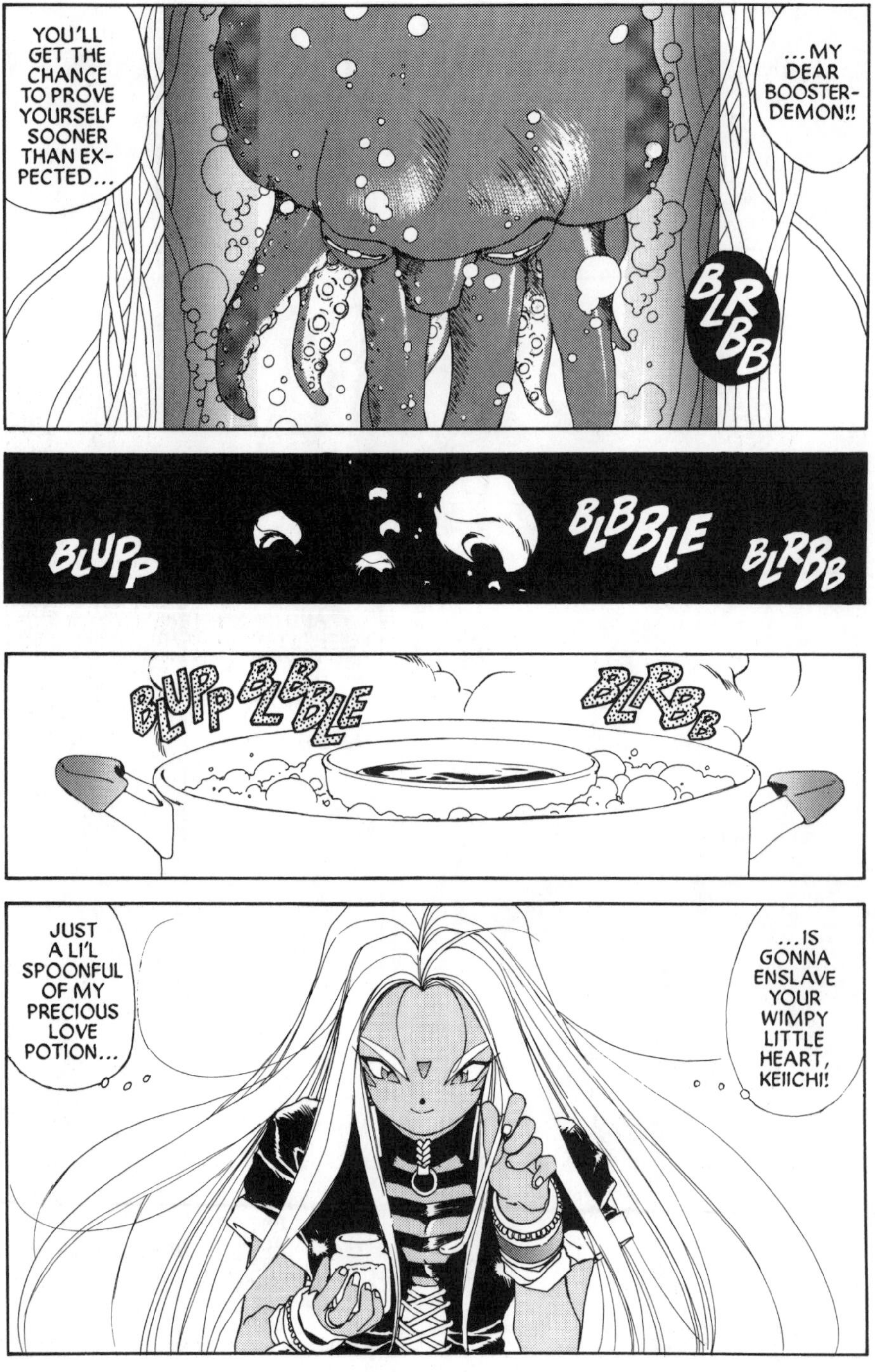
YOU'LL GET THE CHANCE TO PROVE YOURSELF SOONER THAN EX-PECTED...
...MY DEAR BOOSTER-DEMON!!
BLRBB
BLUPP
BLBBLE
BLRBB
BLUPP
BLBBLE
BLRBB
JUST A LI'L SPOONFUL OF MY PRECIOUS LOVE POTION...
...IS GONNA ENSLAVE YOUR WIMPY LITTLE HEART, KEIICHI!

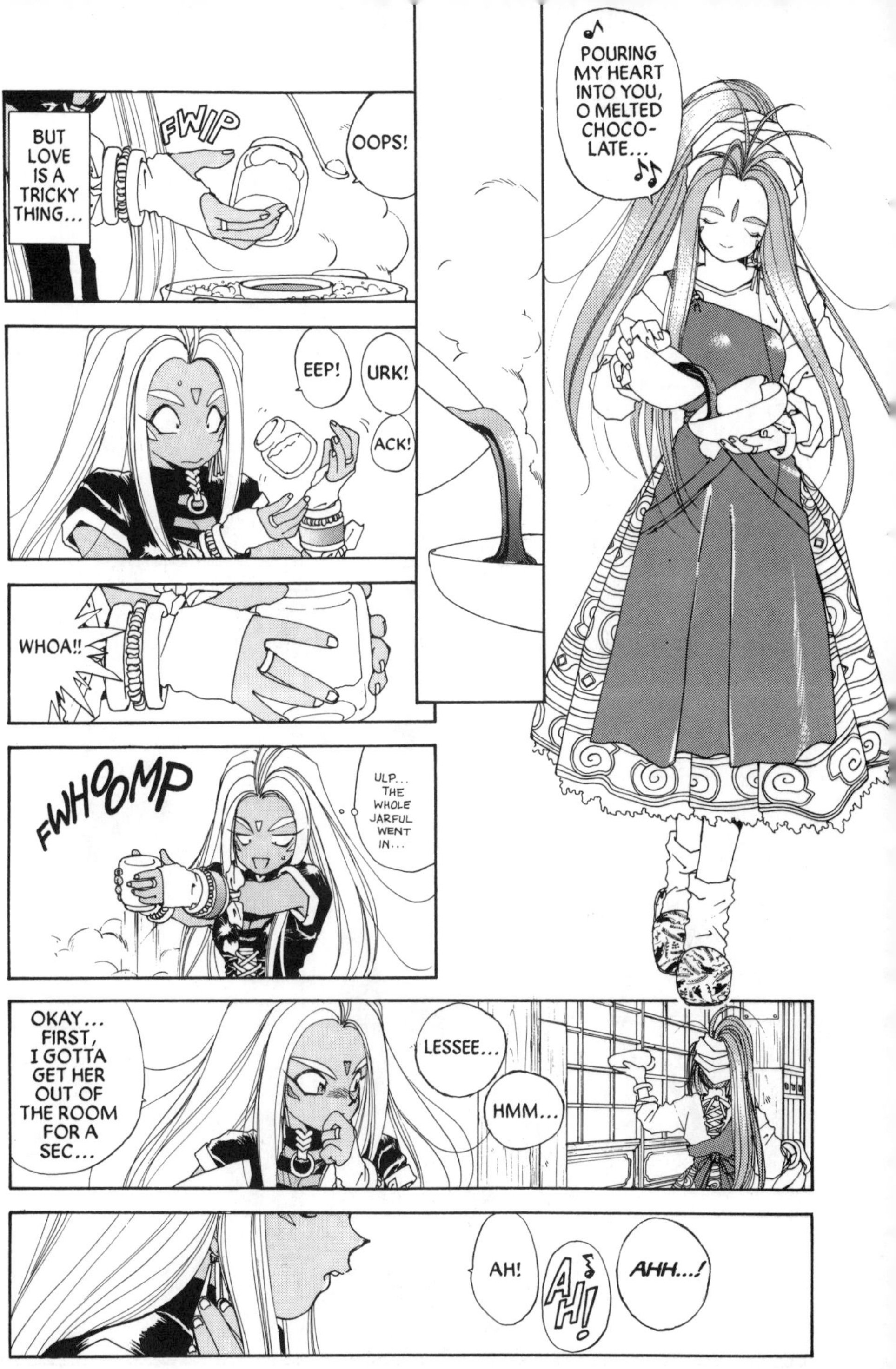
BUT LOVE IS A TRICKY THING…
FWIP
OOPS!
EEP!
URK!
ACK!
WHOA!!
FWHOOMP
ULP… THE WHOLE JARFUL WENT IN…
POURING MY HEART INTO YOU, O MELTED CHOCOLATE…
OKAY… FIRST, I GOTTA GET HER OUT OF THE ROOM FOR A SEC…
LESSEE…
HMM…
AH!
AH!
AHH…!

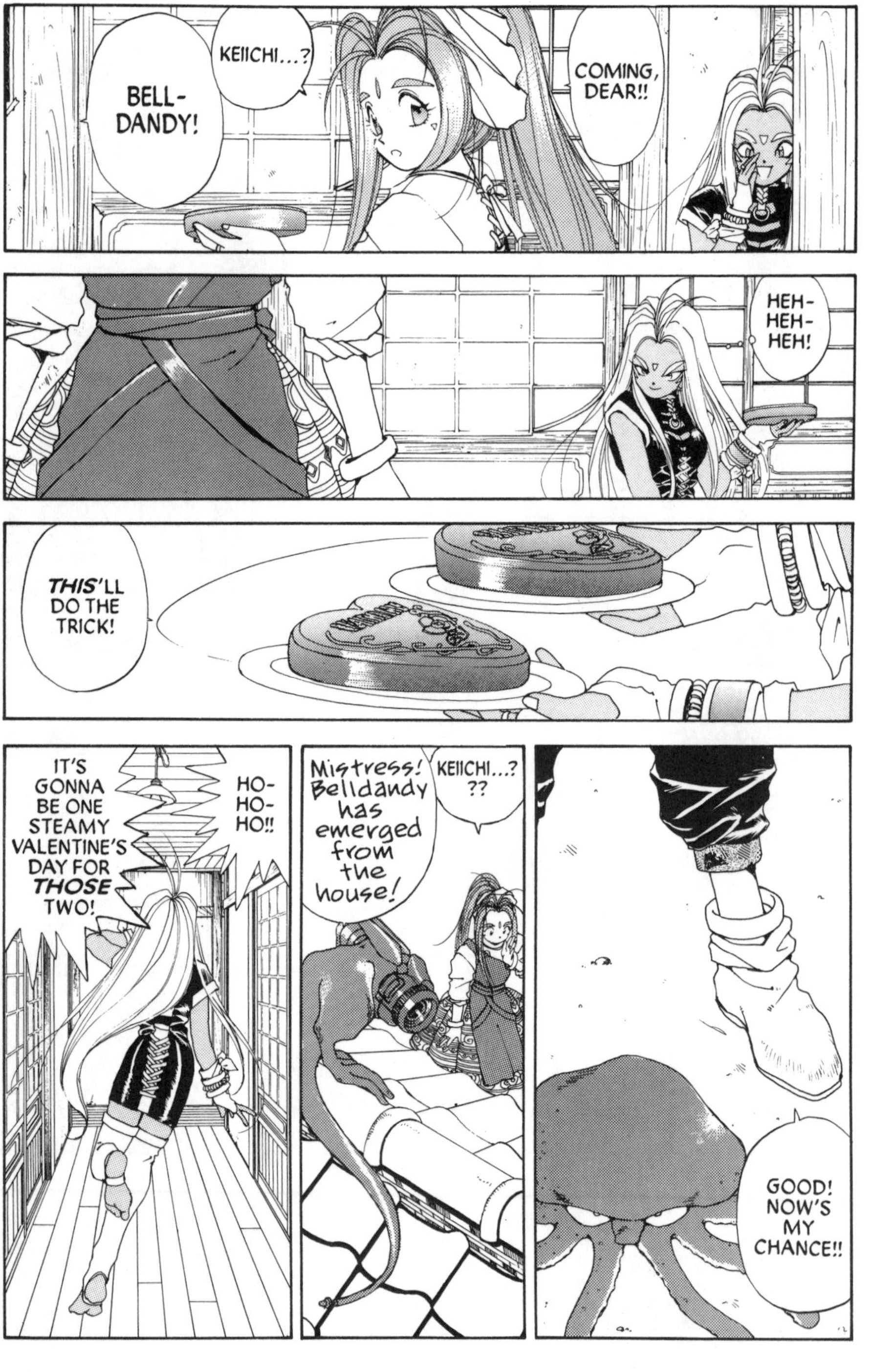
BELL-DANDY!
KEIICHI...?
COMING, DEAR!!
HEH-HEH-HEH!
THIS'LL DO THE TRICK!
IT'S GONNA BE ONE STEAMY VALENTINE'S DAY FOR *THOSE* TWO!
HO-HO-HO!!
Mistress! Belldandy has emerged from the house!
KEIICHI...? ??
GOOD! NOW'S MY CHANCE!!

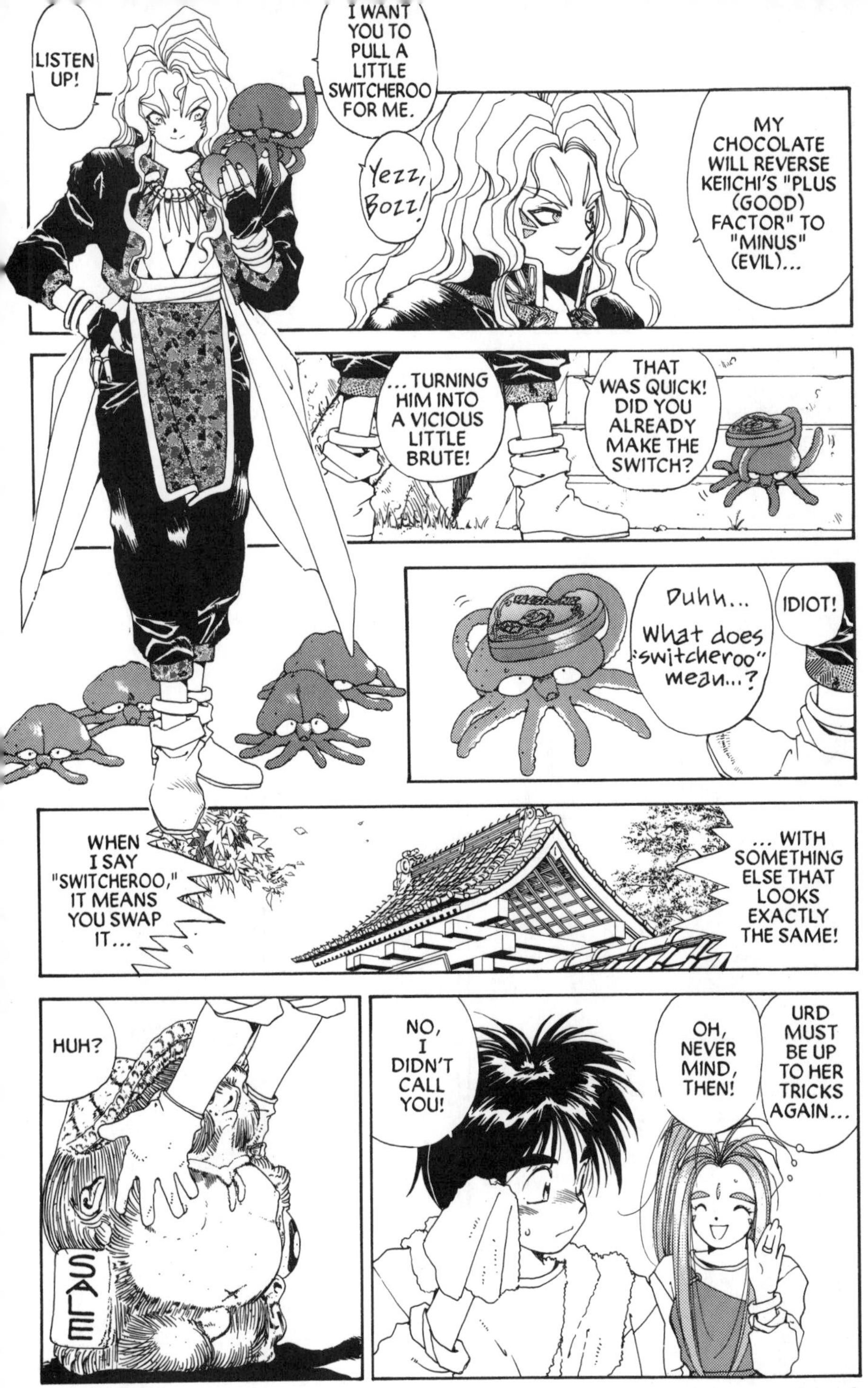
LISTEN UP!
I WANT YOU TO PULL A LITTLE SWITCHEROO FOR ME.
Yezz, Bozz!
MY CHOCOLATE WILL REVERSE KEIICHI'S "PLUS (GOOD) FACTOR" TO "MINUS" (EVIL)...
...TURNING HIM INTO A VICIOUS LITTLE BRUTE!
THAT WAS QUICK! DID YOU ALREADY MAKE THE SWITCH?
Duhh... What does "switcheroo" mean...?
IDIOT!
WHEN I SAY "SWITCHEROO," IT MEANS YOU SWAP IT...
... WITH SOMETHING ELSE THAT LOOKS EXACTLY THE SAME!
HUH?
SALE
NO, I DIDN'T CALL YOU!
OH, NEVER MIND, THEN!
URD MUST BE UP TO HER TRICKS AGAIN...

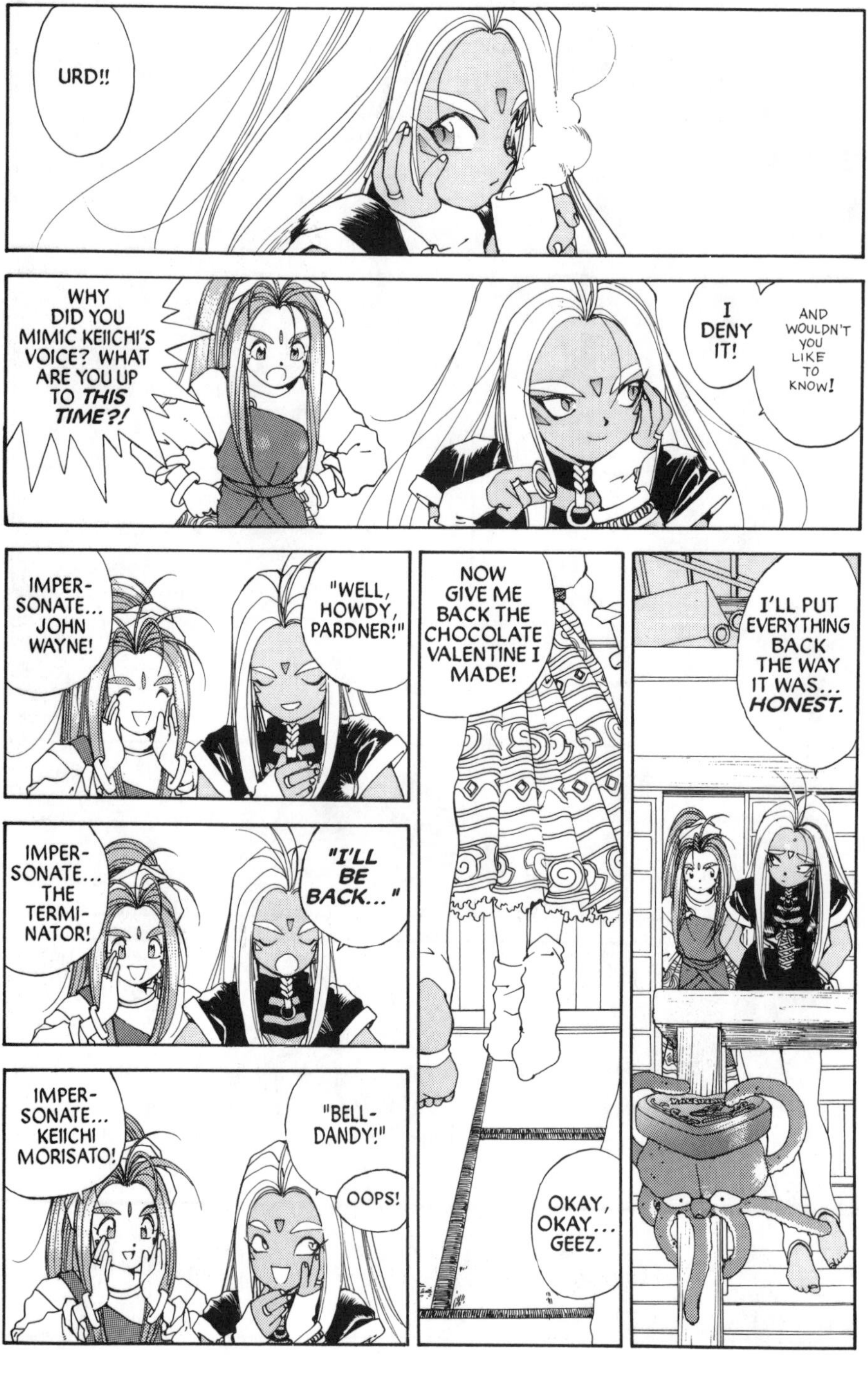
URD!!
WHY DID YOU MIMIC KEIICHI'S VOICE? WHAT ARE YOU UP TO *THIS TIME?!*
I DENY IT!
AND WOULDN'T YOU LIKE TO KNOW!
IMPERSONATE... JOHN WAYNE!
"WELL, HOWDY, PARDNER!"
IMPERSONATE... THE TERMINATOR!
"I'LL BE BACK..."
IMPERSONATE... KEIICHI MORISATO!
"BELL-DANDY!"
OOPS!
NOW GIVE ME BACK THE CHOCOLATE VALENTINE I MADE!
OKAY, OKAY... GEEZ.
I'LL PUT EVERYTHING BACK THE WAY IT WAS... *HONEST.*

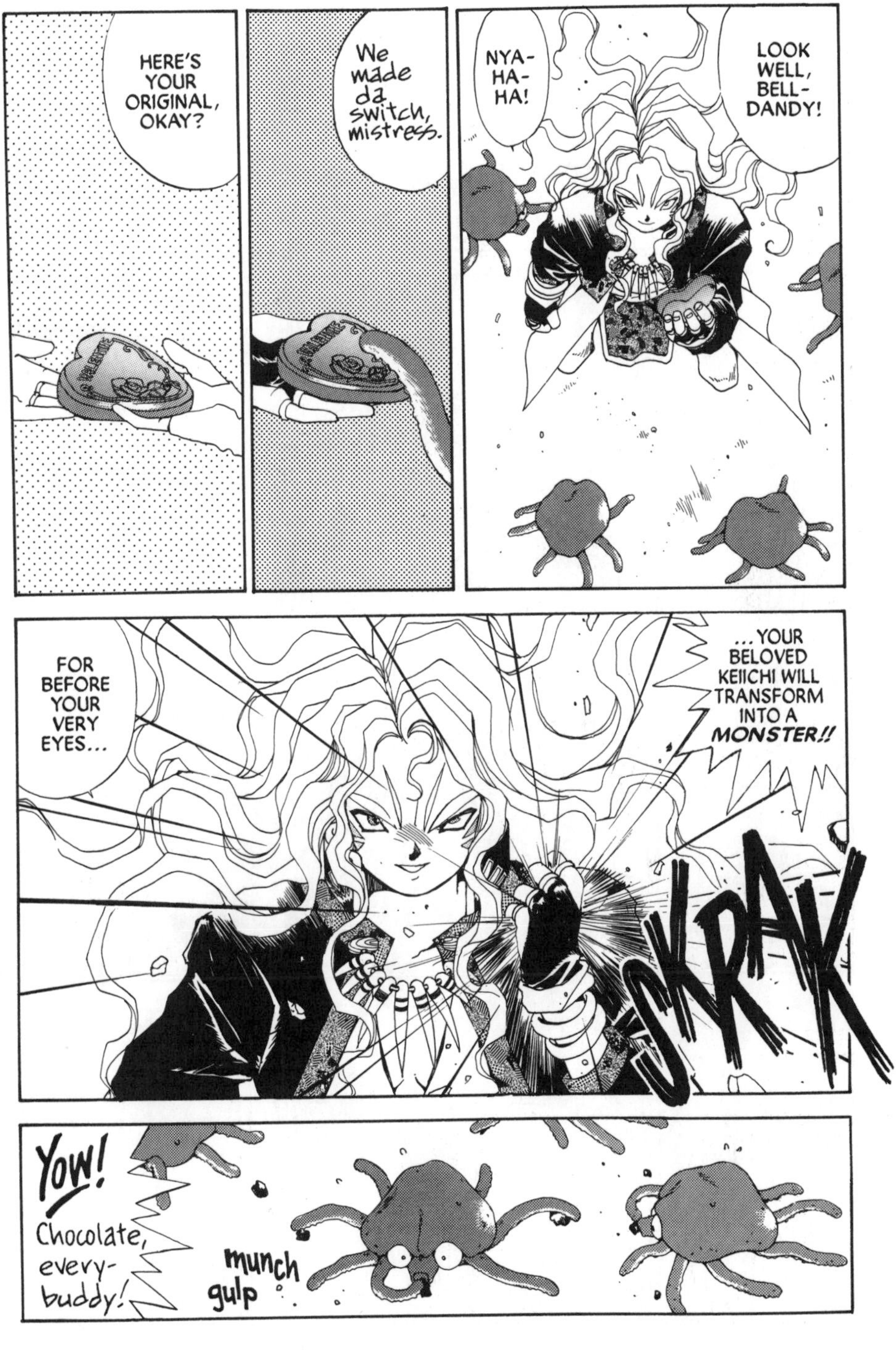
HERE'S YOUR ORIGINAL, OKAY?
We made da switch, mistress.
NYA-HA-HA!
LOOK WELL, BELL-DANDY!
FOR BEFORE YOUR VERY EYES...
...YOUR BELOVED KEIICHI WILL TRANSFORM INTO A MONSTER!!
SKRAK
YOW!
Chocolate, every-buddy!
munch
gulp

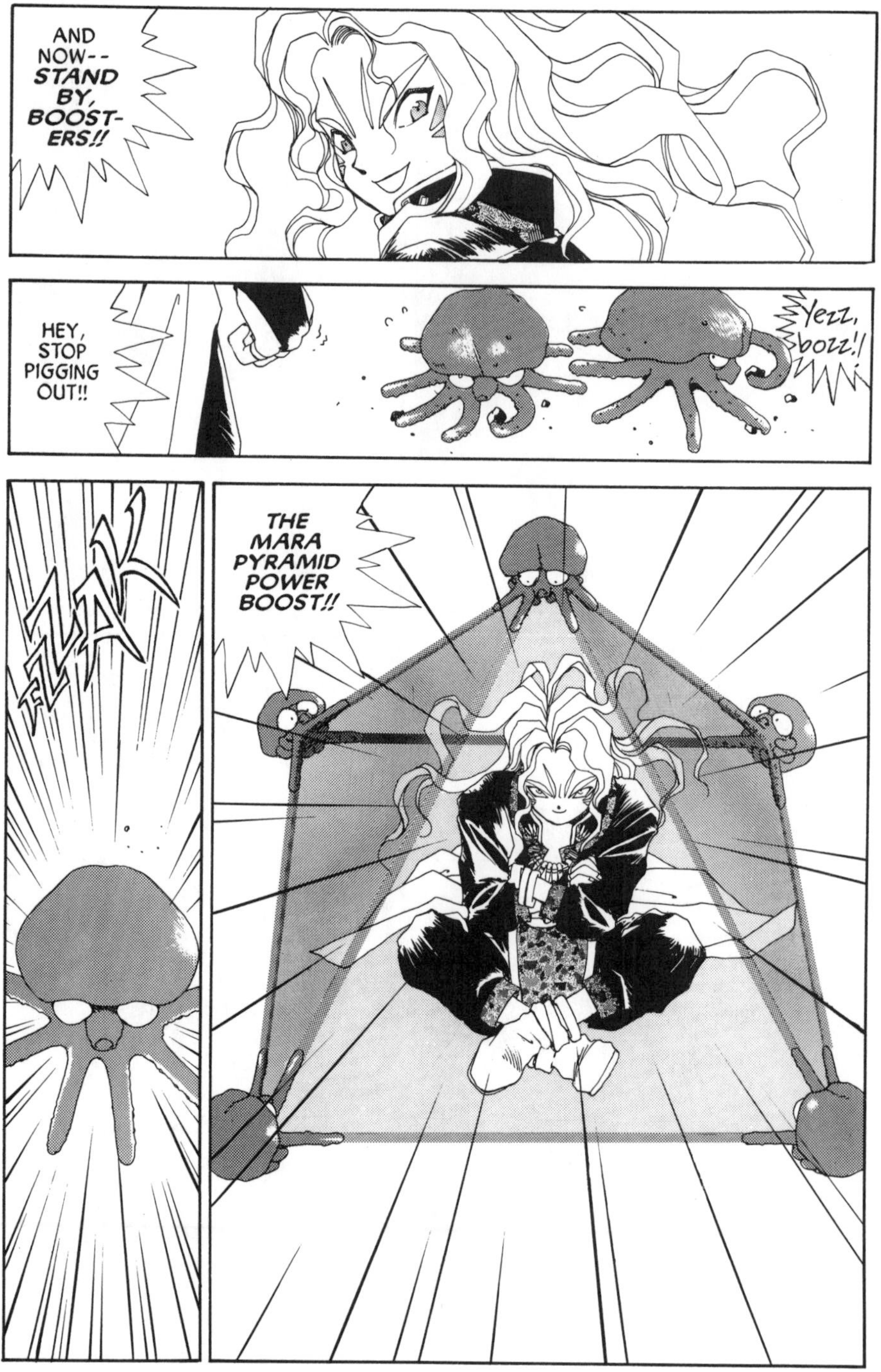
AND NOW-- STAND BY, BOOST-ERS!!
HEY, STOP PIGGING OUT!!
Yezz, bozz!!
FZZAK
THE MARA PYRAMID POWER BOOST!!

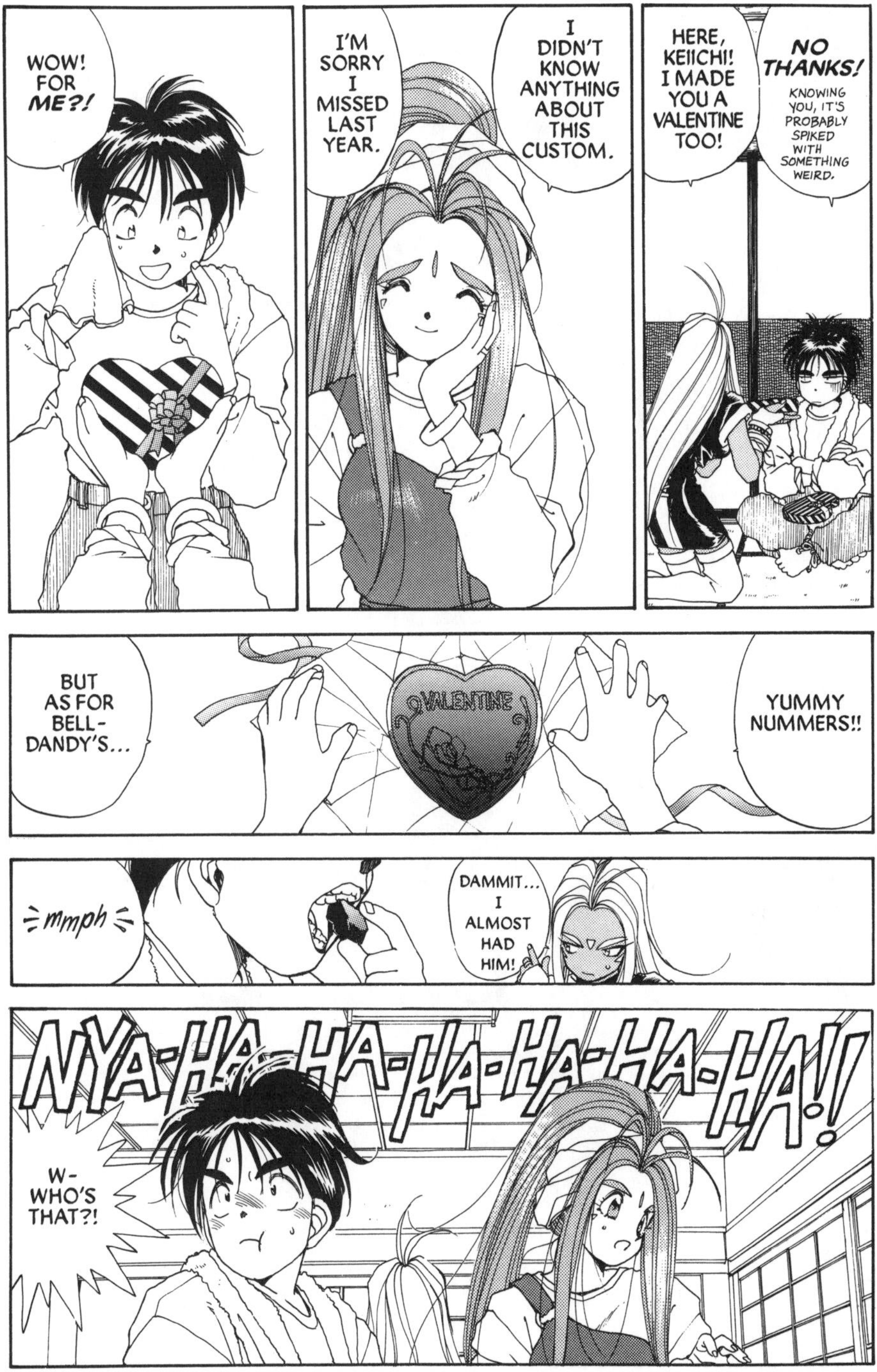
WOW! FOR *ME?!*
I'M SORRY I MISSED LAST YEAR.
I DIDN'T KNOW ANYTHING ABOUT THIS CUSTOM.
HERE, KEIICHI! I MADE YOU A VALENTINE TOO!
NO THANKS!
KNOWING YOU, IT'S PROBABLY SPIKED WITH SOMETHING WEIRD.
BUT AS FOR BELL-DANDY'S...
VALENTINE
YUMMY NUMMERS!!
mmph
DAMMIT... I ALMOST HAD HIM!
NYA-HA-HA-HA-HA-HA-HA-HA!!
W-WHO'S THAT?!

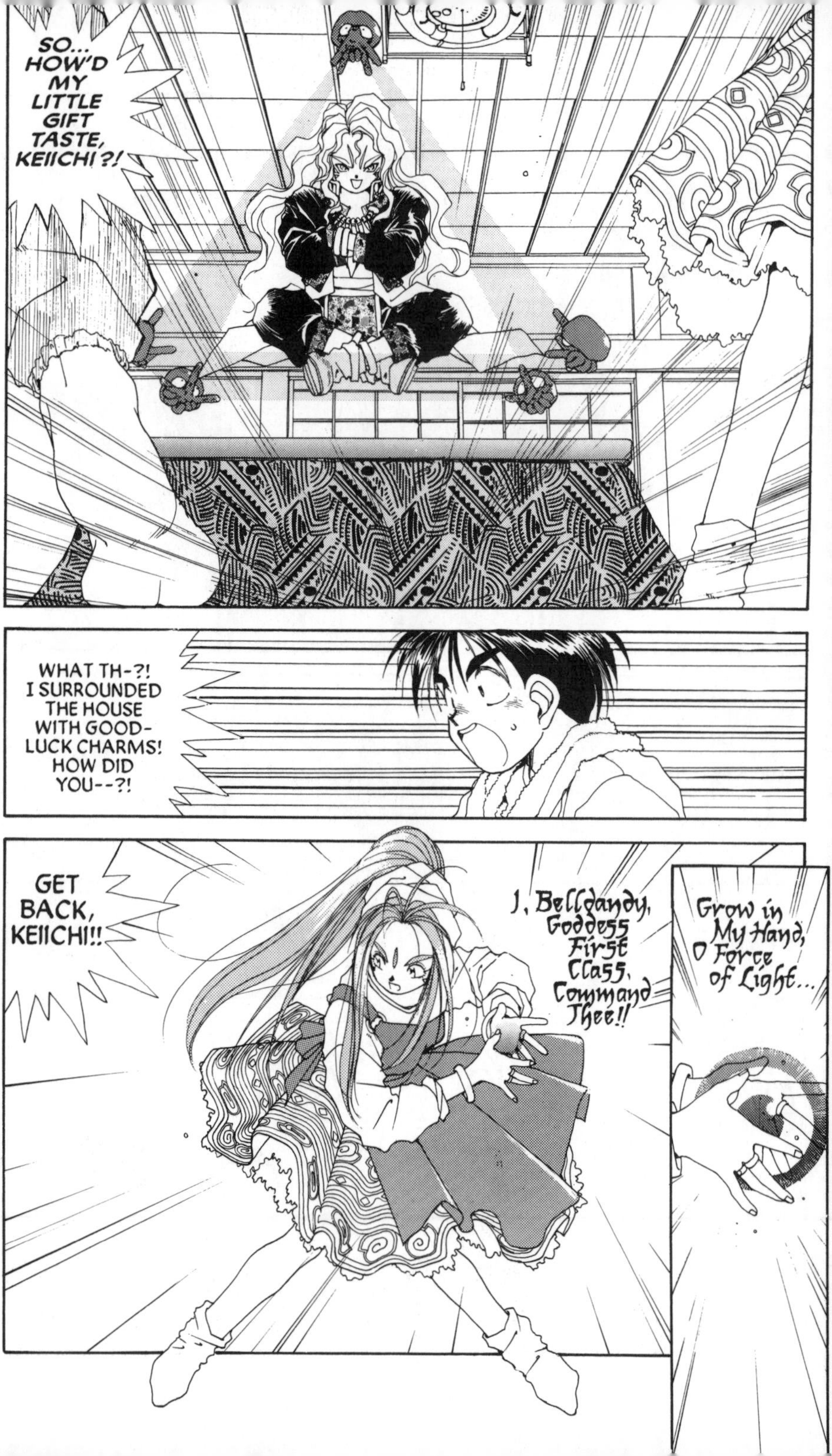
SO... HOW'D MY LITTLE GIFT TASTE, KEIICHI?!
WHAT TH-?! I SURROUNDED THE HOUSE WITH GOOD-LUCK CHARMS! HOW DID YOU--?!
GET BACK, KEIICHI!!
I, Belldandy, Goddess First Class, Command Thee!!
Grow in My Hand, O Force of Light...

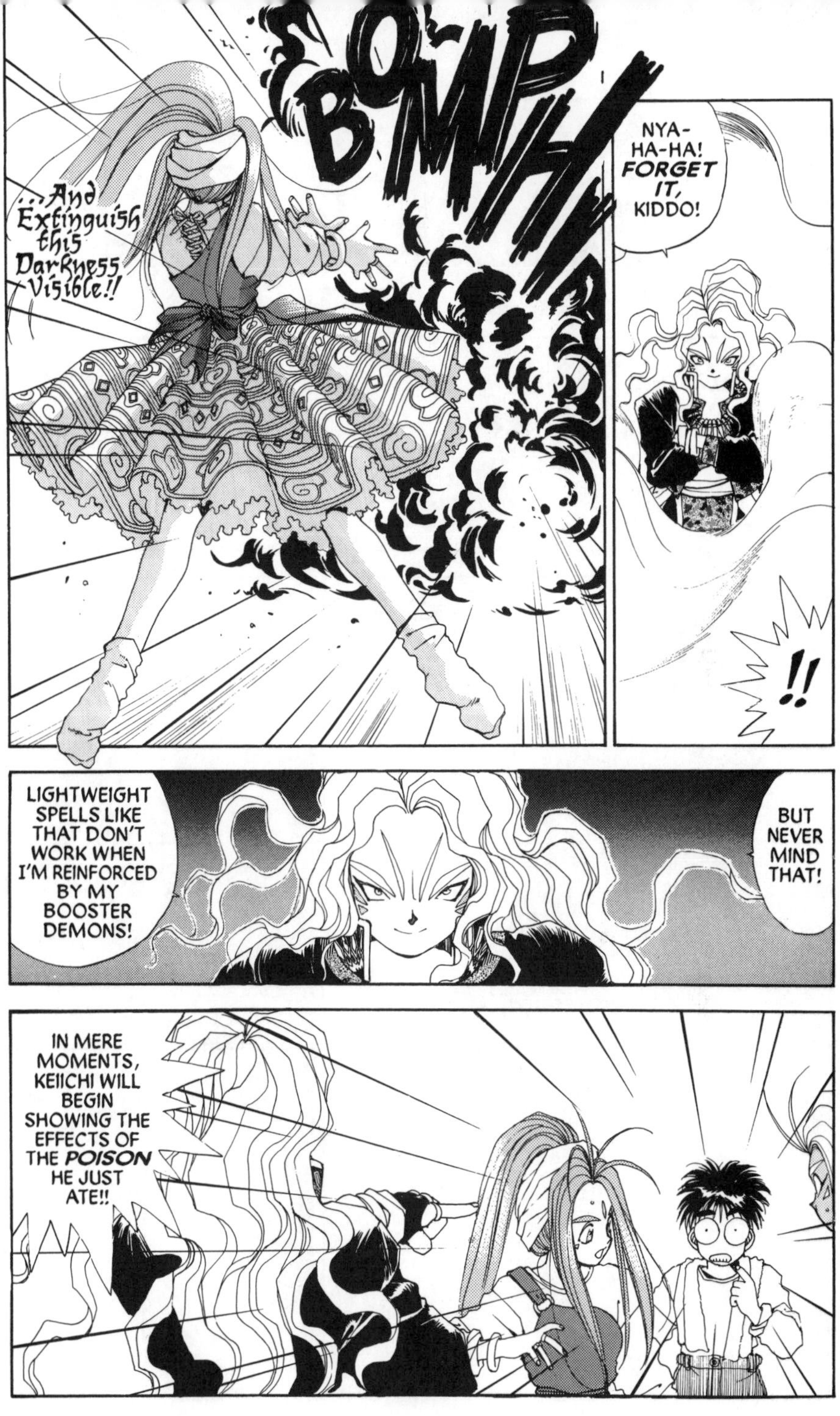
BOMPH
...And Extinguish this Darkness Visible!!
NYA-HA-HA! FORGET IT, KIDDO!
!!
LIGHTWEIGHT SPELLS LIKE THAT DON'T WORK WHEN I'M REINFORCED BY MY BOOSTER DEMONS!
BUT NEVER MIND THAT!
IN MERE MOMENTS, KEIICHI WILL BEGIN SHOWING THE EFFECTS OF THE POISON HE JUST ATE!!

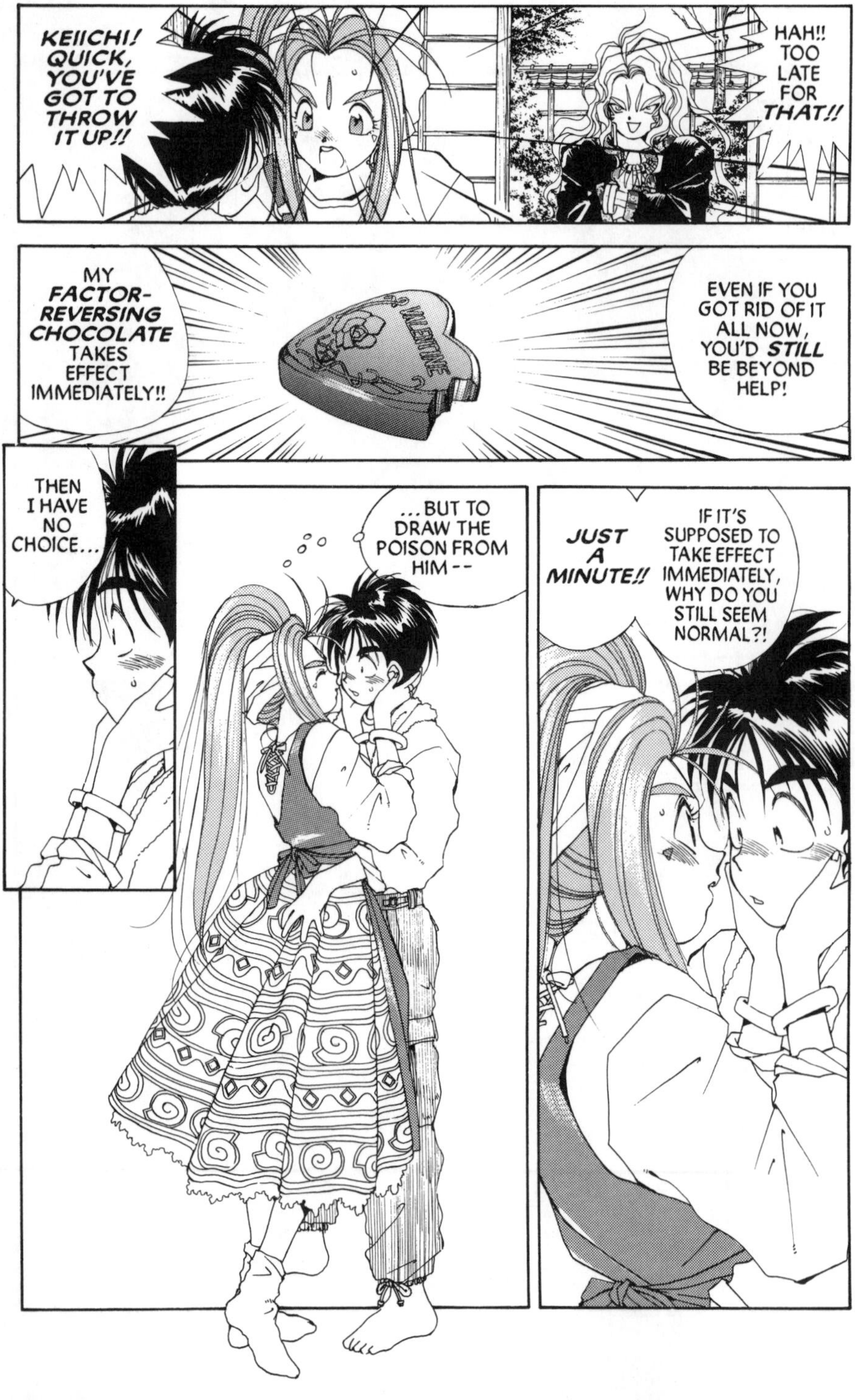
KEIICHI! QUICK, YOU'VE GOT TO THROW IT UP!!
HAH!! TOO LATE FOR THAT!!
MY FACTOR-REVERSING CHOCOLATE TAKES EFFECT IMMEDIATELY!!
VALENTINE
EVEN IF YOU GOT RID OF IT ALL NOW, YOU'D STILL BE BEYOND HELP!
THEN I HAVE NO CHOICE...
...BUT TO DRAW THE POISON FROM HIM--
JUST A MINUTE!!
IF IT'S SUPPOSED TO TAKE EFFECT IMMEDIATELY, WHY DO YOU STILL SEEM NORMAL?!

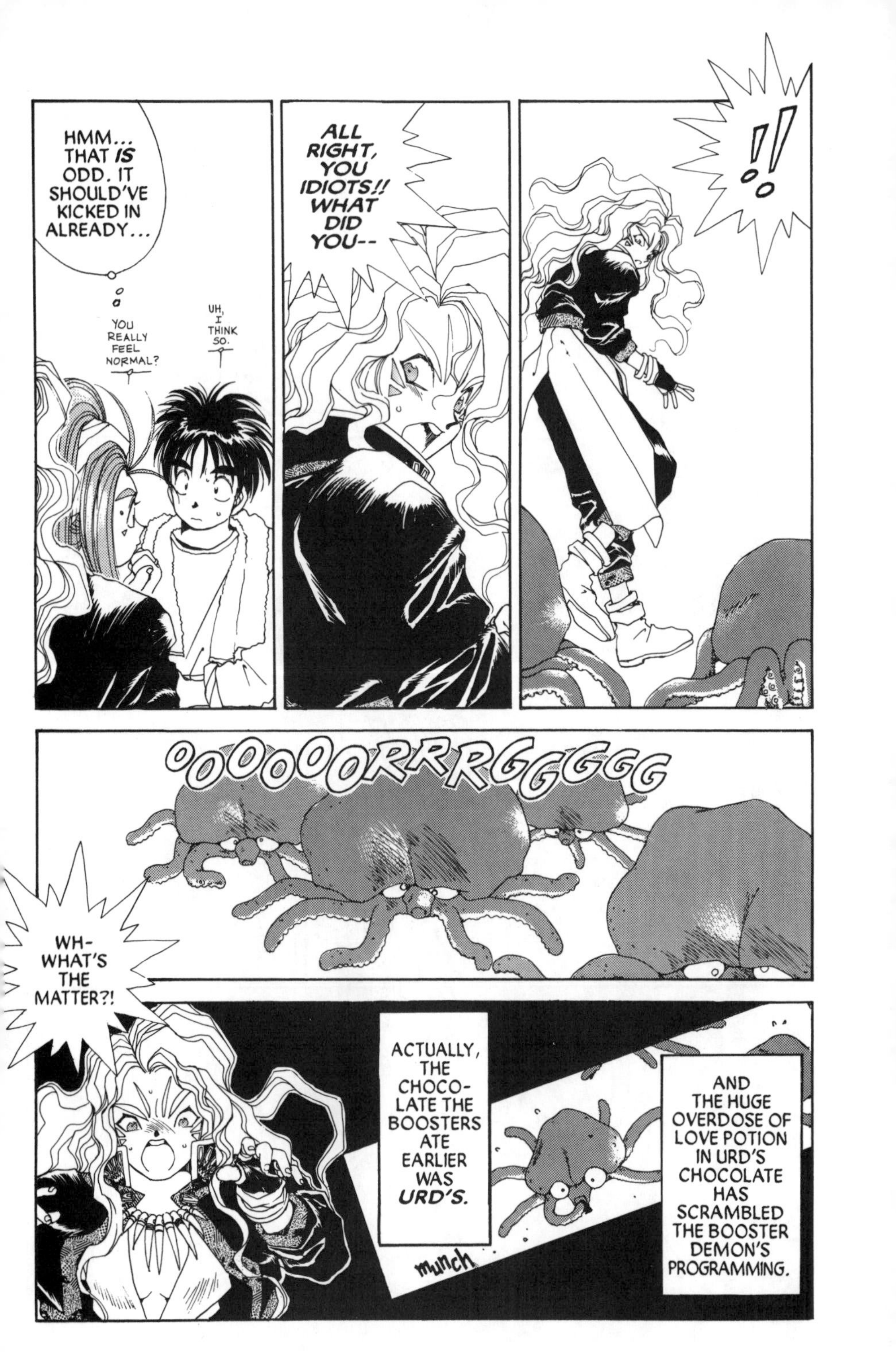
HMM... THAT *IS* ODD. IT SHOULD'VE KICKED IN ALREADY...
YOU REALLY FEEL NORMAL?
UH, I THINK SO.
ALL RIGHT, YOU IDIOTS!! WHAT DID YOU--
!!
OOOOOOORRRRGGGGGG
WH-WHAT'S THE MATTER?!
ACTUALLY, THE CHOCO-LATE THE BOOSTERS ATE EARLIER WAS *URD'S*.
munch
AND THE HUGE OVERDOSE OF LOVE POTION IN URD'S CHOCOLATE HAS SCRAMBLED THE BOOSTER DEMON'S PROGRAMMING.

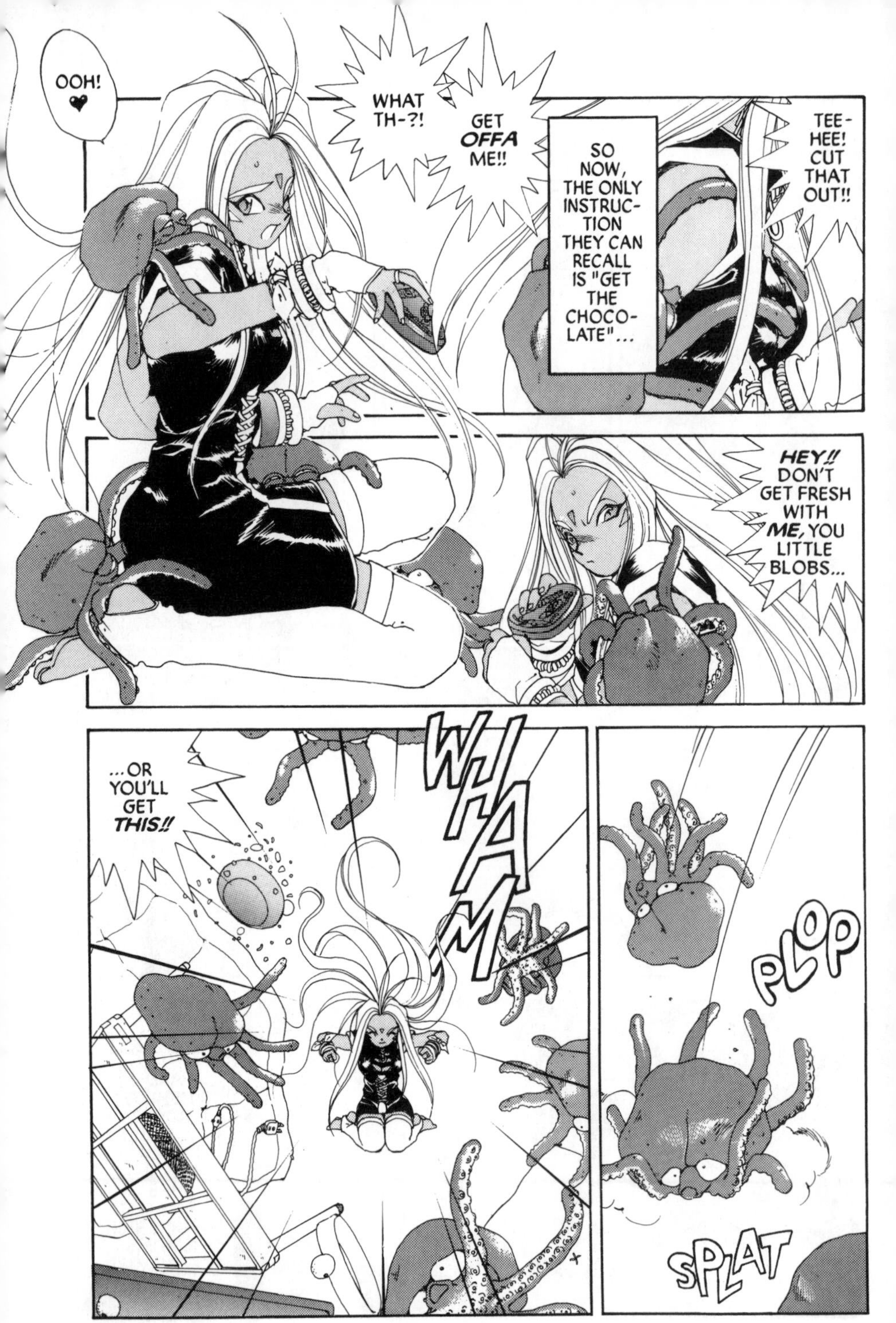
OOH! ♥
WHAT TH-?!
GET OFFA ME!!
SO NOW, THE ONLY INSTRUCTION THEY CAN RECALL IS "GET THE CHOCOLATE"...
TEE-HEE! CUT THAT OUT!!
HEY!! DON'T GET FRESH WITH ME, YOU LITTLE BLOBS...
...OR YOU'LL GET THIS!!
WHAM
PLOP
SPLAT

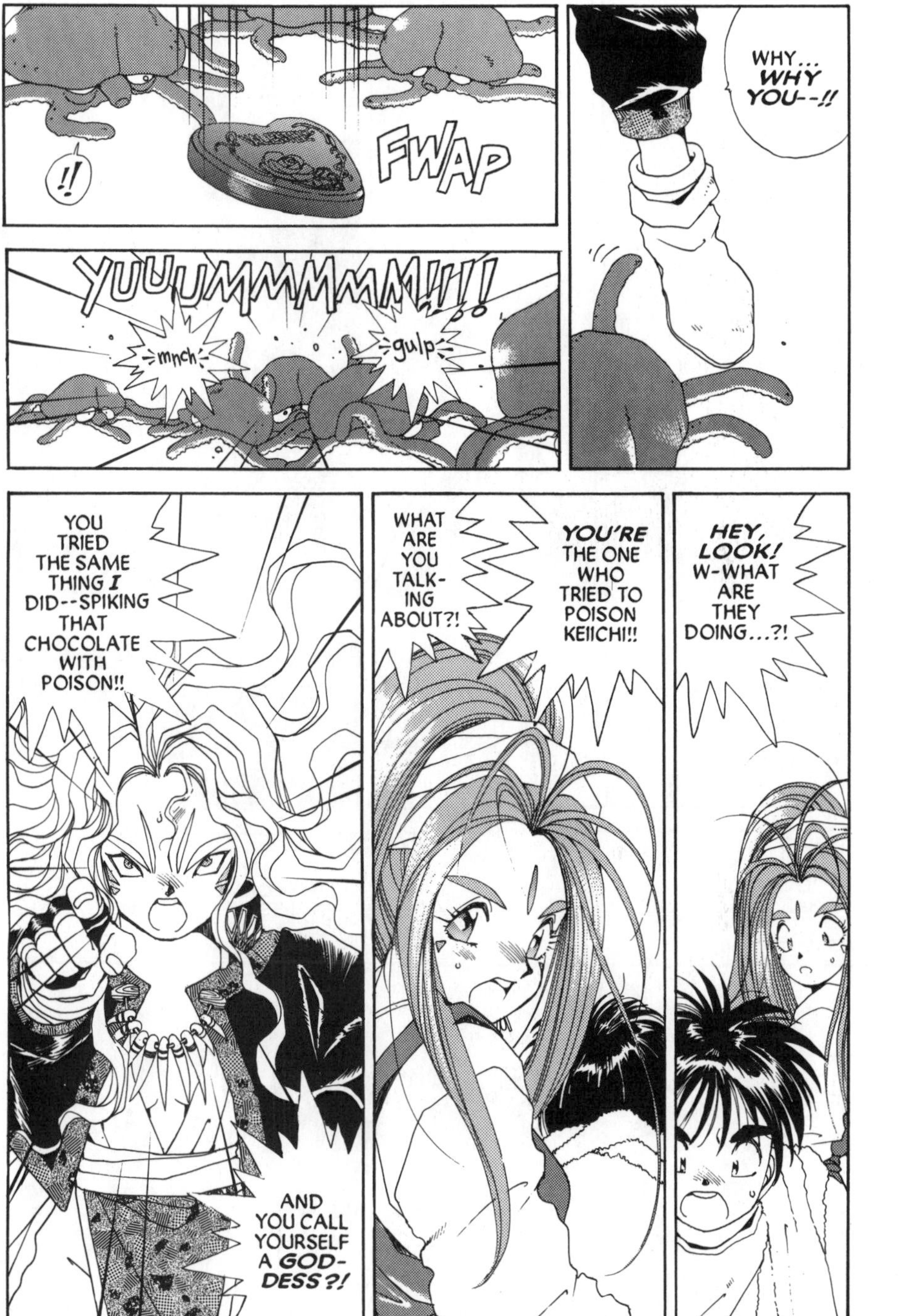
!!
FWAP
YUUUMMMMMM!!!!
mnch
gulp
WHY... WHY YOU--!!
YOU TRIED THE SAME THING I DID--SPIKING THAT CHOCOLATE WITH POISON!!
AND YOU CALL YOURSELF A GOD-DESS?!
WHAT ARE YOU TALK-ING ABOUT?!
YOU'RE THE ONE WHO TRIED TO POISON KEIICHI!!
HEY, LOOK! W-WHAT ARE THEY DOING...?!

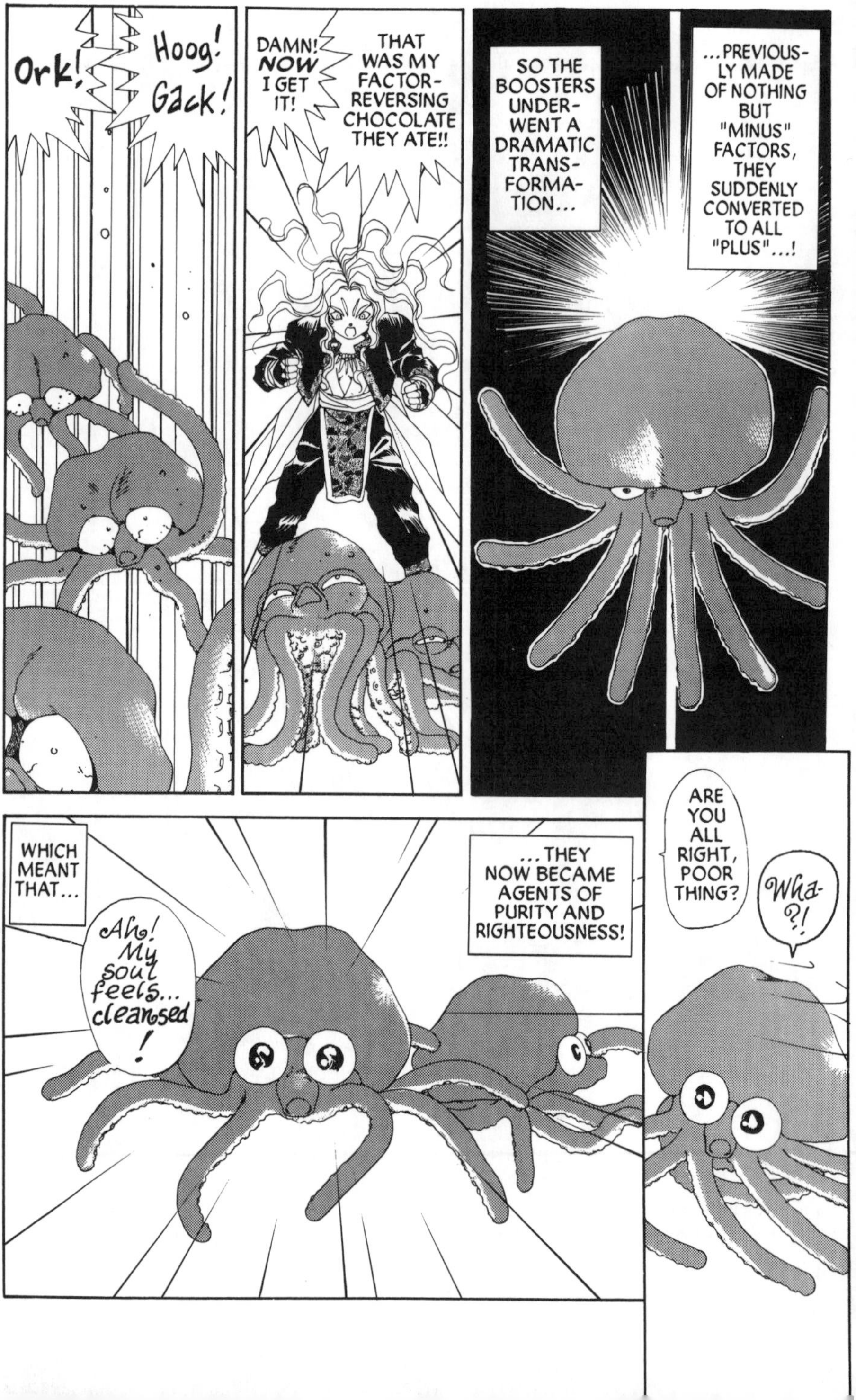
Ork!
Hoog! Gack!
DAMN! NOW I GET IT!
THAT WAS MY FACTOR-REVERSING CHOCOLATE THEY ATE!!
SO THE BOOSTERS UNDERWENT A DRAMATIC TRANSFORMATION...
...PREVIOUSLY MADE OF NOTHING BUT "MINUS" FACTORS, THEY SUDDENLY CONVERTED TO ALL "PLUS"...!
WHICH MEANT THAT...
Ah! My soul feels... cleansed!
...THEY NOW BECAME AGENTS OF PURITY AND RIGHTEOUSNESS!
ARE YOU ALL RIGHT, POOR THING?
Wha-?!

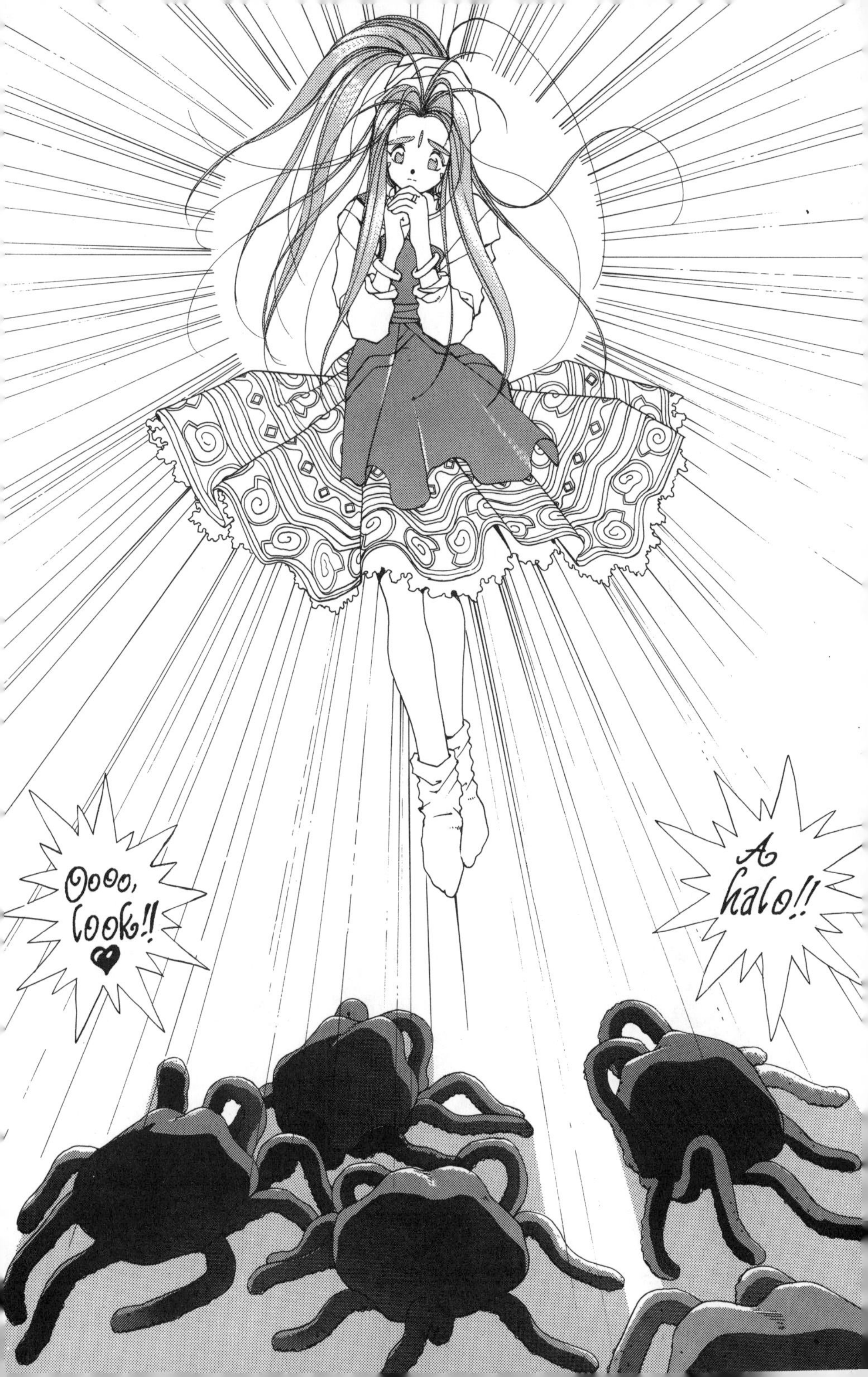
Oooo, look!! ♥
A halo!!

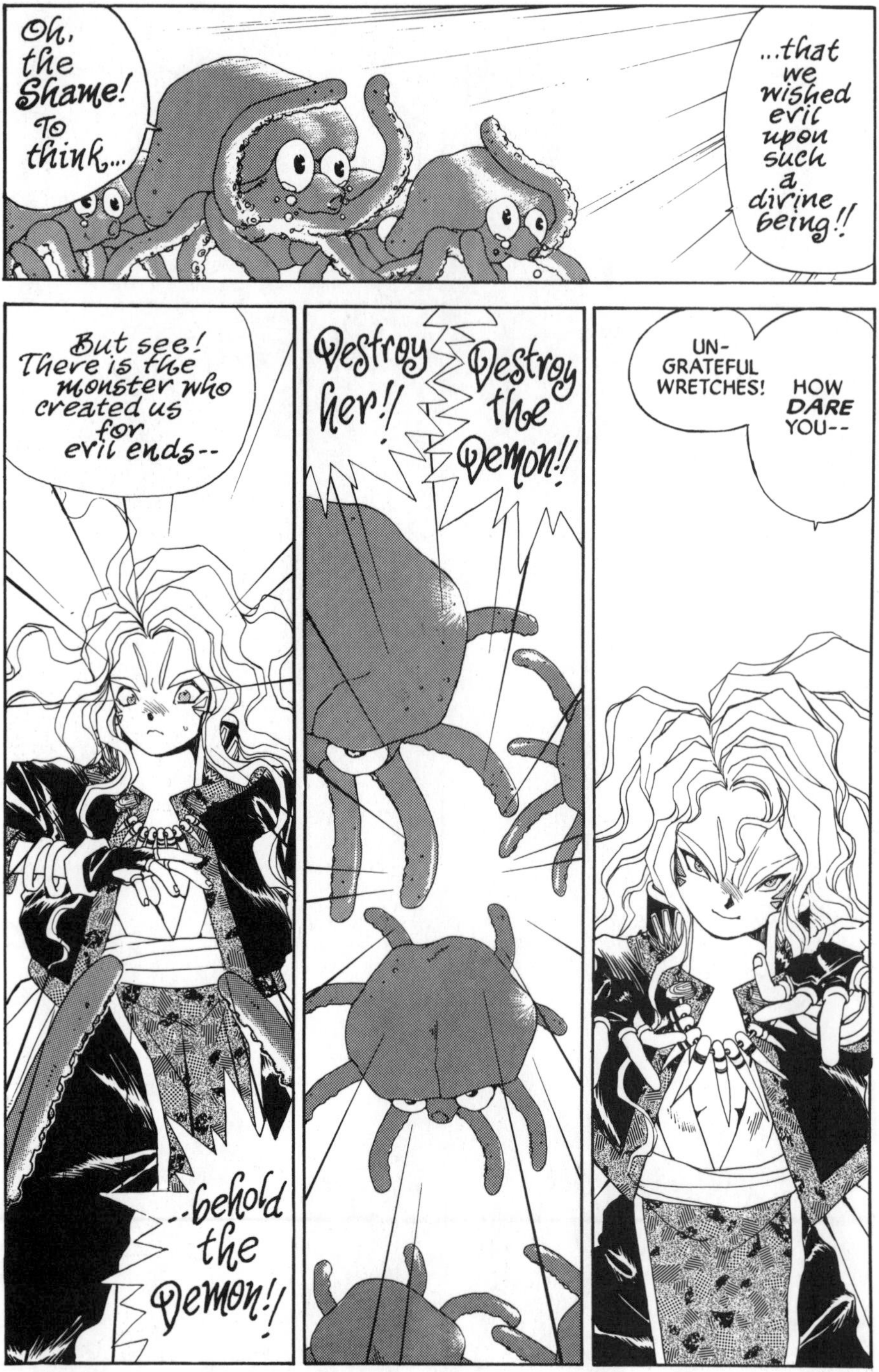
Oh, the Shame! To think...
...that we wished evil upon such a divine being!!
But see! There is the monster who created us for evil ends--
--behold the Demon!!
Destroy her!!
Destroy the Demon!!
UN-GRATEFUL WRETCHES!
HOW DARE YOU--

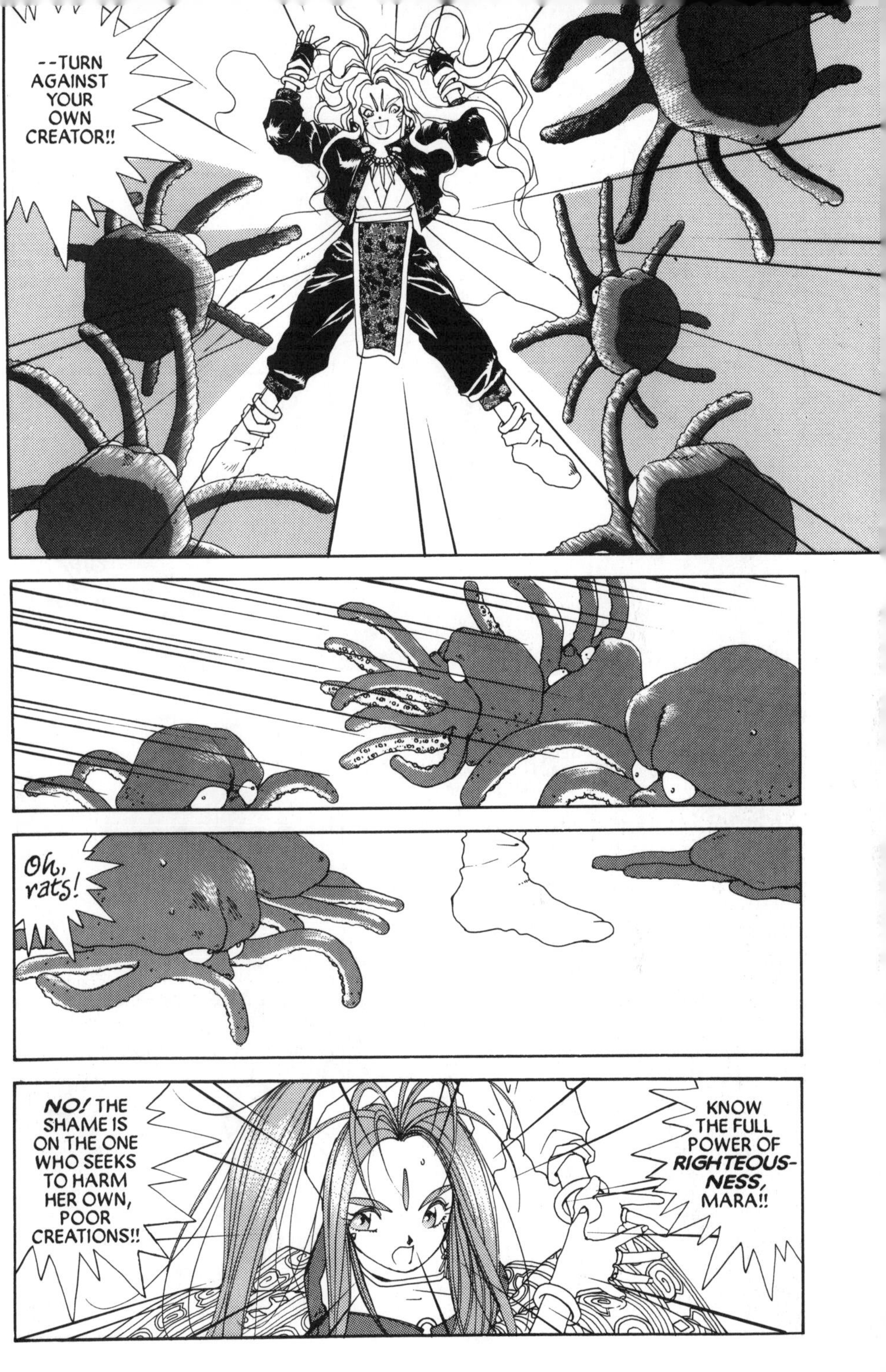
--TURN AGAINST YOUR OWN CREATOR!!
Oh, rats!
NO! THE SHAME IS ON THE ONE WHO SEEKS TO HARM HER OWN, POOR CREATIONS!!
KNOW THE FULL POWER OF RIGHTEOUS-NESS, MARA!!

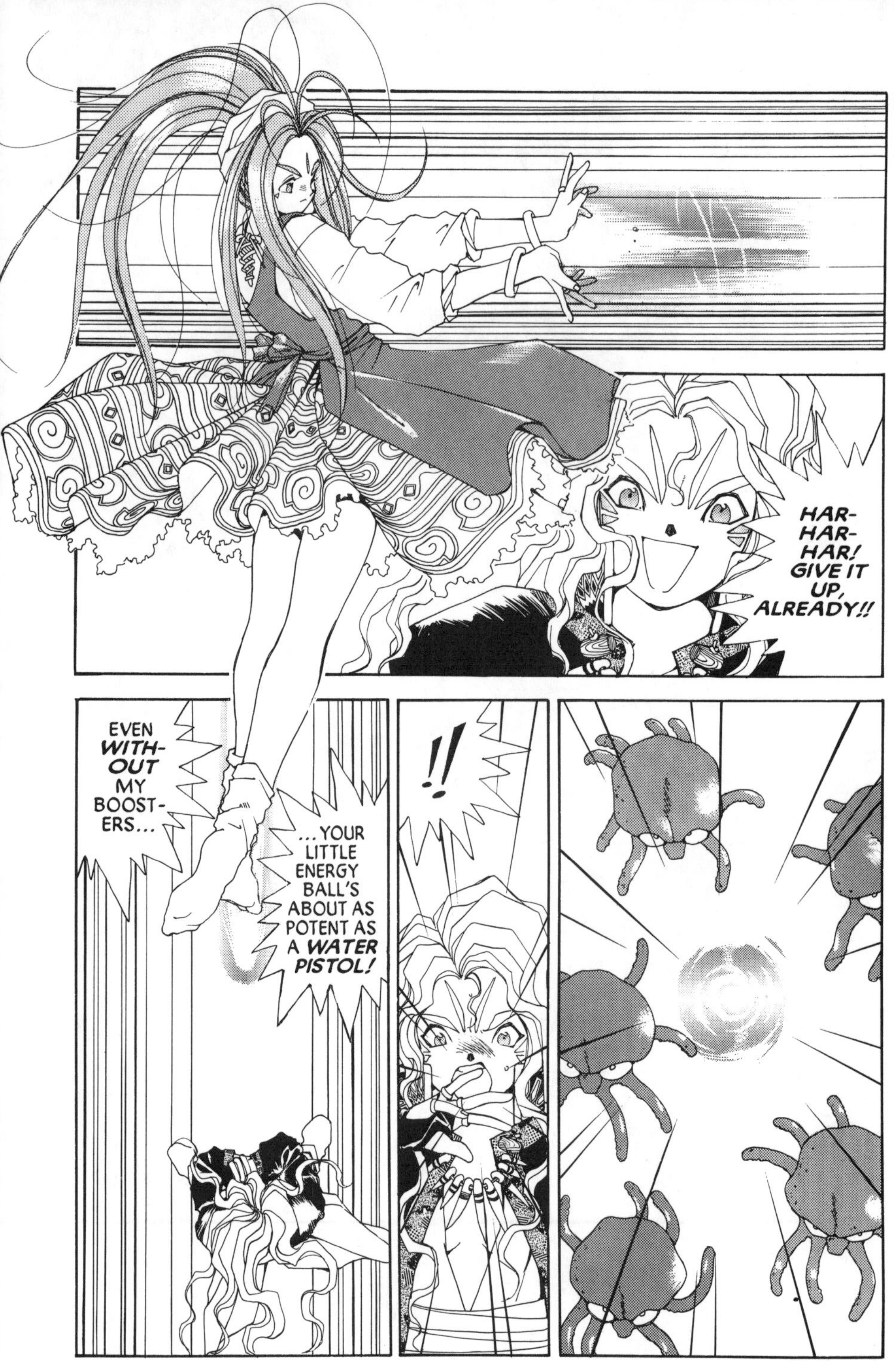
HAR-HAR-HAR! GIVE IT UP, ALREADY!!
EVEN WITH-OUT MY BOOST-ERS...
...YOUR LITTLE ENERGY BALL'S ABOUT AS POTENT AS A WATER PISTOL!
!!

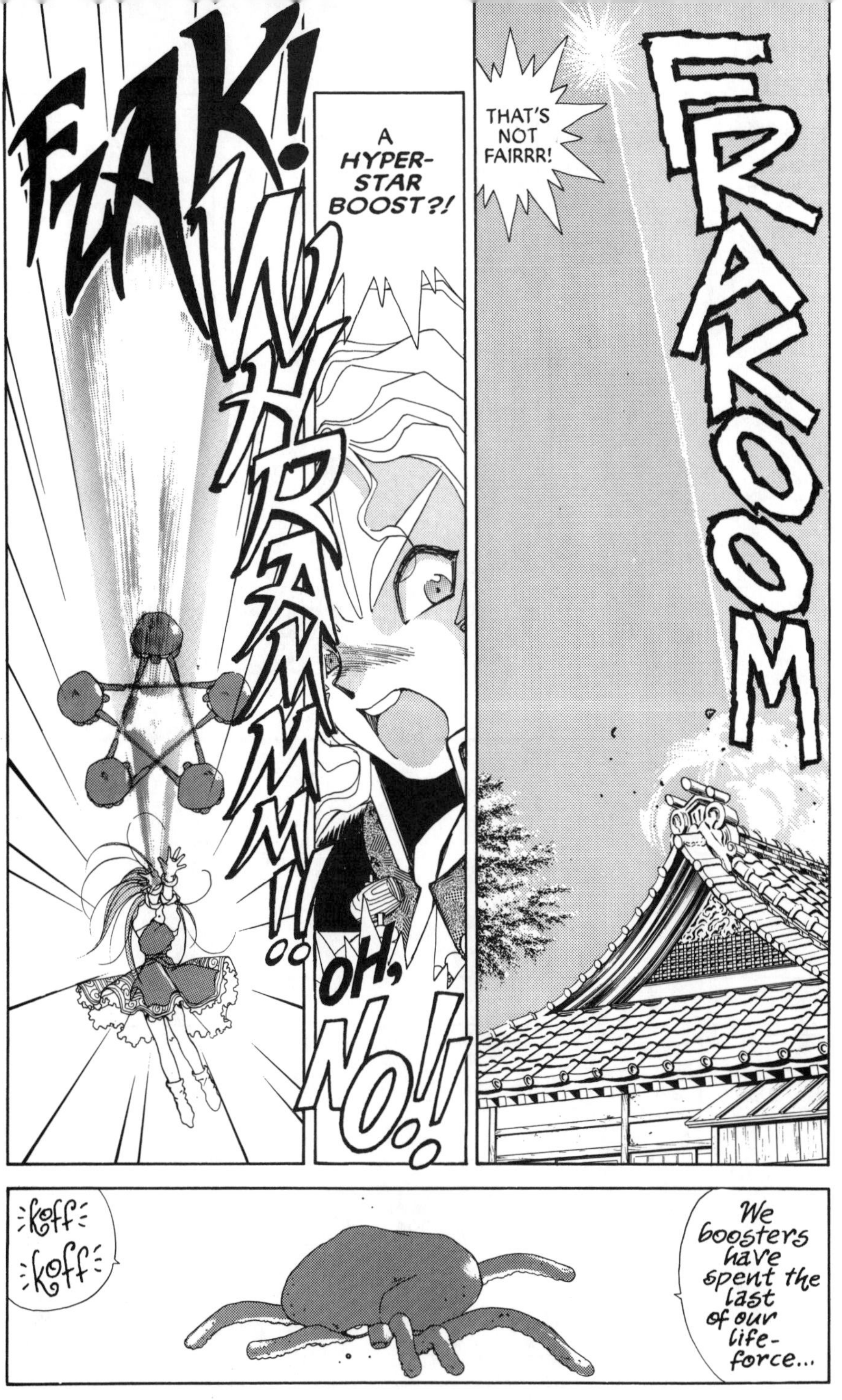
FZAK!
WHTRAMMM!!
A HYPER-STAR BOOST?!
OH, NO!!
THAT'S NOT FAIRRR!
FRAKOOM
koff koff
We boosters have spent the last of our life-force...

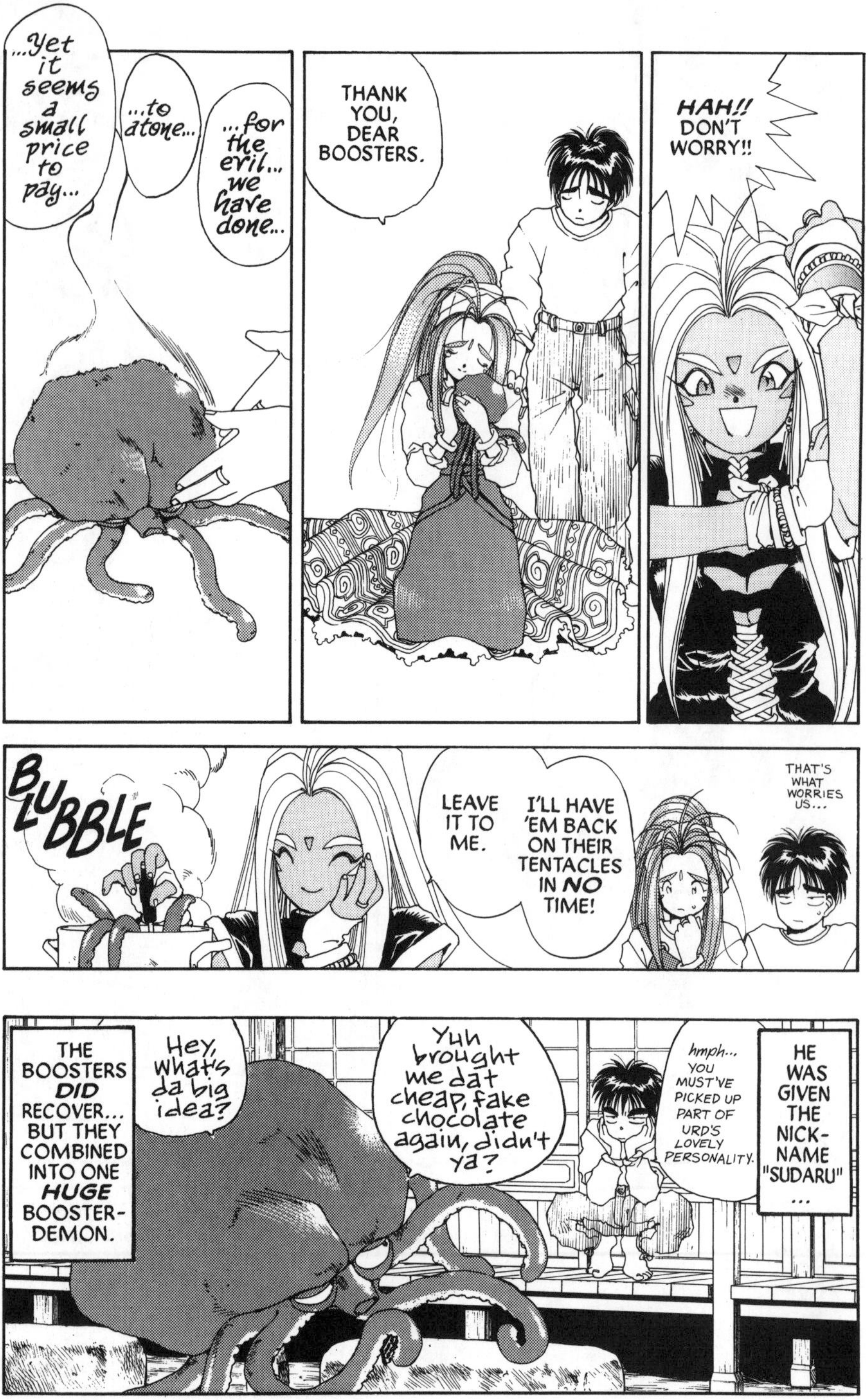
...Yet it seems a small price to pay...
...to atone...
...for the evil... we have done...
THANK YOU, DEAR BOOSTERS.
HAH!! DON'T WORRY!!
BLUBBLE
LEAVE IT TO ME.
I'LL HAVE 'EM BACK ON THEIR TENTACLES IN NO TIME!
THAT'S WHAT WORRIES US...
THE BOOSTERS DID RECOVER... BUT THEY COMBINED INTO ONE HUGE BOOSTER-DEMON.
Hey, what's da big idea?
Yuh brought me dat cheap, fake chocolate again, didn't ya?
hmph... YOU MUST'VE PICKED UP PART OF URD'S LOVELY PERSONALITY.
HE WAS GIVEN THE NICK-NAME "SUDARU" ...

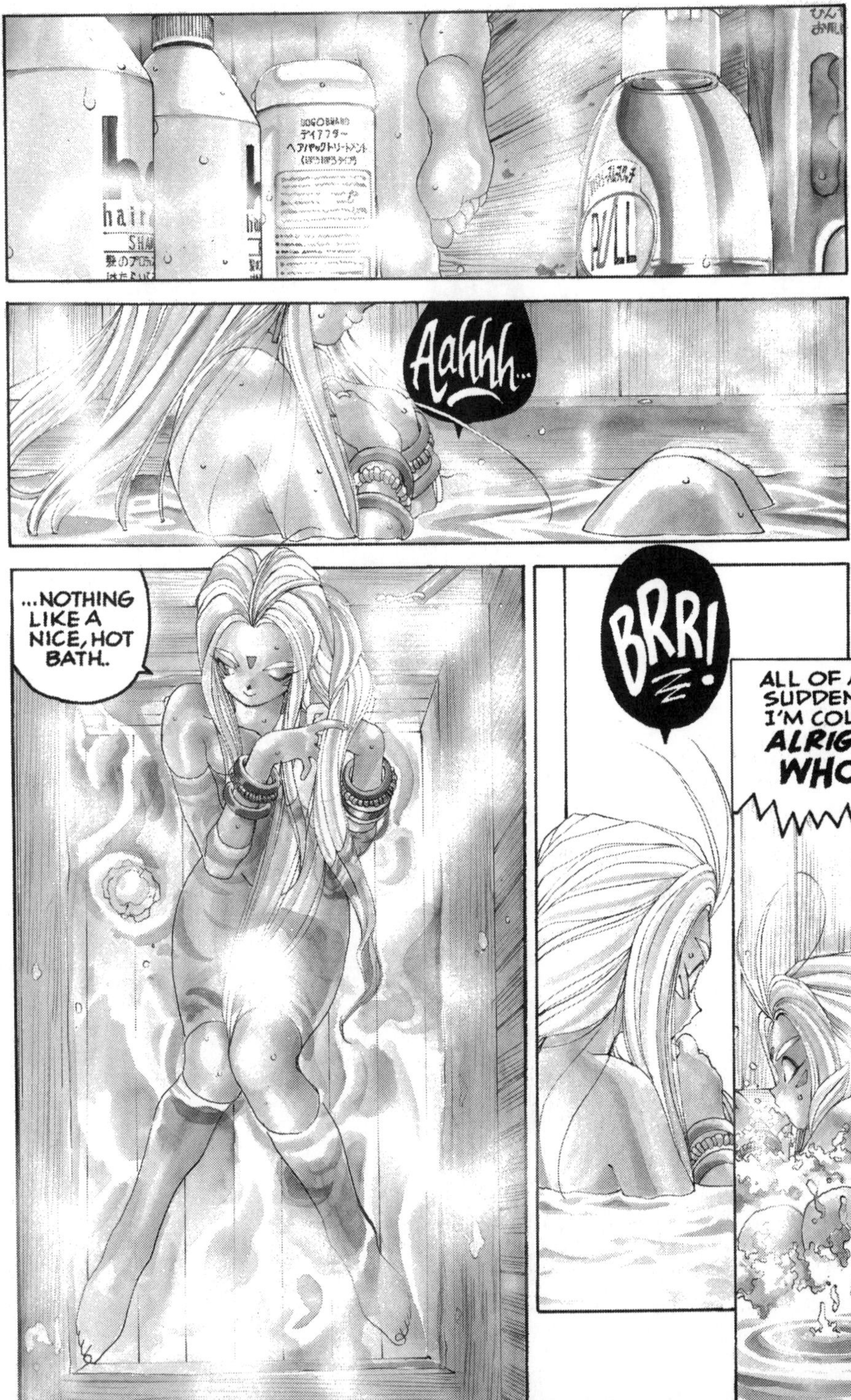
Aahhh...
...NOTHING LIKE A NICE, HOT BATH..
BRR!
ALL OF A SUDDEN I'M COLD! ALRIGHT, WHO--

The Third Goddess

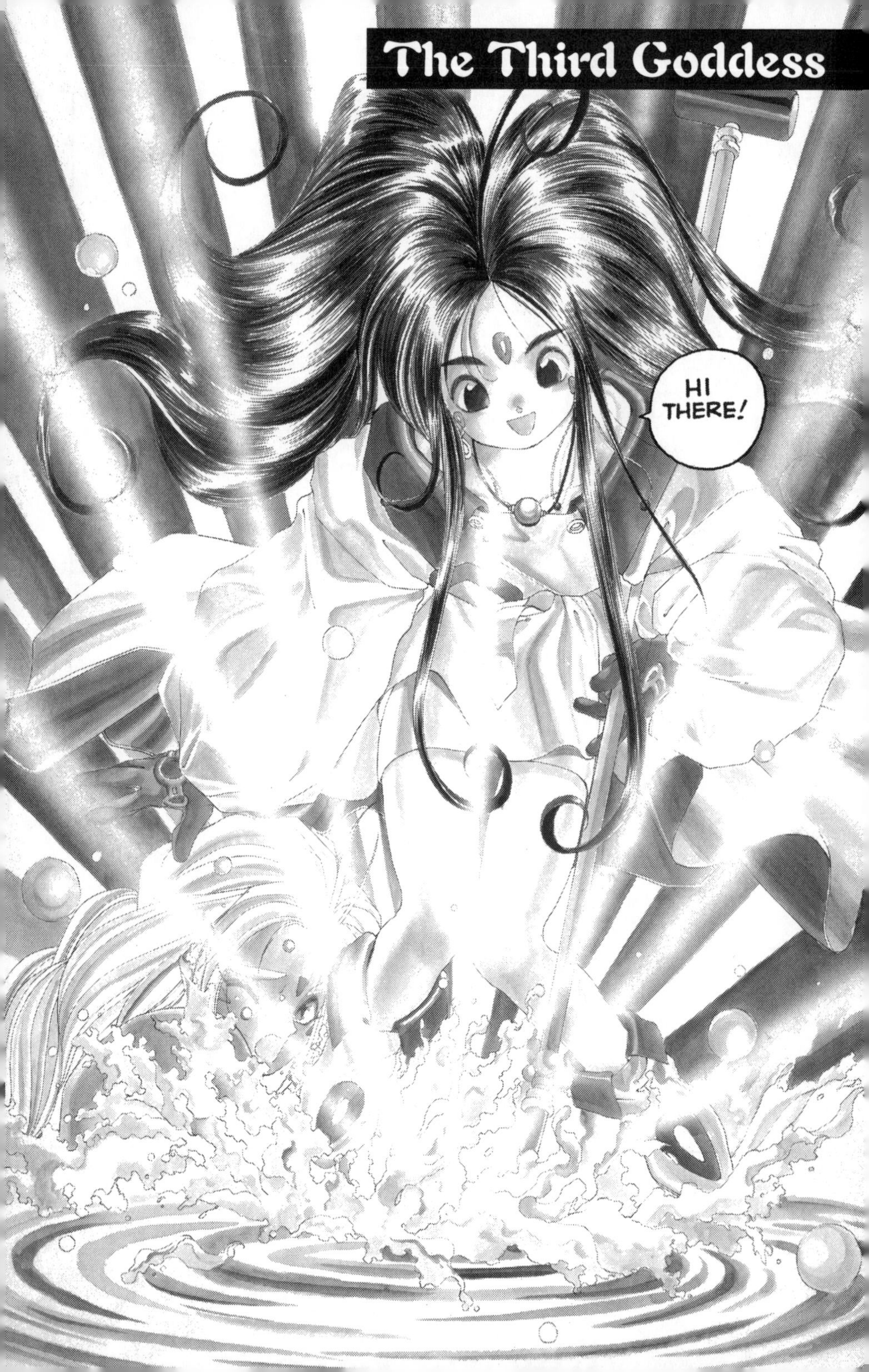
HI THERE!

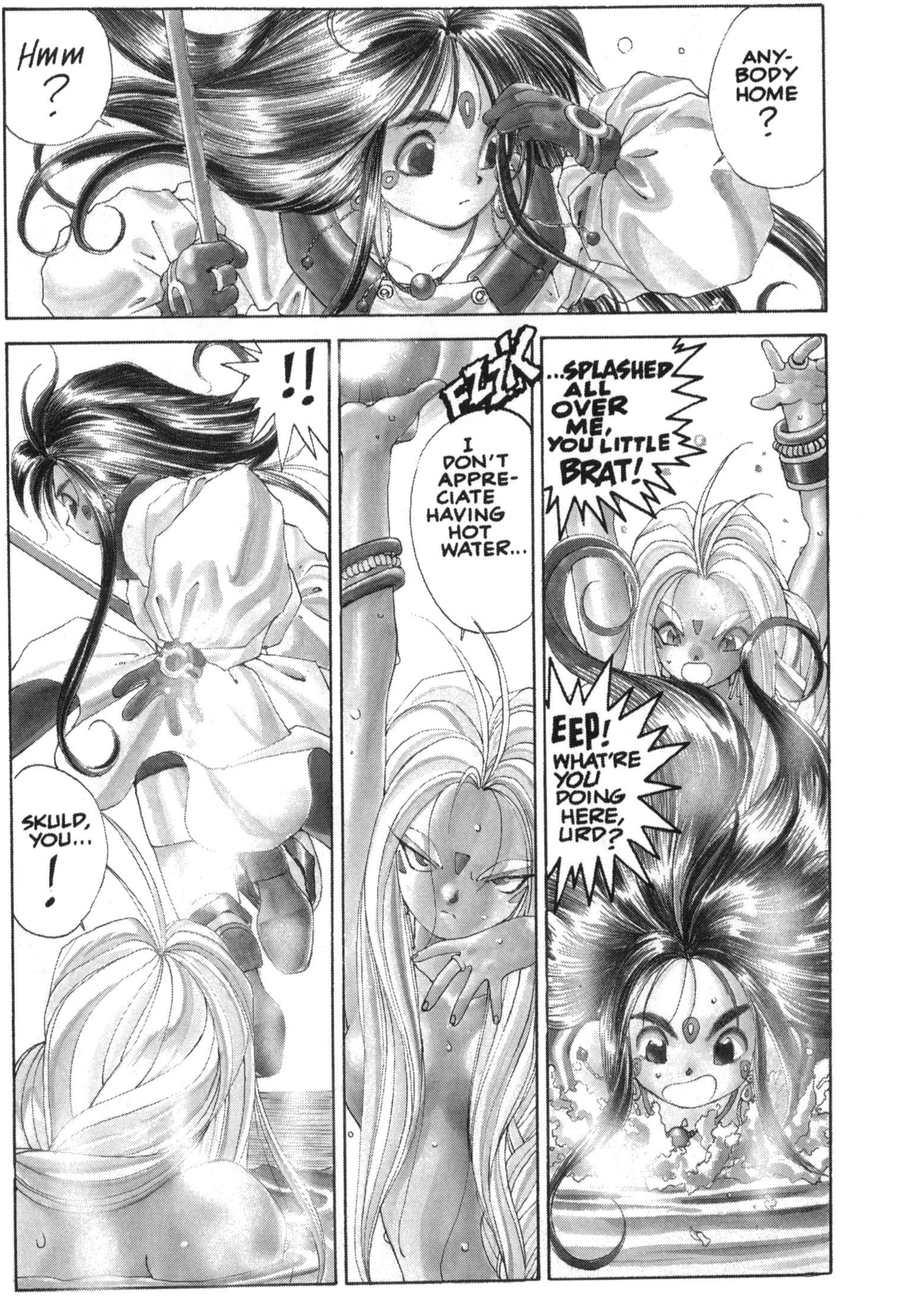

Hmm ?
ANY-BODY HOME ?
!!
SKULD, YOU... !
FZZK
I DON'T APPRECIATE HAVING HOT WATER...
...SPLASHED ALL OVER ME, YOU LITTLE BRAT!
EEP! WHAT'RE YOU DOING HERE, URD?

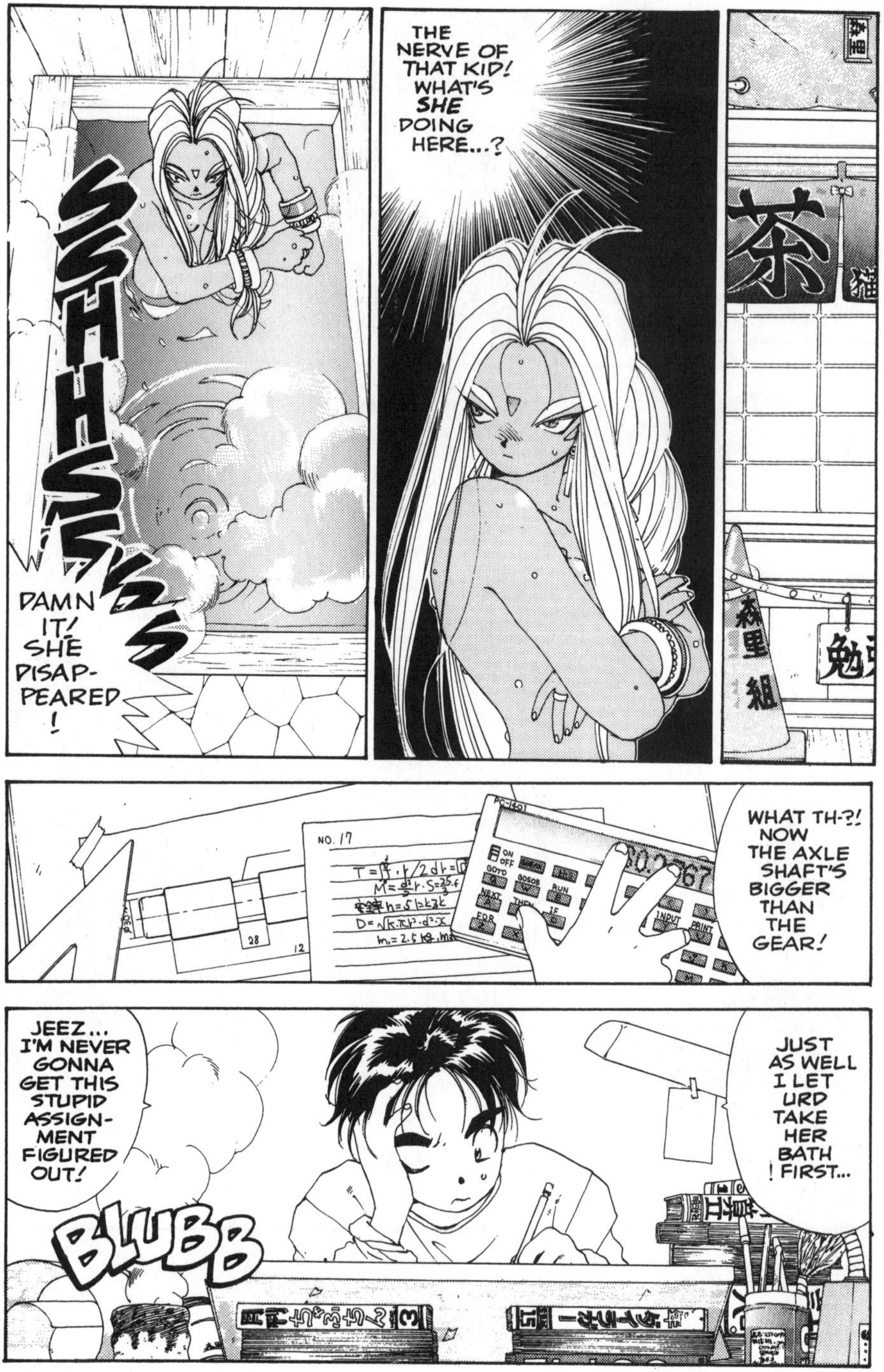
SSHHHSSSSS
DAMN IT! SHE DISAPPEARED!
THE NERVE OF THAT KID! WHAT'S SHE DOING HERE...?
WHAT TH-?! NOW THE AXLE SHAFT'S BIGGER THAN THE GEAR!
JEEZ... I'M NEVER GONNA GET THIS STUPID ASSIGNMENT FIGURED OUT!
BLUBB
JUST AS WELL I LET URD TAKE HER BATH FIRST...

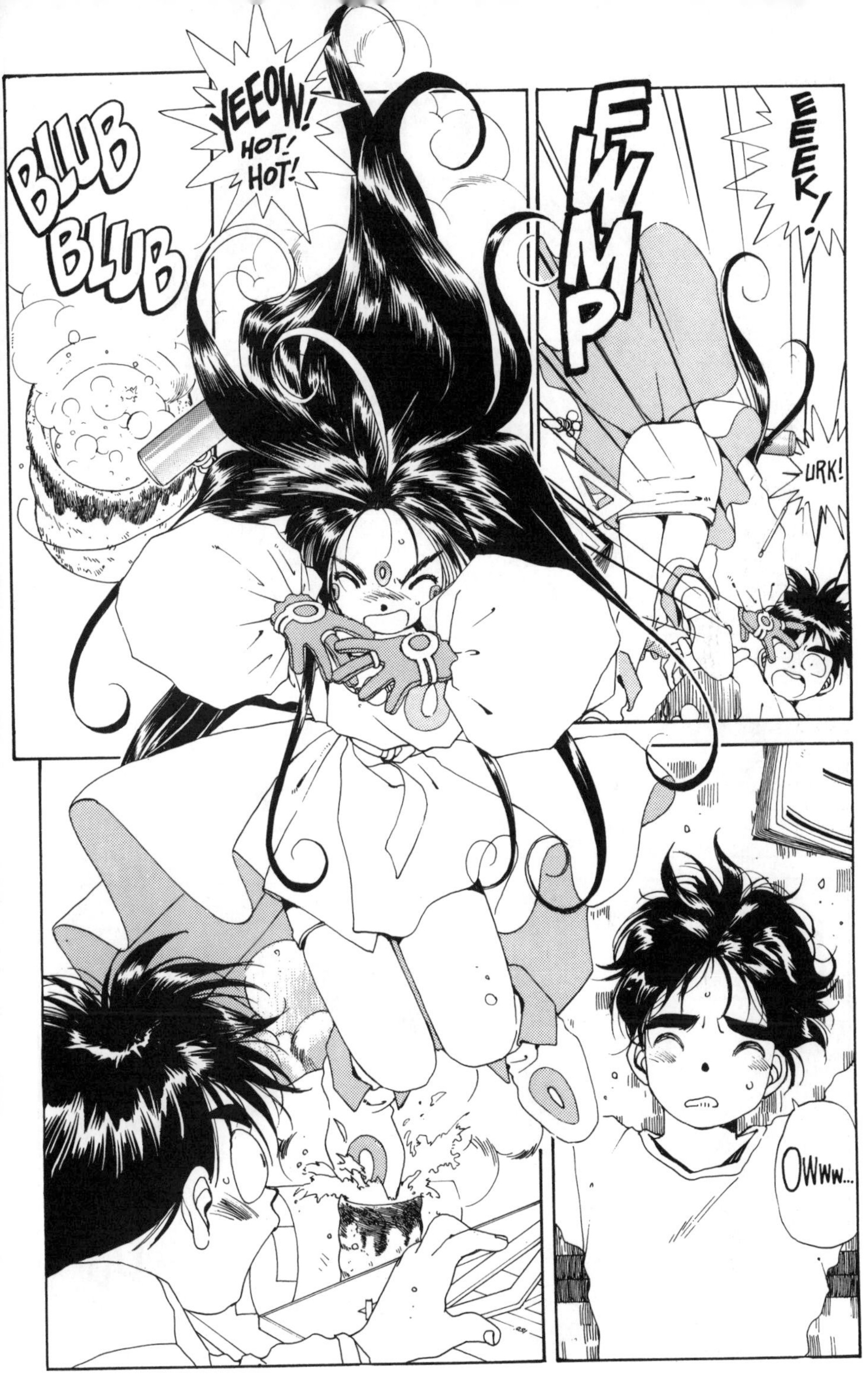
BLUB BLUB
YEEOW! HOT! HOT!
FWMP
EEEK!
URK!
OWWW...

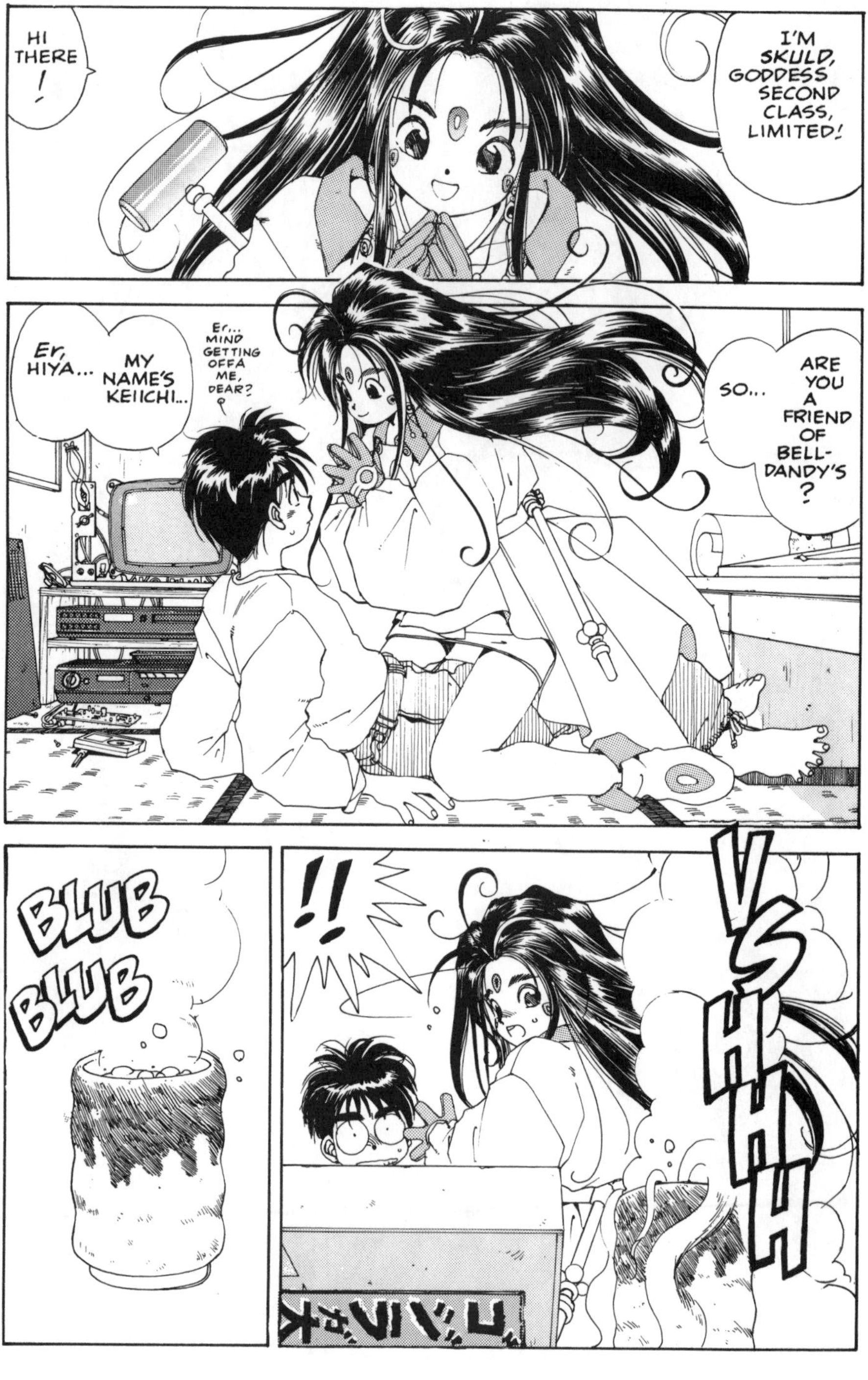
HI THERE!
I'M SKULD, GODDESS SECOND CLASS, LIMITED!
Er, HIYA... MY NAME'S KEIICHI...
Er... MIND GETTING OFFA ME, DEAR?
SO... ARE YOU A FRIEND OF BELL-DANDY'S?
BLUB BLUB
!!
VSHHHH

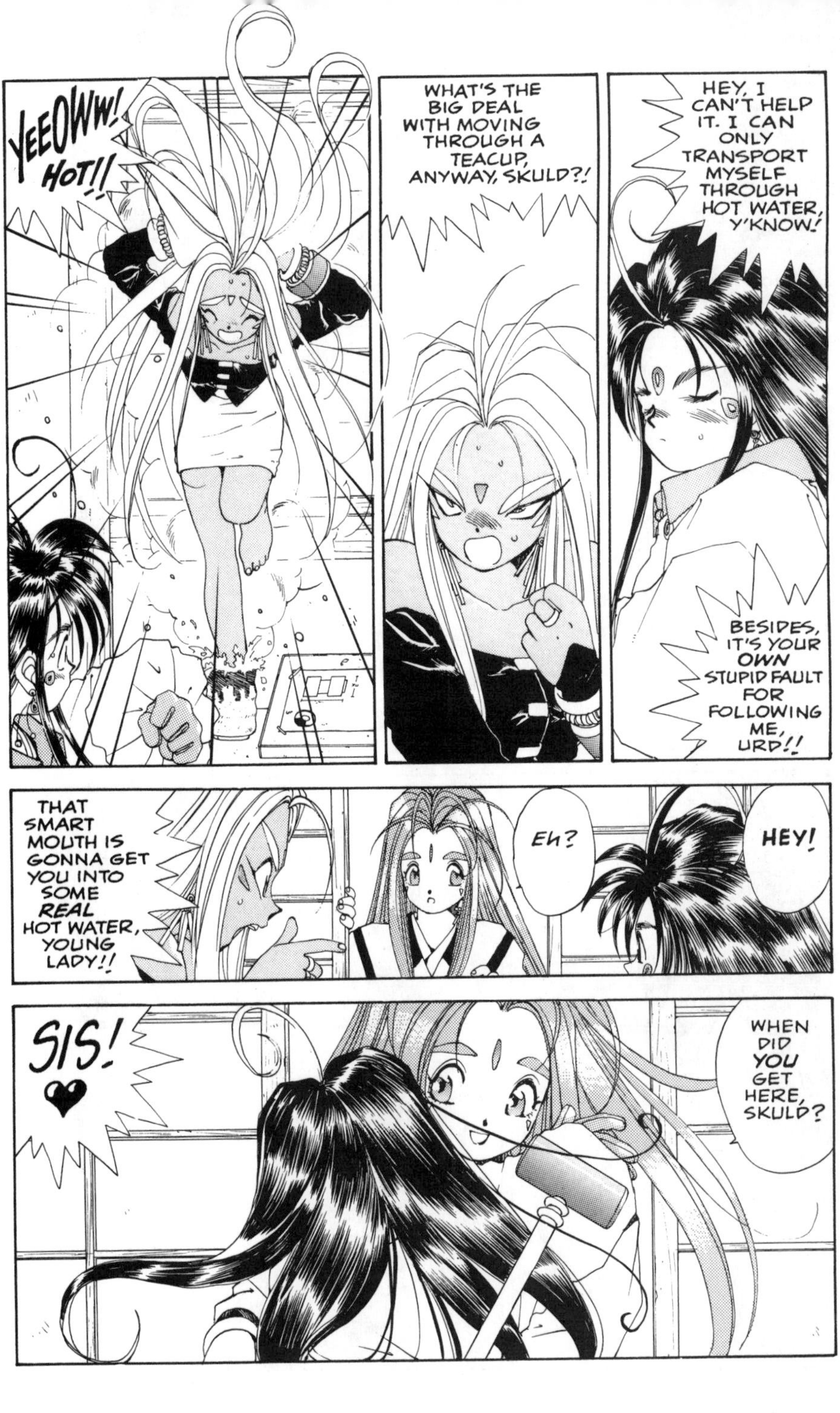
YEEOWW! HOT!!
WHAT'S THE BIG DEAL WITH MOVING THROUGH A TEACUP, ANYWAY, SKULD?!
HEY, I CAN'T HELP IT. I CAN ONLY TRANSPORT MYSELF THROUGH HOT WATER, Y'KNOW!
BESIDES, IT'S YOUR OWN STUPID FAULT FOR FOLLOWING ME, URD!!
THAT SMART MOUTH IS GONNA GET YOU INTO SOME REAL HOT WATER, YOUNG LADY!!
Eh?
HEY!
SIS!
WHEN DID YOU GET HERE, SKULD?

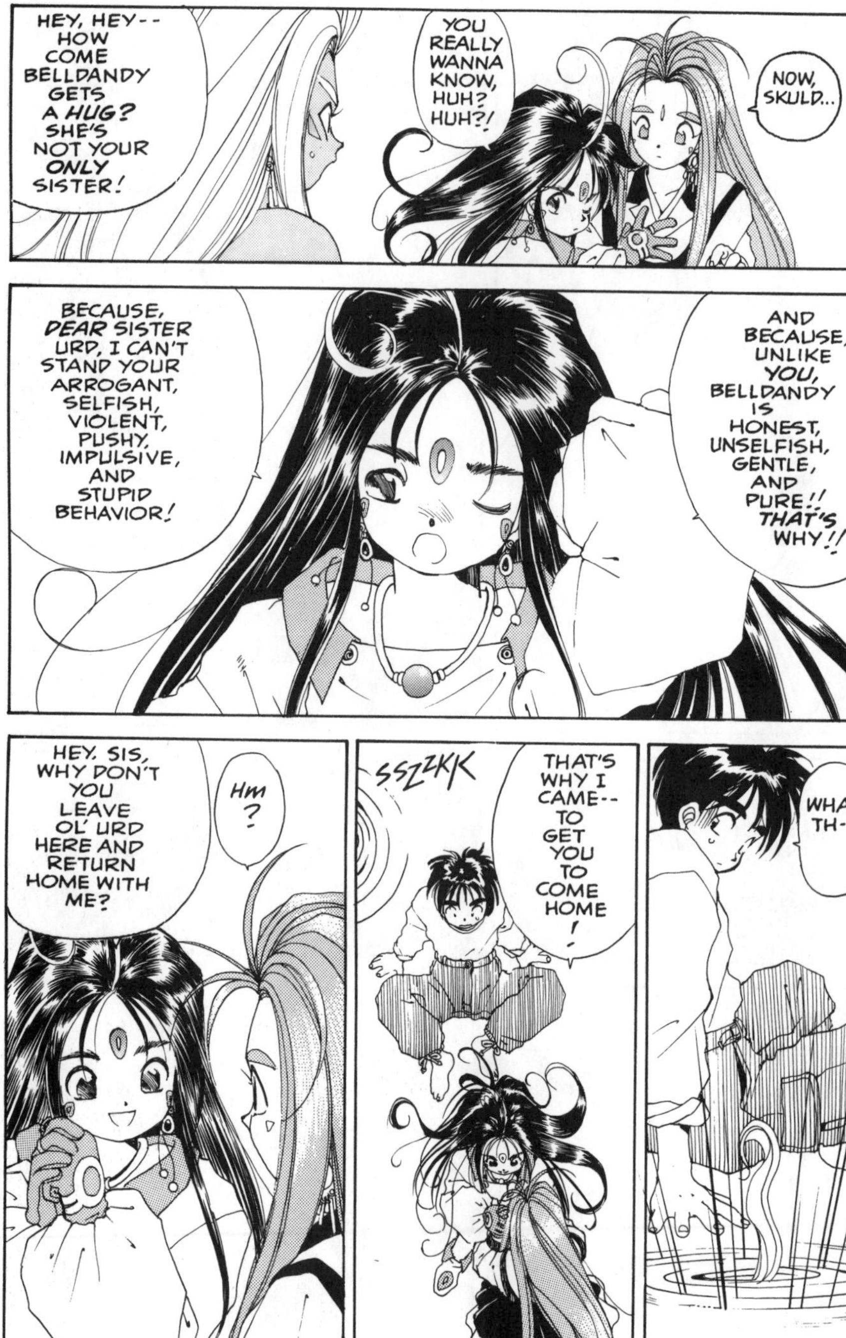
HEY, HEY-- HOW COME BELLDANDY GETS A *HUG?* SHE'S NOT YOUR *ONLY* SISTER!
YOU REALLY WANNA KNOW, HUH? HUH?!
NOW, SKULD...
BECAUSE, *DEAR* SISTER URD, I CAN'T STAND YOUR ARROGANT, SELFISH, VIOLENT, PUSHY, IMPULSIVE, AND STUPID BEHAVIOR!
AND BECAUSE, UNLIKE *YOU,* BELLDANDY IS HONEST, UNSELFISH, GENTLE, AND PURE!! *THAT'S* WHY!!
HEY. SIS, WHY DON'T YOU LEAVE OL' URD HERE AND RETURN HOME WITH ME?
Hm?
SSZZKK
THAT'S WHY I CAME-- TO GET YOU TO COME HOME!
WHAT TH-?

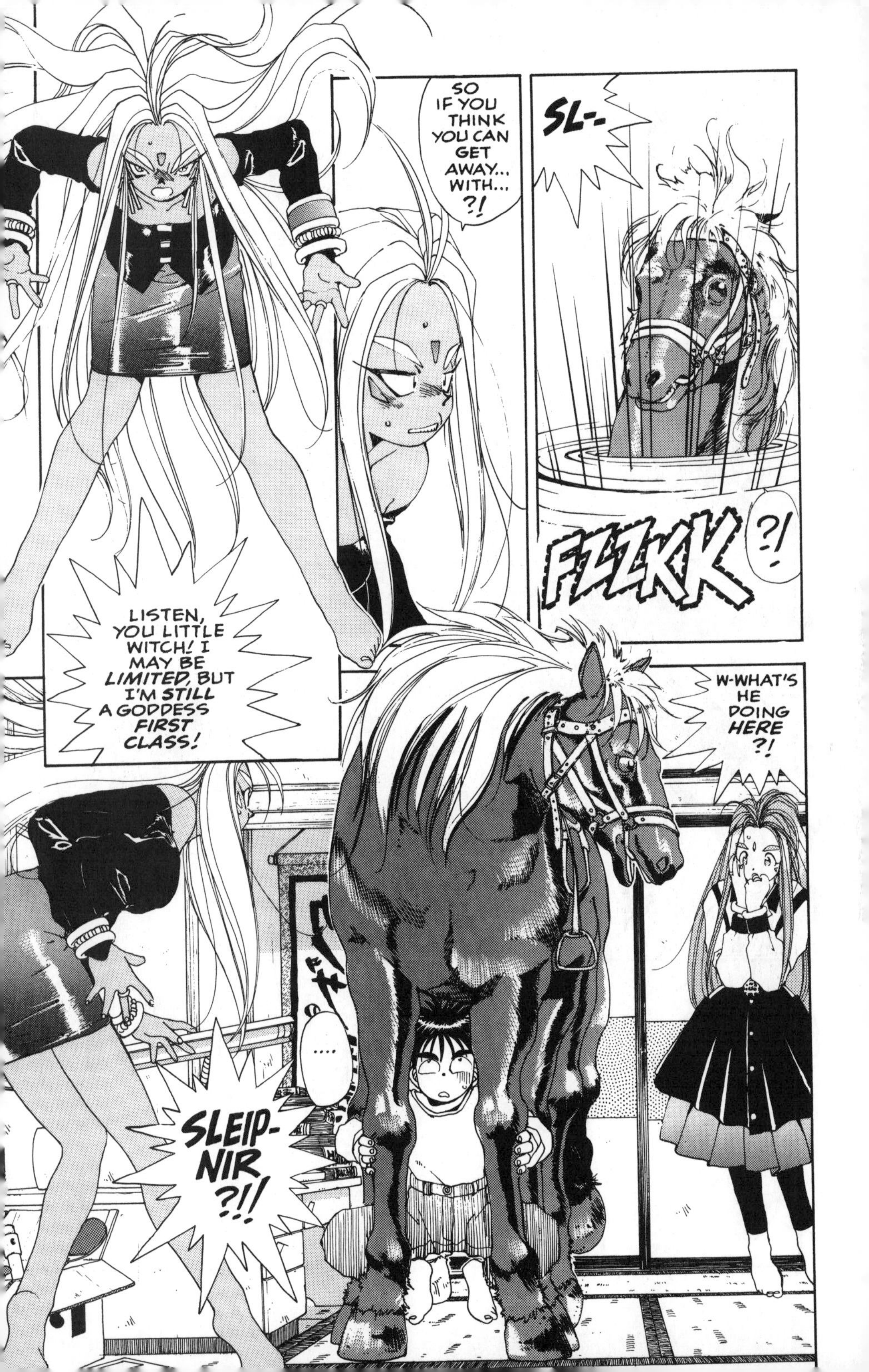
LISTEN, YOU LITTLE WITCH! I MAY BE *LIMITED*, BUT I'M **STILL** A GODDESS ***FIRST CLASS!***
SO IF YOU THINK YOU CAN GET AWAY... WITH... ?!
SL--
FZZKK
?!
W-WHAT'S HE DOING **HERE** ?!
....
SLEIP-NIR ?!!

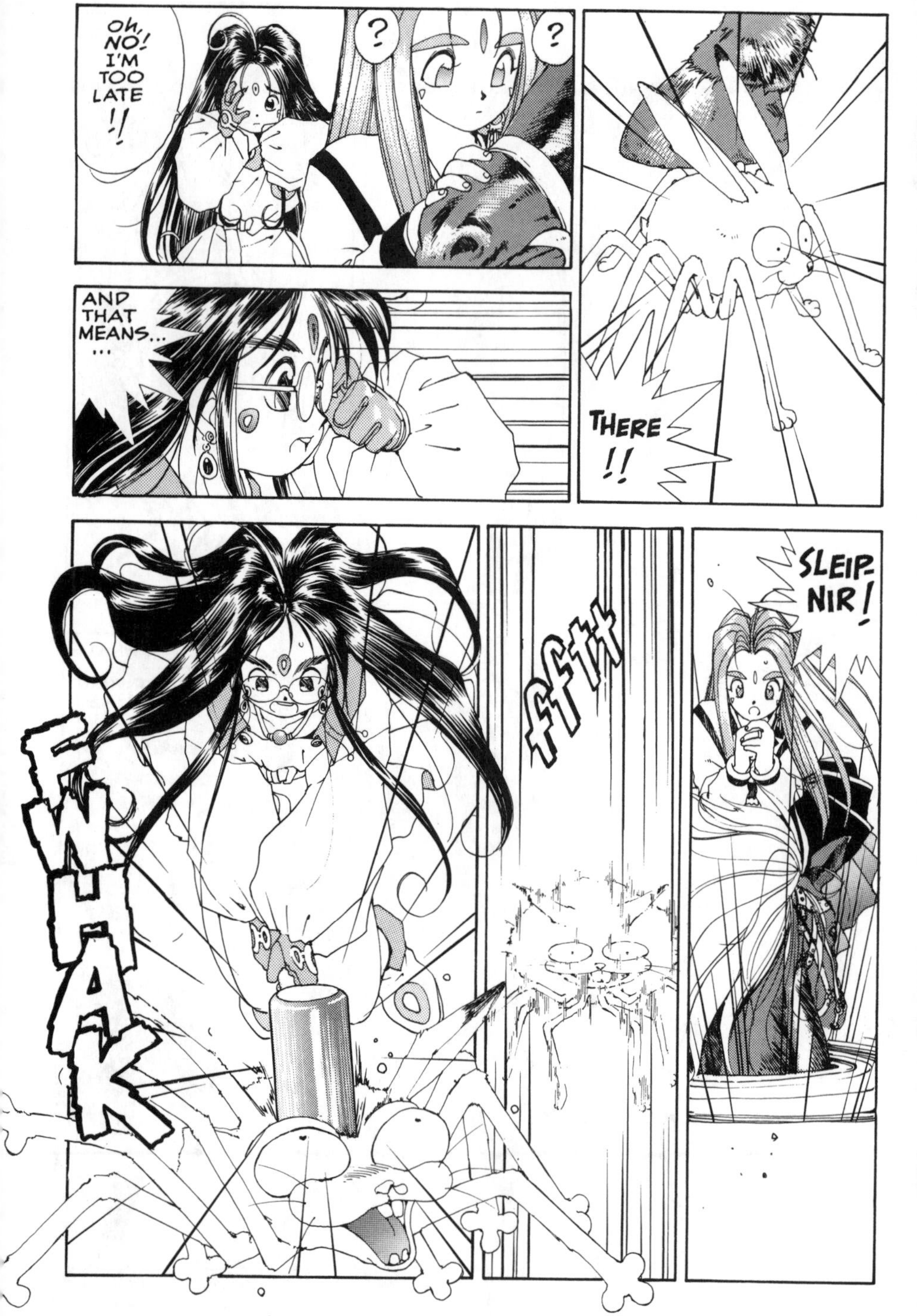
?
?
Oh, NO! I'M TOO LATE !!
AND THAT MEANS... ...
THERE !!
FWHAK
ffft
SLEIP-NIR!

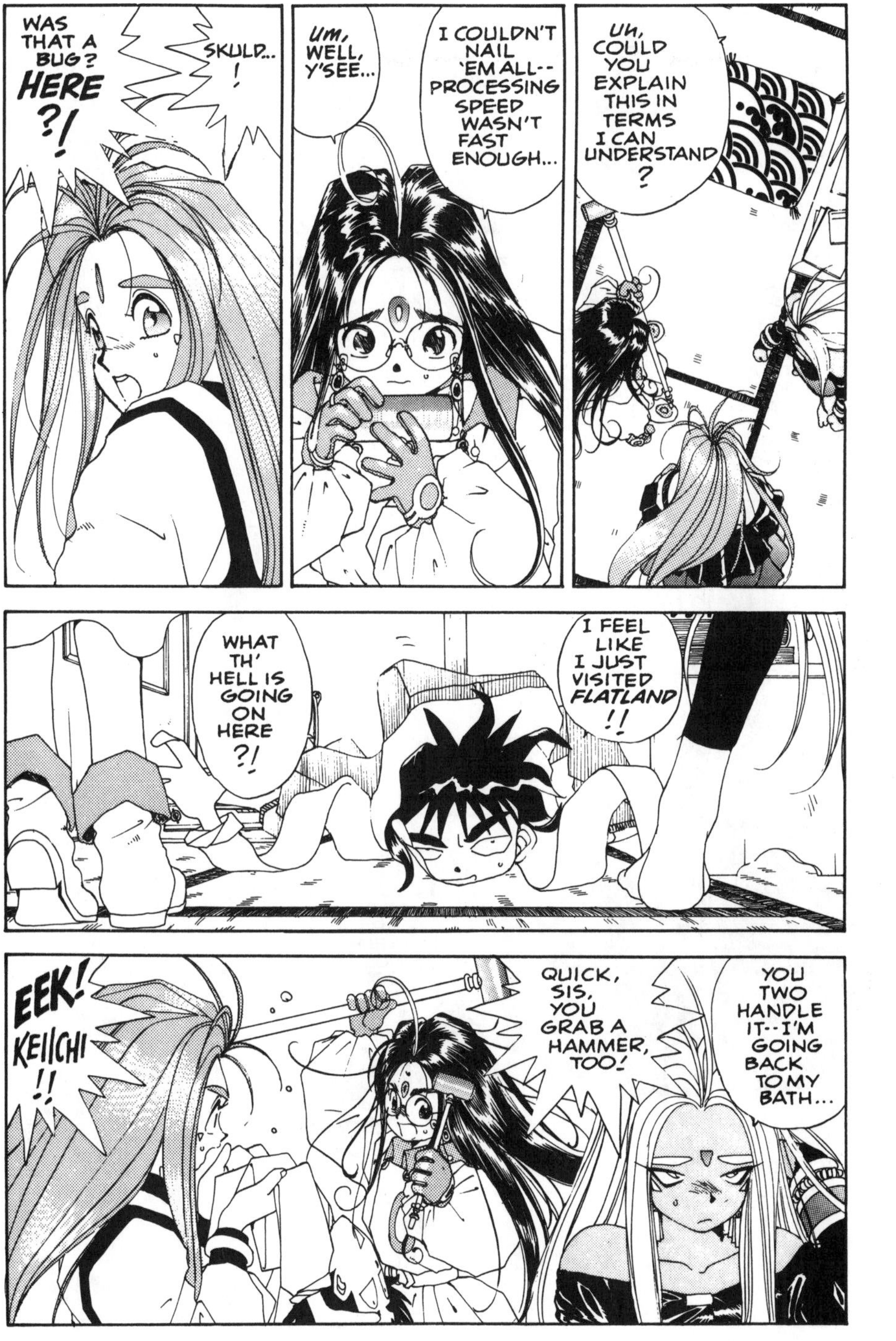
WAS THAT A BUG? HERE ?!
SKULD... !
UM, WELL, Y'SEE...
I COULDN'T NAIL 'EM ALL-- PROCESSING SPEED WASN'T FAST ENOUGH...
UH, COULD YOU EXPLAIN THIS IN TERMS I CAN UNDERSTAND ?
WHAT TH' HELL IS GOING ON HERE ?!
I FEEL LIKE I JUST VISITED FLATLAND !!
EEK! KEIICHI !!
QUICK, SIS, YOU GRAB A HAMMER, TOO!
YOU TWO HANDLE IT--I'M GOING BACK TO MY BATH...

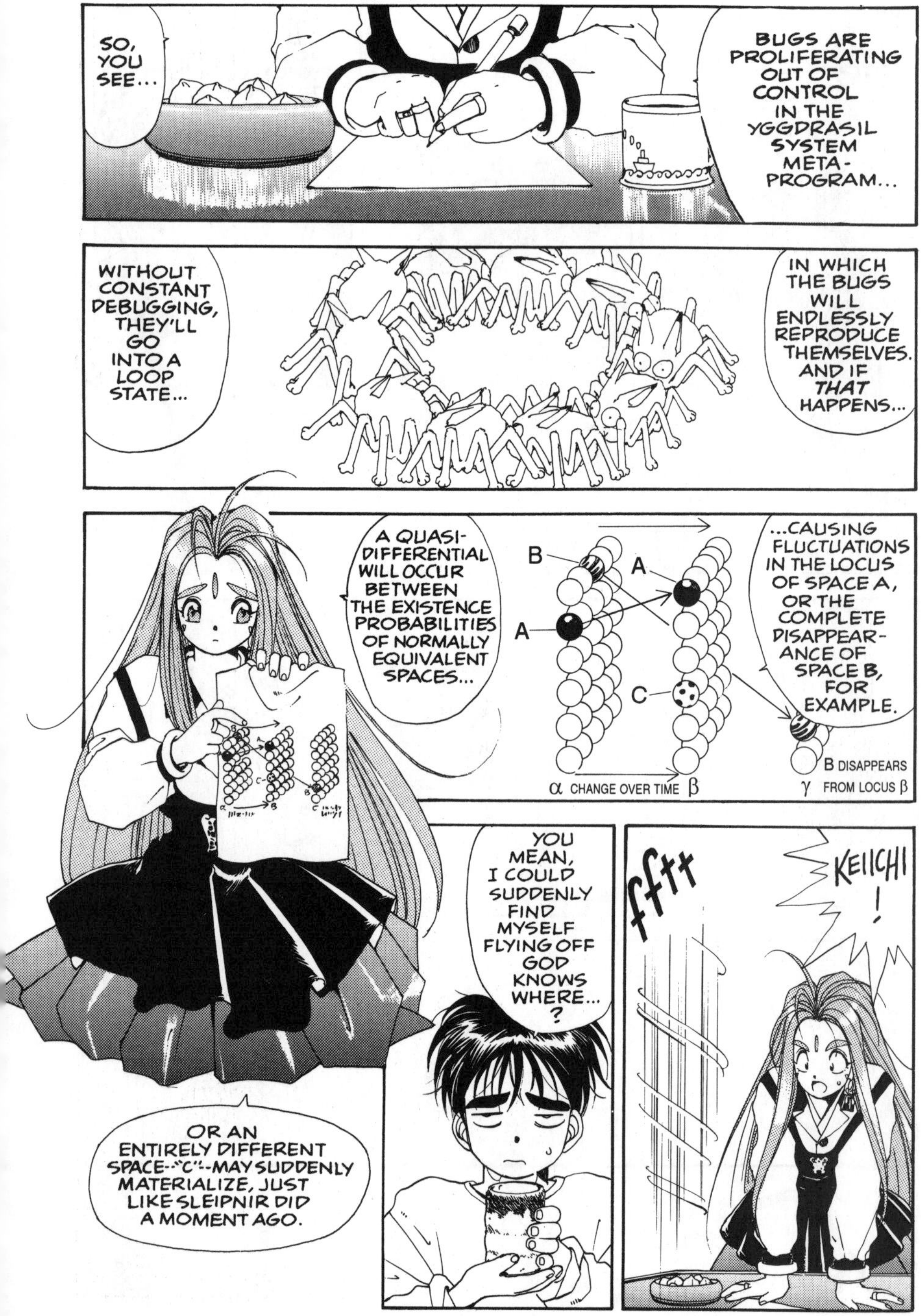
SO, YOU SEE...
BUGS ARE PROLIFERATING OUT OF CONTROL IN THE YGGDRASIL SYSTEM META-PROGRAM...
WITHOUT CONSTANT DEBUGGING, THEY'LL GO INTO A LOOP STATE...
IN WHICH THE BUGS WILL ENDLESSLY REPRODUCE THEMSELVES. AND IF *THAT* HAPPENS...
A QUASI-DIFFERENTIAL WILL OCCUR BETWEEN THE EXISTENCE PROBABILITIES OF NORMALLY EQUIVALENT SPACES...
B
A
A
C
α CHANGE OVER TIME β
γ
B DISAPPEARS FROM LOCUS β
...CAUSING FLUCTUATIONS IN THE LOCUS OF SPACE A, OR THE COMPLETE DISAPPEARANCE OF SPACE B, FOR EXAMPLE.
OR AN ENTIRELY DIFFERENT SPACE--"C"--MAY SUDDENLY MATERIALIZE, JUST LIKE SLEIPNIR DID A MOMENT AGO.
YOU MEAN, I COULD SUDDENLY FIND MYSELF FLYING OFF GOD KNOWS WHERE...?
fftt
KEIICHI!

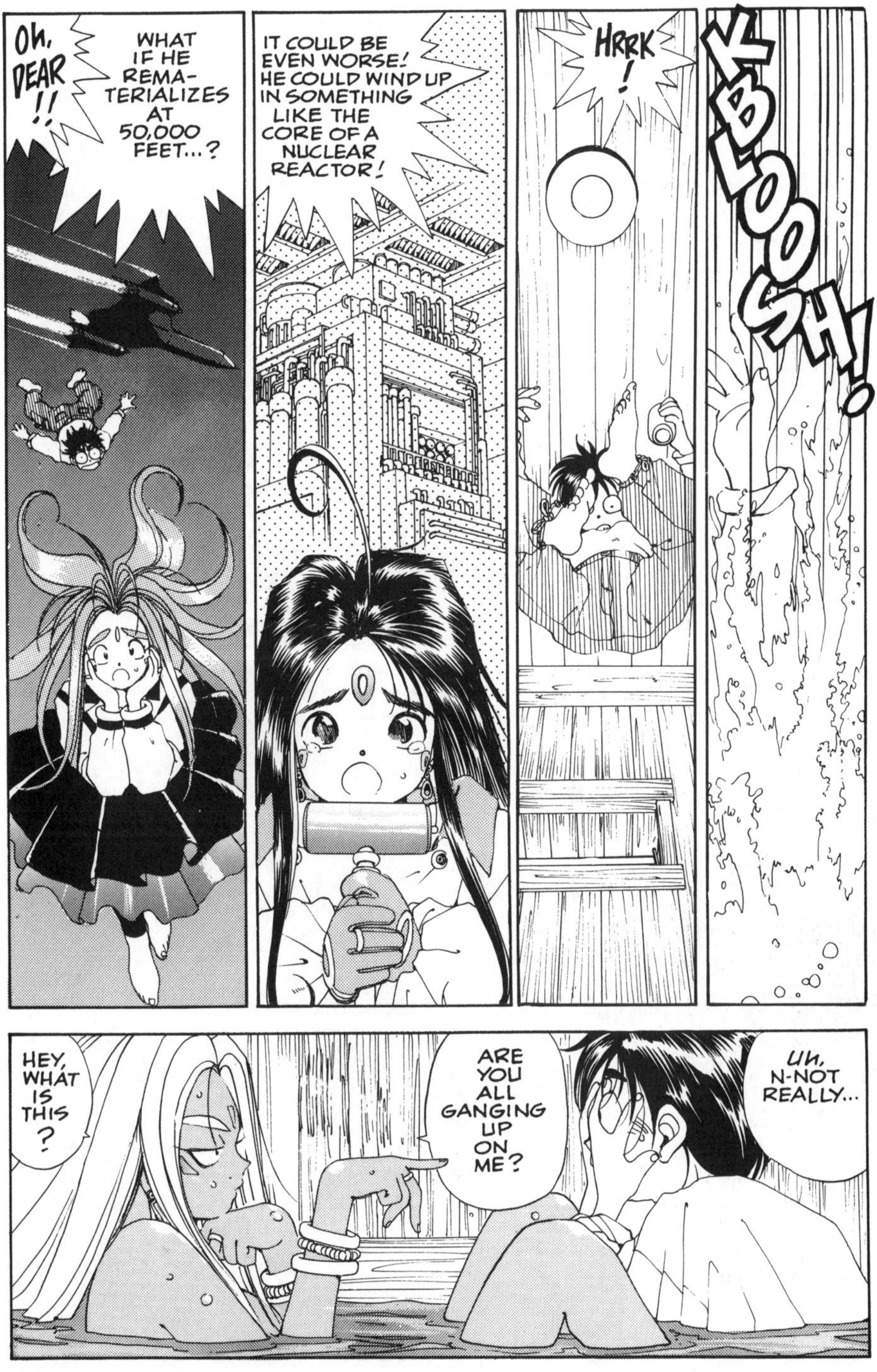

OH, DEAR!!
WHAT IF HE REMATERIALIZES AT 50,000 FEET...?
IT COULD BE EVEN WORSE! HE COULD WIND UP IN SOMETHING LIKE THE CORE OF A NUCLEAR REACTOR!
HRRK!
KBLOOSH!
HEY, WHAT IS THIS?
ARE YOU ALL GANGING UP ON ME?
UH, N-NOT REALLY...

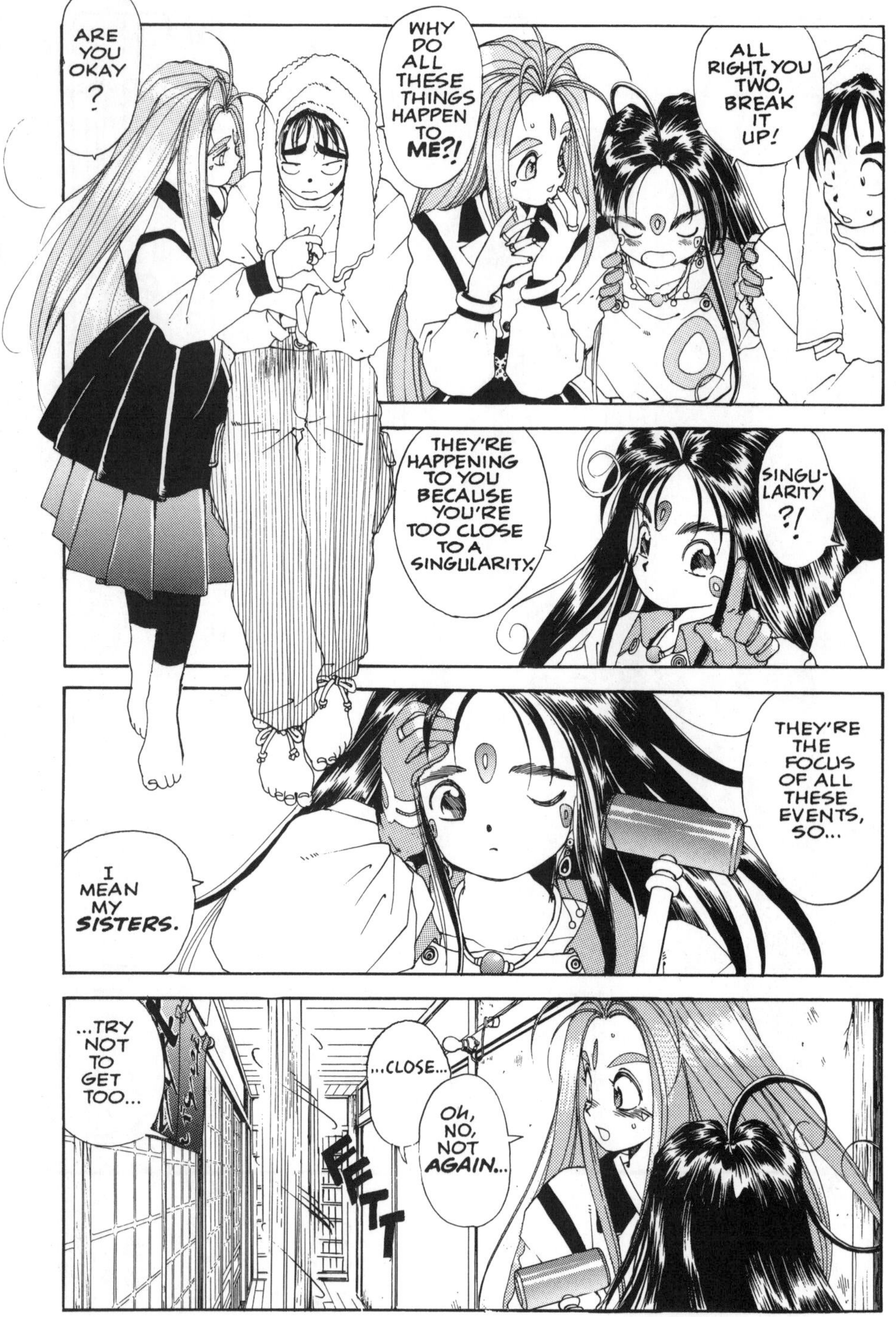
ARE YOU OKAY?
WHY DO ALL THESE THINGS HAPPEN TO ME?!
ALL RIGHT, YOU TWO, BREAK IT UP!
THEY'RE HAPPENING TO YOU BECAUSE YOU'RE TOO CLOSE TO A SINGULARITY.
SINGULARITY?!
I MEAN MY SISTERS.
THEY'RE THE FOCUS OF ALL THESE EVENTS, SO...
...TRY NOT TO GET TOO...
...CLOSE...
OH, NO, NOT AGAIN...
FETT

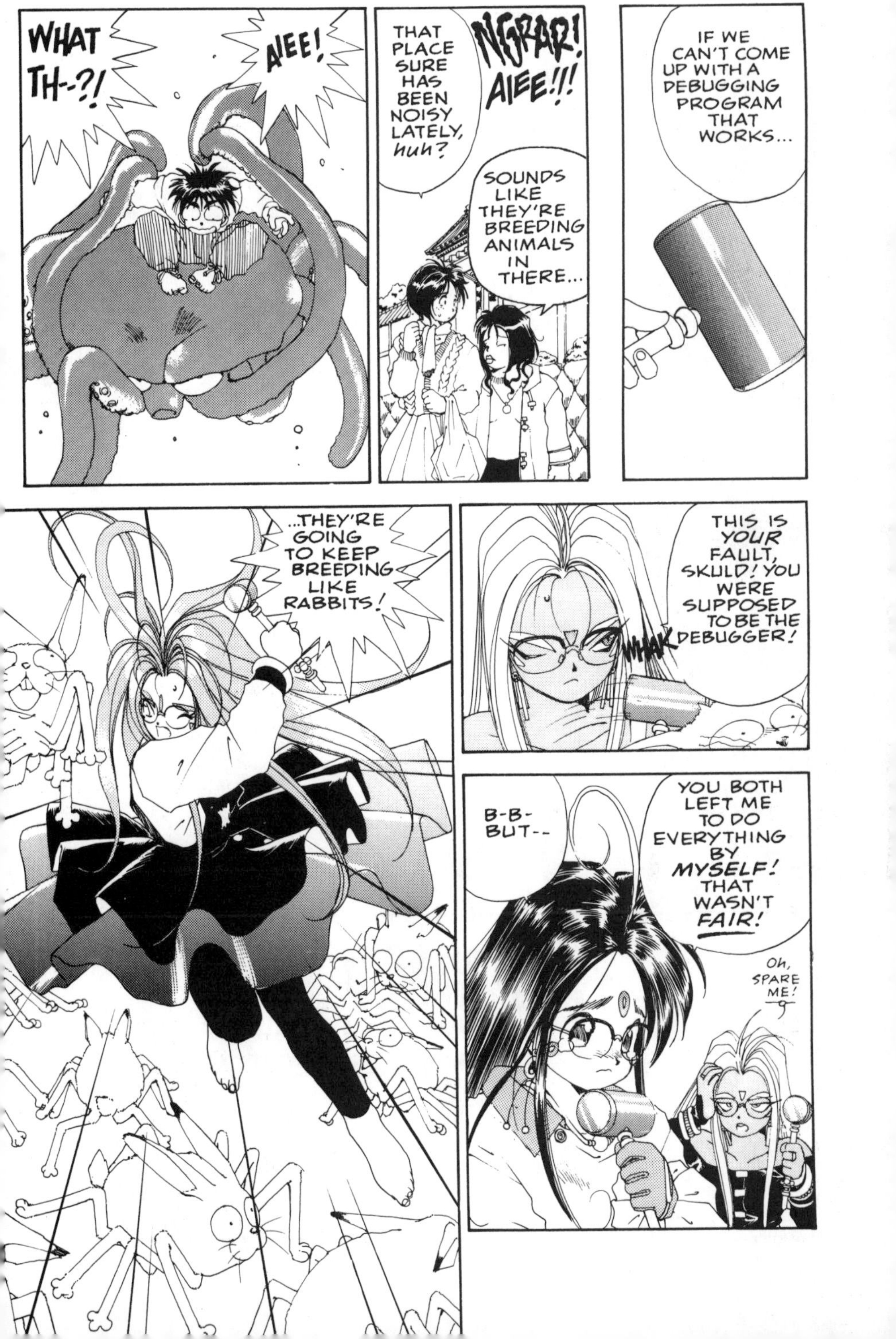
WHAT TH-?!
AIEE!
THAT PLACE SURE HAS BEEN NOISY LATELY, huh?
NGRAR! AIEE!!!
SOUNDS LIKE THEY'RE BREEDING ANIMALS IN THERE...
IF WE CAN'T COME UP WITH A DEBUGGING PROGRAM THAT WORKS...
...THEY'RE GOING TO KEEP BREEDING LIKE RABBITS!
THIS IS YOUR FAULT, SKULD! YOU WERE SUPPOSED TO BE THE DEBUGGER!
WHAK
B-B-BUT--
YOU BOTH LEFT ME TO DO EVERYTHING BY MYSELF! THAT WASN'T FAIR!
Oh, SPARE ME!

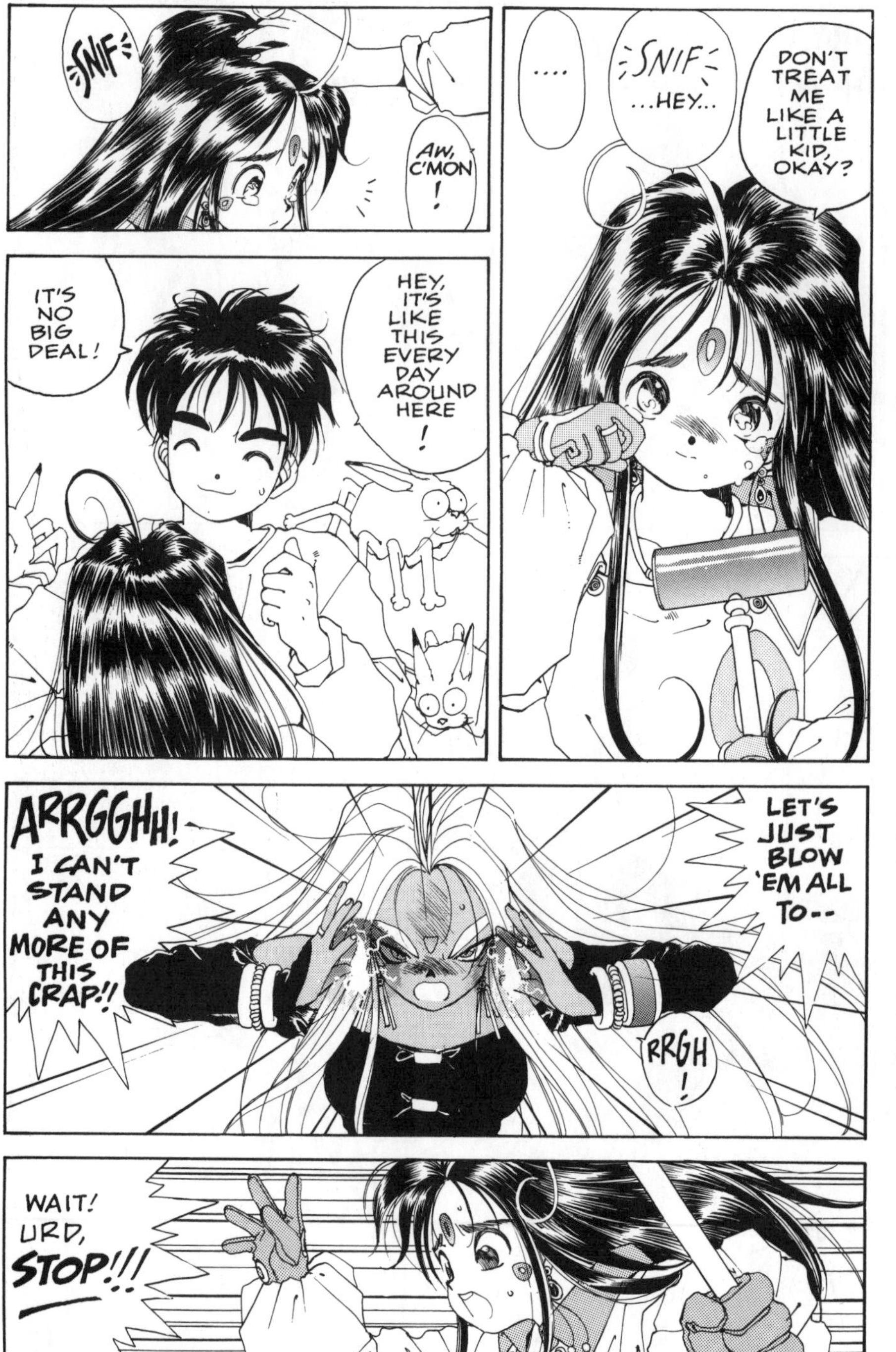
SNIF
AW, C'MON!
IT'S NO BIG DEAL!
HEY, IT'S LIKE THIS EVERY DAY AROUND HERE!
....
SNIF ...HEY...
DON'T TREAT ME LIKE A LITTLE KID, OKAY?
ARRGGHH! I CAN'T STAND ANY MORE OF THIS CRAP!!
LET'S JUST BLOW 'EM ALL TO--
RRGH!
WAIT! URD, STOP!!!

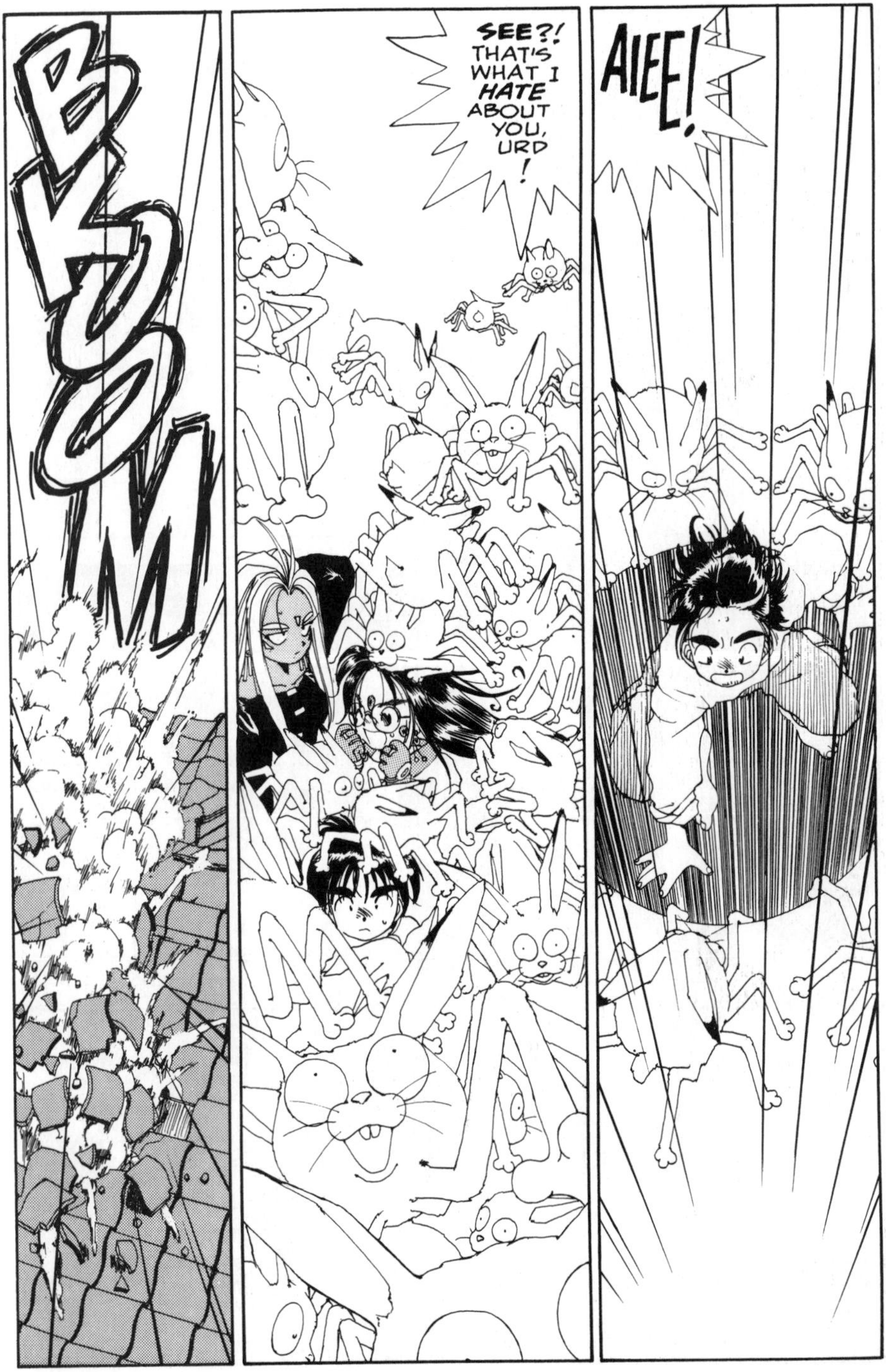
BOOM
SEE?! THAT'S WHAT I HATE ABOUT YOU, URD!
AIEE!

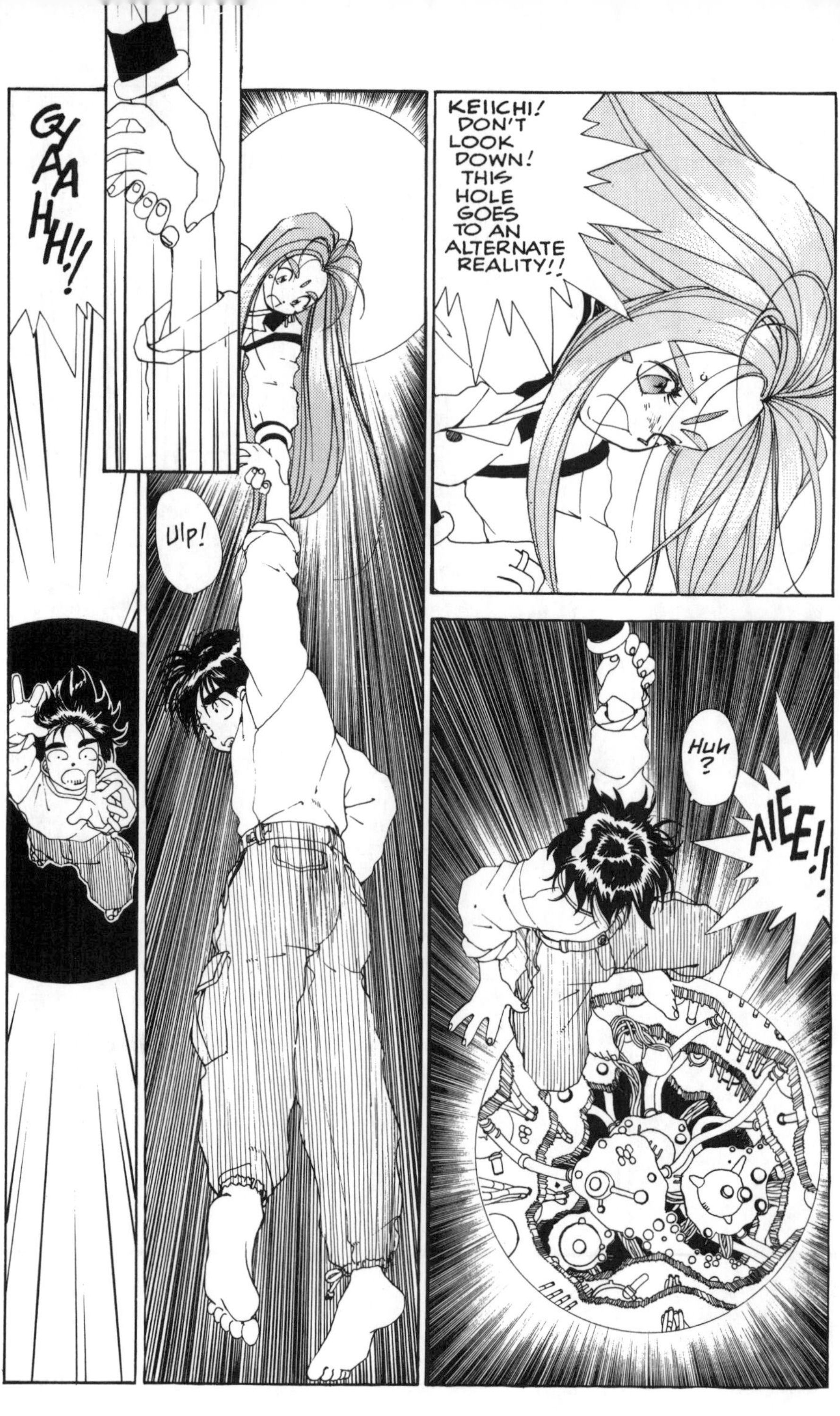
GYAAHH!!
Ulp!
KEIICHI! DON'T LOOK DOWN! THIS HOLE GOES TO AN ALTERNATE REALITY!!
Huh?
AIEE!!

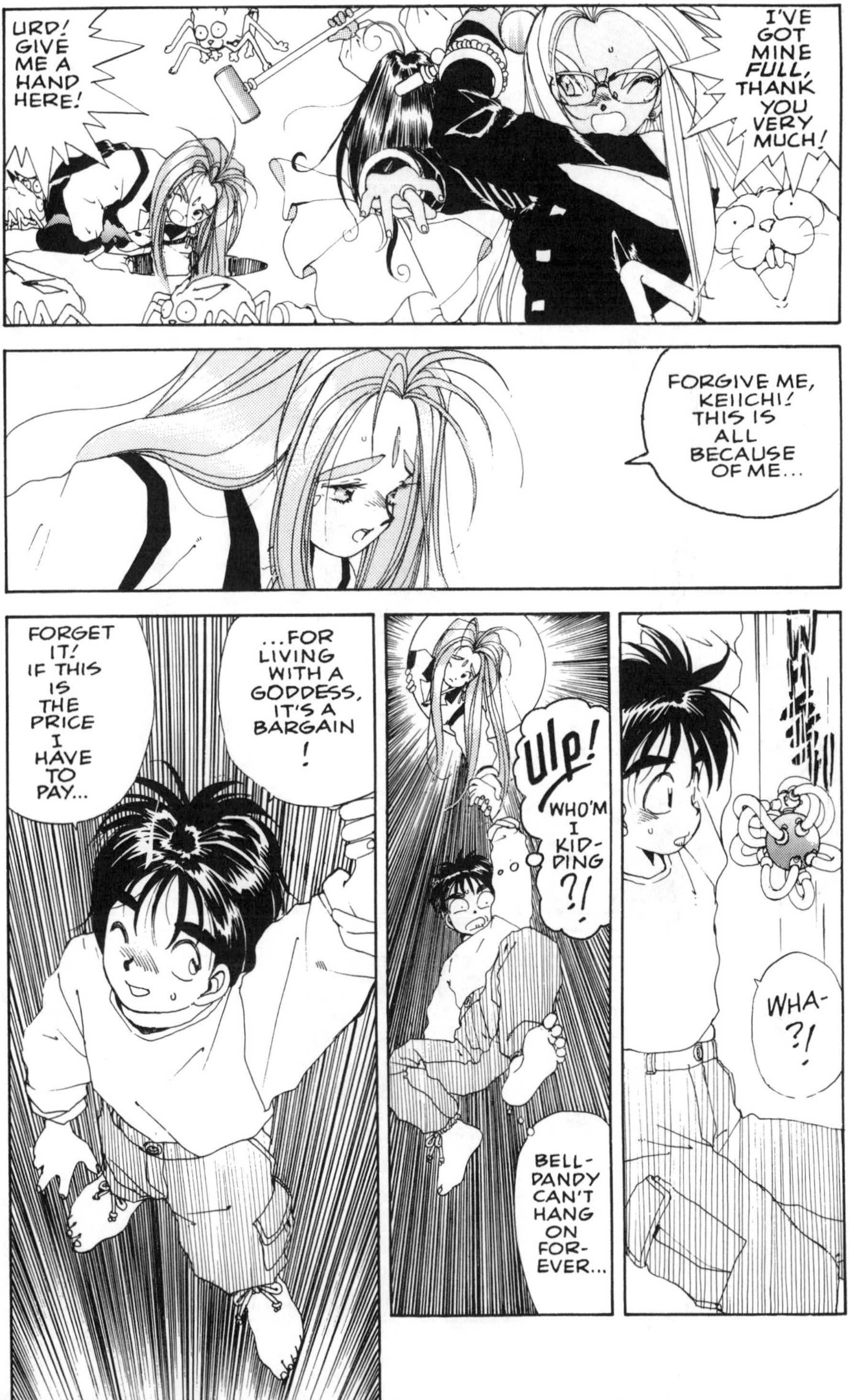
URD! GIVE ME A HAND HERE!
I'VE GOT MINE *FULL*, THANK YOU VERY MUCH!
FORGIVE ME, KEIICHI! THIS IS ALL BECAUSE OF ME...
FORGET IT! IF THIS IS THE PRICE I HAVE TO PAY...
...FOR LIVING WITH A GODDESS, IT'S A BARGAIN!
ULP!
WHO'M I KID-DING ?!
BELL-DANDY CAN'T HANG ON FOR-EVER...
WHA- ?!

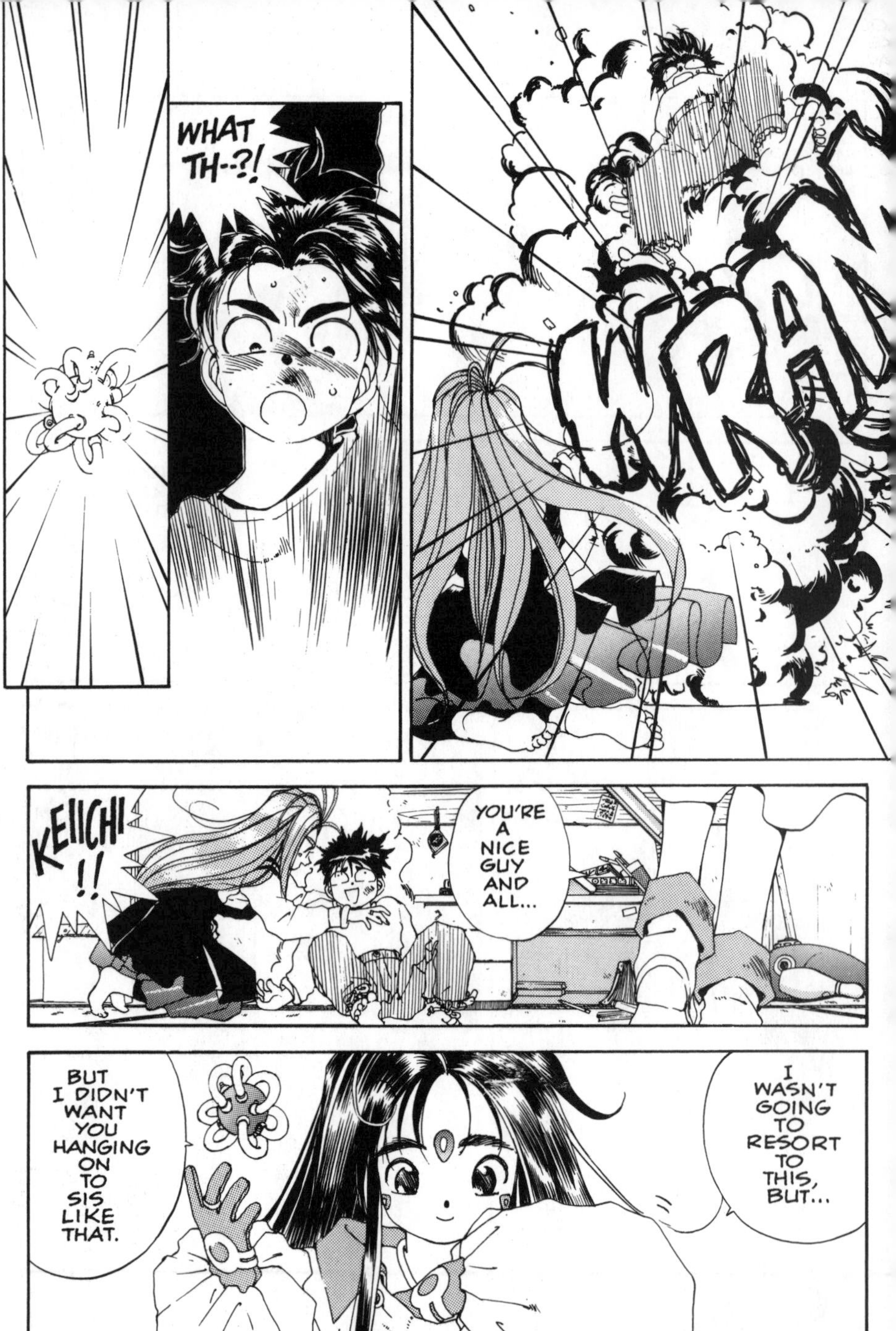
WHAT TH--?!
WRA
KEIICHI !!
YOU'RE A NICE GUY AND ALL...
BUT I DIDN'T WANT YOU HANGING ON TO SIS LIKE THAT.
I WASN'T GOING TO RESORT TO THIS, BUT...

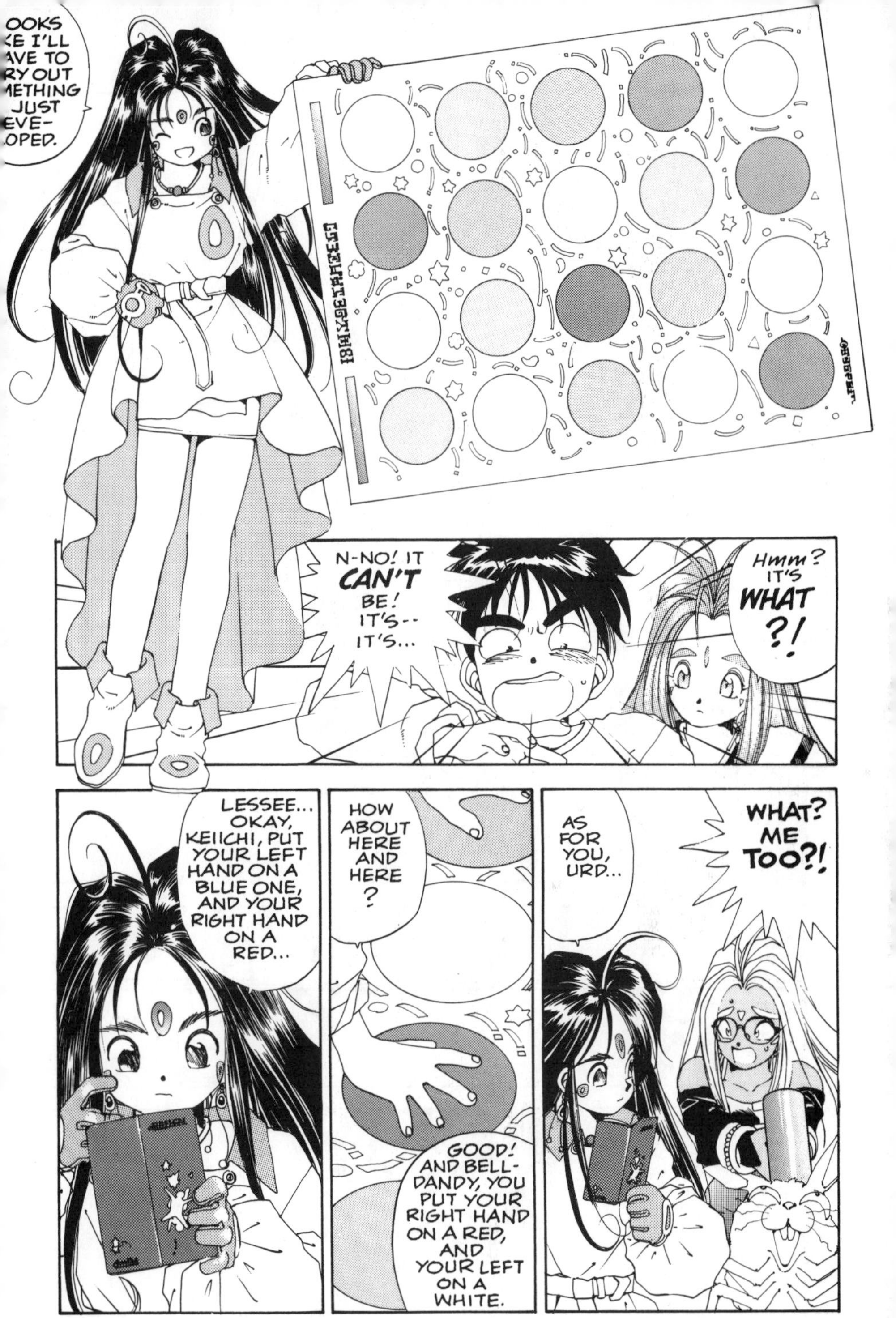

OOKS ᴇ I'LL AVE TO RY OUT METHING JUST EVE- OPED.
N-NO! IT CAN'T BE! IT'S-- IT'S...
Hmm? IT'S WHAT?!
LESSEE... OKAY, KEIICHI, PUT YOUR LEFT HAND ON A BLUE ONE, AND YOUR RIGHT HAND ON A RED...
HOW ABOUT HERE AND HERE?
GOOD! AND BELL-DANDY, YOU PUT YOUR RIGHT HAND ON A RED, AND YOUR LEFT ON A WHITE.
AS FOR YOU, URD...
WHAT? ME TOO?!

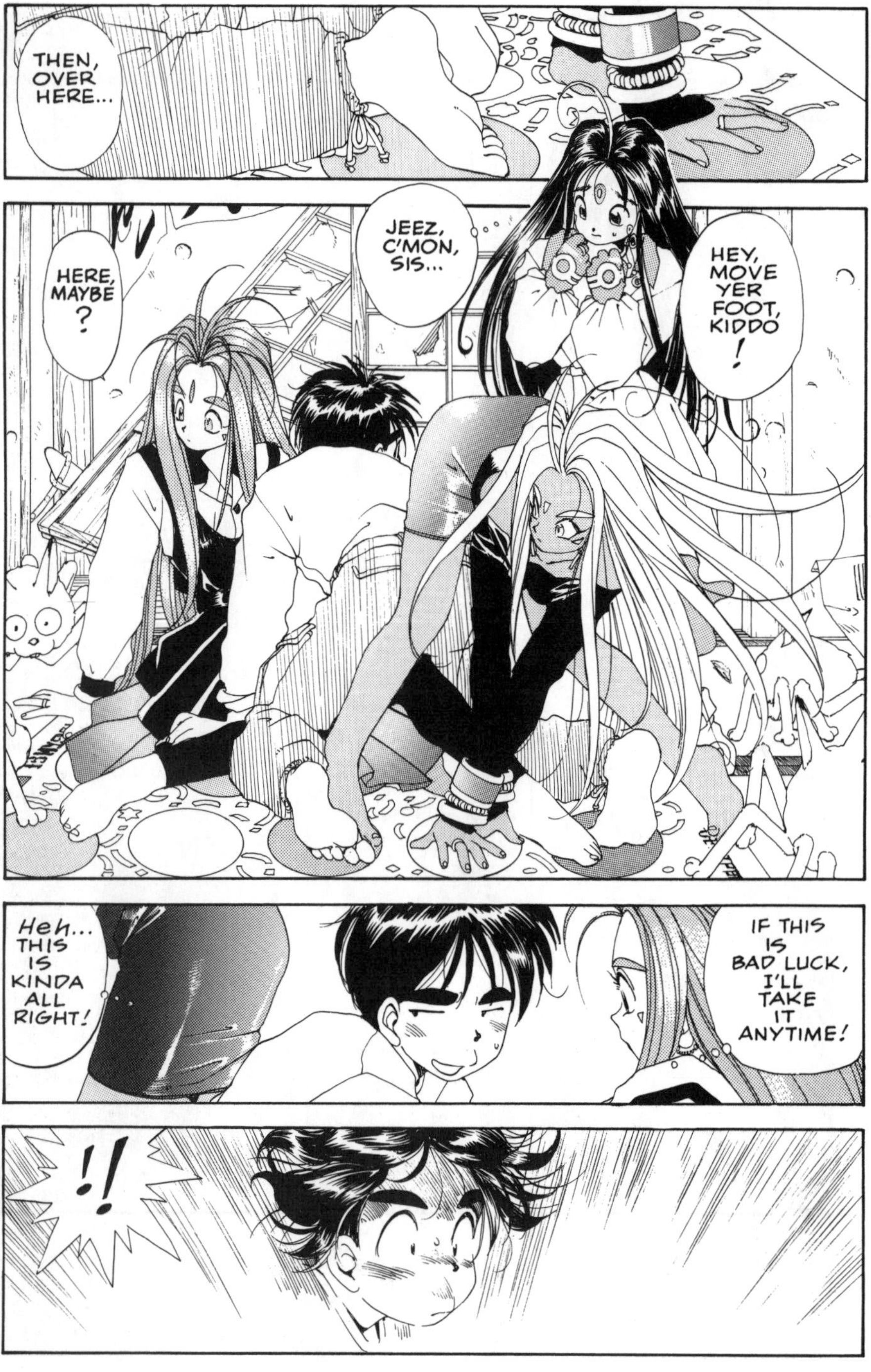
THEN, OVER HERE...
HERE, MAYBE ?
JEEZ, C'MON, SIS...
HEY, MOVE YER FOOT, KIDDO!
Heh... THIS IS KINDA ALL RIGHT!
IF THIS IS BAD LUCK, I'LL TAKE IT ANYTIME!
!!

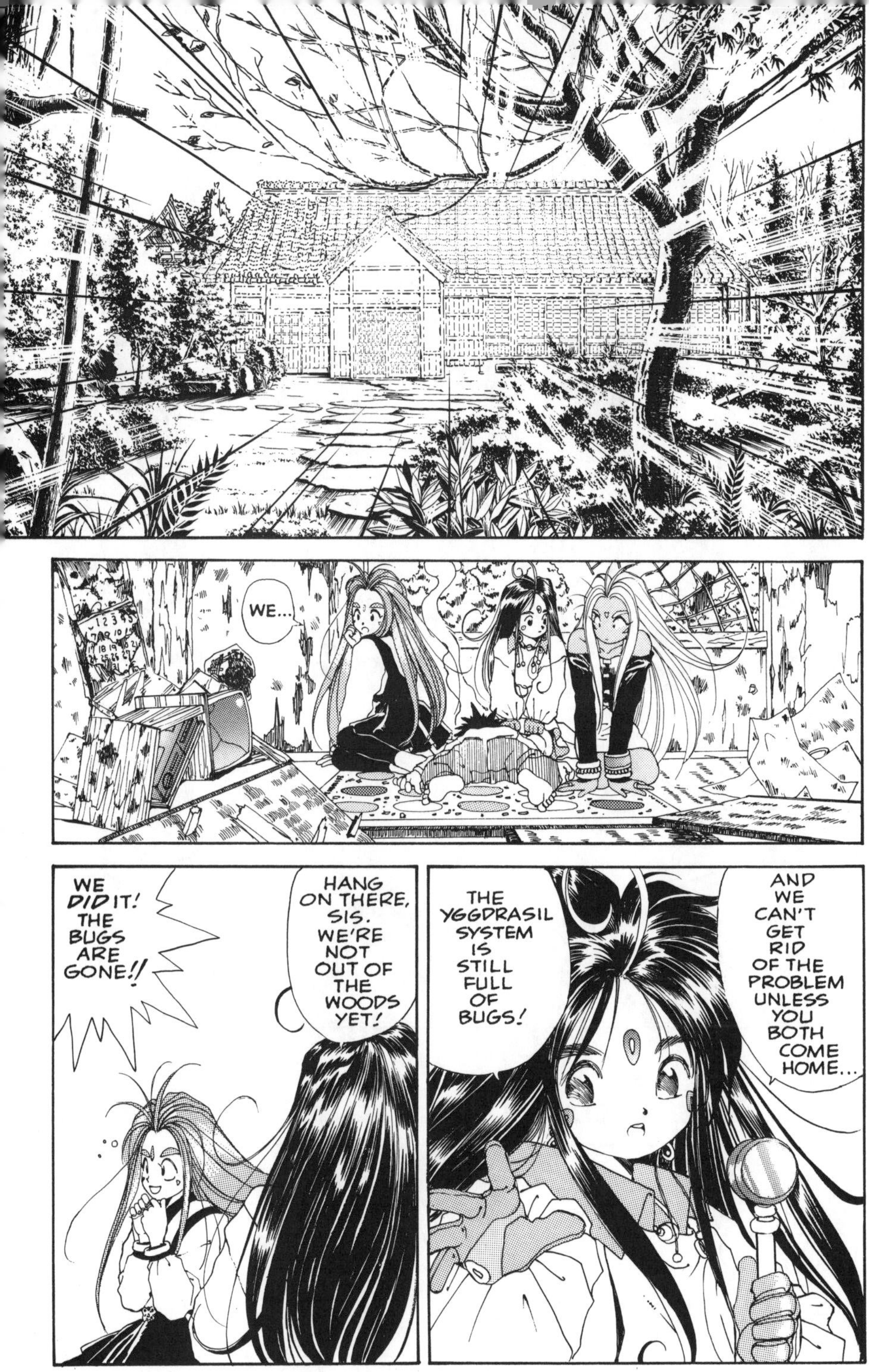
WE...
WE DID IT! THE BUGS ARE GONE!!
HANG ON THERE, SIS. WE'RE NOT OUT OF THE WOODS YET!
THE YGGDRASIL SYSTEM IS STILL FULL OF BUGS!
AND WE CAN'T GET RID OF THE PROBLEM UNLESS YOU BOTH COME HOME...

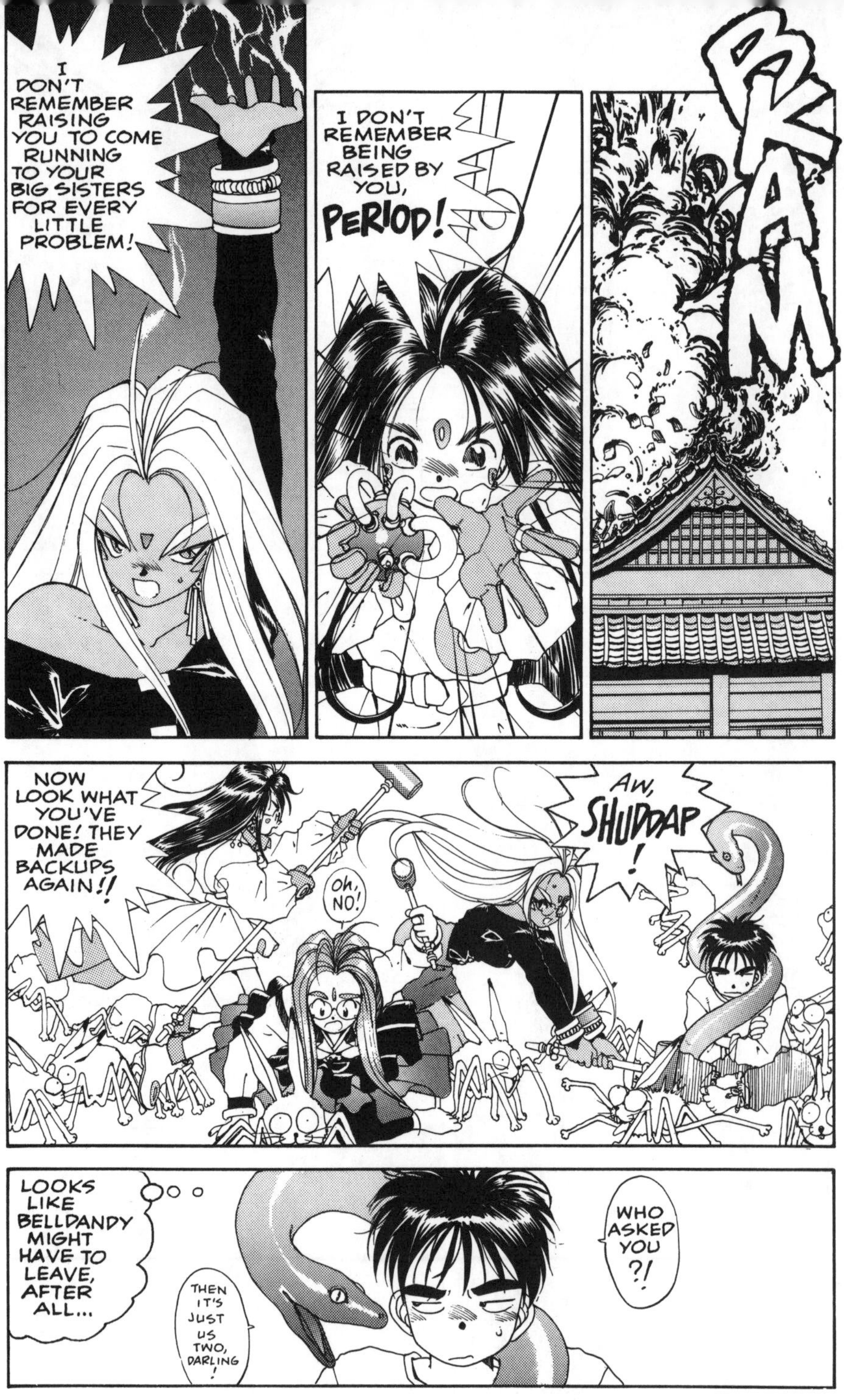
I DON'T REMEMBER RAISING YOU TO COME RUNNING TO YOUR BIG SISTERS FOR EVERY LITTLE PROBLEM!
I DON'T REMEMBER BEING RAISED BY YOU, PERIOD!
BLAM
NOW LOOK WHAT YOU'VE DONE! THEY MADE BACKUPS AGAIN!!
Oh, NO!
AW, SHUDDAP!
LOOKS LIKE BELLDANDY MIGHT HAVE TO LEAVE, AFTER ALL...
THEN IT'S JUST US TWO, DARLING!
WHO ASKED YOU?!

The Goddesses' Big Crisis

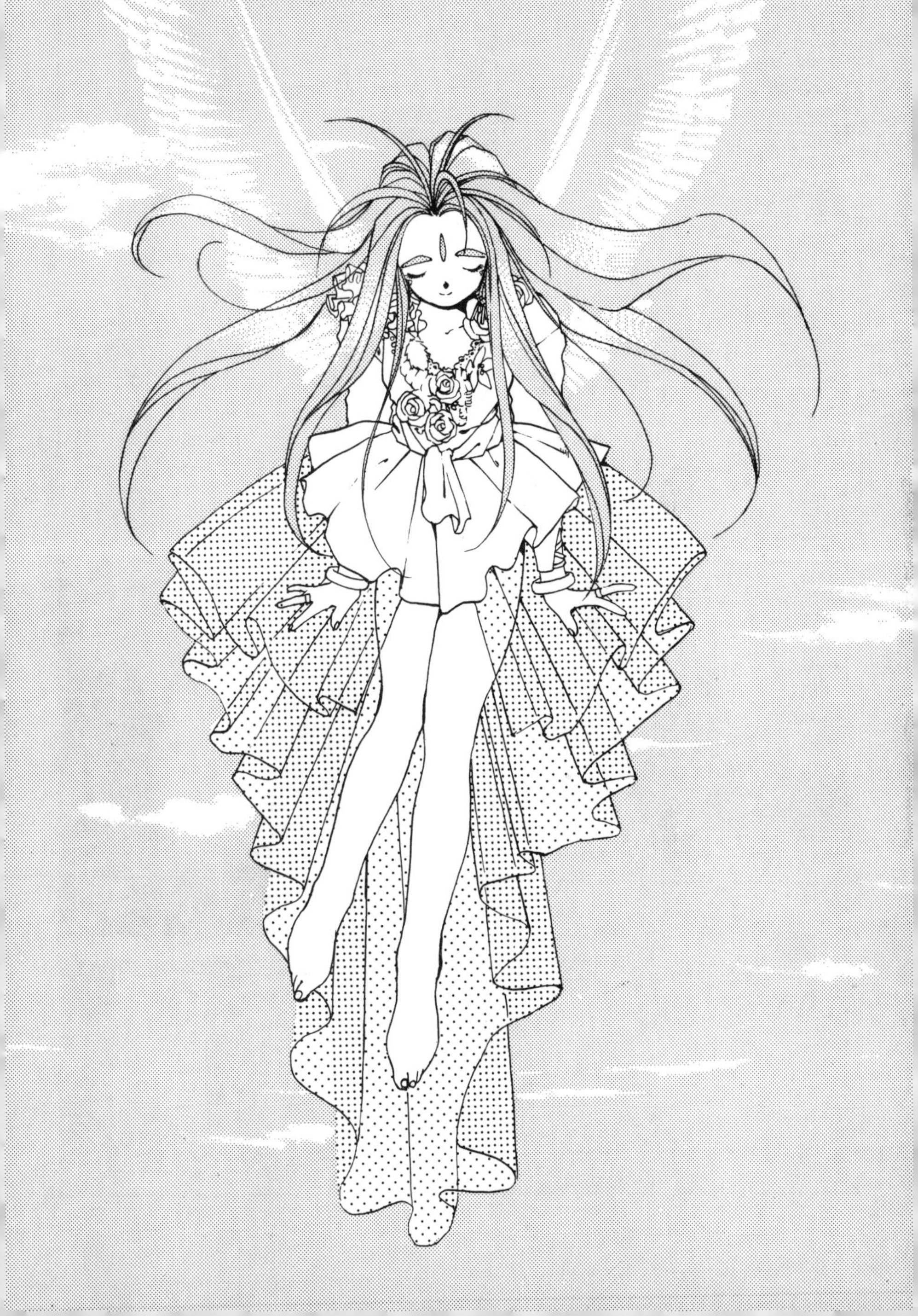

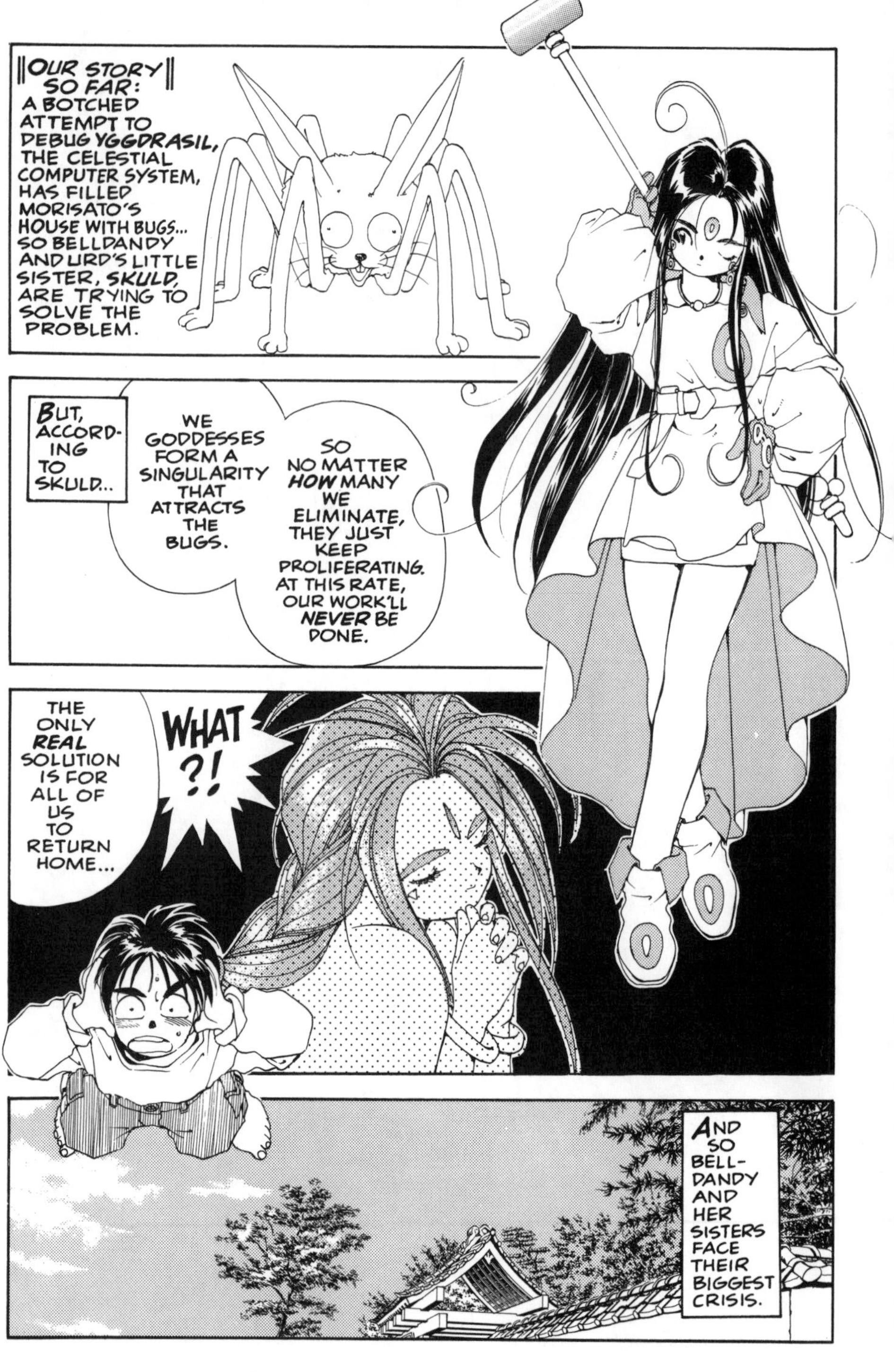
OUR STORY SO FAR: A BOTCHED ATTEMPT TO DEBUG YGGDRASIL, THE CELESTIAL COMPUTER SYSTEM, HAS FILLED MORISATO'S HOUSE WITH BUGS... SO BELLDANDY AND URD'S LITTLE SISTER, SKULD, ARE TRYING TO SOLVE THE PROBLEM.
BUT, ACCORDING TO SKULD...
WE GODDESSES FORM A SINGULARITY THAT ATTRACTS THE BUGS.
SO NO MATTER HOW MANY WE ELIMINATE, THEY JUST KEEP PROLIFERATING. AT THIS RATE, OUR WORK'LL NEVER BE DONE.
THE ONLY REAL SOLUTION IS FOR ALL OF US TO RETURN HOME...
WHAT ?!
AND SO BELLDANDY AND HER SISTERS FACE THEIR BIGGEST CRISIS.

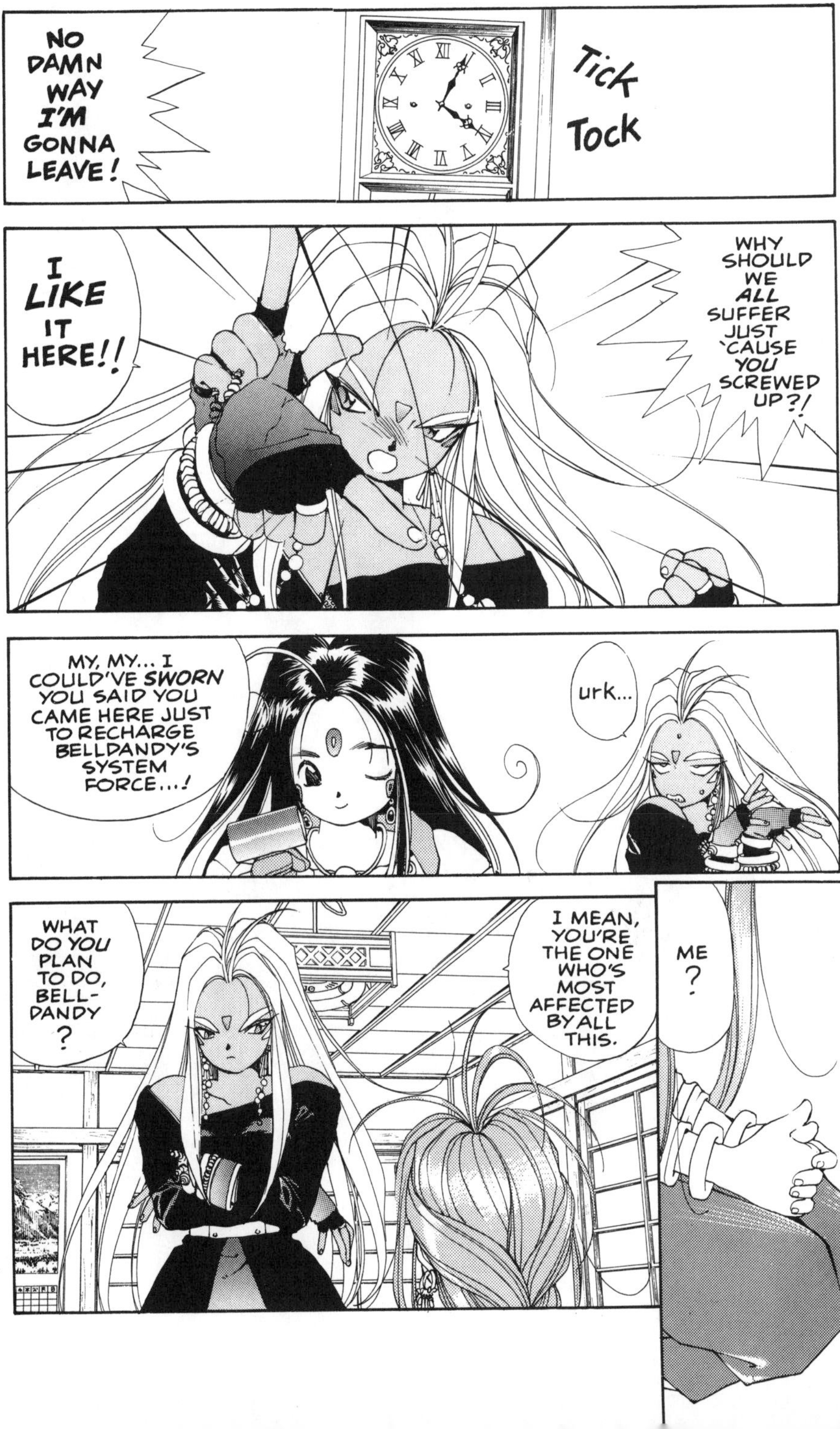
NO DAMN WAY I'M GONNA LEAVE!
Tick
Tock
I LIKE IT HERE!!
WHY SHOULD WE ALL SUFFER JUST 'CAUSE YOU SCREWED UP?!
MY, MY... I COULD'VE SWORN YOU SAID YOU CAME HERE JUST TO RECHARGE BELLDANDY'S SYSTEM FORCE...!
urk...
WHAT DO YOU PLAN TO DO, BELL-DANDY?
I MEAN, YOU'RE THE ONE WHO'S MOST AFFECTED BY ALL THIS.
ME?

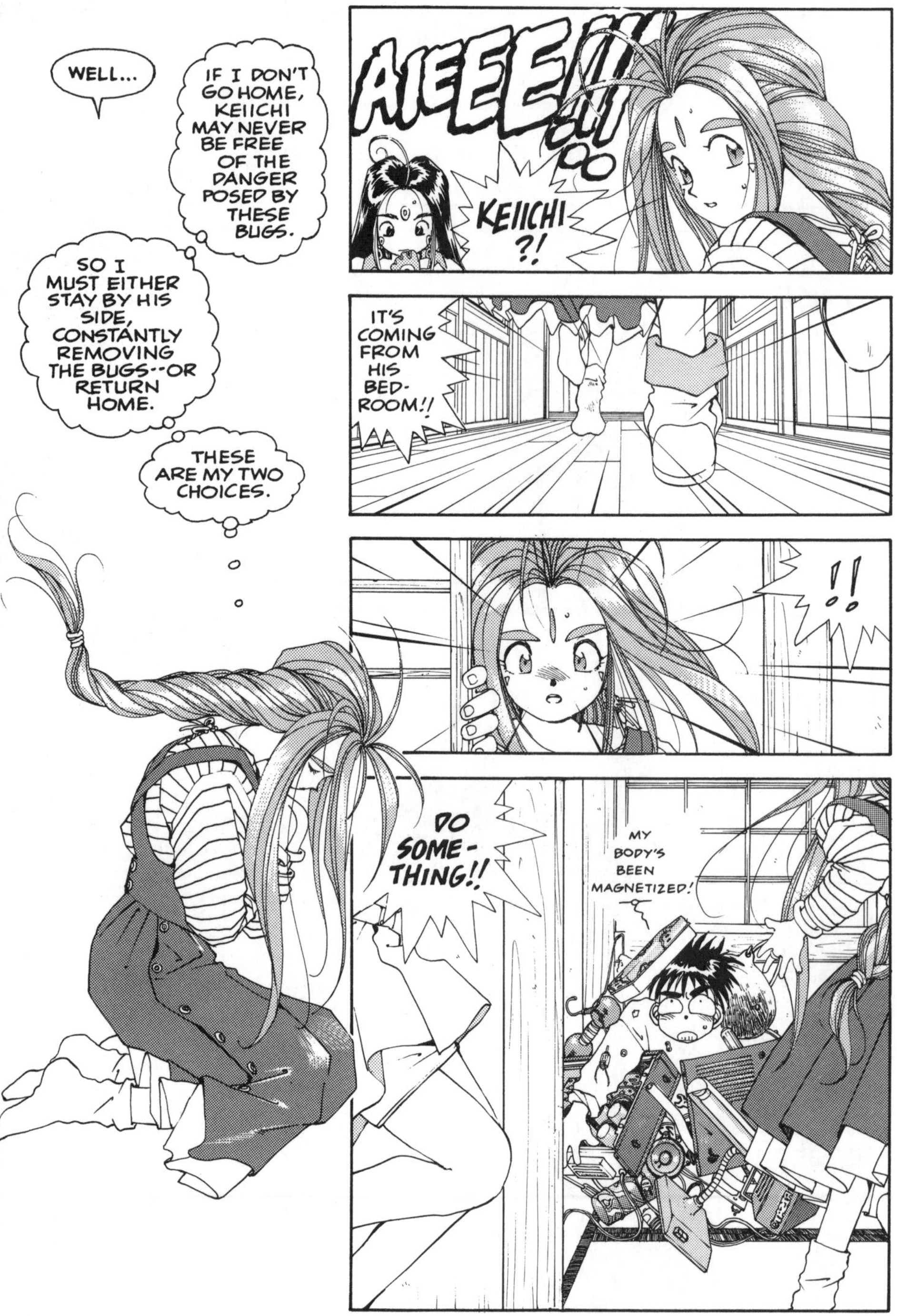
WELL...
IF I DON'T GO HOME, KEIICHI MAY NEVER BE FREE OF THE DANGER POSED BY THESE BUGS.
SO I MUST EITHER STAY BY HIS SIDE, CONSTANTLY REMOVING THE BUGS--OR RETURN HOME.
THESE ARE MY TWO CHOICES.
AIEEE!!!
KEIICHI?!
IT'S COMING FROM HIS BED-ROOM!!
!!
DO SOME-THING!!
MY BODY'S BEEN MAGNETIZED!

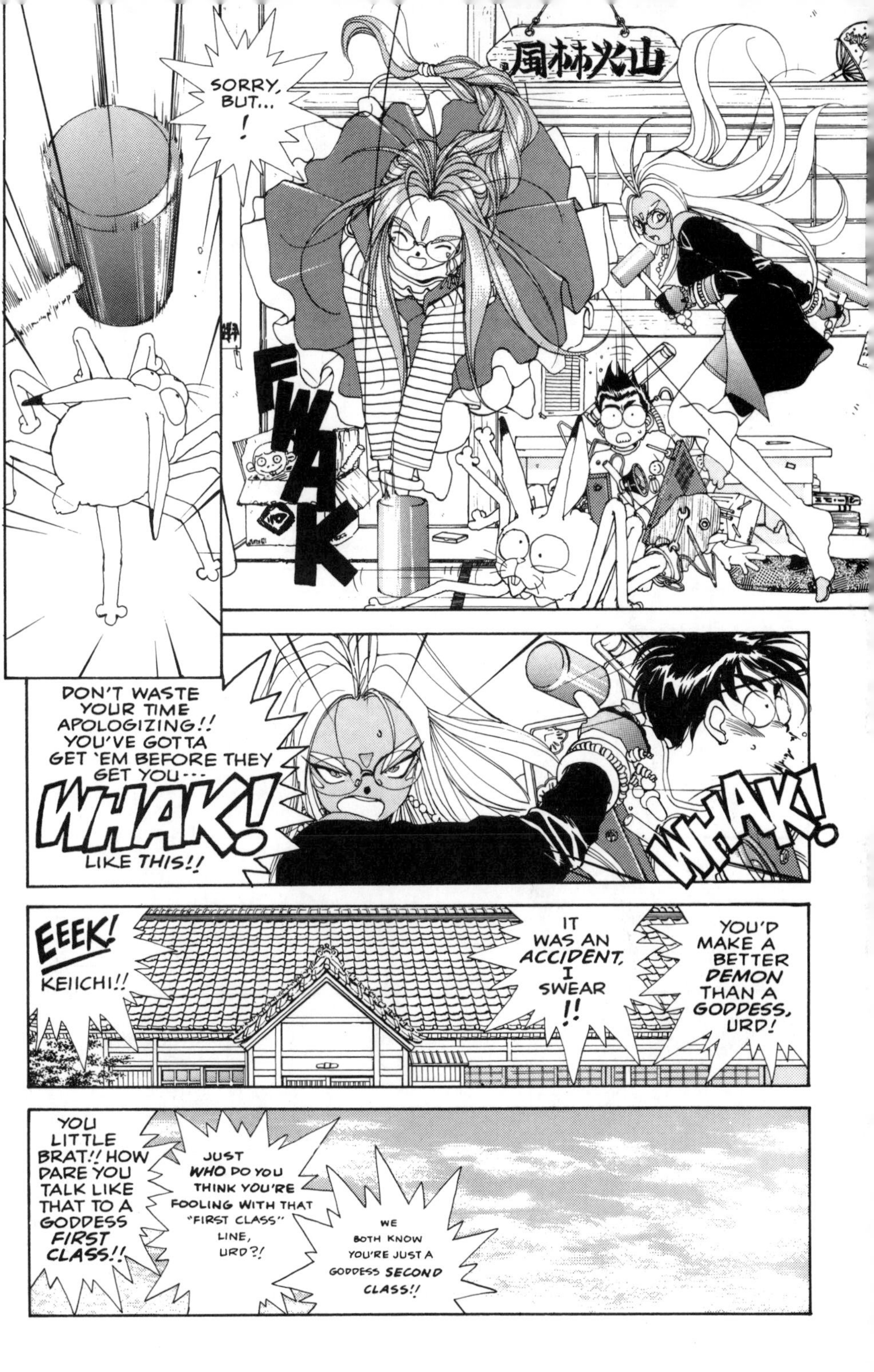

SORRY, BUT... !
FWAK
DON'T WASTE YOUR TIME APOLOGIZING!! YOU'VE GOTTA GET 'EM BEFORE THEY GET YOU---
WHAK!
LIKE THIS!!
WHAK!
EEEK!
KEIICHI!!
IT WAS AN ACCIDENT, I SWEAR !!
YOU'D MAKE A BETTER DEMON THAN A GODDESS, URD!
YOU LITTLE BRAT!! HOW DARE YOU TALK LIKE THAT TO A GODDESS FIRST CLASS!!
JUST WHO DO YOU THINK YOU'RE FOOLING WITH THAT "FIRST CLASS" LINE, URD?!
WE BOTH KNOW YOU'RE JUST A GODDESS SECOND CLASS!!

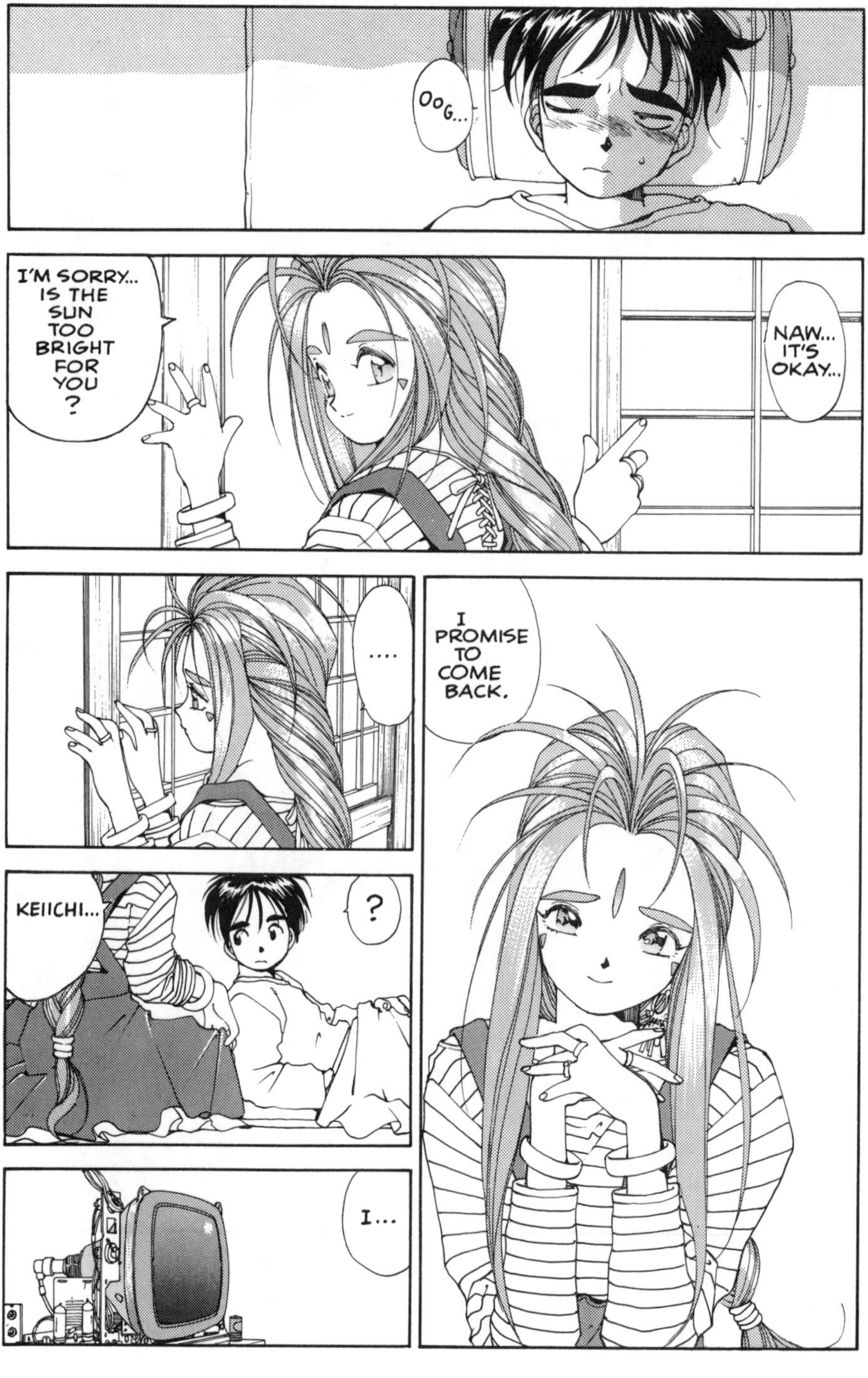
OOG...
I'M SORRY... IS THE SUN TOO BRIGHT FOR YOU?
NAW... IT'S OKAY...
....
KEIICHI...
?
I...
I PROMISE TO COME BACK.

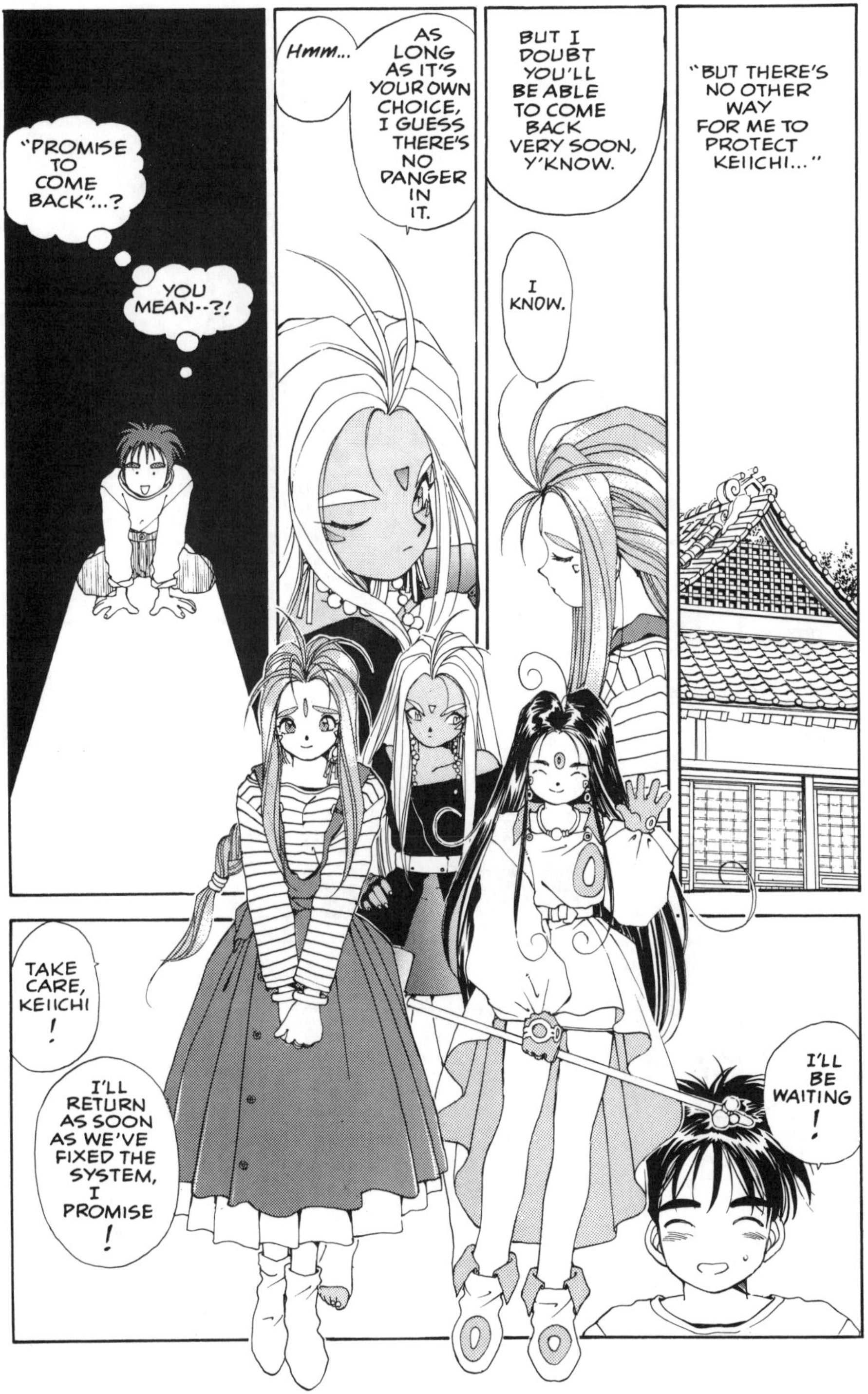
"PROMISE TO COME BACK"...?
YOU MEAN--?!
Hmm...
AS LONG AS IT'S YOUR OWN CHOICE, I GUESS THERE'S NO DANGER IN IT.
BUT I DOUBT YOU'LL BE ABLE TO COME BACK VERY SOON, Y'KNOW.
I KNOW.
"BUT THERE'S NO OTHER WAY FOR ME TO PROTECT KEIICHI..."
TAKE CARE, KEIICHI!
I'LL RETURN AS SOON AS WE'VE FIXED THE SYSTEM, I PROMISE!
I'LL BE WAITING!

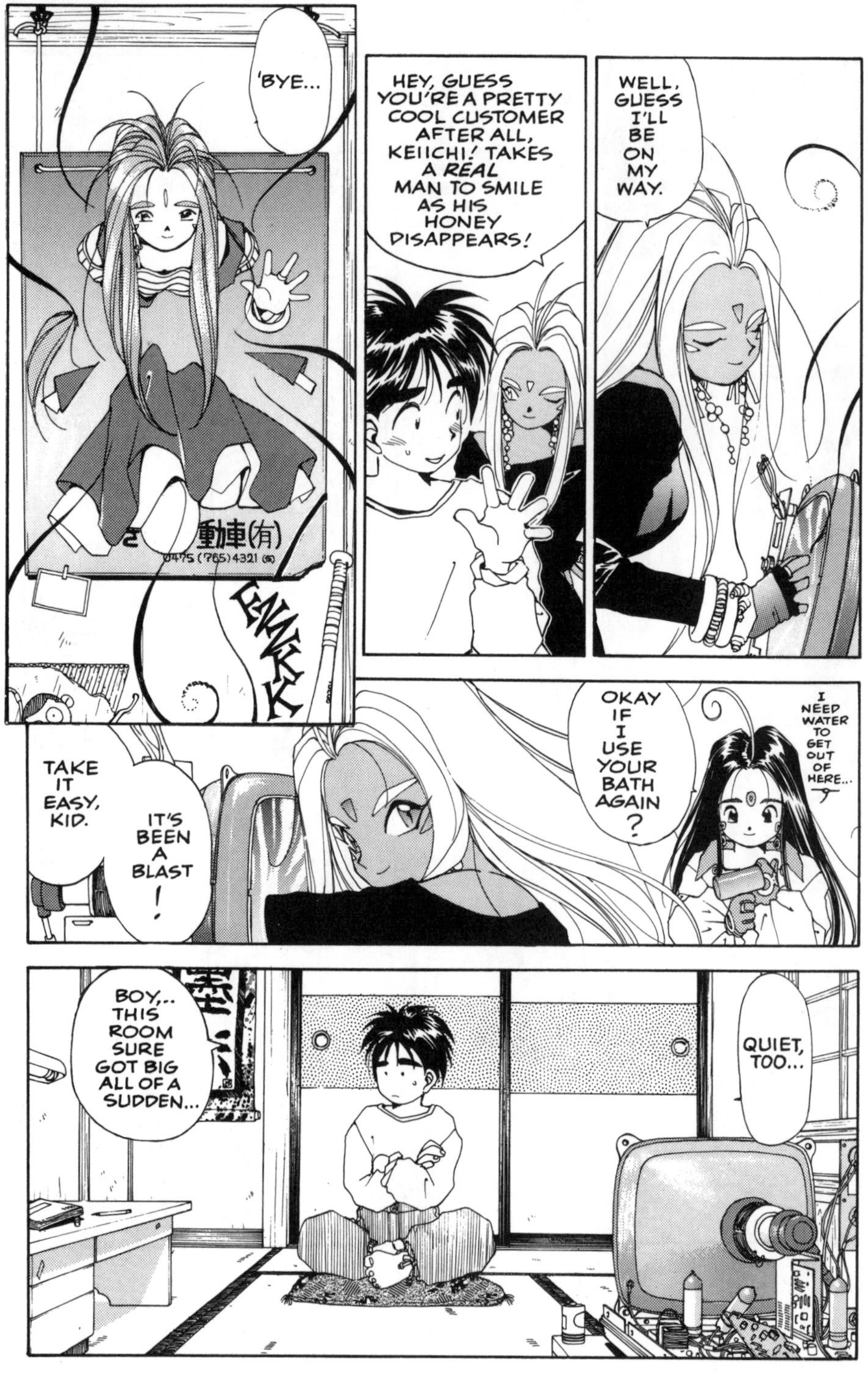
'BYE...
HEY, GUESS YOU'RE A PRETTY COOL CUSTOMER AFTER ALL, KEIICHI! TAKES A *REAL* MAN TO SMILE AS HIS HONEY DISAPPEARS!
WELL, GUESS I'LL BE ON MY WAY.
TAKE IT EASY, KID.
IT'S BEEN A BLAST!
OKAY IF I USE YOUR BATH AGAIN?
I NEED WATER TO GET OUT OF HERE...
BOY,.. THIS ROOM SURE GOT BIG ALL OF A SUDDEN...
QUIET, TOO...

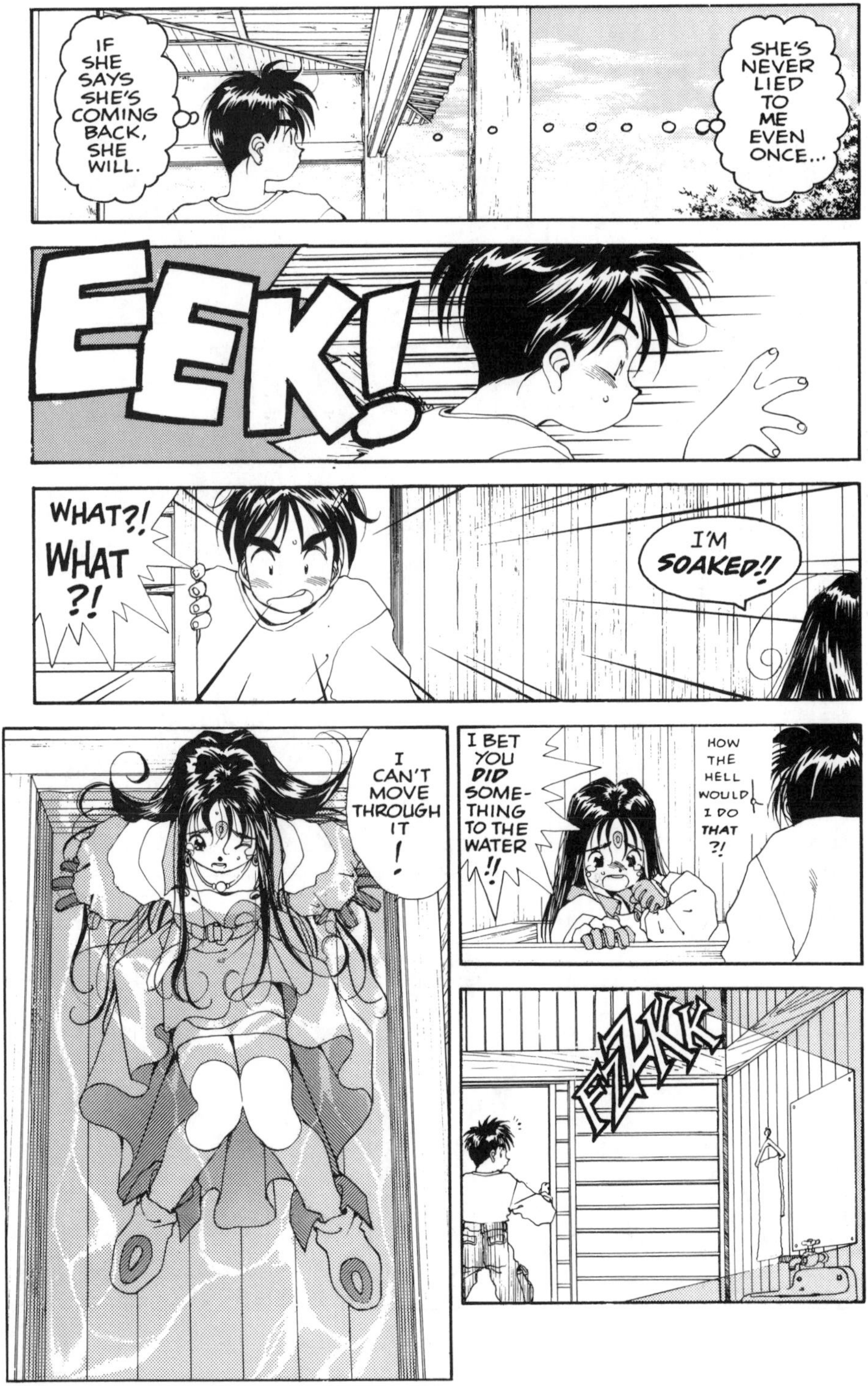
IF SHE SAYS SHE'S COMING BACK, SHE WILL.
SHE'S NEVER LIED TO ME EVEN ONCE...
EEK!
WHAT?! WHAT ?!
I'M SOAKED!!
I CAN'T MOVE THROUGH IT !
I BET YOU DID SOMETHING TO THE WATER !!
HOW THE HELL WOULD I DO THAT ?!
FZZKK

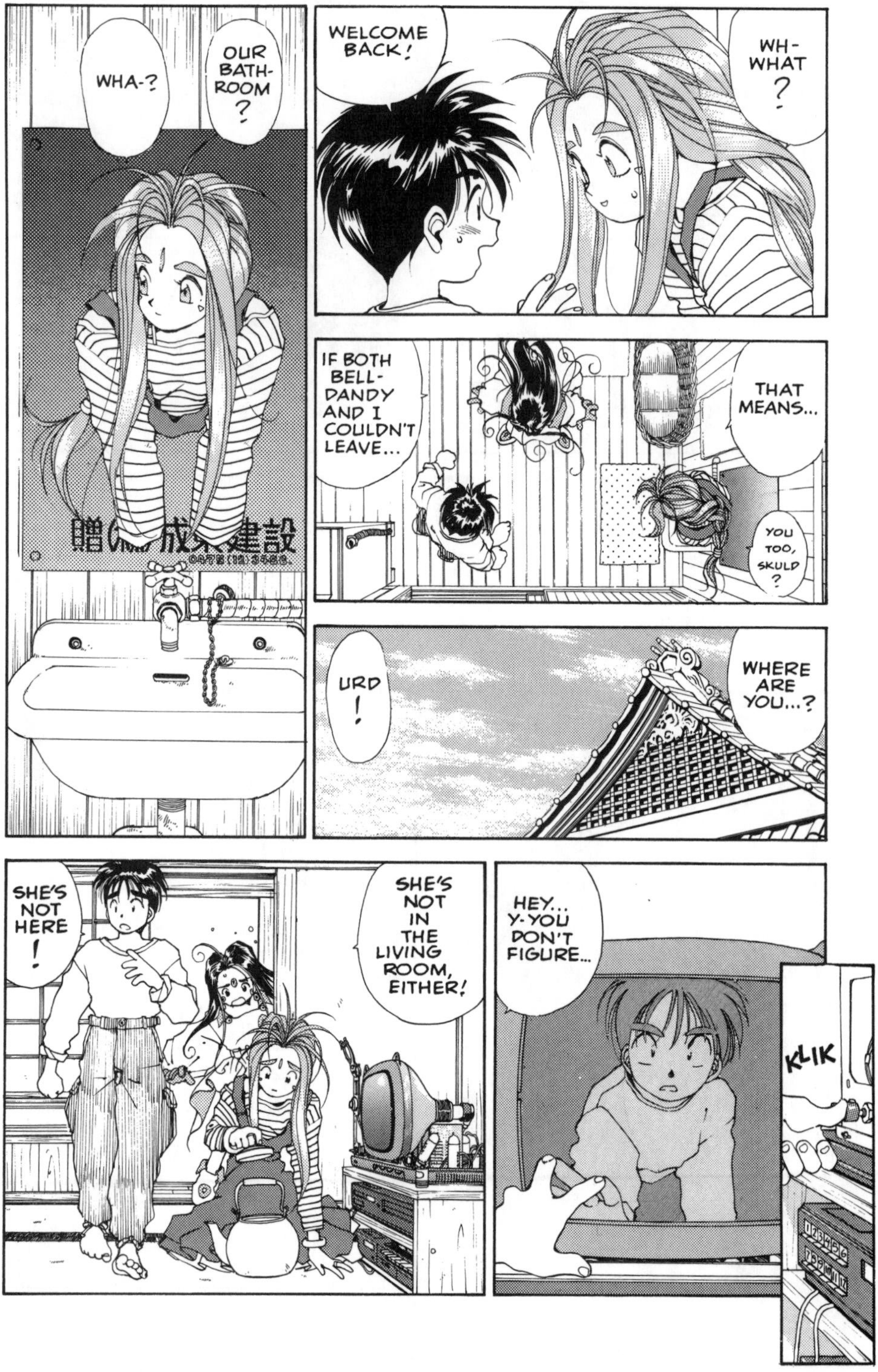
WHA-?
OUR BATH-ROOM?
WELCOME BACK!
WH-WHAT?
IF BOTH BELL-DANDY AND I COULDN'T LEAVE...
THAT MEANS...
YOU TOO, SKULD?
URD!
WHERE ARE YOU...?
SHE'S NOT HERE!
SHE'S NOT IN THE LIVING ROOM, EITHER!
HEY... Y-YOU DON'T FIGURE...
KLIK

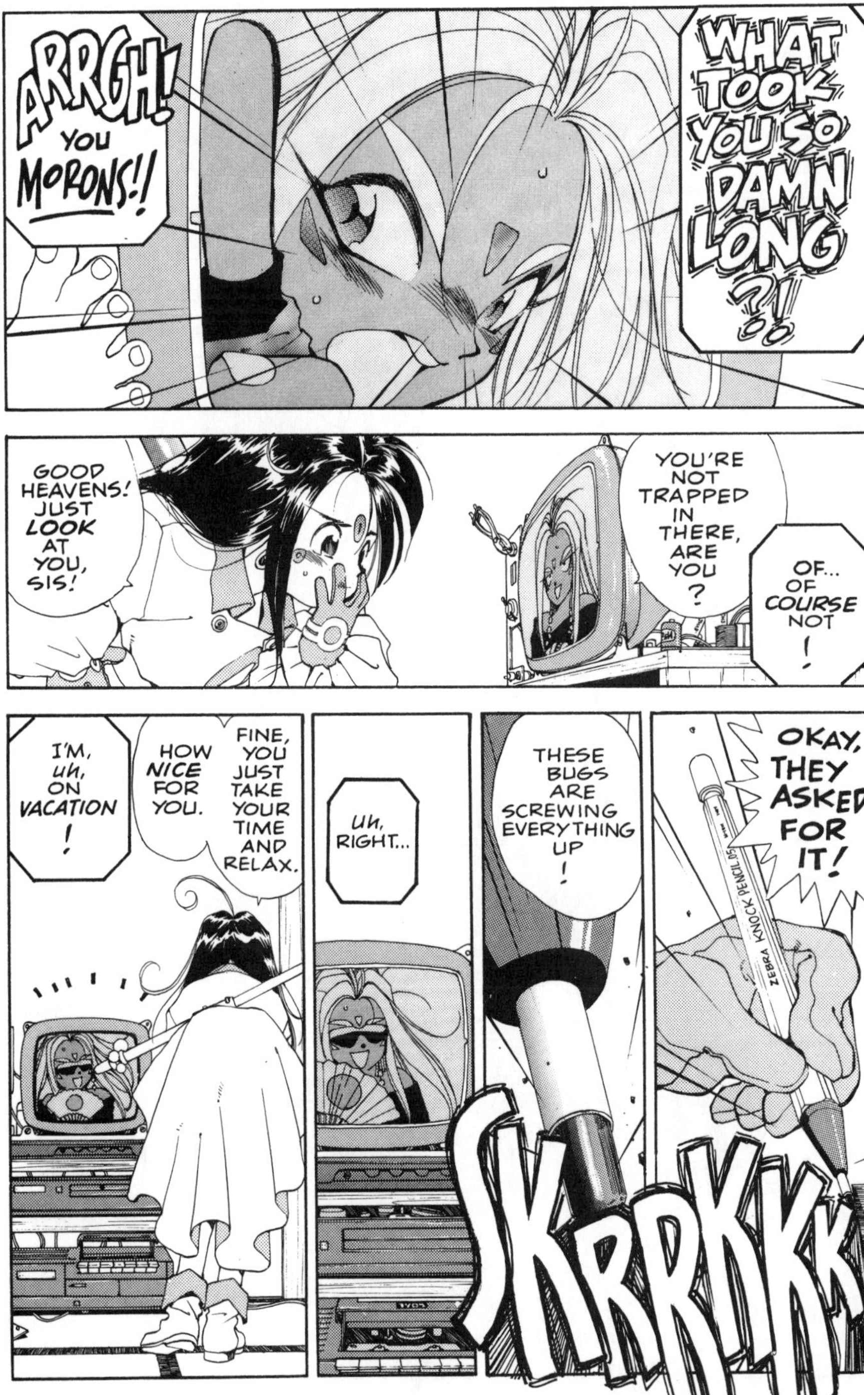
ARRGH! YOU MORONS!!
WHAT TOOK YOU SO DAMN LONG ?!
GOOD HEAVENS! JUST LOOK AT YOU, SIS!
YOU'RE NOT TRAPPED IN THERE, ARE YOU ?
OF... OF COURSE NOT !
I'M, uh, ON VACATION !
HOW NICE FOR YOU.
FINE, YOU JUST TAKE YOUR TIME AND RELAX.
uh, RIGHT...
THESE BUGS ARE SCREWING EVERYTHING UP !
OKAY, THEY ASKED FOR IT!
ZEBRA KNOCK PENCIL 05
SKRRKKK

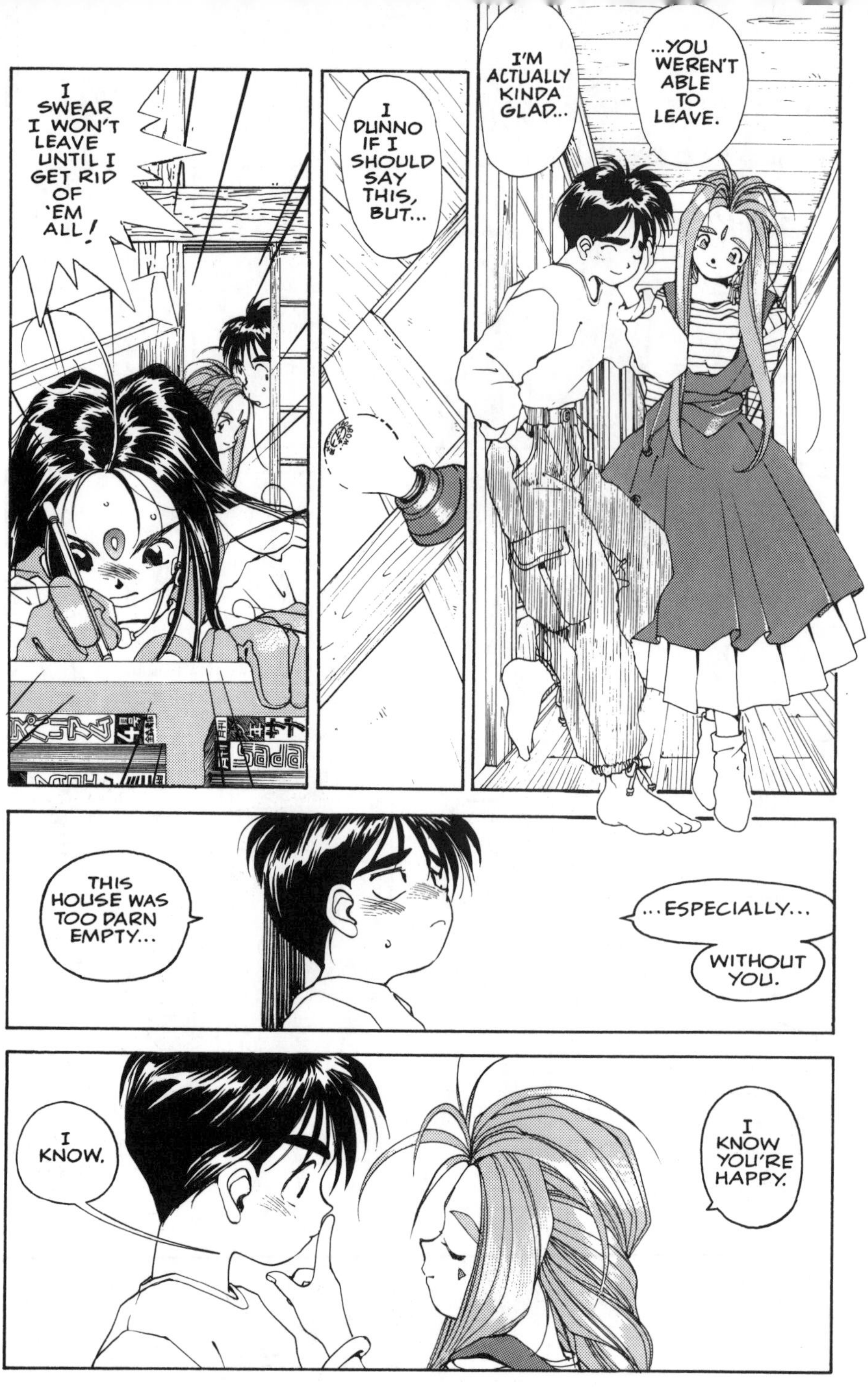
I SWEAR I WON'T LEAVE UNTIL I GET RID OF 'EM ALL!
I DUNNO IF I SHOULD SAY THIS, BUT...
I'M ACTUALLY KINDA GLAD...
...YOU WEREN'T ABLE TO LEAVE.
THIS HOUSE WAS TOO DARN EMPTY...
...ESPECIALLY...
WITHOUT YOU.
I KNOW.
I KNOW YOU'RE HAPPY.

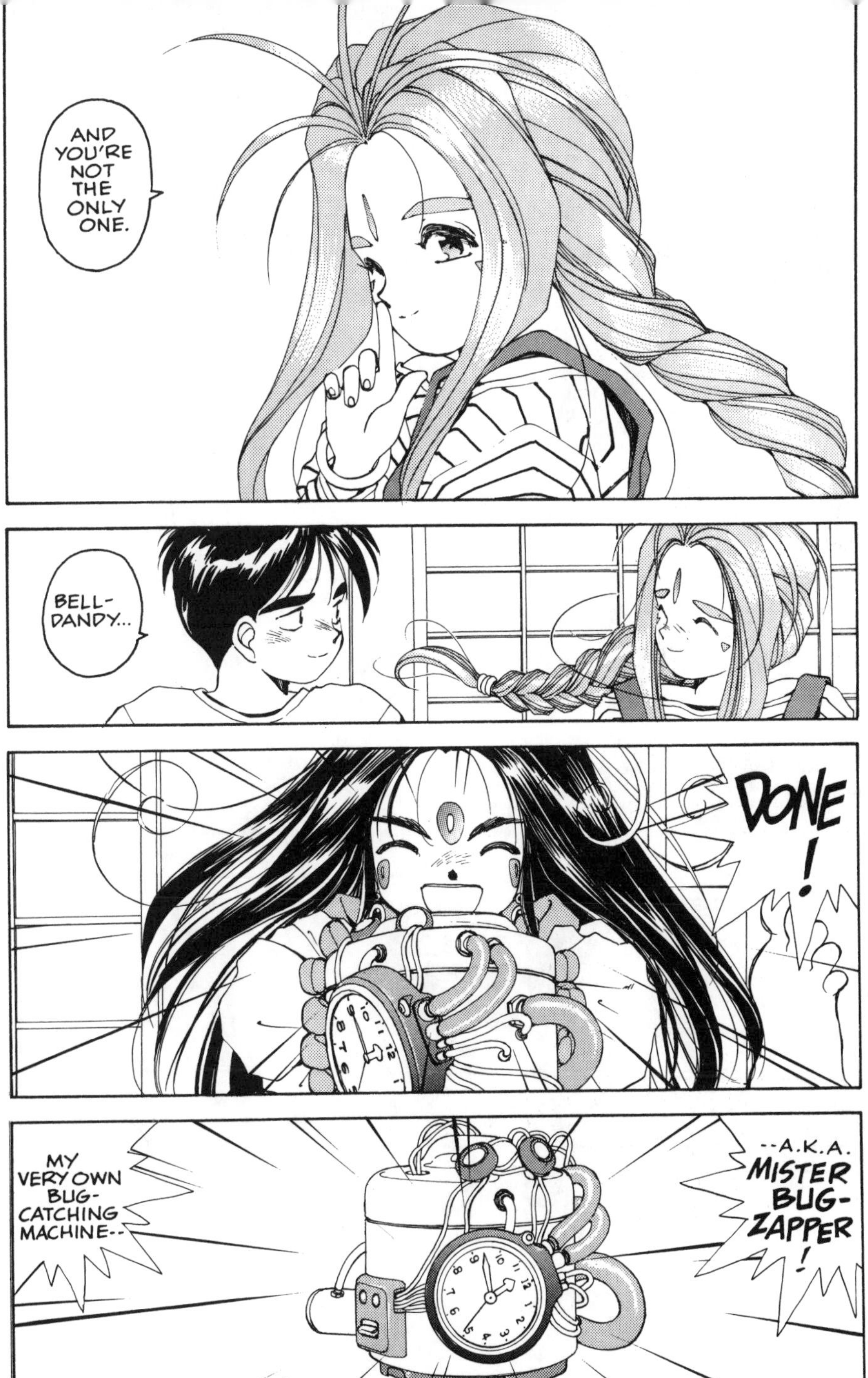
AND YOU'RE NOT THE ONLY ONE.
BELL-DANDY...
DONE!
MY VERY OWN BUG-CATCHING MACHINE--
--A.K.A. MISTER BUG-ZAPPER!

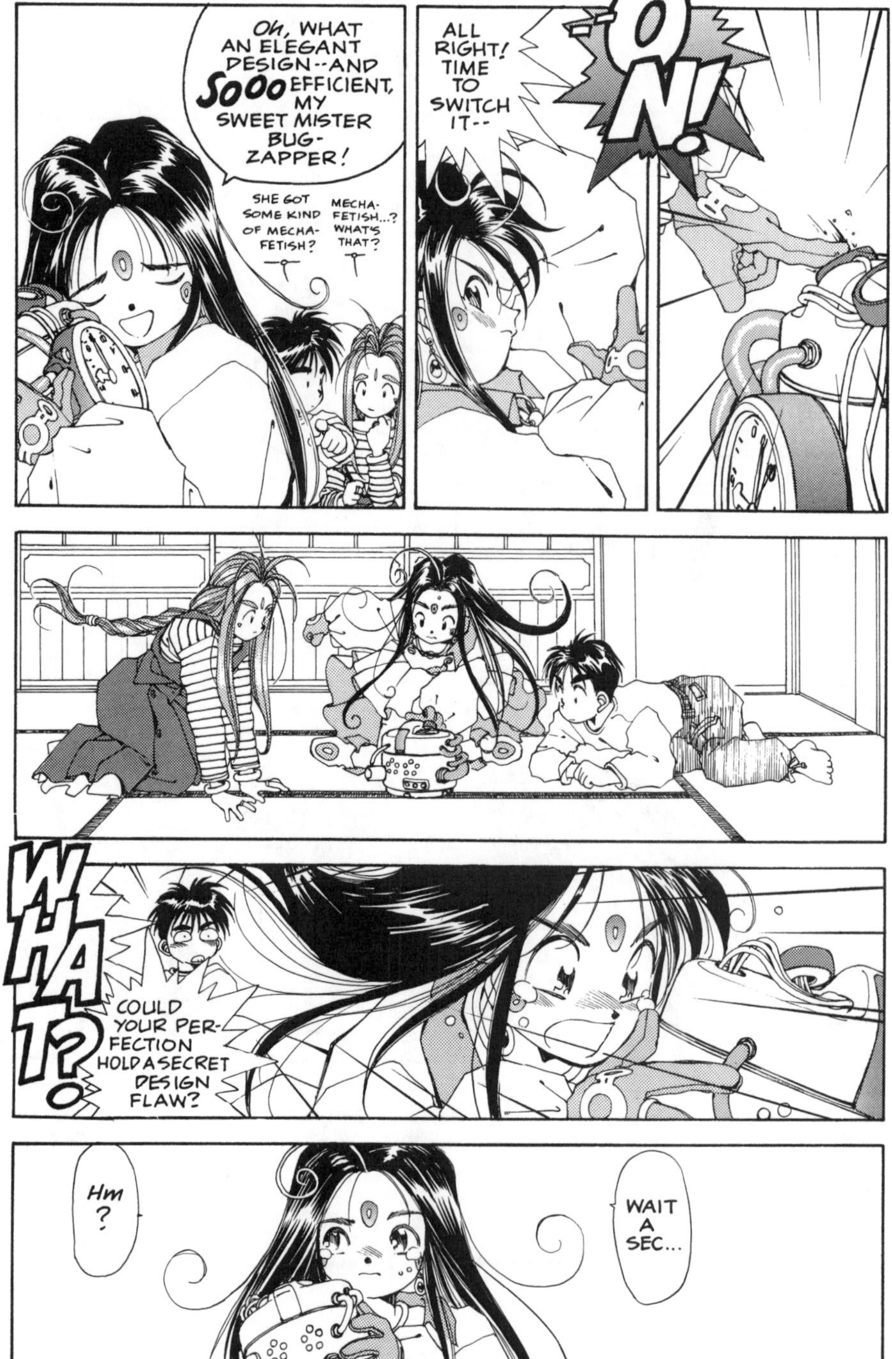

OH, WHAT AN ELEGANT DESIGN--AND SOOO EFFICIENT, MY SWEET MISTER BUG-ZAPPER!
SHE GOT SOME KIND OF MECHA-FETISH?
MECHA-FETISH...? WHAT'S THAT?
ALL RIGHT! TIME TO SWITCH IT--
--ON!
WHAT?
COULD YOUR PERFECTION HOLD A SECRET DESIGN FLAW?
Hm?
WAIT A SEC...

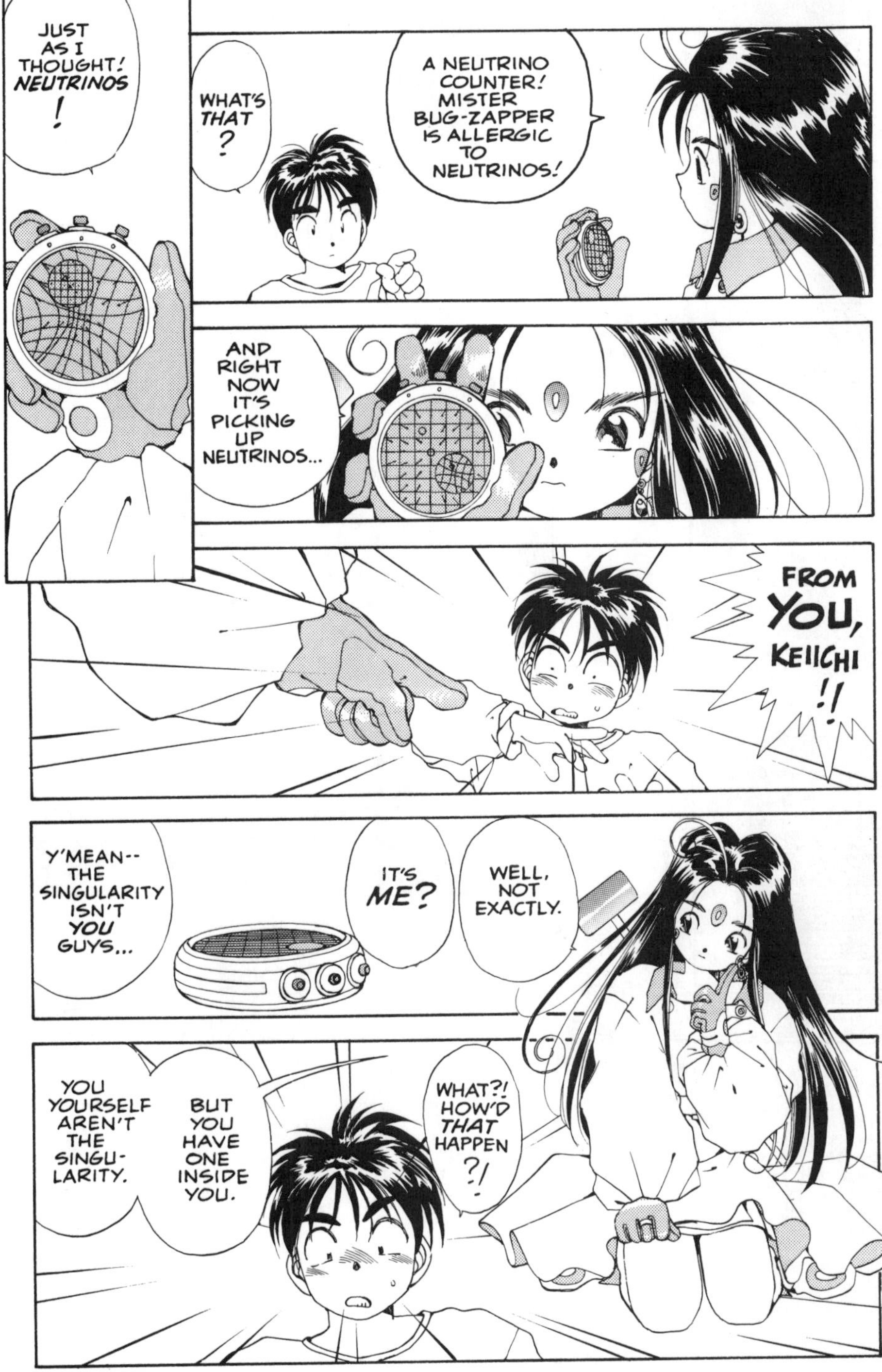
JUST AS I THOUGHT! NEUTRINOS!
WHAT'S THAT?
A NEUTRINO COUNTER! MISTER BUG-ZAPPER IS ALLERGIC TO NEUTRINOS!
AND RIGHT NOW IT'S PICKING UP NEUTRINOS...
FROM YOU, KEIICHI!!
Y'MEAN-- THE SINGULARITY ISN'T YOU GUYS...
IT'S ME?
WELL, NOT EXACTLY.
YOU YOURSELF AREN'T THE SINGU-LARITY.
BUT YOU HAVE ONE INSIDE YOU.
WHAT?! HOW'D THAT HAPPEN?!

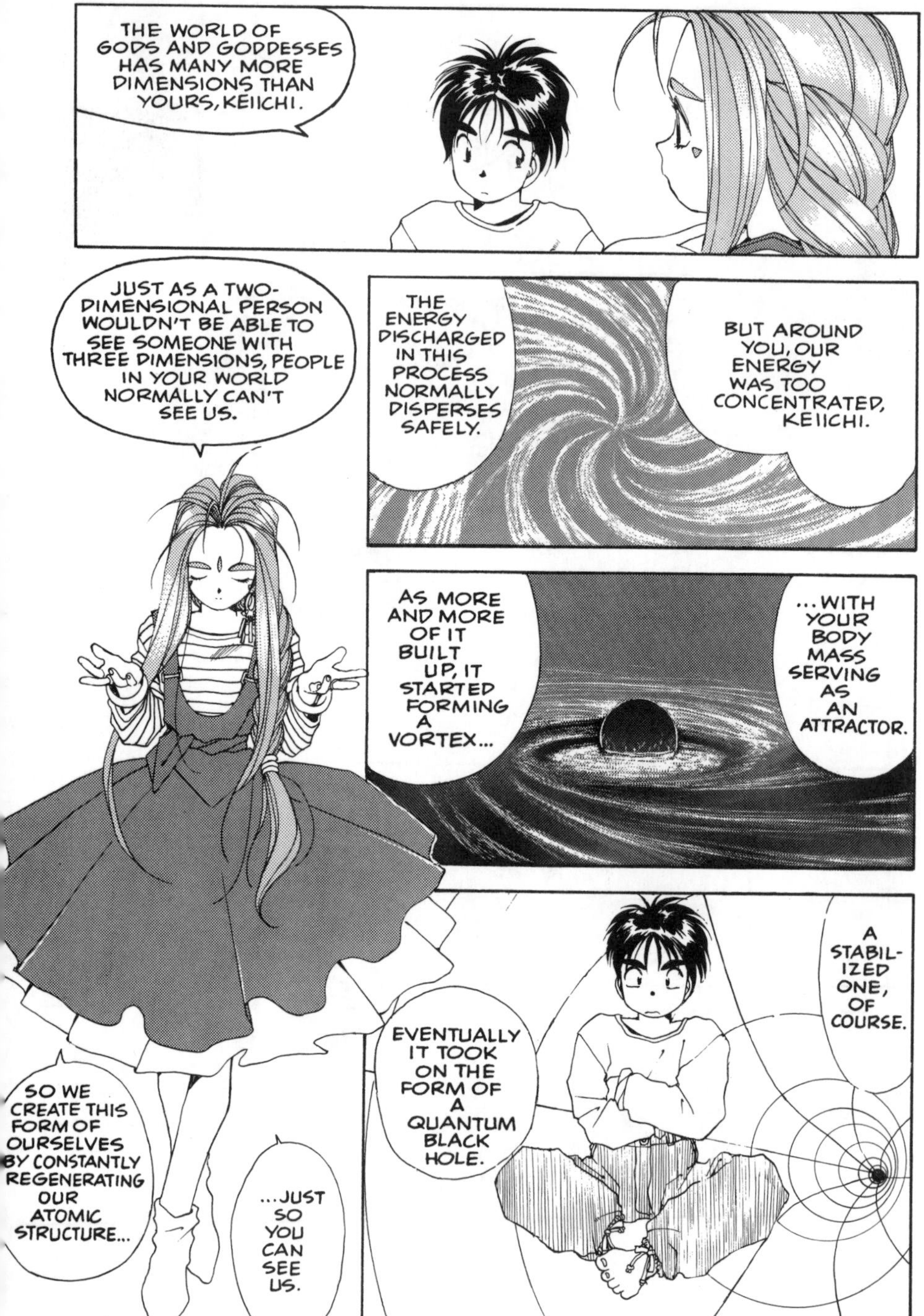
THE WORLD OF GODS AND GODDESSES HAS MANY MORE DIMENSIONS THAN YOURS, KEIICHI.
JUST AS A TWO-DIMENSIONAL PERSON WOULDN'T BE ABLE TO SEE SOMEONE WITH THREE DIMENSIONS, PEOPLE IN YOUR WORLD NORMALLY CAN'T SEE US.
SO WE CREATE THIS FORM OF OURSELVES BY CONSTANTLY REGENERATING OUR ATOMIC STRUCTURE...
...JUST SO YOU CAN SEE US.
THE ENERGY DISCHARGED IN THIS PROCESS NORMALLY DISPERSES SAFELY.
BUT AROUND YOU, OUR ENERGY WAS TOO CONCENTRATED, KEIICHI.
AS MORE AND MORE OF IT BUILT UP, IT STARTED FORMING A VORTEX...
...WITH YOUR BODY MASS SERVING AS AN ATTRACTOR.
EVENTUALLY IT TOOK ON THE FORM OF A QUANTUM BLACK HOLE.
A STABIL-IZED ONE, OF COURSE.

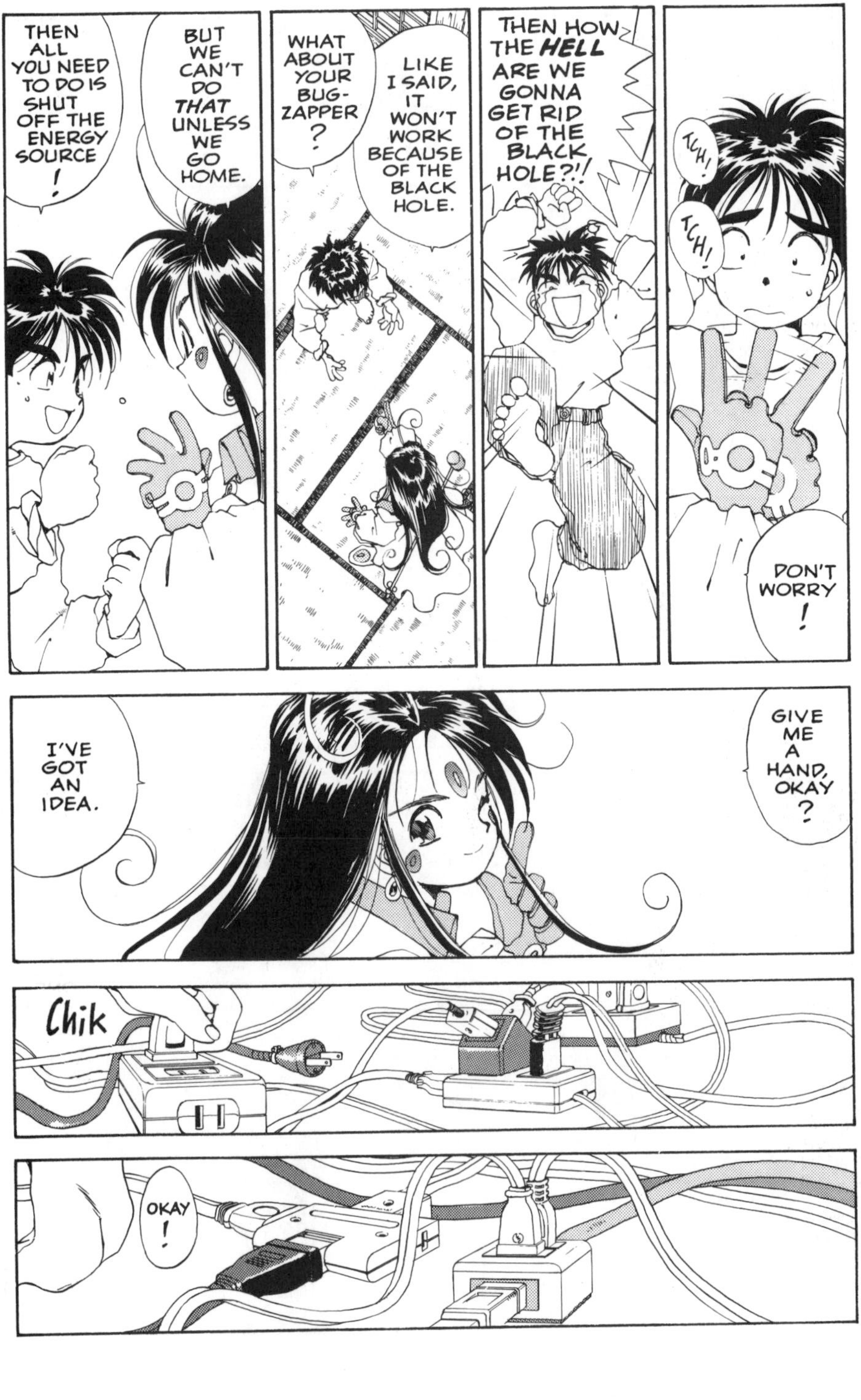
THEN ALL YOU NEED TO DO IS SHUT OFF THE ENERGY SOURCE!
BUT WE CAN'T DO THAT UNLESS WE GO HOME.
WHAT ABOUT YOUR BUG-ZAPPER?
LIKE I SAID, IT WON'T WORK BECAUSE OF THE BLACK HOLE.
THEN HOW THE HELL ARE WE GONNA GET RID OF THE BLACK HOLE?!!
TCH!
TCH!
DON'T WORRY!
I'VE GOT AN IDEA.
GIVE ME A HAND, OKAY?
Chik
OKAY!

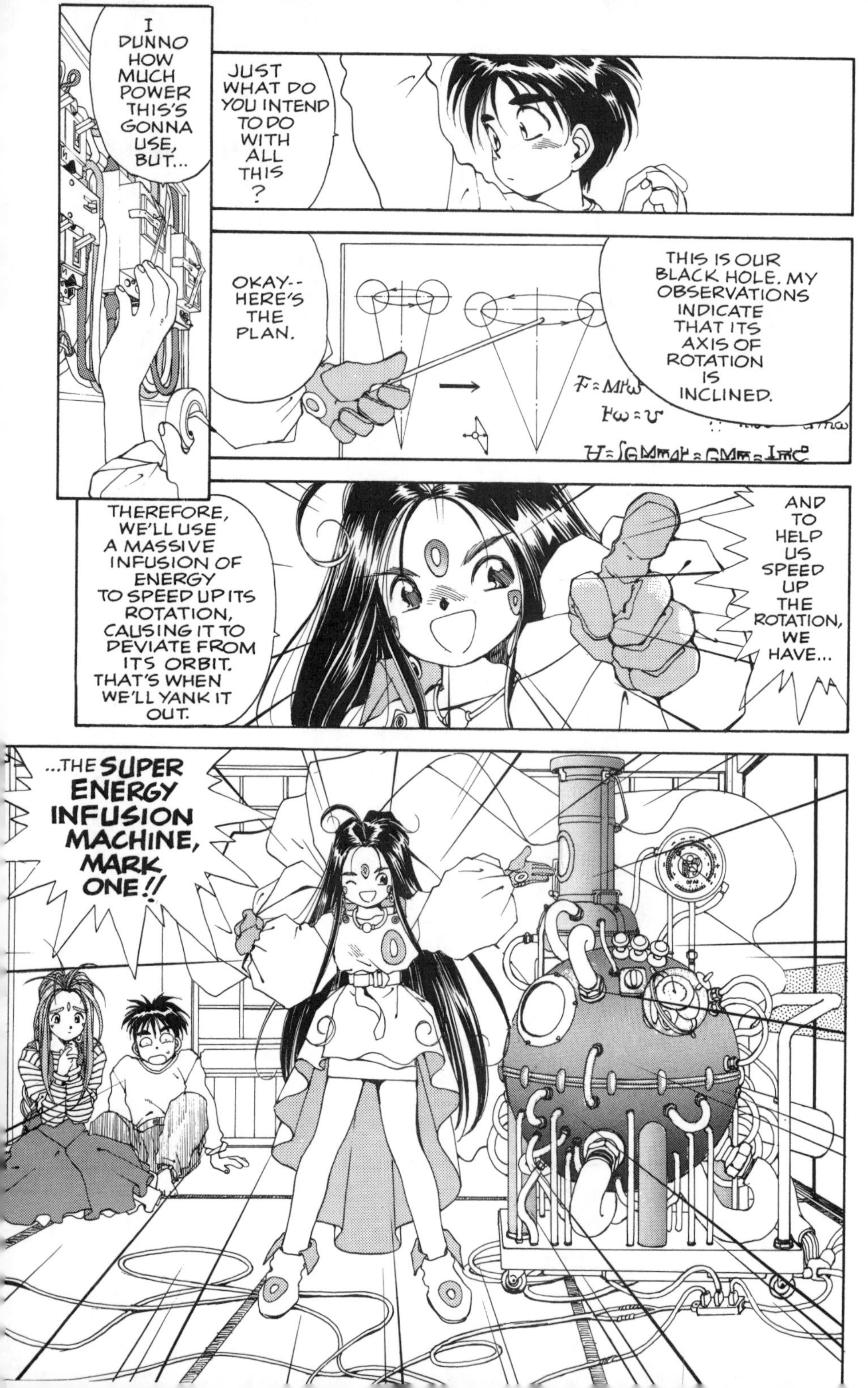
I DUNNO HOW MUCH POWER THIS'S GONNA USE, BUT...
JUST WHAT DO YOU INTEND TO DO WITH ALL THIS?
OKAY-- HERE'S THE PLAN.
THIS IS OUR BLACK HOLE. MY OBSERVATIONS INDICATE THAT ITS AXIS OF ROTATION IS INCLINED.
THEREFORE, WE'LL USE A MASSIVE INFUSION OF ENERGY TO SPEED UP ITS ROTATION, CAUSING IT TO DEVIATE FROM ITS ORBIT. THAT'S WHEN WE'LL YANK IT OUT.
AND TO HELP US SPEED UP THE ROTATION, WE HAVE...
...THE SUPER ENERGY INFUSION MACHINE, MARK ONE!!

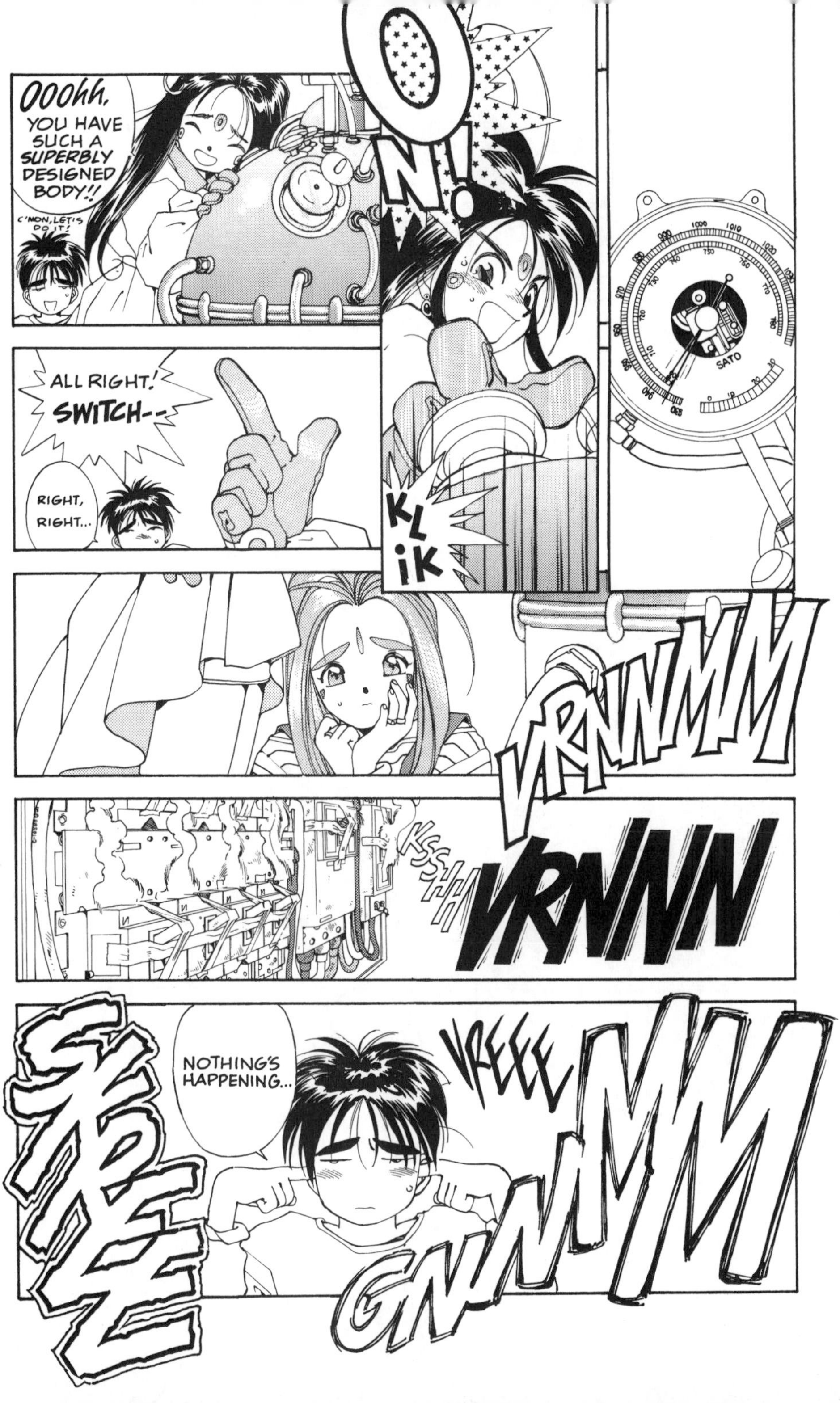
OOOhh, YOU HAVE SUCH A SUPERBLY DESIGNED BODY!!
C'MON, LET'S DO IT!
ALL RIGHT! SWITCH--
RIGHT, RIGHT...
ON!
KLiK
SATO
VRNNMM
KSSHH
VRNNN
NOTHING'S HAPPENING...
VREEE
GNMMM

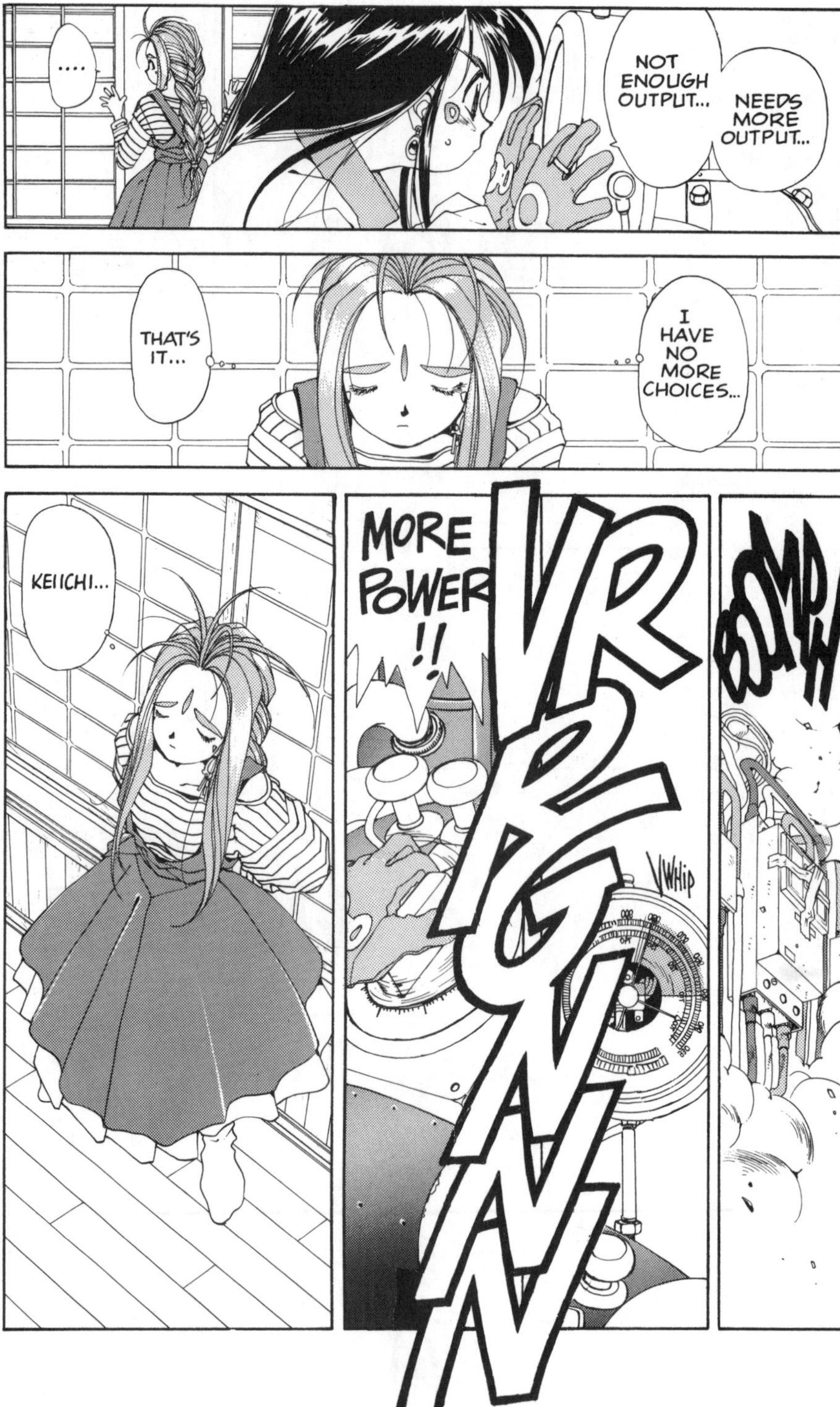
....
NOT ENOUGH OUTPUT...
NEEDS MORE OUTPUT...
THAT'S IT...
I HAVE NO MORE CHOICES...
KEIICHI...
MORE POWER !!
VRRRGNNNNN
VWHIP
BOOMPH

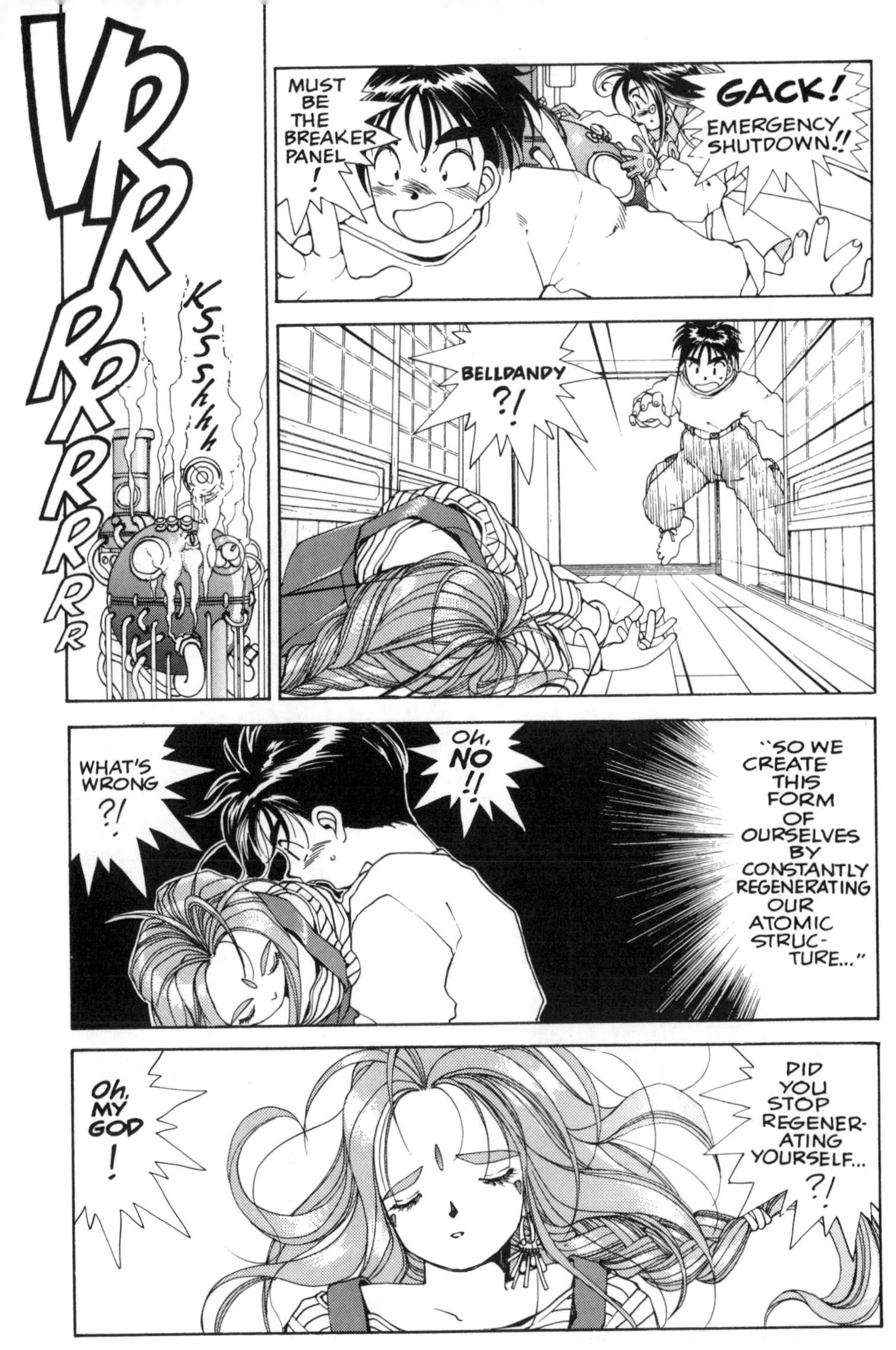
VRRRRRRRRRR
KSSSSHHHH
MUST BE THE BREAKER PANEL !
GACK!
EMERGENCY SHUTDOWN!!
BELLDANDY ?!
WHAT'S WRONG ?!
Oh, NO !!
"SO WE CREATE THIS FORM OF OURSELVES BY CONSTANTLY REGENERATING OUR ATOMIC STRUC-TURE..."
Oh, MY GOD !
DID YOU STOP REGENER-ATING YOURSELF... ?!

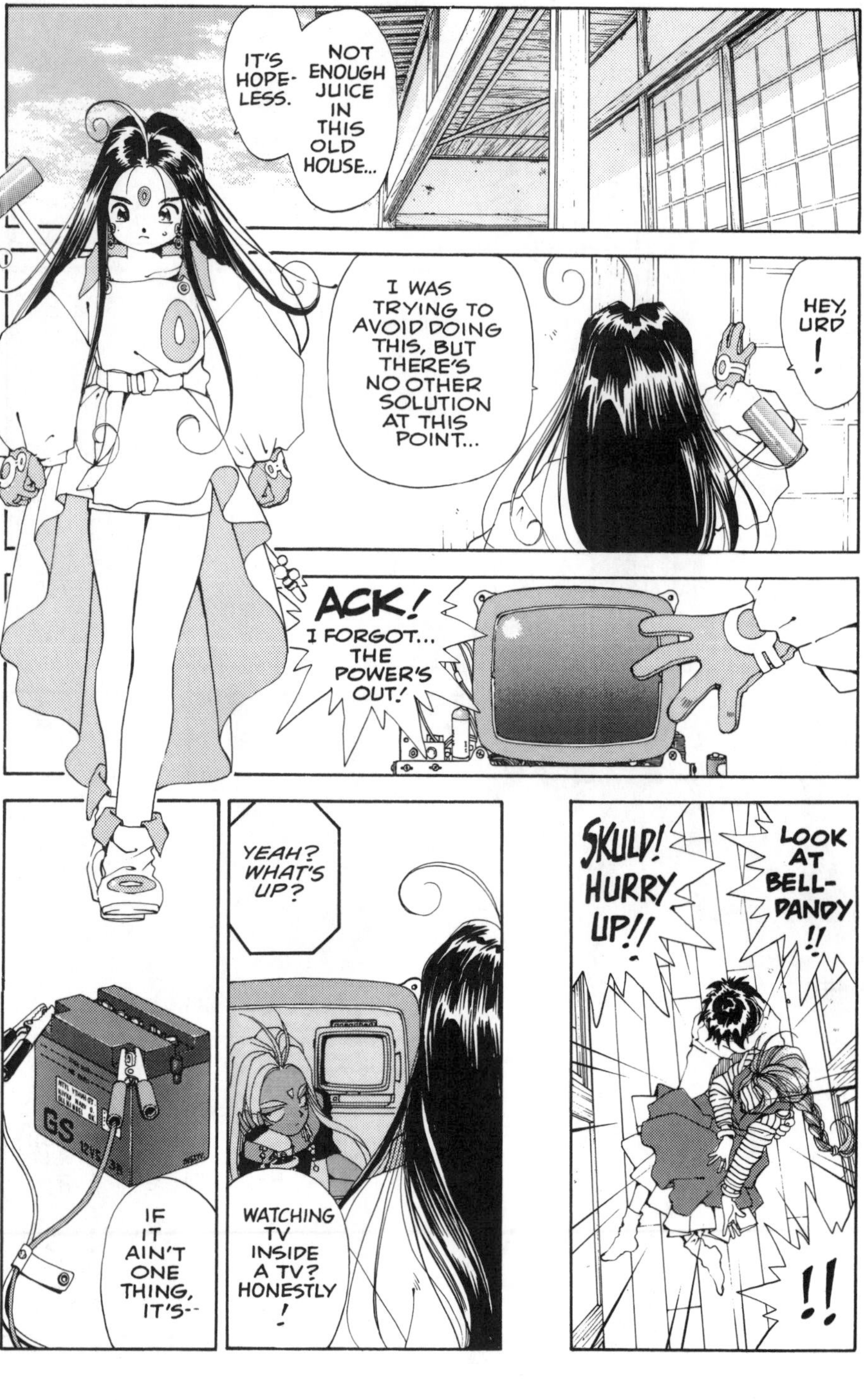

NOT ENOUGH JUICE IN THIS OLD HOUSE... IT'S HOPE-LESS.
I WAS TRYING TO AVOID DOING THIS, BUT THERE'S NO OTHER SOLUTION AT THIS POINT...
HEY, URD!
ACK! I FORGOT... THE POWER'S OUT!
IF IT AIN'T ONE THING, IT'S--
YEAH? WHAT'S UP?
WATCHING TV INSIDE A TV? HONESTLY!
SKULD! HURRY UP!!
LOOK AT BELL-DANDY!!
!!

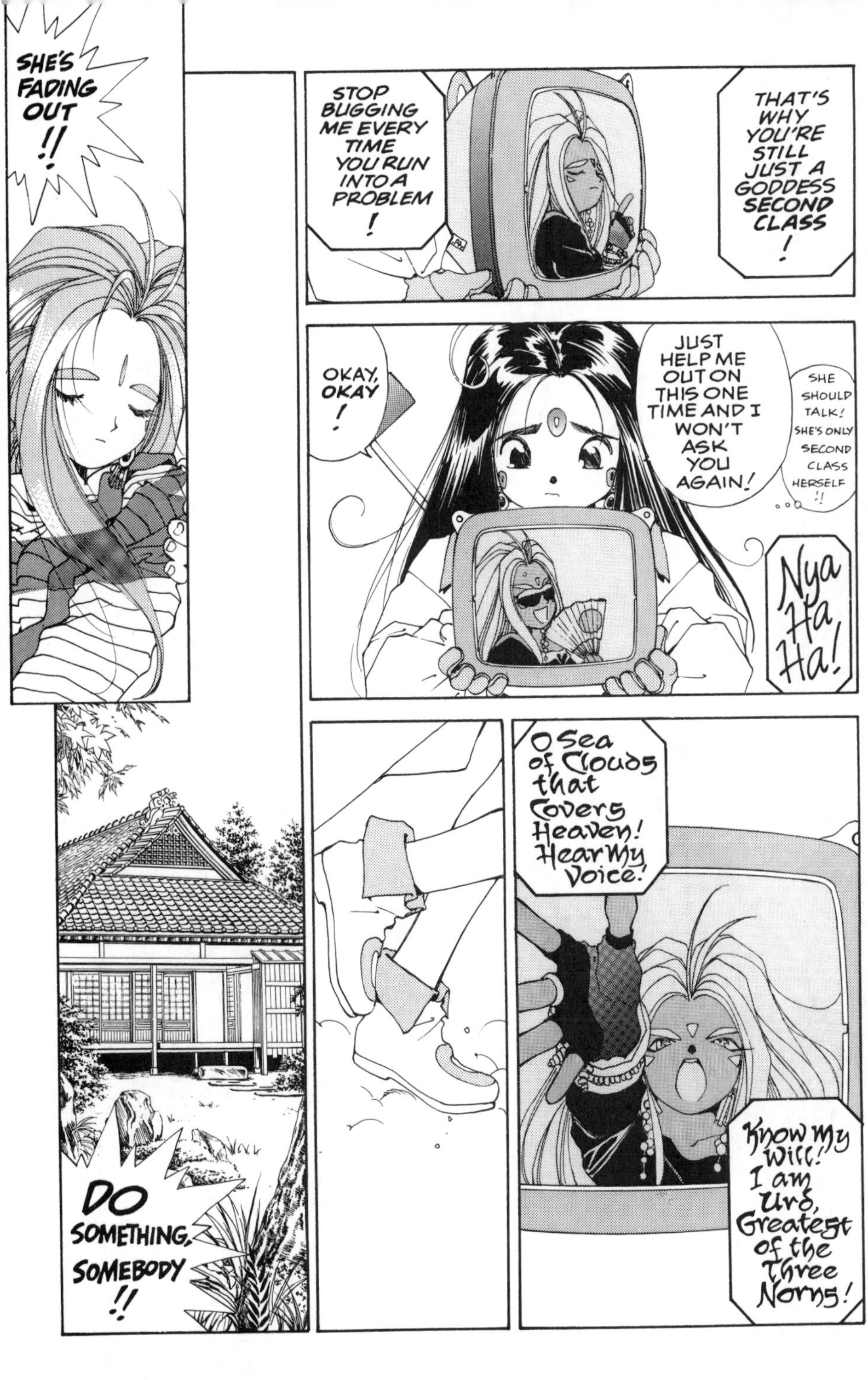

SHE'S FADING OUT !!
DO SOMETHING, SOMEBODY !!
STOP BUGGING ME EVERY TIME YOU RUN INTO A PROBLEM !
THAT'S WHY YOU'RE STILL JUST A GODDESS SECOND CLASS !
OKAY, OKAY !
JUST HELP ME OUT ON THIS ONE TIME AND I WON'T ASK YOU AGAIN!
SHE SHOULD TALK! SHE'S ONLY SECOND CLASS HERSELF !!
Nya Ha Ha!
O Sea of Clouds that Covers Heaven! Hear My Voice!
Know My Will! I am Urd, Greatest of the Three Norns!

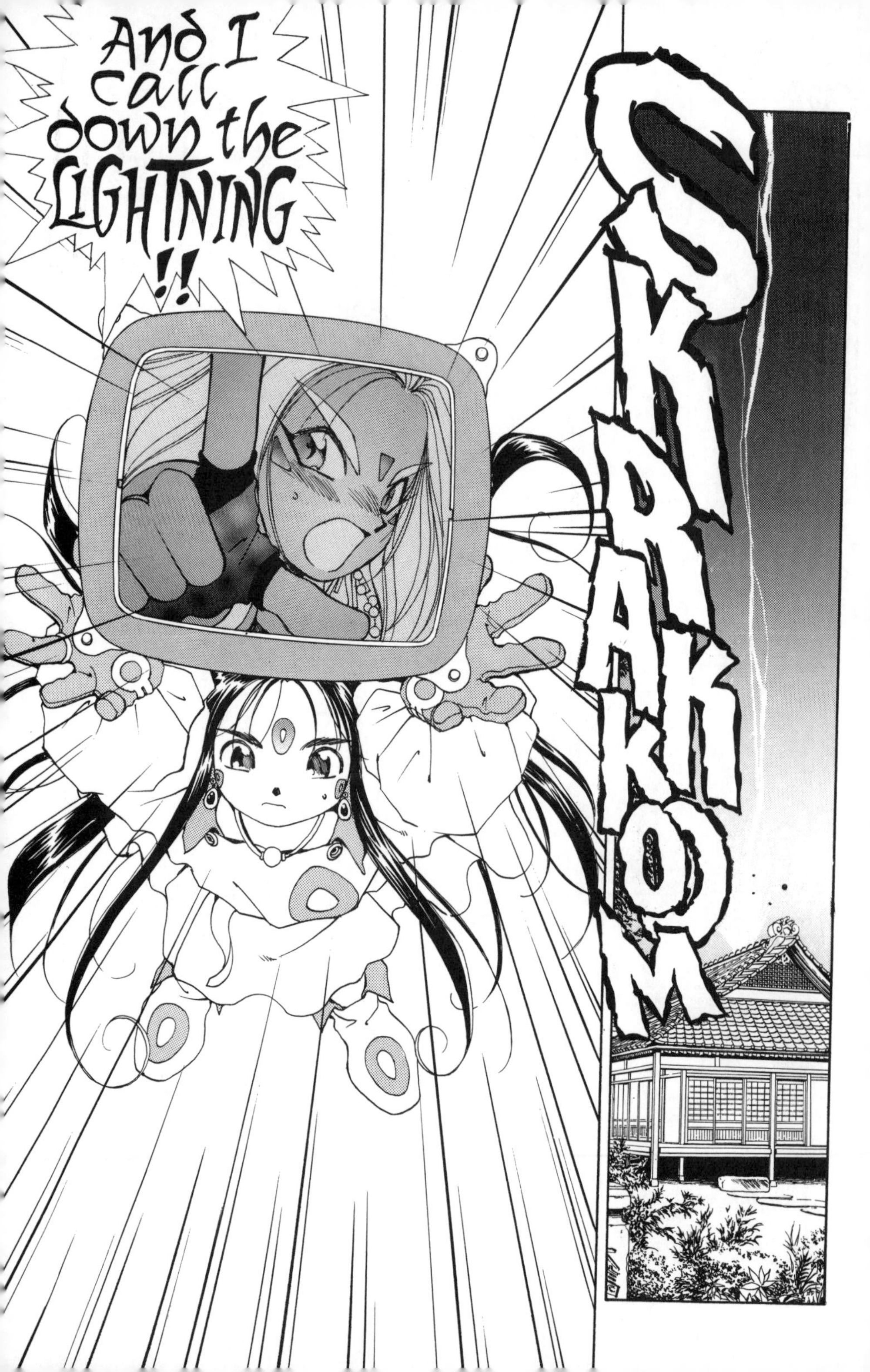
And I call down the LIGHTNING!!
CRAKOOM

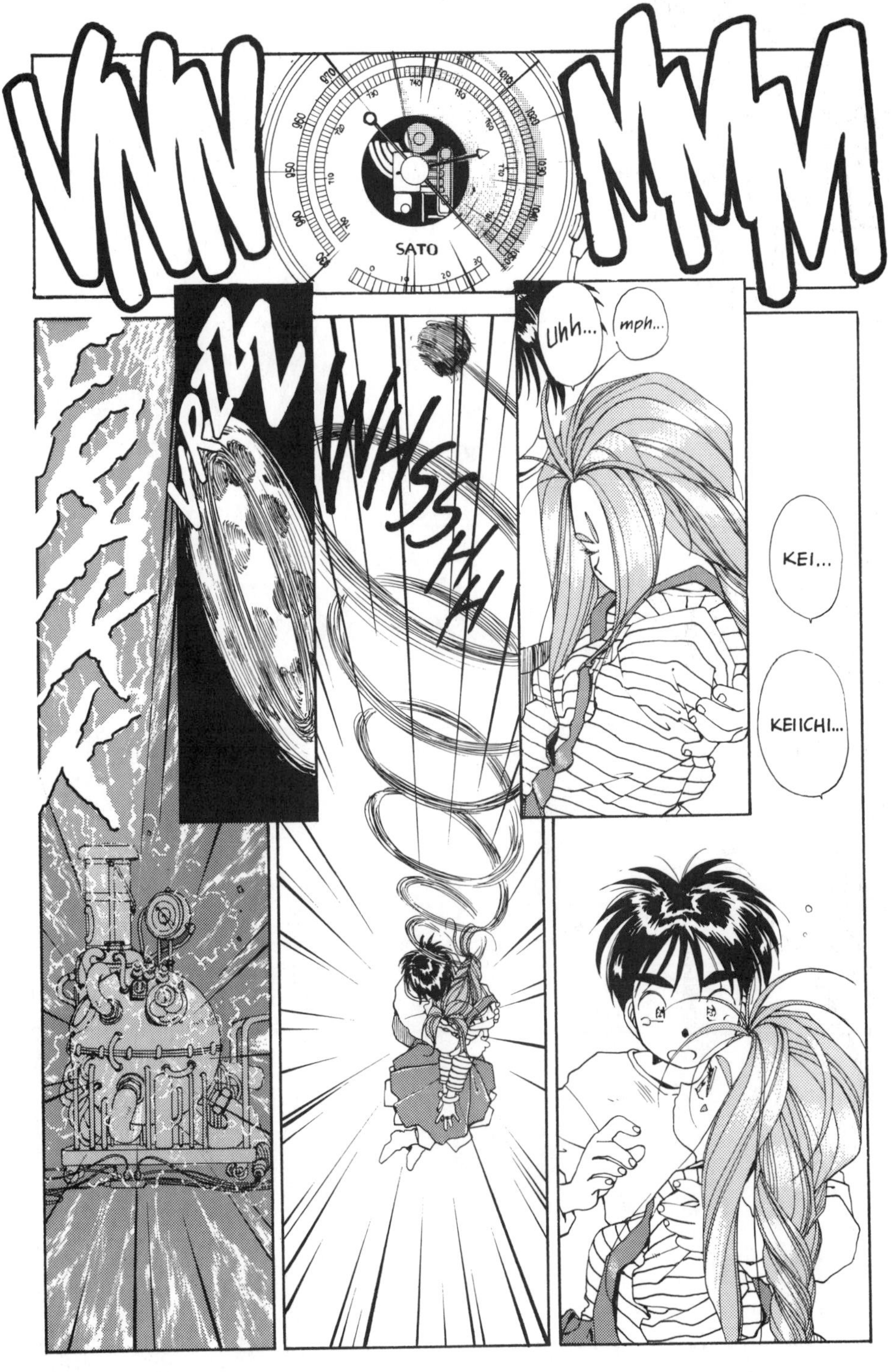
VMN
SATO
MMM
VRZZZ
WHASSHH
uhh...
mph...
KEI...
KEIICHI...

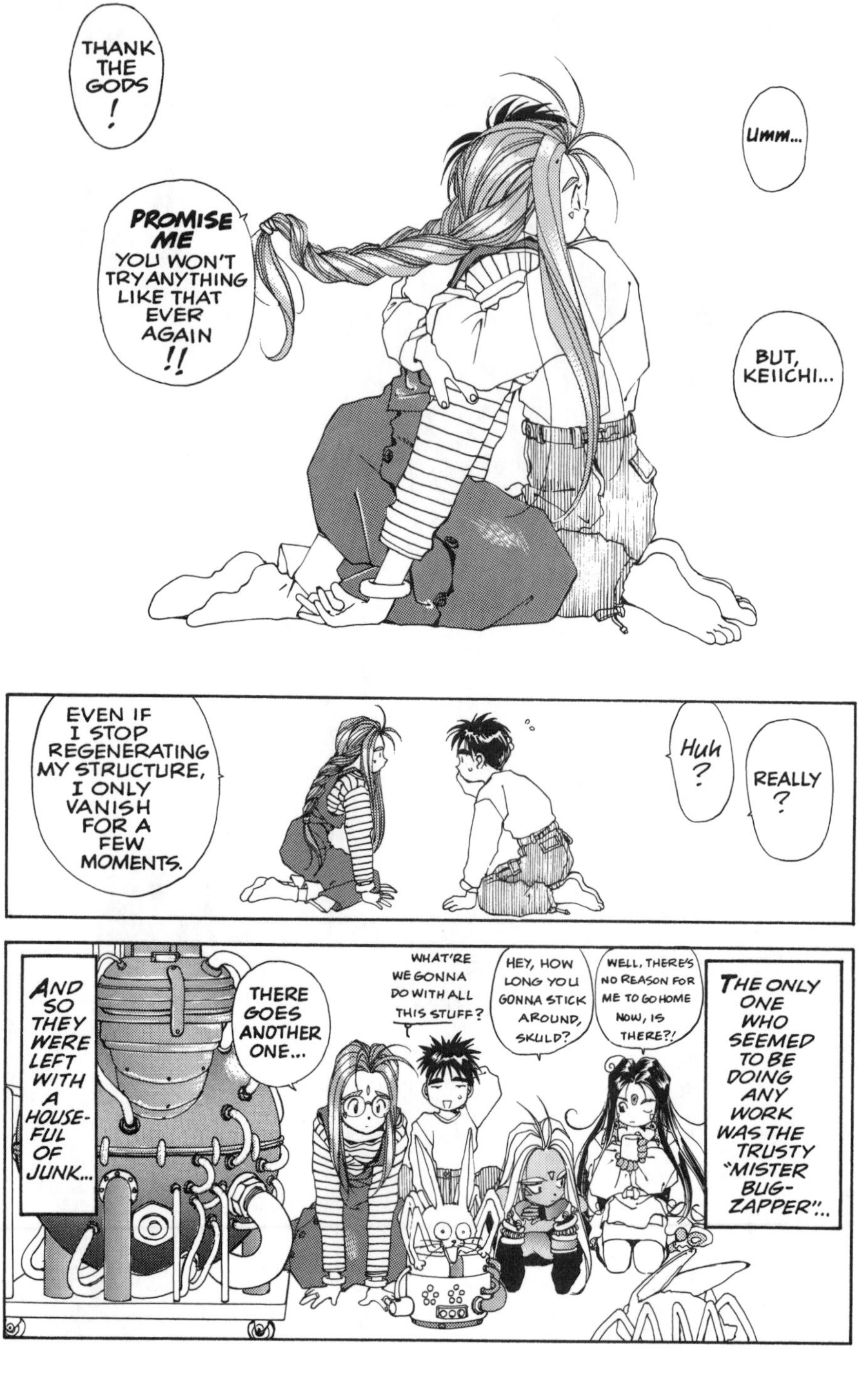
THANK THE GODS!
PROMISE ME YOU WON'T TRY ANYTHING LIKE THAT EVER AGAIN!!
Umm...
BUT, KEIICHI...
EVEN IF I STOP REGENERATING MY STRUCTURE, I ONLY VANISH FOR A FEW MOMENTS.
Huh?
REALLY?
AND SO THEY WERE LEFT WITH A HOUSE-FUL OF JUNK...
THERE GOES ANOTHER ONE...
WHAT'RE WE GONNA DO WITH ALL THIS STUFF?
HEY, HOW LONG YOU GONNA STICK AROUND, SKULD?
WELL, THERE'S NO REASON FOR ME TO GO HOME NOW, IS THERE?!
THE ONLY ONE WHO SEEMED TO BE DOING ANY WORK WAS THE TRUSTY "MISTER BUG-ZAPPER"...

Oh My Goddess!

ああ女神さま **Sympathy for the Devil**

Cover Gallery

Following are some of Kosuke Fujishima's covers
from the comics collected here.

Oh My Goddess! Part III issue 3

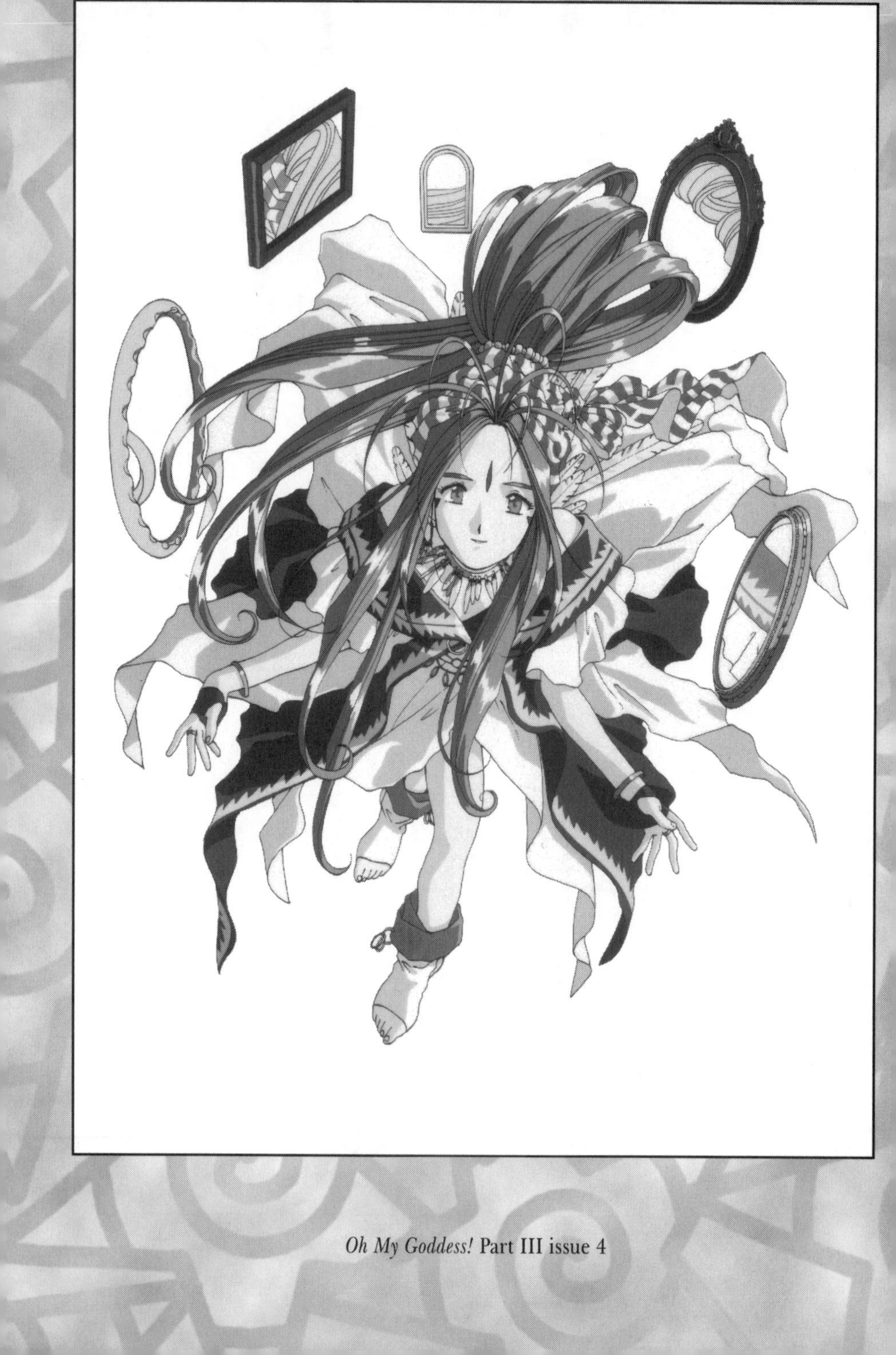

Oh My Goddess! Part III issue 4

Oh My Goddess! Part III issue 5

Dark Horse Comics: Mike Richardson publisher • Neil Hankerson executive vice president • Tom Weddle vice president of finance • Randy Stradley vice president of publishing • Chris Warner senior books editor • Michael Martens vice president of marketing • Anita Nelson vice president of sales & licensing • David Scroggy vice president of product development • Mark Cox art director • Dale LaFountain vice president of information technology • Darlene Vogel director of purchasing • Ken Lizzi general counsel